COUNSELING
Group Theory and System

Daniel W. Fullmer
University of Hawaii

tbook Company
College *Educational Publishers*
nto · London

The Intext Series in
GUIDANCE AND COUNSELING

Series Editor

the late R. WRAY STOWIG

Department of Counselor Education

University of Wisconsin

ISBN 0-7002-2325-8

To My Continuing Experimental Group:
Pat, Dan V. and Mark

Perhaps there is no greater corruption of a person's self-determination than the well-intentioned managing of his motivation by another.

Foreword

This book is good because the author makes an original contribution to both counseling theory and practice. The book is stimulating because one cannot passively absorb what has been set forth in these pages due to Professor Fullmer's insistence that the reader think about applying the concepts which are presented. He does this both through examples and with questions that challenge. With the writer's help the reader should perceive his role differently and feel the need to behave differently.

The ideas and concepts which Professor Fullmer discusses have been examined clinically and experimentally for over a decade. There are few writers who have so well honed their ideas through a combination of research, instruction and practice. I believe both beginning and experienced counselors will feel they have learned a great deal after sharing the writer's experiences, observations, and conclusions which are set forth in COUNSELING: GROUP THEORY AND SYSTEM.

PHILIP A. PERRONE
University of Wisconsin

Preface

The urge for a feeling of community has nudged me along the path of Group. The primeval origins of man seem to resist the isolation of an urban community. To be alone in the crowd of others, nameless, faceless, anonymous, is to be without any way to validate one's own identity.

The concept of group holds the potential for being an antidote to anomie. Group counselling has the promise of being a method of reestablishing the feeling of community in a school. The polar opposite is defined as a jungle, a people jungle, where no one is safe from becoming nobody. Community or jungle is a choice to be made by any human organization, whether family, school, church, or social agency. Businesses and industries have used the contemporary group methods to achieve a working community in their human organizations. Schools, churches, and social agencies have increasingly moved toward the use of group methods, particularly in the 1960's. In the 1970's we will need more than just a good feeling about group experiences. We will need some definitive data about groups and how best to use them in our human organizations. The central purpose of this book is to set the basis for research models to investigate the concept of group as well as the method and/or technique. The reader should get beyond some of the mystical aspects of the cult phenomenon to see what forces are manipulated. It is true, I think, that every group is shaped in the image of the leader's personality and basic character. I can't prove it yet, but between Chapter 7 and Chapters 8 and 9 I have the basis of an empirical test using control groups. I have just completed a pilot run with six leaders. The results encourage me to tighten up the design and get a more rigorous test of the basic hypothesis. If groups acquire the characteristic behavior of the leader, we can use what we know to probe further the problems of alienation and intimacy.

Edgar Lee Masters in his 1915 *Spoon River Anthology* described the personal-social community of rural Midwestern (Illinois) America. I grew to adulthood along the banks of the Spoon River, where the fishing was good and the spring floods were terrible. The nostalgia for a group —a community like that—was to prompt some counterattack on the urban anticommunity-community. The concept of a group is a method against the alienation of the anticommunity, the city. The city itself is no villain. The city is an ingenious invention because in no other human organization can so many persons be in such close geographic array and still be free to move about at will. The city puts all of man's talents, resources, services, and knowledge within the immediate environment and even the reach of each person. However, to do this there must be maintained strict parameters for separation of one individual from another. Separation is alienation but it affords freedom of movement for each person. Community is a feeling of interrelatedness—an identity, loyalty to basic values, a oneness of existence. To achieve a feeling of community in the city requires a highly sophisticated person. Again, the difficulty is compounded by the pattern of migration from rural to urban society. The least able persons collect in the inner city, which in turn demands the most sophisticated behavior to avoid anomie.

Group can help the person create an opportunity for community. The feeling of mutual support, because of the understanding derived from skilled participation in the complex urban community, is an expected product from the process of group methods. The talents for achieving the product need to be developed. We need people to lead groups, but much more urgent is the need to help people learn to use a group to achieve the more complex levels of socialization necessary to achieve the concept of community in an urban environment. Like so many others, my origins were rural. Spoon River is rural American, so my skills were rural. I had to learn urban skills. As a concept, group has helped me to learn these skills.

I'm sometimes disquieted at the need for having others need me. But my chosen profession rests close to the edge of that pali (cliff). Counseling is a profession built on the edge of someone's need for help. The helping professions generally respond to the needy conditions of people in a social system that is too complex for anyone to handle alone. In a group, each of us has a better chance for success. Needs, as gaps in our knowledge and skills, come to be closely related to our way of living. Because of the city, my rural needs had to go and I had to learn urban needs to replace the rural set. To live successfully we must have the right needs. Group is a good place to learn new needs.

Our society has traditionally depended upon the family and the school to bridge the developmental gaps in our learning. Our parents and our teachers have gaps in their skill development. Those who cannot use a group to create new learning environments to learn what they need to know are handicapped if they live in a modern urban milieu.

The task of this text is to show how groups are the basic building blocks of a community. A community is the human organization essential to the operation of our social system. My students and I have a working model of the concept of group. One former student, Darold E. Engebretson, prepared the chapter on the contemporary group methods. The proliferation of group methods in recent years makes it especially important to treat contemporary group methods as a separate topic. Darold not only contributed the chapter but gave his energy and time to reading the manuscript. Lucretia Norberg Jaye typed the original draft as well as most of the final manuscript. Judy Miller, Ann Stanton, and Esther Onaga rendered aid in the closing round of manuscript preparation. *Mahalo* (thank you) to all of them, and to Phil Perrone, *aloha* and *mahalo* for your continued encouragement.

DANIEL. W. FULLMER

Mahalo Nui

February, 1971
Honolulu, Hawaii

Contents

Group: A Human Fix

The most profound things I know seem to be the most simple. Group is the concept in human organization I find valuable because of the parallel nature of the relationship between a group's organization and the culture's parameters for organization. Group as a concept seems to reduce the culture rules and parameters for behavior to proportions I can comprehend.

Reductionism. Reductionism is the process of shrinking all complex systems to a matter of formula. The shrinking of complex relationships factors to a formula has the effect of creating a new system and bypassing the established system. The reductionism in titles or slogans like "Games People Play" or "Make Love not War" and "Virginity Causes Cancer" each represents a kind of magic detour across the uncertain grounds of complex human relationships. Reductionism is a useful pragmatic strategy. The difficulty may come when the second generation utilizes a reductionism formula without any real comprehension for the underlying complex human relationships. This is a very complex area. The telephone is a good example of reductionism. I do not need to know how to make a telephone in order to use one. I do not need to know how to make pencils in order to write with one. There are an infinite variety of practical applications of specific ideas that have been reduced to formulas that have exceptionally important applications in our society.

There are other reductions however, particularly in the human-relations field, that completely denude our basic democratic society structure by the way in which they erase the humaness of the individual and make a thing or robot of him. It is in this area that counselors and teachers need to have an exceptionally keen alertness to the subtlety of the formula construct. For example, most group techniques are a kind of formula, a way of thinking, a way of talking, listening, interacting, and interpreting. The latter—interpreting—assumes values and a frame of reference in which to apply them. The way of talking may define what the formula idea is. The language we use defines the behavior we use (Bernard, 1970). We tend to develop the feelings that go with our words. Our words reflect our beliefs—both the beliefs we have and the beliefs we are acquiring from the group. If I can control the formula for talking in a group, I have control of considerable power over a process with potential for changing behavior. The formula is a way of structuring social-personal power. The person with the formula has power, and the formula is a way of managing power among group participants, once the process of interacting is begun. Reductionism has significance in the process of group organization and action. I always like to know how all of the diverse elements, discussed here in part, act as variables to produce a unity of purpose and action in most groups. The formula for talking is a major variable in the complex set of elements.

Alienation. Dundes (1969) points to the possibility that as the world increases in its urbanization and as specialization of labor continues to build, alienation probably will increase. Alienation is separation from others and/or their ideas. If alienation increases there will be a continuing need to develop some effective countermove to assist people in combating the negative aspects of separation from a group. One way this might happen is to increase the frequency and availability of self-help groups, counseling groups, and other task groups designed specifically to bring people together for meaningful encounter.

Ethnocentrism and Cultural Bias

The way we do things is right and natural. The way other people do things may be unnatural, strange, and possibly wrong. This belief is probably held by most peoples of the earth today (Hall, 1959). The chauvinistic nature of beliefs may be characteristic of a given group of persons. We speak of international, intercultural, interpersonal cultural exchange. The East-West Center at the University of Hawaii promotes cultural exchange among some thirty distinct national groups and nearly the same number of cultures. However, the students do not engage in intercultural exchange. More frequently, as reported by Low (1967, p. 20) in a study of Asian grantees, almost all of them spend their time intrachanging with members of their own culture usually limited to their own national group. Food is safe for interaction among most of the grantees and they use it to express their identity with their culture. Food is one vehicle for cultural interchange. People of nearly every nationality will express themselves by sharing their national dish or special food. However, interpersonal problems, such as sex, have many hazards due to differences in behavior across cultures. Not only is the cue system different from one culture to another, but so is the response system. Thus each East-West Center grantee tends to seek the familiar, to be found in his own national group. The interpersonal encounter is less frequently an expression of cultural interchange.

Students in most American schools are found to be of divergent cultural origins. Ethnocentrism and chauvinism provide the psychological set for counselors, teachers, administrators, and other responsible adults. With the civil rights revolution of the 1960's in the United States we have only achieved recognition of some differences. Racial, cultural, and socioeconomic differences are major hangups because we assume equality. We react to others equally and those who cannot respond appropriately because they are different—become ignored.

Cultural bias exists in nearly all social institutions. This truism is based upon the fact that institutions are the products of a given culture. In a very real way institutions are an extension of the values and beliefs systems in a society or culture. Individual persons join together in groups to deliver a given service or actualize a particular belief system. When the complex system is formalized and maintained over long periods of time, an institution is created. The school is one example. The religious institutions are other examples. Institutions form the support for stability in the basic human organizations through services to individual and to other institutions. Educational, financial, and cultural-social institutions form complex organizations to maintain the delivery systems for services at many levels in the society. Some institutions are private, parochial, public, or nonpartisan. The school is an example of one social institution locked into the cultural bias of middle class legitimacy. The bias of legitimacy manages to define all other biases as illegitimate (Hamilton, 1969). What about the teacher in Hawaii? Oriental cultures meet Hawaiian and American cultures. (We say *meet* because cultures do not mix—Hall, 1959.) It is possible for a teacher to have, in the same classroom, new immigrant children from the Philippines, a third-generation Japanese, a Korean, a Samoan, an American black or white, and one or two Hawaiians. In addition, there may be children from mixed racial or cultural families. How can a teacher handle such diversity? There is one common factor. They are, or aspire to be, *middle class!* If they do not have the middle-class bias, the chances are increased in favor of cultural conflicts of values and consequently of behavior. The manifestation of such a condition will be seen in the teacher's request for transfer to another school, the removal of the child from her classroom, or simply a request to the counselor, "Please, fix this student!" The bland ignorance about the effects on behavior of culture differences might lead a teacher to act with situational impropriety.

According to Goffman (1967, p. 141), situational impropriety may define psychotic behavior. The fact that a teacher associates wrongly with another human being further supports the harsh label *psychotic behavior*. Whether or not you wish to go this far, it is mentioned to alert the student of group human behavior to the subtle situational character of most all behavior, especially the behavior experienced out of a cultural bias. It is extremely important to understand the folklore or belief system of the students with whom we work (Dundes, 1969).

Group Counseling or Group Training

Group counseling and training groups have evolved over the past twenty years to be two of the most significant developments in human relations work. Group counseling and group psychotherapy are treated as the same phenomenon except that each has a distinctive setting and a unique relationship to the network of persons in the group. Group counseling takes place largely in educational and social institutional settings. Group psychotherapy is used in hospitals, clinics for mental health, and private practice by professional psychologists and psychiatrists. In group counseling and group psychotherapy the personal, social, and emotional behavior of any individual may become the focus for treatment.

Training groups are concerned with the human organization as represented in a particular human group. The T-group (training group) as developed by the National Training Laboratories described by Bradford, Gibb, and Benne (1964) is the most widely used method. Many newer variations have evolved in recent years and are discussed at greater length by Engebretson in Chapter 12.

The idea that work with the human group may serve a wide variety of different specific goals has been taken as the theme of this first chapter. Perhaps the reader will find the concept of group is nearly representative of the human fix. Because of the nature of the culture organization, the human group is needed if the individual is to find his way in life. The human group is the organization I think most nearly replicates the culture rules and parameters, so far as the individual human being directly encounters the culture's organization structure. The work we have done with groups of families has demonstrated the efficacy of the group as a replication of the culture parameters for organization. Groups form into larger collections of people we call *communities*. The communities make up the society of a given culture. There are up to sixteen levels of community in a modern society—i.e., the urban center or city (Doxiadis, 1966).

A community may be defined as a group of persons who share a similar system of beliefs. The community of scholars make up a university, for example. The community is a group that is too large for every member to encounter every other member on an intimate basis. The fact is important to my idea of group as a phenomenon. The fact is that behavior is the expression of a system of beliefs. The meaning a given person tries to actualize by his behavior is based upon the shared system of beliefs in the group and community. This condition permits a given group to act on a belief; to act as though the behavior based on the belief is a fact, and achieve the phenomenon of a self-fulfilling prophecy. A shared *myth* is another way of describing the self-fulfilling prophecy phenomenon. If everyone *acts* as if a belief system is true, the behavior in that group will confirm and validate the belief. Here is the reason any systematic work in human relations will appear to be a success, if, everyone in a given group *goes along.* In Chapter 7 I give an example to demonstrate how the formula for leading a group and a community of believers happens. The happenings in the community confirm and validate the belief system. The belief system is expressed as a way of talking and behaving. Because everyone has to depend upon everyone else to carry out the appropriate behavior competently, I use the test of *competent behavior* as the measure of the *health* of a group. A sick group has a *deviant* member. Deviant members are sometimes created by the group or community, i.e., delinquents or scapegoats in a family. Deviant behavior may be effective, but I do not define it as competent behavior in the reference to group health. The behavior of each member in a group is *expected* to confirm the belief system, or shared myths, just as the culture system for behavior sets parameters and rules to guide behavior. If I come from a different culture I can see the differences in the behavior, but I cannot predict the next happening in a sequence of life events. Prediction implies precise anticipation of future events. Forecasting may be a more accurate concept for what I have in mind. A forecast is probably going to happen within some set of limits like weather forecasting, e.g., "partly sunny or snow on Mauna Kea." Predicting is more characteristic of scientific research endeavours.

Forecasting, Predicting, and Preventing. Where are we? Where are we in the business of managing our future, living our present, and remembering our past? The science of human behavior has created a capability for predicting future events based upon data from the past and the present. The science of human behavior has brought forth new myths and facts to explain individual and group behavior. The sources range from cultural anthropology (Hall, 1959) to psychoanalysis (Freud, 1938) and beyond.

The massive measurement of human talent continues. Predicting the future performance for a given group by the application of probability techniques has become routine ever since computer scoring and analysis of scores became possible. The entire personnel industry profits from the accumulated wisdom derived from hard facts based on individual performance on test instruments matched to evaluation of performance on the job. Going to school is analyzed in similar fashion. We can predict for the *group* but not the *individual,* at least not in scientific terms.

Demands for improved efficiency in performance of persons on the job, particularly in management, led to group training. The task was to improve performance by increasing the quality of the human organization. Group dynamics came into its own when the *National Training Laboratories in Group Development* (NTL) began in 1947 (Bradford, Gibb, and Benne, 1964, p. 2). The focus was upon the behavior of each person *in relation to* other persons (group dynamics).

Recent developments during the 1960's brought a new focus. Each person is asked to look at *himself in relation to* other persons (personal, social, emotional development). This shift in emphasis from group dynamics to personal development has given rise to group models that focus upon the *individual.* The training groups continue to be used by NTL and others for human organization improvement through encounter group, sensitivity and awareness group, body-awareness (nonverbal) group, or other derivations, including marathon and nude encounter groups.

Therapy treatment models are important forms for group use. The group methods used in therapy gave us ways to treat the community of other persons. The milieu or environment was to become a legitimate target for treatment (Yablonsky, 1965). The community of significant others becomes therapeutic when each person joins the treatment function. The therapeutic community may consist of multiple groups representing different levels of community organization.

In fact, therapeutic community was found to be ineffective if the person were to return to the same family, neighborhood or community. Thus halfway-house concepts were tried. Family treatment became a common and routine procedure in some sectors (Fullmer, 1969a). The major shift in the late 1960's seemed to be from treating the individual in isolation to treating the entire group of significant others (Mowrer, 1968; Fullmer, 1971).

Fullmer (1971) has studied the use of a group model for family therapy called Family Group Consultation. The more than ten years work has revealed the efficacy of treating the group as well as the individual. The principle that *a problem group must treat itself* has been tested and has been found to be valid. Whether one is treating drug addicts, alcoholics, or families, the target group is identical to the treatment group (Farson, 1968; Whitaker, 1970; Fullmer, 1971). The idea of helping a group with a problem is not new. What is unique is the finding in research and practice that it is the dry alcoholic and the rehabilitated drug addict who can help the alcoholic or drug addict. Therefore, any treatment group should contain representatives from the target group—the persons help each other so that the new community can maintain the new behavior instead of reproducing the previous (old) behavior. We treat the family group so that new relationships can be defined in it. The new relationships will produce and support new behavior in the identified patient.

Psychotherapists and counselors gradually have been accepting these new forms of treatment. One can still find practitioners who prefer the individualized models for treatment. In the past decade of rapid change, innovations for treatment ran well ahead of the science of verification. Currently the 1970's provide fertile fields for the research-inclined professional. Group research or research on group models can be done legitimately, only by the qualified practitioner. The clinical virgin will be fearful at meeting such powerful social pressures as a group produces. Penetration would be painful for the clinical virgin.

Group Focus: Personal Behavior—Human Organization

Bradford, Gibb, and Benne (1964, p. 2) speak of two innovations in education and reeducation. (Education is used to denote all learning exposed to an individual, including formal schooling. However, schooling is not the total concept of education.) The T-group or training group is one innovation and training laboratory is the second innovation. The T-group is a technical training arena for directing behavior under controlled conditions. The laboratory is a community designed to shape the environment necessary to stimulate and protect the learner in his experimental attempts at change (new behavior).

Two major branches of group work emerged from T-group training. One is T-group or training to modify the human organization through improved interpersonal communication achieved by application of group dynamics principles. Second is the group that emphasizes the modification of the individual as a personal force in the community of others. Here the training laboratory has become an end as well as a means. The social-personal environment does affect behavior, and the individual as a part of the environment can be aware of his impact on others and be sensitive to the impact on him of other's behavior.

Modification of the individual's personal, social, and emotional behavior has been more closely associated with group counseling and group psychotherapy models. The rapid expansion in recent years seems to indicate the popular acceptance of the human laboratory methods. There are multiple examples of human laboratory methods including sensitivity and awareness training. Marathon, encounter, body awareness, Synanon, venture, gestalt, and nude groups are among the better-known popular forms for human laboratory types. These vary in intensity of encounter and confrontation from the total social system of Synanon to the self-help encounter of Venture groups.

Why Group? Dundes (1965 and 1969) and Brunvand (1968) have underlined some of the major reasons why we have need for group methods of working with people in the 1970's. If an individual belongs to a group, it is part of his basic identification. If he is separated from his group, he is in an alienated state. This can happen when the individual rejects his group or when the group rejects the individual. Dundes (1969) points out that in recent history there has been a major change in American society regarding the transitional patterns of group membership.

Until fairly recently in most parts of the world, the abundance of tradition helped to maintain the stability of the individual's emotional belongingness. The United States has experienced some rapid changes in regard to existing traditions and the development of new traditions. Americans have a value which places the *new* above the *old* or change for the sake of change. The idea extends into the personal lives of people. In the American family the child is encouraged to leave home, seek a new home of his own away from his parents, and perhaps even away from his friends. The practice of neolocal residence is widespread and serves to separate the young married couple from both sets of parents.

In the American ideology it is the individual who is to be rugged, autonomous, and strong. The group is relegated to a support function and definitely a secondary status. For example, I can well remember my initial introduction to group and being concerned particularly with the submission of my individual identity to the possible supremacy of a group. That particular idea persisted for some years and was not relieved easily by assurance, reassurance, and accumulated experiences to the contrary. It was an idea that had come out of the role the family had provided in my early development. The family had identified its role as being one of support and encouragement, sort of the launching-pad concept rather than the central foundation on which a permanent structure or relationship could be built. The skill to be able to establish and maintain a long-term interpersonal relationship had to be learned in a group. The peer group provided the milieu for the initial exposure.

The first peer group was a sibling peer group. Then age-mates at play and later at school created the lasting relationships. The teen years brought the opportunity to have a long-term relationship with a member of the opposite sex. If all goes well, each person should gain exposure to learning experiences in groups all the way through his life.

Issues in Group

The issues in group cover many more areas of conflict and synthesis than I will be able to treat here. I have included those areas of concern which seem vital to the students' understanding of material in this text. The theory and research problems in group are very difficult issues because of the way some of us develop our knowledge about group. Other issues seem to be derived more from ethnocentrism than from vital concerns, but even this statement is an example of the biased writer. Thus it is an example of what it purports to report. Groups are a *natural* form used in the culture organization to order the essential behavior and avoid being dependent upon random behavior, impulsive behavior, or chance happenings. Because people live so close to groups, there is an issue about whether a given collection of persons is or is not a group. I maintain that every contrived collection of persons is *not* necessarily a group. You may take *issue* with that notion. If you do, we could have a lively debate. Each of us should be free to conform to our own group experience.

Freedom-Conformity. The freedom-conformity issue in group revolves around the idea of whether the behavior of the individual is a product of the pressures induced by the group toward conformity or whether the behavior is the consequence of facilitated freedom by group social action. The issue of conformity and freedom may be a purely academic one. An academic difference between coercion and nonchoice condition may be all I can identify. The old freedom and responsibility issue was similar. I can see some parallel in viewing responsibility as a response to the rules in a culture, community or group. The response could be called *conformity* or *compliance*. This reason is the one I use to justify going beyond responsibility to *accountability*.

Accountability is what action I did take. Freedom, on the other hand, has to do with choice. Choice points occur ahead of the conformity, responsibility, accountability functions. If I choose to join a given group, the new social matrix will present me with a new set of nonchoices. My social maturity level will influence my feelings about the new expectations in the group. But in any case, at the point of entry, I relinquish any further control, directly or indirectly, over the so called nonchoice conditions to which one will be pressured to conform, or become responsible. The action I take in response to the new conditions is what I become accountable for in any group.

Philosophically, one could pay his money and take his choice. In actual practice the individual is by no means clearly distinguishing between the social pressures of the social matrix of the group and the forces that are unleashed upon him as he makes his individual choice. It is conceived of as an autonomous act. However, it is carried out far less in isolation from the group than may be apparent on the surface. Perhaps it is more realistic to look at the life condition as an individual who does not enter a group. Such a person is in no way directly coerced by any of the social pressure to conform to the internal group norms. However, the person who does choose to enter a group does sign in or accept a contract, whether overtly or covertly stated, implying that one will abide by the rules set by the group and respond positively to group norms as they evolve. In matters of philosophy it is necessary to ask each person to make a choice on his own terms prior to entering into a dialogue concerning the relative nature of freedom and conformity within a group structure.

Schneider (1949) would argue that behavior which conforms and the concept of freedom within a social system is not necessarily a contradiction. At this point it would seem one should bring in the variable of the individual's development level and ask a question about whether at a given level the individual would find conflict where later at a more mature level he might find integration in the same forces. The reverse is also possible and is perhaps more common. The poet who writes in the sonnet form probably is not the immature poet. The poet who writes in free verse may of necessity have to have been a poor poet, a neophyte, or an extremely naive fellow. The assumption would be that the more experienced poet might have enough skill to utilize the ambiguity of a nonformula. A nonformula formula like free verse may shift us too far from our point of focus. The individual who is behaving in a less mature way will usually be caught up in the basic paradoxes and contradictions of every day relationships. The more mature and experienced person may experience the relationships that apparently are in conflict in a broader perspective. The individual is able to comprehend interdependencies and interrelationships that nullify the more immature constructs of conflict.

From birth, each person is exposed to group. Each person for most of his life is actively exposed to family groups and peer groups. Therefore it is assumed that groups are vital to all ages at all levels in the culture. For example, the Eskimo uses ostracism to condition a high degree of conformity into the behavior of the child.

Divergent and Convergent Thinking. Another issue is whether in group we follow too much the direction of the divergent thinker. As contrasted with the convergent thinker of science and technology, we tend to broaden beyond the scope of comprehension the variables and the complexity of their relationships to be considered in the milieu of the individual social setting. In other settings where the convergent view is central, the individual is narrowed to a manageable and comprehensible size. Variables are dealt with in small clusters rather than all at once. In human behavior and particularly in group work, this gives the illusion of being precise, and consequently more credible.

Level of Knowing. The level of knowing is essentially a consequence of the amount of information that can be included in the concern under consideration in a group.

A significant contribution by Rogers (1962, p. 311) indicates that opinion leaders frequently conform more closely to the social norms in the social system than do the average members of a given social system. The paradox retards change because the leader may be unable to risk nonconformity. The member safe enough to risk nonconforming is not powerful enough to effect acceptance of an innovation.

Information Sources. The sources of information used by persons in a given social system represent one of the dimensions necessary to understanding the quality of behavior in a given group. Information sources may be classified in any one or combination of the categories:

- Personal-impersonal
- Technically accurate old wives' tales, fairy tales, folklore, myth.
- Cosmopolitan, local or provincial.
- Higher status–lower status.
- Earlier adopters of innovations, later adopters of innovations.

It seems to follow that opinion leaders occupy higher status in the social system than do followers. The level of social participation is higher for opinion leaders than for followers. Because of the high level of conformity in opinion leaders it is frequently apparent that innovativeness depends to a large degree upon the norms for such behavior in the social system.

It is apparently true that human organizations did not gain a freer flow of communication between individuals within the same social group because of the addition of modern rather than traditional norms. Modern norms do not enhance any more than traditional norms the communication between persons within a given social system (Springer, 1968). Traditional organization within a human social system allows for blocks to occur between superior and subordinate. These seem to be replaced by interpersonal barriers between individuals, defined as simply differences in innovativeness. Both the above are true when modern rather than traditional norms are characterizing the social system.

Definition of Man

It is axiomatic to claim all systems for modifying human behavior contain some definition of the nature of man. Either assumptions or explicit statements spell out a definition of man as an autonomous element or a part of the society of other persons. A man may be defined as an end product. Man may be defined as an integral part of a social unit in the process of becoming. However man is defined makes a difference in the way behavior is perceived. Most systems for modifying behavior reject the assumptions on the nature of man.

The nature of man is a metaphysical question more closely related to our cultural parameters than to our metaphor in an atomic machine age. Dependence upon others and independence for oneself must be accounted for by the definition of normal and pathological behavior. Which interventions are legitimate and which are illegitimate? The preference for one or another system of intervention is ultimately based upon the definition of man. Differentiation and nondifferentiation of man as an autonomous being is decided by the point of departure that one chooses. The verbalizations vary but the issue of man's nature is an essence with consequences for any concept of group and the formula utilized in the interaction within the group membership.

Theory is based upon a definition of man. Whether man is a free unit existing only in relation with other free units, the nonchoice is social existence. Whether expressed as I-thou or some more abstract symbolic level, the relationship is the way man exists. Adjustment and coping behavior define the quality of social living. Conformity is pathological to the degree it permits inadequate social behavior to persist.

Man is basically an active and reactive being. Man is above the lower animals and below the gods—he is human. This is a unique category of living organisms because he has learned to encode—i.e., receive, organize and communicate—his meanings and experiences. The symbol is the product of the encoding process. Symbols may be combined into even more abstract symbols apparently all the way to infinity. In this sense there does not seem to be any particular limit to the potential knowledge development of man.

There are, however, some limiting factors in his existence. The one that is foremost has to do with his animal nature, the actual body in which man lives and has his being. This body is a kind of chemistry set and requires constant refueling and attention to maintain functions. The substance of man's existence should meet the promise of the symbol. Symbol without substance leads to alienation, as in a marriage that ends in divorce.

In addition to symbolic formulations which allow mankind to retain accumulated knowledge and to pass it along from one generation to the next, he has the ability to use institutions as extensions of the individual, social values, and beliefs. These institutions become living entities in the life space of man because institutions are extensions of man and become part of the social nature of man.

Man forms social ties. Or, as folklore describes man, he is a political animal and therefore forms human organizations with highly intricate and complex relationships defined into the functions and the roles of the persons who populate the human organizations.

One of the major tasks in today's society is to build into the individual the necessary skills to utilize the knowledge that he acquires through the educational system, family, and experience in the community.

All of these attempts to define man in terms of his *products* or in terms of his *essence* create a matter for choice on the part of any professional human behavior specialist. In theory development, we are interested in the nature of man only so far as it helps to create the parameters of the contexts in which he moves and in which he has his being. Therefore, if the essence of man is a metaphysical question it had best be left to those whose interests and concerns lead them in that direction. For group counseling and psychotherapy, it is important to understand the nature of man in his organization matrix with other human beings.

Social Being: The Group Form of Existence

The social being is essentially the result of a necessity created by the completeness of the individual unit. The basic human *social* unit in human groups is two or more people.

Defining or describing the individual in finite terms to accommodate the process of isolated specific variables is of no particular consequence in the current material about group. It has remained popular in the psychological and behavioral sciences to deal with the individual as a monad. In group we are concerned with the *relationships* between the individual and other individuals who complete the matrix out of which all behavior comes, or in which it takes place.

The basic framework within which all observations are taken must include the nature of the individual human being and the nature of the cultural context defining the rules by which interaction can occur. In the family in American culture the pattern of interaction is carefully controlled by a set of rules which are not immediately obvious to the participants (Hall, 1959). There is a consistency within the culture as one observes behavior from one person to another, one family group to another, one peer group to another. The nature of this code seems to be uniform in all levels of human interaction. When the code is learned and well known to the participants in a group, the communication and the behavior flow in what would be defined as normal or healthy. But when the methods of behavior are confused by the absence of complete knowledge and an incomplete set of skills regarding the application of rules, there is the inability to apply a uniform code. The human interaction is disturbed or confused, and perhaps even insane or sick. Anything that disrupts or destroys or handicaps the codified system of interpersonal communication will result in behavior that does not adapt adequately or does not conform in productive and undisturbed ways in the social system of the culture.

Basis of Group Theory

There is no escaping the subjective, personal orientation of the theory builder. The personal bias in group theory is the notion that social systems of behavior of individuals are reproduced from the social system of the model group, usually family, formulating the personality of each individual. There is no small difficulty trying to fit this concept into the reality that some families produce criminals and others produce saints. For that reason the personal bias is only a small part of the total figure when one includes all underlying bases of a theory.

The attempt has been made to observe the phenomena occurring in groups, particularly family groups, in counseling settings. The second concept has been equally difficult. The attempt is to formulate a theory that will explain the majority of the observed behavior. The theory is useful if it is tested and discovered to be valid and a reliable basis for prediction of behavior in given life situations. Because exceptions are continuously discovered, it is necessary to make the theory-building process a continuous learning and developing phenomenon.

In the behavioral sciences our theory building has progressed about to the point where theory building was in the physical sciences about five hundred years ago. Emotional attachments and belief systems are prominent in theory building in the behavioral sciences. As behavioral scientists we may never escape the problems of emotional attachment.

Systematic investigation of group based on any theory is further handicapped by the impossibility of systematic data gathering without somehow, and in unknown ways, influencing the "objective" reality. All current theory in the behavioral sciences seem to assume there is an "objective reality." In group we do know there are multiple subjective realities.

Intervention Strategies as Variables. In carrying out research activities the interventions themselves become variables which must also somehow become accounted for in final analysis of the data-gathering process. The search continues for interventions that can be utilized with a minimum of contamination of the "objective" reality. There is an assumption in much of the literature that an *objective reality* exists.

Because this theory deals with people in groups, it is necessary to be concerned about the ethical rightness and wrongness questions regarding a theory and its applications (Theobald, 1961).

The Sociological and Anthropological Bases of Theories

Americans are particularly prone to order everything. Theories attempt to impose an order upon phenomena that may normally be in a natural state and without any apparent social order where relative weighting of the variables is of concern. All theory is a point of departure, because the hope for progression of knowledge is short-lived. As soon as I learn something new, it seems to reorganize all previous knowing, so that now I am on a new level of knowing. One goal is to build a model or a theory around which one can collect additional knowledge. The anthropological and sociological bases of theories account for the matrix of culture as well as for the personal context of the model builder.

A model for group work with one group will not always function with a culturally different group. The reasons for saying anything about sociological and anthropological differences are based on the obvious fact that each culture's pattern of human group organization is a complete social system. Hall (1959) has pointed out that cultures do not mix. The reason seems to be connected to the above fact. If a culture is complete, it needs nothing else.

An example of the above was experienced in working with a newly formed group of college graduates. The task of the group was to complete a program in teacher education. The group consisted of persons from mainland, Caucasian middle-class backgrounds and also people from middle-class Oriental backgrounds living in Hawaii. They were placed in an economically and culturally deprived community. Culturally different people have a complete culture nonetheless. The cultural difference was vast indeed between the group of college graduates, embarking on a two-year program to learn to be teachers of the disadvantaged, and the culture and environment of the people with whom they would work. But the problem of launching the group was much less defined by the differences between the groups' basic cultural patterns (middle-class American and the deprived community) than it was a problem *within* the group to adapt to different concepts of reality within their own communication form or code. The mainland students were unable to understand why the local Hawaiian of Oriental extraction middle-class college graduates, tended not to support their "wonderful" suggestions and their energetic attitudes toward aggressive action. Further, they did not understand the reluctance of the local Hawaiian-Oriental person to make overt suggestions or become intensely involved in the ideas that the group pondered. If the Caucasian students from the mainland remained quiet so did the local Hawaiian students. If the Hawaiian-Oriental spoke up, the verbal mainlander sent up a flood of words which seemed to cut off further communication.

You might imagine the complications experienced in attempting to initiate a seminar on group procedures with this very real problem of group differences existing within the class membership. The students had successfully utilized their power to neutralize the usual instructional methods of three professors in previous courses. There was no doubt that any strategy to make overt teaching approaches to this group would be doomed to a similar tragedy. In brief the following things occurred. The class was convened by the Director and the initial session was spent in getting acquainted and explaining the potential parameters of the course. The first session went generally well except that an extended break was taken and there seemed to be little or no concern for covering the course material. I observed the length of the break and wondered if the meanings might be interpreted by my concurrent projections.

The second session of the class was a catastrophe. The initial presentation had to do with some relatively simple material concerning American culture folklore as a means of getting a look at the way an individual experiences his reality in life. The idea is taken from the technique used by cultural anthropologists to study a different culture. Folklore is the system of beliefs shared in common by all members of a group, community, or social system. When the appeals came from three of the students that the material was too difficult for them to understand, I was aware that some adjustments would have to be made immediately in the program. The question I asked, "What is the process happening right now?" formulated the new beginning of the course. I ask the question in any new group when I want to focus on the here-and-now in the process of a group. It is a technique for bringing into verbal conscious awareness what each member is doing with his behavior in the group. Almost no one likes to be exposed this way.

The response to this was ambiguous because they had no language to express any awareness of the intricacies of each member's role and function in the group. Definitions of relationships they were attempting to find within the class became the immediate focus. Whereupon I laid a proposition before the class. I should welcome their participation in determining both the direction and the content of the course. They seemed able to go along with the idea until they encountered their differences within the group. The task, as far as I was concerned, was merely to get behavior that is real and involved in the immediate here-and-now context of the group. The group agreed to help work out this plan and discussed something about their dissatisfaction with previous experiences at utilizing their power to neutralize the professor and his program.

After a relatively brief break the group reconvened itself, I took an inconspicuous position on the periphery of the group and waited. A spokesman emerged and propositioned the group to decide whether it would stay in one large group or subdivide into three smaller work groups. The discussion was mixed and the desires remained conflicting about whether they would (1) break into three small groups, or (2) remain in the large group. As arguments were reported pro and con a spokesman moved for a vote. The vote was taken and the group divided 12 for and 13 against, subdivision. This was the first time many members of the group were aware of the conflicts within the group. Following some dismayed reports from those members surprised by the confrontation, they returned to ask me for some evaluation and interpretation of their current status. The question was asked, "What happened?"

The only comment that seemed appropriate was that the group apparently got along no better without a professor than it did with one. This realization allowed the group to explore a further point about the nature of their internal structure. The spokesman who had originally asked for the vote decided to take some action. His action called for subdividing the group and removing himself physically from the territory currently occupied by the large group and inviting those interested to come along. Those who followed him were without exception mainland Caucasians. One other group formed in another location and the remainder sat without any visible order to follow. It was at this point that the group began to learn something about itself. I was able to continue to observe the group through nearly two years of their life together. Almost 20 percent dropped out. Group action remained a function of dyads and triads. As individuals, the group was a very well-endowed collection of students. As a unit, it remained fragmented.

Commentary

The group's problem revolved initially around the fact that members used and assumed different formal codes. The technique is to surface them into conscious awareness and communicate about them within the group. The errors of perception had to be examined. The most glaring error is the error of choice of adversary. The professor (myself) is not the adversary but the opposing view held by individual members within the group is the adversary. This adversary had remained hidden and therefore could not be attacked. This group of students never succeeded in learning how to deal with each other.

The outcomes of this situation have been recorded many times in many groups and are not different in this case. As soon as individual members of a group learn to recognize the discrepancies between their own assumed code for communication and that being used by others, the process of compromise, integration and synthesis can take place relatively quickly. Because the group was together for two years it was necessary for them to do more than resolve a temporary cease-fire, if they wished to have peace. They needed to allow some integration process to occur. This process became the central subject matter of the course. Because the course was fifteen weeks long it was necessary to help the group learn to manage its own learning beyond the termination of the course so that in future encounters within the group there would be a plan or a code on which they could base their actions. They were unable to fully achieve an integrated group level for functioning. They remained a divided group and practiced mostly by self-defeating methods.

The code became the parameter by which the evaluation of behavior was managed. The basis for validation and the evaluation of behavior requires a common parameter. The parameter should be identified within the group and available to each member. Each member in this group remained isolated with his own unique code.

The definitions of man and of the individual have considerable importance when we look at a systematic framework or context or matrix in which to learn about the intricacies and operations of a group. A group eventually develops a life of its own. The life of a group is experienced by individual members and as such is really a fiction for the group conceived as an entity. The individual is the only entity that exists and he collects together with other individuals in what we define as a group. The social intercourse is prescribed according to a set of very strict rules provided by the cultural context. It is this matrix or framework or model that we want to expand and define for use in further discussions about group and human behavior.

The Human and His Behavior As Two Variables

When human behavior occurs in isolation it is artificial. Human behavior is a variable. A variable has no meaning of its own except as it relates and is connected with other variables.

The individual human being is usually not treated as a variable except in group. The controversy surrounding the issue of whether an individual has absolute magnitude of value and is an entity that should never be studied except in isolation, has not yet achieved resolution in the behavioral sciences.

In group work it is necessary to treat both the behavior and the behaver (person) as variables which have meaning only in relation to other behavior and/or behavers.

Human behavior happens all at once. In order to impose some order on the ambiguity of the variables and the events it is necessary to contrive a structure that can be used as a map. This map is called a *theory.*

Theory is not always made explicit. It is always a point of departure in research and in practice of group counseling and therapy. There is never a question about whether group-counseling practice operates from theory but only a matter of what explicitly is the theory? The original theory I developed for group counseling is described for you in this text. It has grown out of empirical practice with family counseling. It is the statement of the bases for the order I impose upon the ambiguous variable in the behavior encountered in family group counseling.

- The theory should include a statement of the understanding of what life is like in the world of the other person or persons.
- The theory should include a clear-cut statement of the goals toward which group and counseling move.
- The role and function of the counselor is important if he is to be a group leader in the processes of group interaction, indeed, *his* role and function.
- There is need to understand the techniques, methods, strategies and working tools of the *counseling* and *group-action* theory.
- These need to clearly relate to the successful process of counseling and treatment in group.

In Chapter 3, I get to the statement of theory. Chapter 2 attempts to line up the reader with parallel theoretical foundations. It should be kept in mind that most theories *follow* practice and precede research. The sequence was similar in family group counseling and consultation.

Summary

Group practice needs a theory to order the ambiguity of unknown variables. Data taking in research needs a theory with explicit assumptions to guide the understanding of relatedness and connectedness among the behavior events and the variables within events. In order to understand a system designed to make explicit the ambiguity of isolated behavior, we presented some ideas about the human in this group. This background is representative instead of exhaustive. The student will want to know about the culture and sociology of *group* behavior. Also, it is important to be familiar with the several systems in psychology which provide explanations for behavior and methods for treatment. These are treated on selected bases in subsequent chapters.

The *human fix* is group. Group is the organization model used in our culture to pattern behavior and events so we can forecast, even predict, subsequent events in nearly every sequence of life events.

Reductionism and chauvinism are the common phenomena to reduce all complex relationships to manageable size and then conclude: "I am right." This summary may be an example of oversimplification.

2

Theoretical Formulations for
the Concept of Group

Counseling and psychotherapy may be defined as a process for restoring self-respect in the life of an individual. Competent behavior is characteristic of a person with self-respect. If these ideas are profound, why does anyone use group? Why not stay with the model for individual counseling and psychotherapy? Individual counseling and psychotherapy continue to be highly regarded by most leaders in professional practice. Most of us who utilize a group model continue to do some individual counseling. The scope of this work does not include an in-depth treatment of the subject of individual counseling and psychotherapy. We are here concerned now with the individual in a group. In group counseling and psychotherapy one of the goals is individual competent behavior. Theoretical formulations are concerned with both the individual and the group as phenomena to be studied as separate variables.

To achieve competent behavior, the person must achieve self-respect. Beyond these broad-gauged purposes it is possible to select highly specific goals and apply, through group action, the forces to shape a given behavior act. The individual remains as the principal target for all group counseling effort (Burks and Pate, 1970).

Theory provides the structure for defining the connectedness among the many variables operating in a group. Most of the variables are beyond our direct control. In research, we cannot assume that if one variable is controlled all others operate as usual. The reason is the massive interdependence among the variables within a system. The kaleidoscopic nature of behavior in a group has influenced the designs used to collect data. Data are taken on very specific variables—e.g., social distance in a series of person-to-person relationships. Relationship is the variable most frequently utilized in the study of group. The forces which define and qualify the relationship are targets for system-

atic study. The culture provides the broad framework to define relationships among persons within it. However, the infinite variations within
the broad framework permit definition of specific levels of knowing.
The how and the why may change places from one level to another in
human behavior. For example, the behaviorist may know how to get a
given reinforcement schedule to operate in a particular relationship,
but be unable to explain why (at another level) teachers won't use it.

The combination of strategies from various doctrines or counseling
systems can help to create healthy environments for human behavior
growth and development. My theory of group has come out of empirical
practice with family consultation and peer-group counseling. Peer
groups included the full range of ages, group origins, and social statuses.
Subgroups form within any complex group and help to create new
arenas and environments for more specialized learning among the
group members. The relationships formed in the groups provide the
arenas for forming new behavior.

The theory range available for application to group and individual
study is apparently as broad as the psychology of human behavior. A central issue has been the choice of doctrine and the method of application.
One side of the issue is *individual* and the other side is *group.* The problem seems to be whether individual theory can be extended to cover
group phenomena. I believe there is a serious gap in the logic of the literature which purports to base group practice on individual theory.

The position taken here is to avoid the issue at its own level and ask
another type of question. In essence, move to another level of concern
and ask, "What happens in group anyway?" My goal is to attempt to
answer that question by theory and practice through analysis of the
system of formula.

Theoretical Formulations for the Concept of Group

How to Know What You Know

The first purpose of this book is to provide a way of knowing—how
to know what you know. Knowing and how to know what *I* know, may
be my own simple self-fulfilling prophecy. However, when the culture
is considered as a complete system of beliefs, and everyone in a given
culture system shares common methods of thinking, is it any wonder the
self-fulfilling prophecy becomes central? Of course, you may feel yourself an exception until *I* examine my own belief system in a group. Then
I can discover that *knowing* is an illusive isolate, like a speck in the eye
—moving with each shift of the glance, seen but nonexistent.

Learning How to Learn

The second purpose of this book is to help each reader *learn how he learns.* When McLuhan (1964) punned *massage* for *message,* the signal was open for realization of more than one level of knowing. The *conditions* under which we learn may be more profound than is the *content* of what is learned (Loukes, 1964). This implies more is happening than mere transfer of informational content. There is an affective mass which needs care and feeding in order to grow. If left ambiguous, the emotional side of learning will remain in the mystical realm of assumption and speculation. There is no resolution of the question: Is learning a unitary process? (Walker, p. 25, 1967)

Group is a method for investigating the affective dimensions of behavior in addition to studying interaction patterns and cognitive interchange. The emotional or affective realm is left undefined and thus in mysticism. Techniques to manipulate outcomes or products of the group take precedence over understanding the process within the group, beyond mapping the communication pattern among members. Many group procedures can be classified at this level of surface manipulation of information flow among members. To move toward the unmapped complexity of depth to levels of abstraction beyond the surface is how we enter the realm of group theory.

Relationship

The most profound concept about group is the complex phenomenon of relationship. Relationship is a dynamic condition consisting of the sum of identity, self-concept, and interpersonal interaction. This idea is at once complex and central to the theory of group counseling and group psychotherapy as used by most professional specialists. I define relationship as the interpersonal contract between two persons, a person and a group, a community, or other identified entity. The contract sets forth the level of commitment each person will expect to give to the other. The commitment level defines the contributions each person will make to the welfare and development of the other person. Montagu (1970) defines such a commitment as love. Because relationships may be negative, the degree of commitment may range from intense emotion to benign neutrality. There is *always* a relationship defined for *each* member of a group. There is no such thing as a nonrelationship. The task is to discover the terms of the interpersonal contract. Like communication, you cannot *not* communicate. You cannot *not* have a relationship. You may wish to redefine the relationship in any given specific instance. Because a person's behavior is *always* an expression of the meaning *I* am experiencing in a given relationship (contract) at any given moment in time, *behavior* is the variable to observe to collect the data which define the existing relationship. Behavior is *always* an expression of the meaning a person gives to the terms of the contract. Further reduction of the relationship concept will be given in chapter (3) three when I set forth my theory of group.

Theory Formulations for Counseling and Psychotherapy

Formal Attributes of a Good Theory. A clear and concise statement of the idea is essential. Differentiation of the unique qualities is presented within a concrete framework to insure preciseness of relationships among the major variables. For example, in group theory it is necessary to have a clear idea of the target as a single person or a collective of persons. Our language is imprecise unless underlying assumptions are made explicit. Key words must be defined by more words and examples. The metaphor sets limits of its own, so we need to reckon with such variables.

In addition to being clear and concise, a good theory is

- comprehensive
- explicit
- parsimonious
- research-generating

Comprehensive coverage of all relevant variables without distortion of any phenomenon is a required task. The theory statement has to be comprehensive enough to serve as a point of departure in research formulations. The verification of major assumptions can be achieved through systematic data gathering and analysis by rigorous research designs. A major problem in research on group phenomena persists because the group social system lends itself to a machine model or black-box phenomenon. We can study input and output of a group without any verifiable data about the internal functioning of the group. Inversely, we can study the group's internal processes and exclude the inputs from external forces and ignore the products or outputs. The alternatives are not limited to these polar examples. The range of choices among possible alternatives may well approach infinity. Ambiguous conditions abound in group. Not the least of these has been the absence of comprehensive theories.*

---

*Because of the complex nature of the human group, it may be necessary to assume that the social system of a group is its own best explanation and the current organization of the system the only basis or methodology for study.

Explicit statements of the idea expressed by the theory are another requirement in the list of formal attributes. How does one define *explicit?* Perhaps the criterion of *explicit* can be met if ambiguity can be reduced to near zero. *Precise, definite,* and *specific* are good synonyms for "explicit."

To be frugal, even stingy, is considered a virtue in theory building. Parsimony means a stringent criterion is placed upon the statement of the theory and the quality of its application. For example, the essence of the entire theory of relativity in physics was expressed in the familiar mathematical formula of $E = mc^2$, yet many refinements for specific ideas and the relationships (connectedness) required volumes. Group has no metalanguage, as mathematics represents for physics, to express the abstract relationships of the variables. Because of this task, our statement and theory will be less parsimonous than Einstein's formula.

Continuing the example of relativity theory, it is extremely important for any theory to generate research. This formal attribute reminds us that theory is a beginning, not an end in and of itself. An untested theory is much like a myth. As long as we act as if the myth is true, the self-fulfilling prophecy phenomenon continues to operate. A good theory may lead to relatively useless information because the central idea isolates a variable and creates an artificial context. In group, isolation is artificial, whether the individual member or the group is isolated. This is why most existing theory and the derived group-counseling systems are without substance, because theories designed to explain relationships of *individual* subjects (whether persons or traits) lose their power when extrapolated to *group* subjects. When form is kept and substance is lost, theory is useless. We refer to this state as *immaculate scientism* —form but no substance.

Underlying Bases of Theory

Theory is characterized by a person and by a name. Freud (1938, 1929, 1935) is the person identified with Freudian psychoanalysis. The neo-Freudians were identified with newer forms and their individual modifications of theory. The personal basis remains a central feature of most theory.

Historical bases rest upon the stage of development characteristic of a given era. Because of the personal dominance, what is popular may be more of a fad than a substantive theoretical foundation. It seems accurate enough to claim the modern conceptualization of man and his behavior began with Freud's formulations about it. Historically speaking, the entire notion of an unconscious has barely outlined the man Freud himself. Already there are numerous theories and systems which deal directly with the human being and his behavior. For more than thirty years the development of group counseling and group psychotherapy has been under way. With the exception of Moreno's role theory in psychodrama and sociodrama, there has been mostly an extrapolation of individual theory to group phenomena (Fullmer, 1969c).

Sociological and anthropological bases of theory may lend considerable depth to the substance of understanding behavior. It is assumed that group as a concept and as a reality began in the social system long before the discipline of psychology. The group must have begun with man as a biological survival vehicle. According to Mowrer (1968), the systematic use of the social group or community was common among the early Christians as a means of restoring self-respect to deviant group members. In light of the prison system's corrections record in America, self-respect has been more frequently shattered than restored. Deviant members are not healed and restored to the community with their self-respect intact.

Human organization is based upon the patterns of group identified by sociological and anthropological systems of analysis. The culture and the social system influence the parameters and set the tolerance limits for group and individual behavior.

Philosophical bases of theory set the definition of man followed by the theory builder. The existentialist deals with man as ultimately free and responsible. The behaviorist sees man as determined by the very limits one might call nonchoices. However, the philosophical point of departure has influence within any system of psychology because it directs the flow of energy and determines the amount of energy employed to actualize the system. We feel the stress as energy is expended if we defend one system of psychology against another system. Such a predicament can drain the energy and waste the resources without producing any systematic development of new knowledge. In addition to a philosophical basis, the personal nature of counseling has spawned discipleships for one theory over another on the basis of the charisma of the mentor. It is important for the student of group to develop a clearly defined and self-conscious understanding of the philosophical foundations of the system of counseling and the theory it is based upon.

Psychological bases for theory take us back to the beginning of the treatment interventions to be employed. These interventions vary with each system, method, and technique. Because psychology grew out of philosophy there may always be a symbiosis. But the level of knowing at the point of action need no longer hang in the balance of philosophical questions such as, Ought we to be doing this? Rather, we wish to ask an empirical question: What are we doing? On the basis of data derived from the empirical question, it is assumed the value balance in the philosophical question will have some substance on which to base a decision.

Empirical Questions in Group Counseling Practice

What is happening *now?* For many years this question has confounded students in classes and clinics, social-personal interaction groups for counseling and therapy. Social-personal interaction, indeed, in each encounter where the task is to teach about group and behavior phenomena.

Analysis of interaction is one way to see the pattern of communication and the behavior outcomes. Watzlawick, Beavin, and Jackson (1967) have put a systematic "systems" analysis to interaction. The hallmark contribution in interaction analysis reported by Bateson and Jackson was the double-bind theory of schizophrenia (Watzlawick et al., 1967, pp. 212–213).

In the analysis of interaction, the key empirical question to be answered is: What is the consequence of each response when it is viewed as a stimulus? For example, if I say to you "How are you?" it is possible for you to reply to the *content* of the message by saying "I am fine." However, if I send simultaneously a message that I don't really care how you feel—this second message defines our *relationship.* If you do not accept the relationship definition, the message response will carry the two distinct levels of meaning—namely, *content* and *relationship.* Therefore it is not only *what* is said, but the *way* it is said that is systematically analyzed in the Interaction Model.

Engineering the Environment. Skinner (1948) set forth the principles and system associated with operant conditioning through his created character Frazier in *Walden Two.* The utopia described in detail by Skinner has spawned systems for managing group behavior by scheduling the individual's behavior. The idea of natural selection was rejected and replaced by design. Accident gave way to a plan, as would be expected in any utopia. Systematic programming of the reinforcement schedule is the hallmark of the behavioristic modification empirical model. Social and environmental engineering has become familiar in a number of applied areas such as juvenile corrections and teaching machines, later known as *programmed instruction.* Unfortunately, most of the behavior modification models have no total environment scope as did the utopia described by Skinner. The reinforcement pattern follows operant principles of rewarding any desired behavior response and ignoring or remaining neutral to all other responses. This in no way covers the entire subject of behaviorism. It does indicate the nature and direction of energy employed by the Skinner point of view.

Prescriptions for response behavior are the central source of Adlerian technique. The model is basically paternal or authority oriented. "I know." If you listen to me and follow these practices, the child will respond in this prescribed way. Empirically, the model works if the prescriptions are followed. The group of parents and counselors formed by the application of the techniques becomes the community of friends for support of each other member. The continuing exposure to the group defines roles and sets expectations for the active participants. Each person is to progress from neophyte to experienced practitioner through the several essential levels. In practice, the observations made indicate that usually a small cadre of professionals form to administer to others the benefits of the system. The fallacy in this is simply that any accrued benefit has been derived from participation in performing the service, not in receiving the service. For practical reasons the reinforcement schedules approximate those encountered in the real world (Dreikurs, Corsini, Lowe, and Sonstegard, 1959; Dreikurs, 1948; Dinkmeyer and Dreikurs, 1963).

The key pattern to behavior emphasizes the *natural consequences* of any act. This assumes an order to the community formed by human organizations in any given culture. The interventions are based on the empirical notion about maladjustment. Maladjustment is treated as a fact. *Natural consequence* as seen to embody the schedules for reinforcement which shape the behavior of the individual. Natural consequence is prescribed as sufficient to modify maladjusted behavior. It is a nonspecific reward and punishment system maintained because each person believes his culture-based behavior is "natural" (Hall, 1959).

Selected Examples of Established Theoretical Formulations Used in Group Counseling and Group Psychotherapy

From among the many theoretical formulations I have selected the following three examples. Psychodrama or role theory is especially basic to group counseling and group psychotherapy because most techniques currently in use come from Moreno's (1946 a and b) work. Behaviorism has spawned a host of eclectic practices in group counseling based on the stimulus-response learning theories derived since Pavlov (1927) reported his work on conditioned reflex. Freud (1929) contributed psychoanalysis, which greatly influenced the direction of development in psychotherapy and later in group counseling.

The student of group will want more information than I can reasonably include in this text. The purpose here is to set up a framework within which to present the bases of a theory of group counseling and to show the interdependence of all theory on the structure or parameters of the culture. Further development of the ideas presented in this text for the first time needs the background of established theoretical formulations to bring out the potential for research and practice. I need to link up with the reader's perceptions through the vehicle of published literature, established group counseling practice, and the developing need for rigorous research. I will postpone until Chapter 3 my theory of behavior based on the concept of group as defined by the culture.

Behavior Therapy and Counseling in Groups

Unique to any theory building created for group applications is the risk of evaluation. Judgment of process and product is common practice in all counseling and therapy strategies. Behaviorists have achieved a convincing strategy by creating a model in which it is possible to observe behavior in parcels small enough to count and consequently arrange in frequency distributions. This virtue permits research designs to be satisfied by objective observations and psychological measurement of clearly defined referents (Krumboltz and Thoreson, 1969).

Beyond empirical practicalities, the issue of *referents* contains some basic differences with other standard and classic therapies. Take the whole issue of *criteria.* Most group therapies use *group norms* as the referent to gauge their progress, evaluate relative value and judge the efficacy of the treatment interventions. This tendency grew out of the psychological measurement movement and consequently shares many of the fallacies of setting criterion variables for group norms on the basis of *group performance.* The norm may be based upon the least common denominator. The major handicap in normative criteria is that all measures are relative to an indefinite referent or norm, and as such become imprecise to measure in meaningful quantitative terms. Qualitative terms are used. Qualitative terms are less likely to satisfy statistical research designs than are quantitative measures.

Behaviorists use criterion measures for their referents. The advantage of criterion measures is immediately evident because a definitive measure is possible. This gives the further advantage of preciseness in measures taken as data in relation to a specific defined criterion instead of a norm ambiguously defined. This type of model fits research criteria with greater precision than any normative data model available for the standard and classic therapies.

Criterion Measures: Advantages and Disadvantages for Group

The most obvious advantage was set forth immediately above. Several more should be mentioned here, even though our purpose is to give only a sketch for each system. The interventions used in behavior therapy require a controlled environment (Lazarus, 1968).

The degree of environment control has a direct impact upon the effectiveness of the procedures applied in behavior therapy. In group settings the degree of control may be reduced because of the number of variables operating simultaneously. Operant conditioning procedures applied to groups need a high degree of control of the actual physical setting in which a given group lives.

Theoretical principles related directly to specific behaviors coupled with criterion measures to demonstrate changes in the subjects' responses provide another major advantage to behavior therapy. The advantage is seen in the precision of evaluation of progress toward specific goals or criterion measures.

Reinforcement is perhaps the most important principle because almost all behavior in a group carries reinforcement potential for one or more members.

Conditioning is the concept necessary to understand how a human being can master so many diverse elements and combine them into meaningful patterns. In one sense conditioning is the process by which two or more stimuli combine to form a more efficient system. Conditioning frees us from being dependent upon self-conscious monitoring of all of our behavior all of the time. It gives behavior the intuitive or unconscious quality, as in walking, talking, or seeing. There are varieties of conditioning defined by the way it occurs. Classical, operant, and instrumental conditioning depict the major varieties.

Pavlov (1927) reported the evidence to substantiate the form of conditioning called *classical*. The process is the capacity to substitute or interchange stimuli and keep the same response. Pavlov's dog experiments are well known for demonstrating this phenomenon. In them, meat powder was the unconditional stimulus which was paired with a metronome bell. The bell became the conditioned stimulus. The dogs would salivate at the sound of the bell, thus changing the unconditioned response to a conditioned response.

Skinner (1938) explained the application of reinforcement to a selected behavior act in an otherwise free environment. The selected response is reinforced until other responses are omitted. Then the response is put on cue so the response can be elicited on command.

Instrumental conditioning happens when one alternative response, among several equal-value responses to a given stimulus situation, is instrumental in goal achievement. The application of instrumental learning models requires some contraints in the subject's environment. However, the practical applications are evident. Random-seeking behavior in a new or novel social milieu is reduced because alternatives *not* associated with goal achievement tend to be ignored in subsequent trials.

In summary of the conditioning principles and processes, it should be noted that several processes of learning might be described as conditioning. From the simplest learning described as classical conditioning to the complex generalization levels of gestalt principles and processes, there is enough substance to contain many volumes. Here, we will select enough to circumscribe the parameters and define the territory necessary to understand group counseling and group psychotherapy practice. The applications of conditioning principles may be used to explain other phenomena in behavior group therapy such as extinction, desensitization, and modeling.

Role Theory and Psychodrama Technique

Moreno (1946a), the undisputed pioneer of group therapy and group psychotherapy, came to the United States from Germany in 1925. His contributions of psychodrama technique and role theory, in association with sociodrama and sociometry, have provided much of the nomenclature in group counseling and therapy. While acceptance of the group concept has gained greater support than the parent technique of psychodrama, this technique continues to appear in practice and in the literature under the guise of new names. Moreno has also influenced the contemporary group movement in its use of role theory concepts and techniques—nonverbal techniques, encounter, tele, spontaneity, confrontation, catharsis, and reality testing.

Role theory is based on the concept that the person *is* the role. The central idea has come to mean that the person is the way he behaves in any given life event. This expression is the tangible form of the self as demonstrated in the role which the person has assumed. Psychodrama and sociodrama are techniques used to apply the role theory idea in working with groups. Because the results are immediately available to all participants, there has been little need for traditional research methodologies. Perhaps this fact accounts for the absence of psychodrama in the academic arena.

Psychodrama is a method of achieving self-disclosure. The central principle is spontaneity. If one can be spontaneous, self-disclosure follows. Self-disclosure is a form of self-confrontation with reality, and is indeed a form of reality testing because others are present in the group to provide feedback for confirmation and validation.

Catharsis has been considered a therapeutic technique because to share responsibility with others builds a relationship which in turn expects support as well as it provides support. However, Mowrer (1968) has suggested another reason why catharsis is therapeutic. His idea is that a secret kept unshared is pathological or sick. Telling a secret or sharing responsibility through catharsis is a way of releasing the barriers to trust. Relationships based on trust lead to spontaneous expression, and thus mental health is attained.*

Evaluation in psychodrama is the direct act of behavior itself. The behavior act provides its own test because the drama of role playing occurs in the theater of reality testing. In this arena the competence level of the behavior is assessed immediately in the drama act. Using the concept of health–disease as a dichotomy tends to shift responsibility away from the behaver, whereas competence as a measure or criterion keeps the responsibility on the behaver. Psychodrama techniques keep confronting the behaver with his level of competence. The treatment is based upon the assumption the behaver will give up the incompetent games and choose competent behavior because it fits the culture's reinforcement schedules.

Trusting others in a group situation is a major developmental task. Mutual trust and safety are antecedent to sharing anything, especially responsibility. But trust and safety are achieved if responsibility for confidential relationship among the members of the group is actually understood as something *we* share.

Role theory is based on the assumption that tangible action or behavior is the directly observable expression of a person's basic identity, ego, self, or way of being in the world. Mysticism, metaphysics, and magic are bypassed for the tangible action immediately experienced. Common-sense knowledge and common culture conditioning permit immediate feedback systems for each person participating.

Psychoanalytic Theory

Psychoanalysis (Freud, 1929) is an elaborate system based upon principles and assumptions which collectively are known as psychoanalytic theory. Historically, Freud's contribution to personality theory was significant because it revolutionized the concepts about human behavior and personality disorders. The system of psychoanalysis provided a more humane basis for treatment of pathological behavior in

---

*The concept of health is used as a concept of the absence of disease. However, Mowrer and others, including this author, feel the disease-health dichotomy should be discontinued in favor of behavior competence.

man (Freud, 1935). While the treatment technique of psychoanalysis has gained wide recognition, it should be noted that other treatment procedures may be based upon the psychoanalytic theory, or more accurately, principles (Hobbs, 1956).

Group therapy and group-counseling methods based upon psychoanalytic principles have developed in response to the trend toward group. The group increases the number of reactions available to each participant in contrast to the one-to-one model for treatment in psychoanalysis. The analysis of behavior is essentially the same in both group and individual models. What is different is the multiple response relationships between the behaver and group members. The relationship between the therapist and the patient in psychoanalysis takes on elaborate dimensions and may be continued for years. In group, the nature of the relationship between the leader (therapist) and the group members is diluted by the numbers of persons present in each session and by the number of sessions that make up the life time of a group. The group provides an expansion in potential alternatives for relationships for each member. It should be noted further that the kinds of concerns and issues vary from individual analysis and group analysis. Sometimes the choice of model (group-individual) rests with the preference of the therapist. Some choose group models; others prefer individual analysis.

There is no attempt here to make explicit the complex system of psychoanalysis and its many elaborate derivations. Anyone interested in further study may begin with Wolf and Schwartz (1962), who elaborate six parameters of group. These include (1) multiple responses from group members, (2) the leader's authority status and the peer status of group members, (3) communication among members and communication within a given member (inter-intra), (4) shifting attention among members, issues and events, (5) alternatives of roles between being helped and helping someone else, and (6) forced interaction of each member and encouraging practice with changed behavior. These above listed six parameters could define the fundamental dynamics of most therapy groups. Combined with psychoanalytic principles, a special type of therapy group could be defined. If these fundamental dynamics are combined with existential principles and theory, a somewhat different group therapy system emerges.

The significant idea about any theory and system of intervention rests with the formula for interacting and the parameters established in the group setting. For example, the family is a group with established parameters defining its purpose and setting. What the family group can do is contained within its definition. Any intervention, whether psychoanalytic, group or family group consultation, follows a formula for interacting that fits into the ongoing dynamics of the family group (Fullmer and Bernard, 1968).

Group Diversity

Each group has a life of its own. The range in diverse types of groups can be as broad as the culture, although groups formed for therapy, counseling, and training limit the range somewhat. There remains an ambiguity about group concepts which promotes a kind of polarization toward one type of group or another type of group to the exclusion of other types. The charismatic leader may spawn a host of followers. At the other extreme is the self-taught, do-it-yourself grouper. In between the extremes we find the ambivalent ambiguous condition among persons interested in group but unsophisticated about just what is involved.

The Form and the Substance

The form for group is essentially dictated by the task it is to perform. Human organization abounds with models for bringing together single units or bodies into a collection or grouping. The most common image for group is the form of collecting members into a common geographic territory. Other group models do not require the convening of a collection of bodies. Such groups are used for decision making when individual bias is important to the judgment. Frequently this model is used without the different members knowing the identity of the other participants.

Sherif and Sherif (1964) described research with reference groups which are similar in many respects to decision-making groups who do not collect in one geographic meeting place. Teen-age idols and groups collect followings which become reference groups for other teen-agers. Reference groups are another example of peer groups the person aspires to join. Conformity and deviation in behavior can be evaluated by studying the patterning of relationships within groups and the values supported by the members. Fads are examples of shared values in a group.

Now we move from *form* to *substance*. Patterning of relationships within a group is *form*. The values defining expectations of behavior in support of specific values is *substance*. Dynamics of groups, or group dynamics, deal almost exclusively with *form*. The behavior of individual members reflects the *substance*.

Summary

Theoretical formulations affecting group may be viewed from two broad categories. One is the theory category including any relevant theory of human behavior concerned with individual personality, learning, and nature (or culture). Second is the dynamics of group, or group dynamics. The principles derived from the theories of behavior constitute a level of the formulations essential to understanding group: theory and practice.

The culture forms a frame of reference for all behavior and group forms, substance, and types. Each use of group as a method of counseling or therapy requires a formula for intervention into the life styles of people commensurate with the cultural parameters defining the group. This fit is the link between theory and practice. Otherwise the dynamics constitute form only.

3

The Concept of Group:
Theory and System

Isolate one Variable. The goal of science is *to know*. The method of science ultimately requires empirical verification. The way of thinking for science as adopted by the behavioral sciences has remained enamored with the single variable criterion. While it is true that controls applied to entire systems of behavior make observation increasingly mystical and at best ambiguous, it is also a fact that to study an isolated variable is to bias the context where groups of humans are concerned. The point is disquieting because of the stated difference between the laws governing the part-whole polarization of units. If the isolated variable cannot hope to explain the whole, the whole cannot explain the part. It is just as illogical to study the whole, which in human behavior is the group. The conclusion is simply to study that unit under question and *not* to generalize to the other unit.

The study of human behavior reflects many attempts to explain its origin, its variables, and its paradoxical predictability. The criterion of individual stability and adjustment based on compliance and conformity to the nonchoices of the cultural rules defined by a community of like-minded members, seems to best epitomize the central themes in much of the group literature. There is the focus on personality. Another, on learning, has built a system called *behaviorism*. The Freudian psychoanalytic movement focused attention upon the effects of early life experiences and later neuroses and even psychoses. Normal behavior was somehow kept defined as stable, adjusted or described by other indefinite labels.

Learning theory was derived in highly restricted, narrowly defined contexts. Nevertheless learning theory explains how human behavior responds to symbols, cues, and stimuli combining the contingencies in one or another form of conditioning. This development has contributed heavily to the knowledge necessary to understand human behavior *in restricted contexts,* narrowly defined. One of the phenomena, experimental neurosis, which has occurred in animals during experimentation, cannot be fully explained by learning and conditioning concepts. Clearly additional conceptualization incorporating higher levels of abstraction are needed to understand new or different explanations beyond those provided by any one limited system. The concept of group is one attempt to go beyond the severely limiting contexts of previous research knowledge to look at a theory of human behavior which includes the total context of the culture as reproduced in microcosm—the small group, namely the family.

Most of the literature assumes behavior exists a priori to a life event, simply being stimulated and given in response to previously conditioned symbols. Such a point of view omits any contingency about how the behavior is formed. Because of this, the operant principle holds that behavior occurs in random fashion and persists only if reinforced immediately following the occurrence. Subsequently, the new behavior may be shaped by changing the stimulus or conditioned symbol. Existing knowledge has led toward the engineering of environments and other social control innovations. These efforts have been most successful with instruction of known subject matter when specific content is to be learned.

Another school of psychology embraces the view that man must be free within the context sanctioned by the social system. This view leads to group procedures of the personal-social training and sensitivity types. The movement toward the use of group to create a milieu which *permits* new behavior to form, is currently widespread. Permission is the *key* and the *limit* of intervention. Now, the claim against this type of group work is leveled at the lack of structured follow-through after the opportunity to form new behavior is set.

Simple logic would lead to setting a model that could capitalize on both systems. Set up the group, create the learning situation, permit the behavior to happen, follow through with operant reinforcement principles, and shape the new behavior into the prameters of the criterion or behavioral goal.

We have been doing the above for some years. However, we have found that simple combining of procedures from discrepant theories can create verbal communication problems because of conceptual discontinuity.

Conceptual discontinuity results from two or more divergent systems based on different orders of complexity and different levels of abstraction. Behaviorism and gestalt psychology form one example.

Because the logic of every system is essentially complete, we began to develop a new theory derived from neither behaviorism nor gestalt psychology, but symbiotic with them and most other existing systems. For research purposes, the use of specific goals permits the utilization of behavioristic or gestalt concepts, depending upon the nature of the phenomenon under study. If the phenomenon is simple conditioning, the behavioristic model is useful. When the behavior under study combines context and individual contingencies, gestalt concepts are helpful.

The fallacy of any system of thought, whether in psychology or another discipline, is the tender trap of creating its own self-fulfilling prophecies. The ideas presented here for your use will probably not be completely free of a similar fallacy.

The Origins of Family Group Theory

Back as far as 1957 there was a restless seeking for a new conceptualization of group therapy and counseling. Dissatisfaction with existing conceptualizations stemmed from the fact that treatment intervention and observed outcome seemed to be only academically related. It was reasoned that any system of therapy that could not explain its failure was probably similarly handicapped to explain its success. Furthermore, most group strategies still focused upon the individual as target patient.

How about the group? What does the group social system have to do with the individual's behavior?

To get an answer to these and other questions it was necessary to establish a program to prepare ourselves to carry on the developmental work. Developmental work was carried on within our staff to conceptualize the use of small groups as a teaching-learning model. Further developmental work was required to achieve the formal program structure. In 1958, the first formal step was taken. A new postdoctoral training program was launched at the University of Oregon Medical School Psychiatric Division. The model was a one-to-one treatment method. Each staff member in counselor education followed in rotation for six months or a full academic year (9 months) of training. By September 1961 I had completed one postdoctoral tour and my turn came up again. Three other staff members were included in the one-year cycle. Two of us were assigned to work with family groups. Each family had one or more members who had been referred to the Medical School for psychiatric evaluation and possible treatment.

The object of our search was to find a method of treatment which would result in changing the behavior of the individual. We were interested in a model that school counselors might use. What happened when we began treating the family group was far too complex for existing theory to adequately explain (Fullmer and Bernard, 1968). We learned many things to share with others interested in group concepts. I continue to study the method under actual, real-life conditions, even though the original group of families was convened for a projected nine months. Many years and many hundreds of families later, there still seems a long way to go before all of the phenomena can be fully explained. Unique among the original goals was the idea that treatment of the entire immediate social system in a family group would change behavior in a target individual. This "unique" notion was clearly demonstrated. What was less "clear" was the nature of the forces that brought about change. The theory and all the principles we have discovered may help the reader begin to understand how behavior begins, how it is shaped, how it is maintained in a group. First, the behavior theory is stated.

Statement of the Theory

Human behavior is formed by the individual person to make explicit his unique experience in a group life event.

- All behavior expressed in a group is the symbolic formulation of the individually perceived relationship between the behaver and the others at a given moment in time.
- Subjective meaning is made explicit by the choice of behavior.
- Behavior expresses the personal definition of relationship. (This is the only motivation principle.)
- Behavior is the symbolic vehicle for communicating subjective meaning.
- Subject meaning, relationship, and basic identity usually designated as role, self-concept, or ego ideal, all form antecedents to behavior.
- Behavior is an explicit expression of the person's goodness-of-fit, relative to others in the group, between the person's ego ideal and the other person's expressed perception of it.
- Relationship is a dynamic variable, not a static fact.
- Behavior is rarely created out of a vacuum of prior exposure to behavior alternatives.
- New behavior is usually a replication of the behavior observed in a prior exposure (modeling).
- The need to meet the expectations of the group is learned in a confidential, intimate, interpersonal relationship. The relationship must exist over a long term, i.e., the mother-infant relationship.

Assumptions

There are a number of significant assumptions underlying the theory. For group, the most significant assumption is that group expectations motivate individual behavior. Stated another way: We assume the individual will want to meet group expectations for his behavior. It follows that when social pressure is enough to get an individual to modify his behavior, the assumption is met. Acceptance is a sufficient reinforcer only with the person who has learned the need for acceptance by others. This capability is learned only in a close confidential relationship with *one* other human being, usually the mother. The need for acceptance is learned. This is the universal antecedent to social control. Social order or control is necessary before a stable confidential interpersonal relationship can build its existence over time.

Time is the essential variable in a relationship if long-term intimacy is to be achieved. Short-term intimacy is relatively easy to achieve, but is disorganizing to the human personality and the human organization, over the long-term.

System of Behavior

The system of behavior based upon the above stated theory consists of the continuing behavior responses within the context of a group. The system is characterized as a response that follows a stimulus in a group context and thereby perpetuates the rules and parameters of the context. There are three variables according to the above: stimulus, response, and context. Each of these variables is extremely complex, but the greatest complexity lies with "context" because it contains the second-order variable "relationship," as well as the *assumed* observable variables of stimulus and response. There are no absolute magnitudes or values, only variables in this communications model of interaction. The principle of relativity and the principle of indeterminacy as described by Hall (1959) are useful to understand the relationships.

The relationships connecting the multiple variables in a system of behavior are further complicated by the fact that each social system contains many subsystems—each complete with its own rules and parameters for interacting. For example, if there are four persons in a family, there are family units of four persons each according to each member's perception. There are four individual perceptions of the family unit. For each counselor added to the group, there is additional complication at the "systems" level.

The system concept of behavior patterns does not simplify the reading of complex behavior. It merely affords a set of rules of its own by which an investigator can impose a structure on what otherwise appears as an ambiguous mass of mystical symbols—namely, undefined behavior. Further, the reader is reminded that what is understood about behavior as a result of imposing the systems model is more representative of the rules and laws governing the *system* than the rules and laws governing *behavior.*

Behavior and interaction may be represented by many different methods. Each method will impose its own laws and offer an explanation in terms defined by the method. Psychoanalysis, existentialism, and behaviorism are three prominent examples of imposed structures, each containing preconceived assumptions and internally consistent rules or laws governing the relative meaning among variables interpreted within the respective frame of reference.

Students of human behavior need to be capable of living with large doses of ambiguity. The patience and fortitude necessary to spend time observing, defining, and restructuring methods of investigation continue to be significant. The chief article of faith remains tied to the ultimate paradox of introspection—understand thyself. The paradox dissolves in group because others can feed back their ideas about you. Thus a criterion is established. You may then compare the other person's idea about you with your own assessment. The results and the process may be validated and confirmed with the additional group membership.

The Group As Isolate

This theory of group is a theory of behavior. The group is used as an interdependent interaction phenomenon. Behavior of the individual within a group is seen as interdependent at the pattern and systems levels, but independent at the isolate and set levels. (See next section, Isolates, Sets, Patterns, and Systems.) The central fact is: *The rules or laws governing relation among variables change when we move from behavior of the individual as isolate to individual as part of a whole group.* The part is governed by specific laws governing specialized parts, as in photosynthesis in a leaf. In General System Theory for example, the parts of a system are governed by rules or laws that are different from the systems's laws. This is the basis of most error in the literature about human behavior.

Whenever the study of behavior requires the isolation of a portion of the whole, the investigator should avoid generalizations beyond the limits of his data. Behavior at every level of abstraction has its own rationale and its own logic. This is true for the individual within the group and the group (family) within the community. There is another source of logic with its own rationale. The source is the context the group gets from the culture. The culture social system is complete and includes all behavior variables permitted within the limits created by the rules or laws governing the relationships among behavior isolates, sets of isolates, patterns and systems.

Isolates, Sets, Patterns, and Systems

Isolates of behavior, like sounds of letters of the alphabet, are the smallest units observable in a given phenomenon. An example of a behavior isolate is the conversation distance you maintain when you are talking to me about a neutral subject. (This distance would be two or three inches less than two feet—about 20 or more inches.) This isolate holds for all persons in a similar culture. Though all isolates are universal for a given culture, it does not follow that all persons will have any self-conscious feeling except when someone violates one of them.

Sets of isolates form the substance of patterns of behavior. Each set has its own function but has no further meaning until it is combined with other sets to form a pattern ruled by the laws or guidelines of a pattern. An example of sets can be given combining the 45 variables of spoken English, the initial teaching alphabet. Isolates are limited (45) but the sets are all of the possible combinations of isolates. Sets combine in almost infinite array into patterns or words.

Patterns of behavior consist of isolates and sets organized and governed by rules or laws. The pattern of a given person can be observed and recorded. The individual's pattern of behavior will be a replica of the pattern found in his culture (Hall, 1959).

Systems of behavior are the product of two or more patterns of behavior functioning as a unit. The social system is one example. The more patterns included, the more complex is the system because of the addition of variables. Systems of behavior are governed by rules and laws.

Group as Interpersonal Model

Behavior can be observed and studied directly in the interpersonal model. The intrapsychic model creates the necessity to rely on inference from observed phenomena. The communications method of studying human behavior is essentially an interpersonal mode. The machine-computer metaphor may be helpful to the understanding of input-output. We can observe and measure input and output without knowing anything about the internal processes of the mind, just as we use a computer. Analysis of behavior in the interpersonal communications method consists of collecting the isolates of behavior. It is possible to keep a permanent record. The observations are collected together. The patterns formed by the isolates lead to a study of what makes the system work. The rules and laws governing the variables can be made explicit.

Levels for Analysis of Behavior

Hall (1959) described the language of the culture as silent and pervasive. Behavior is a language. The task is to learn how to read it. The following system has been useful in learning and teaching. The system consists of categories. The categories are progressive in the level of generalization each one contains. Hall (1959, p. 96) gives three categories for verbal language: isolates (specific sounds), sets (of isolates, like words), and patterns (the way words are put together, grammar). To this basic list of categories may be added *systems* (such as social systems) and *culture.* However, the broad inclusiveness of the latter two categories do not help in the analytic processes.

The isolates of behavior include all of the specific behaviors an individual knows about. What is the inventory of behavior isolates? It may be presumed to be potentially infinite in a given culture, but not for a given individual. The potential may be infinite for an individual, but the redundancy in the actual life of a person delimits the repertory to a finite number.

An isolate of behavior is of no consequence except as a tool leading to sets of isolates. We study and take data at all levels of behavior. Sets and patterns take most of our time and attention. An isolate, like personal distance in conversation, is observed in isolation but used in sets—i.e., relationship definition (Engebretson and Fullmer, 1970).

Sets are of use because patterns are found by observing how the sets go together. The order combined with the pattern yields a system. The job is the systematic search for the isolates of behavior (Engebretson, 1969). These will be of the same level as sounds in a language. Like the sound system of language, the isolates of behavior will form a social system. The social system will hold from individual through groups and community, indeed throughout all social-cultural human organization. Social literacy is the function of mapping the behavior system of the group. This procedure is reflected in the initial stages of getting acquainted in a new group. Once these mapping exercises are completed, the group is predictable for each member and consequently safe.

Paradigm for the System Based on the Theory

The system based on the theory of behavior stated earlier in this chapter is presented in the following pages. The student of group concepts needs to learn to differentiate among the major and minor uses of these phenomena. (1) The group is a target of study as well as a tool for working with behavior development, training, counseling and therapy. (2) The system of thinking and acting out group procedures based on the theory of behavior is sufficient for research and practice. If research and practice are separated, the products of such efforts would be mostly academic or philosophical. (3) The group may be the vehicle for study of the individual human being. (4) The combination of target behavior for study and procedural study may combine as a family is combined. Any separation of individual and group for study is a violation of the behavior model of the family group.

The rule to use as a guideline follows from the question of whether or not the group is contrived by someone, convened for a period of time for a specific purpose, and terminated; or whether the group is a natural (cultural) phenomenon occurring spontaneously in the community, i.e., family group, peer group, and other groups that form and remain intact for extended periods of time.

The reason for concern about a group's term—whether long-term or short term—is the nature of the impact which length of group life has on the participants.

1. Short-term groups lead to short-term intimacy, a form of alienation.
2. Long-term groups create long-term intimacy, the substance of community.

The assumption in small group practice with T-group, sensitivity, awareness, encounter, and similar models is that a person who learns to achieve intimacy for the short term can transfer this skill to long-term groups such as family, work group, friendship social group, etc. The seed of disreputation lies in the above assumption because it is a false premise. Only over long-term exposure can the *stability* develop to achieve the noble hope of community. Small group, short-term, is form; long-term group is substance. Long-term group experience maintained intimately (over time) is the test of competence. (See next section, The Concept of Competence.) Form without substance is like symbols without substance—a hollow ritual, a cruel substitute for the real thing, which is, authentic intimacy that creates experience opportunities where new behavior may form.

The paradigm has roots in the culture. The parameters for all group concepts come from within the frame of a given culture. Picture a tree as the paradigm. The metaphoric quality of a tree, including roots and limbs connected by a trunk, is used in the hope that the essence of theory and system will better be understood.

Roots are culture because they supply the basic human organization rules and patterns. Tree trunk is the concept of community. The connecting and sustaining fluids pass from roots to limbs and leaves while holding the entire plant intact. The limbs symbolize subgroupings from family to great human institutions like church and school. The branches extending from the limbs represent the multiple potential of small groupings and dyads an individual may acquire as he grows over time. The needles or leaves are the individual-person-units in the paradigm.

The metaphor is complete in all essential details. The system is complete because all necessary functions are being performed. Each function is unique and connected to the interdependent whole. The laws governing the whole tree are different from the laws unique to its context. The whole is governed by laws governing the whole system (Bertalanffy, 1962). The rules governing my behavior may change when I enter a group.

Any logical analysis explaining the system based on the theory *must* be tied into the larger frame of culture. The task is to know the parts, the whole, and the inter–intra relationships connecting it all together. This metaphor is preferred over a machine metaphor because it contains the vulnerability of living protoplasm to the consequence of natural and man-made (culture) laws. The hazard is simply poetic license to become carried away by a powerful metaphor. Consider the contingency if the tree grows on the Kona coast of Hawaii and produces a product like macadamia nuts, perhaps. Yet, like trees, group products range from life-sustaining fruit to ornament to poison, while maintaining essentially similar basic processes in the body of the plant. One is tempted to go on to use stunting, blight, disease, drought, etc., because the metaphor potential could carry it. Metaphorically I prefer the giant redwood.

Whenever it is not possible to explain something in simple terms, a metaphor is utilized to help characterize relationships and specialized functions. Imagine the shared complexity between individual human behavior and photosynthesis in the leaf. Is there a chlorophyll of individual human behavior?

The Concept of Competence

Criteria

1. The major criterion for behavior is *competence.* Competence is submitted instead of disease, illness or health as a way of defining behavior in the individual. The medical model lifts responsibility and accountability from the patient because of the paternalism in the model. The medical model creates an alibi and an escape from health. The competence criterion gives a goal that can be achieved without placing a ceiling on the degree of competence. This compares to the criterion of absence of disease as used in the medical model for establishing the degree of health in a given individual.

2. Each person uses everything he knows all of the time. This idea could be used as a basic theory. Many propositions flow from it. The usefulness of the idea is seen in its application to observations of a person's behavior. If the assumption is made that the behavior represents the best effort a person can make in a given life situation, it is possible to measure the relative competence between the behavior performed and the criterion of competence. Discrepancies found may be used to infer what it is the person knows and does not know. This procedure leads to the discovery of gaps in the learning and behavior patterns of an individual's system of behavior.

3. Competence as a criterion has two main reference points—the person and the context.

A person, competent in a familiar context, may be handicapped in a new and unfamiliar context. In a culture noted for mobility in both horizontal (rural-urban) and vertical (lower to middle class), there is a high incidence of dislocated persons. Horizontal (rural-urban) mobility is frequently associated with poverty or disadvantagement. Vertical (lower to higher class or socioeconomic level) is frequently associated with emotional disorders.

4. Individual behavior patterns persist even beyond the time when the individual acquires information or evidence contrary to his belief associated with a given behavior.

The smoker keeps smoking. The alcoholic keeps on drinking. The drug addict goes on popping or mainlining. The professor keeps on lecturing, maybe even teaching. Behind the behavior is a third-order premise. The premise is based on relationship meanings believed to represent the "way it is." This belief will persist even in the face of countermanding (?) evidence (Blachly, 1969 and Watzlawick, et al., 1967).

5. Communication (verbal-nonverbal content) or behavior is a con-

stant phenomenon. Metacommunication (communication about communication) is an extremely rare phenomenon.

How to get there from here is the key question. When communication becomes a ritual or game, the substance or meaning must be supplied by the receiver. In group, the feedback system takes over. It is not always a simple matter to come to common understanding between two persons, and virtually impossible to achieve unity of understanding among more than two persons at a given moment. For example, consensus is merely the absence of explicit conflict, not the presence of unity in understanding. This is a major reason why many groups need a strong leader to submerge conflict and maintain the ritual of compliance.

6. Acceptance is a significant reinforcer in social control.

The person who has not learned the need to meet group expectations (see theory statement principles) will not be controlled by acceptance. Because most persons learn this need early in the first months of life, the use of *acceptance* as a powerful reinforcer is successful in achieving social control.

7. Needs are learned in the exposure in a group to the life styles of significant others.

The concept of motivation as response to satisfying needs has an antecedent. It is the concept of *need acquisition*. Needs must exist as a part of the life condition of the person before they can be significant as motivators. Needs are acquired from group exposure. Shared needs lead to group action based upon mutual satisfaction of the expectations of the group members.

8. A system is the connecting *rules* that perpetuate the group context.

9. In the study of any group, the system is the only explanation of itself, the group (Bertalanffy, 1962).

The only appropriate methodology is to study the human organization forming the system. For example, a family must be studied from within its own group system. To impose any externally based structure on a family group will corrupt the unique system each family maintains. The phenomenon helps to make each family a unique culture of its own. Generalization across families is extremely hazardous to accurate knowledge.

10. The human group is ruled by cultural parameters and the process of the social system.

This is why quite different family systems yield similar results. Unless the family violates a cultural parameter, i.e., incest, symbiotic parent-child relationship, the same results in terms of group product may happen even though the initial conditions and origins were different. Admission practices that screen applicants for a human organization are mostly ritual or rites of passage. The determining forces are in the ongoing process within the social system organization. A long-standing example is the recruiting of insurance salesmen, especially life insurance salesmen. The following statistic is intended to convey an effect, not accuracy: only about four in one hundred of those screened ever stay and become agents. Some companies spend substantial sums on the testing and screening admissions procedure without knowing the arrogance of the above principle. It is what process comes *after* selection and continues over the first two years that would determine (and indeed does determine) the results. For contrast, examine the apprenticeship programs in the skilled trades. The programs have a continuing process consisting of formal classes, informal groups, and supervised on-the-job training. When you wonder about results in human group, look to process.

11. Process is the involvement over time while contributing to perpetuation of the rules of the social system of a given group.

Dynamics constitute the form in group process. Substance comes to the form only through perpetuation of the rules of the system. No group will need to terminate if substance is maintained. Good management in a human organization is based on the success with perpetuating the rules that constitute the parameters of the system.

Summary

This chapter has presented the theory of human behavior developed out of empirical study of family groups engaged in family group consultation—a method of group counseling. The theoretical formulations underlying the theory were presented in the previous chapter. The concept of group has been developed and made explicit to provide the backdrop and frame of reference for the theory presented. The system, based on the theory, is detailed in terms of a paradigm displaying the major principles, assumptions, and criteria for measuring progress in human behavior change and development.

In summary, a paraphrase of the foregoing material would say: Human behavior is created anew within the context of a group. The behavior is all-at-once, the symbol and the personal experience. The motivation for behavior is the need to express a meaning defined by the perception of the relationship in the individual's personal experience of the moment. The behavior act is the symbol used in communicating to significant other persons. Feedback and confirmation from others completes the process. When all of the antecedents and consequences are considered in the context of a group life event, the necessary parameters and rules for understanding "what is happening" do exist. Good hunting.

4

The Concept of Group: Experience,
Intimacy and Alienation

The Frame of Reference.

Experience is something I bring to the group. It may lead to intimacy or to alienation. I am standing in the middle of an idea. It is the concept of group. For ten years and more I have been pursuing the concept of group as if it were something that one day I would be able to share in writing as I am now doing. Instead of a gestalt or a terminal point at which I could turn and share with you, I have evolved a seemingly endless series of *transitions* that continue to blend more with life itself than with an idea *about* life. Transitions are temporal dimensions of change. To be different than you are requires *time to change* (Tyler, 1969). Time implies an interval and an interval permits a process. The process engages the members of a group in a continuing series of interpersonal relationships. The interpersonal relationships are defined through the process and constitute its major outcome. Relationship may be subdivided into components of forces and conditions that help to explain the etiology and meaning of behavior—master-slave, superior-subordinate, symmetrical-complementary—within a given context or situation defined in a culture. The behavior act is a piece of communication. Its message and its meaning must be brought into one's subjective reality. In my theory of group, the essence of group is intimacy. Intimacy implies a closeness, a kind of interrelated, interdependent condition that involves both geography and psychological touching. The concept of commitment and the interwoven involvements of the interaction patterns of people, serve as metaphor to explain the complex and the intricate dynamic condition in a group.

The way I think, the way I act, the way I speak, can all be modified or changed in group.

When we speak of the concept of group, the word *group* is used as its own subject, a phenomenon apparently universal in the culture. Group, used to define a cluster of people, is something else. The individual in a group has been the object of study because of the availibility of direct observation. The inferential nature of the concept of group as a subject-object paradox has been generally passed up for the more concrete group techniques of manipulation. The training and sensitivity type group procedures abound in the manipulative techniques. The language of group process can be learned in training groups. Further understanding is necessary if one is to use group in a controlled way in psychotherapy and counseling.

Controlled groups are formal social systems and require a leader. Self-help groups are informal social systems characterized by equal status among the membership. Individual members must have quite diverse skills to function effectively in both. All groups do not fall neatly into the formal-informal dichotomy. Contrived groups may form a third category. The primary and secondary status of a group adds more complexity to an already complicated system for defining "groups" because the level of commitment is dependent upon the formal-informal nature of the group.

Much of the new knowledge we have acquired in the past ten years has come from our experiences and research with family group consultation. This continuing, systematic study of group counseling for a decade or more has served two general purposes: (1) to show how the concept of group has formed a powerful training method, and (2) to show the treatment effect of the concept of group when a network of significant other persons can participate. The process in each leads through transitions for each person in relation to the human organizations.

Human organizations seem to use group as a system for socialization and survival. The individual human being somehow functions alone and in cooperation with others through group.

Group structure leads to order and meaning in the relationships among persons where the absence of group promotes ambiguity, confusion, and alienation. Group somehow makes a myth of directive-nondirective concepts in counseling (Tyler, 1969), (Fullmer and Bernard, 1971).

There are multiple forms of group-interaction treatment and healing procedures. Allan A. Glatthorn (1966) classified group in terms of its major task or function for its membership as task, didactic, tutorial, discursive, heuristic, and Socratic.

Will Durant might hypothesize that civilization began when man learned to inhibit impulse. If man lived entirely alone instead of in groups, it might be conceivable that he could live without any inhibitions placed upon his impulses. Because the word *group* is an abstraction the same as individual or culture or personality, there's a need for definitions. Definitions are given in the form of nomenclature which serves as the language of group. The central theme or focus and principle that guides the logic of the group process helps one to understand the treatment and healing nature of group. There's a need for the definition of man as an individual and as a social being, if the philosophical foundations of groups are to be clearly stated. One must understand the definition of a social system such as the society, the individual or the group, and the community. The roles, probabilities, identities, realities, and essences of existence in a social system must be clearly outlined. The inferential system of existence is a phenomenon in analysis of meanings of behavior events and constitutes the source of meaning.

The concept of systems has provided additional assistance in the analysis of groups. The major share of our social system related to material in the following pages will bring forth an order and a sequencing of the events, living as experienced, in the limited context of a culture (Bertalanffy, 1968).

The concept of a group deals directly with a conflict in the literature concerning the verbal conditioning that accompanies the group counseling system or phenomenon. Concept of group deals with the proximity factors, the social-distance factors, and the touching conditions maintained in a group. The verbalizations become secondary and indeed almost completely irrelevant as healing forces in group behavior. The phenomenon of group or the concept of group is itself a factor for study in this book. The restrictions of the verbal model are shown clearly in those examples of the acting-out models of group. The family seems to incorporate both the acting-out models and the verbal models, but the acting-out models take precedence in all meaningful and directional determining situations. Acting-out models include behavior modification and sensory awareness, as well as the direct-intervention models—i.e., the one advanced by Fullmer and Bernard (1964) under the three I's: interrupt, intervene, and influence methods.

The concept of guidance as applied to individuals has been altered considerably in recent years. The idea is that an environment in which an individual can learn may be managed in such a way as to predict rather accurately the type and kind of behavior developed by an individual. Guidance of the individual through the management of his environments, his social environment, his economic environment and his personal-social environment will somehow affect the literature on group by the way interventions occur in group counseling. It is speculated here that management of group is perhaps more important in the guidance of an individual than has been the notion of testing and other technological advances in the field of personnel work. The concept of group has an interesting relationship for the idea of spectator roles and participant roles in the social system. People seem to have a kind of pathology that is characterized by the spectator sport and the idea that others are playing the game but I am only *watching,* and therefore I have no power to influence whatever the participants are doing.

The Idea of Continuous Social Revolution

Social revolution seems to be a continuous provider of transitions that lead to greater and greater acceptance of differentness in people, events, behavior, and the established methods of behaving or conducting our affairs. We frequently find change comes as if on a schedule— new models for cars, new styles in dress and grooming, new books on group counseling. The change is planned and becomes a primary force in life. Change is defined as dislocation by Peter Drucker (1968). Dislocation may happen to people and to things. People are mobile, and urban renewal may move entire communities of families to rebuild a portion of a city. Every dislocation creates a need for transitions to get from where I am to where you are. Contemporary life seems filled with a continuing series of transitions that require increasing tolerance for differentness.

Methodology in Group Research

Group concepts are based upon the culture's defining limits through individual and collective behavior. There are a number of established formulas for studying individual behavior, role behavior, and small group dynamics. Additional methodologies from cultural anthropology are available. Most useful for group work is the participant-observer method for data gathering. All acquired knowledge and skill one can bring to group research should enhance the probability for successful work.

The formula is unique in every instance. The more precise the measure of relationship on one level, the less precise will be the measure on another level—thus indetermined yet relative. However, the level of specific verification means more than just interdependence. Interdependence is the judgment of good by one standard and bad by another standard. Indeterminacy and relativity, of behavior in group, require a new formula in every instance.

The researcher must be able to take a measure of behavior in event

1, group 2, and compare directly with event 2 in group 1.*

The analysis of data begins with a definition of specific relationships within a given group. Data gathering in each life event within a group consists of all variables necessary to account for the observed behavior. To do this task, each force influencing behavior must be identified and measured.

The detailing and explaining necessary to understand the formula and the analysis leading to interpretation of individual behavior must be taken up from this point. The student has a structure of his own. Here is a structure used to explain the gap between theory and practice in group.

Self-Disclosure in a Group

Self-disclosure is a projective technique happening in continuous sequence in all behavior. This assumption covers the less inclusive arena of group counseling and group therapy. The family group can be studied by projective techniques but it is difficult to manage the massive data build-up.

The methodology for group research has been largely a study of antecedent treatment and subsequent outcome. The yield in new knowledge has brought two main features: (1) elaborate techniques for group manipulation, all the way to complete denial of manipulation under the force of permission, and (2) the simple castrating fact that equifinality is the reality—that different techniques for group manipulation yield similar results: persons report success in group participation or in therapy and counseling groups. The individual, identified as patient, improves because of common culture parameters in the behavior of the treatment group. The fact remains that no one can say why or how the change came about, or even if the change would have happened anyway with no therapy. We conducted one experiment when the family groups under consultation were matched with a group of families awaiting treatment, and a control group of families not seeking help. The results confirmed that if the process of interaction can be stimulated within the group, the outcomes may be similar *whether or not* a professional specialist is present in the group (Irish, 1966). Pre- and postmeasure consisted of a Q-sort for measuring attitude changes among family members during family counseling. These results seemed parallel with the studies of different counseling systems reported in the early 1950's (Fiedler, 1950 a and b). The differences between systems

---

*This formula concept is based on Hall's schema for social scientists (Hall, 1959, pp. 169–170).

based on different theories was less than the difference between experienced counselors and therapists and neophyte practitioners.

The above seems to confirm that the quality of process within a group of two or more human beings is more significant than the manipulations prescribed in the formula of interaction (Bertalanffy, 1968). When no professional is present, if a new process is introjected, the results change if the relationships develop in accordance with cultural parameters for behavior.

The apparent undisputable fact seems to be: Process is more important than is the intervention. Process defines relationships, intervention is equated with content in communication. Verbal self-disclosure is zero because it is similar to talking to oneself. Relationship definition sets the limits on behavior. The target of study is relationship and the forces, beliefs, conditions, and other variables that define it.

Cultural Parameters for Behavior

The reason behavior within a given group within a given culture is predictable at all is that the individual member persons have a common culture. The parameters or boundaries for acceptable adequate behavior are established and maintained by each culture. Each child learns these isolates, sets, and patterns of behavior in his family as a part of his basic acculturation process. Every subdivision within a culture shares a slightly different program of isolates, sets, and patterns of behavior with slightly different values, attitudes, and belief systems. These differences may be ever so slight and subtle that at formal and official levels of interpersonal intervention, convention and standard operating protocol or common courtesy will be enough to permit the uninterrupted flow of meaningful communication. However, the group therapy, group counseling, and encounter-group interpersonal interaction will require a formula to negotiate these subtle differences in personal parameters of behavior. Social, economic, class, and caste status differences may be so great that it is not possible to negotiate and reconcile the differences. For example, in a secondary school in Hawaii the students have gathered in their respective ethnic and racial groups at certain "corners" of buildings on campus. These demarcations of territories define the social boundaries for each group. The violations and transgressions are treated with ostracism. A similar pattern is true for East-West Center students from the Philippines and some other countries at the University of Hawaii. They do not use territory to express their cohesiveness but they do ostracize any member who becomes personally involved with an American. The examples are given at the general level because the behavior is easily observed. The point here is that a similar pattern holds at the person to person level in a small group. It is the substance and the form of what is called relationship.

The Task in Research

The task in research on group is clearly a complex venture. Initially, the direct comparison of event 1 in group 2 with event 2 in group 1 requires a criterion variable (this is the cultural parameter for a given behavior) and the identification of significant variables to be studied. All behavior is a variable. All values, attitudes, and beliefs are variables. All external reinforcers are variables. The culture parameter is a variable *only* when more than *one culture* is involved. In microcosm, the socio-economic, class, caste, and family group differences *may* be treated as culture variables. The cultural message systems were identified by Hall (1959, pp. 174–175) and displayed as a map.

Whenever a group achieves a common culture, the human organization will function productively as a survival group. Culture is defined here as the *formula for group behavior* parameters and values, attitudes, and belief systems held in common. The formula is a set of rules governing the behavior sequence that defines relationships within the group between and among individual members. The primer-level formula at the verbal interaction level is: Each person speaks for himself and no one else. (1) The person hears himself and the responses of others in the group. From this exercise one can learn to read one's own behavior. (2) The person listens to another person speak of his meanings. He also hears other persons and himself, respond to the person talking or verbally self-disclosing. From this exercise, a person can learn to read the other person's behavior. The entire process is designed to produce a more refined awareness and sensitivity to the emotional climates of the self and of others.

Learning to Read Behavior

Behavior, like any language, is influenced by the context in which it is expressed. Taken out of context, behavior may have no relevant meaning in isolation. In group, behavior context is visible at one level, in the here-and-now of the group. At another level, the person in his own world, the context is not visible. (Context and relationship are one; see Chapter 5.)

The formula used to direct the interaction sets up qualifiers as parameters on what is said and what is left unsaid in the verbal context.

However, the nonverbal message system may be carrying the significant behavior expressed to amplify and further qualify what is verbally stated. The verbal interaction may be analyzed by using the Watzlawick et al. (1967) model. The model will cover only the verbal expressions. The large portion of behavior that is nonverbal is left in the realm of mysticism. The task of learning to read behavior is a major project and must include extensive exposure to direct supervised practice in a human behavior laboratory. Yet many of the skills are a matter of making explicit what children seem able to do intuitively—spot a phony, recognize an authentic human being, and pick up a very accurate "reading" of your emotional climate at any given moment. Beyond the intuitive level much of what is understood can be explained and shared with the person capable of third and fourth level abstractions.

Levels of Knowledge

- The first level is knowledge gained by direct sensory experience —e.g., the thing was hot.
- Second level is knowledge *about* first level knowledge. The iron was hot because it was plugged in and turned on.
- Third level is knowledge *about* second-level knowledge and is necessarily a premise or hypothesis about the order of relationship that would account for the iron heating up when plugged in and turned on and cooling when turned off and unplugged.
- Fourth-level knowledge is knowledge *about* third-level premises and reaches the preconscious levels usually labeled as intuitive thinking, because all the premises used to reach a conclusion are not in the conscious awareness.

These levels of metaknowledge (knowledge *about* knowledge) may proceed to infinity. We could, but usually do not have any knowledge beyond the third or fourth levels.

As one moves from second-level knowledge acquisition to learning at increasingly abstract levels, a process sets in that makes learning progressively easier. This process is sometimes called *learning to learn*. Insight is one experience shared by many persons that may serve as a general example of the above. Suddenly, by some restructuring and reordering the arrangement of relationships, a new concept or perception happens at the conscious awareness level. Insight may happen at any level beyond first-level sensory perception. It is most commonly experienced at third level.

Firsthand Information

The source of information and the way it flows within a group must be regulated by the formula for interaction. Very little information is gained in firsthand experience. Most information comes to us from others. This defines the information as, at best, secondhand.

The goal in group is to get firsthand information for oneself.

In the American social system it is usually necessary to rely on some *authority* for valid information. Information required beyond what we can get firsthand or from an authority may have to be created. This can happen in a group. The contrast between the open group and the prison is essentially one of firsthand information. The prisoner has only second- or third-hand information. Severe consequences may result from acting on unvalidated information—thus the prisoner's dilemma. The group is an information generating source if one can create firsthand experiences through direct encounter with other members in the group. This condition would meet the goal stated above and set the stage for firsthand information. Once information passes to secondhand status, the reliability becomes dependent upon the authority relaying it.

One-Trial Learning

Every culture contains a systematic pattern sometimes called *learning to learn,* or *learning how to learn.* The experimental demonstration of the phenomenon referred to above is simply the record of reduced trials for similar material to be learned. The fact that most learning is *one-trial learning* has largely been ignored in the education and psychology literature. Because of this, most people are unaware that most of what one learns is learned with one trial. The fact of one-trial learning is significant to group because it accounts for most of the important events in a group.

One-trial learning is possible because of the common or shared learning accumulated within a given culture. Beginning with imprinting of sounds, rhythms, and sights, the child gets a consistent continuous sequencing of order of grunts and groans. Eventually the form of sound symbols becomes a language of substance (meanings). The cultural pattern for learning how-to-learn is built up bit by bit over a continuing exposure to other persons using the same pattern. The pattern is repeated by everyone in the same culture. A group of persons does a similar thing by initiating a new pattern.

The phenomenon referred to here is most easily observed when a new person enters a group that has met for six or more times. Before the group moves ahead, it must help the new person learn how to learn in this new or unique way currently used in the group. If it takes too long, the social stress may cause a minor crisis in the group. If the group doesn't understand what is happening, the new person may need to leave.

Mowrer (1966) maintains that secret confession has not healed the sickness of guilt nor caused the self-respect to grow. Whether priest or psychiatrist, Mowrer questions the value of secret confession because the healing record is not good. He thinks a group or community is an improvement.

The concept of self-help is quite another matter. Here the person is encouraged to be radically honest with persons significant to him. Instead of confessing his sins in private to someone unknown, impersonal, and neutral in feelings toward him, he hears himself speak the truth. Mowrer thinks the integrity of this process is more healing than any other treatment laid on a person from outside. He bases the idea on empirical demonstration of positive healing results with persons treated in this type milieu. To give the idea historical significance, Mowrer (1968) found that the early Christians used a group method of restoring self-respect to wayward members. The essence of the process was complete self-disclosure to one or two other members followed by sharing with a group and then the community, the *radically honest* report. Hearing oneself speak the truth was coupled with group support and love, and intimate experience. Courage to confess was not enough. The wayward one was required to do penance. This introduced an interval of time. Following the restitution, restoration to full membership in the community was accomplished with self-respect intact. We have found a method similar to the above in nearly every healthy family group with whom we have worked over the past ten years.

Self-Authentication

Only you and your conscience know for sure. Some persons have been phony so long that even they come to believe they are the facades they present. A child can spot a phony and so can most other authentic persons. The alienated person is the opposite extreme from the authentic person. The alienated cannot achieve an intimate relationship experience with others.

Self-disclosure is the sacred paradox. The person who claims inability to self-disclose in a group is merely expressing self-disclosing alienation. Intimacy in relationship comes only from authentic self-disclosure. If I am ever to change the behavior of another human being, I must first change myself. This condition is not achieved by any automatic process. The courage to be authentic is a rare gift. It is easier to take the short-term gain, like short-term intimacy, than to hold out for the authentic consequence. Blachly (1969) has equated short-term gains to *seductive* dependency. It looks easy and the reward is there. However, for the drug addict and the alcoholic, the consequences in the long term are inescapable; to remain a drug addict or to remain an alcoholic. This seduction concept fits into the rationale of Mowrer's integrity concept. The person combines behavior, reward, time, and punishment. Seduction is a good descriptive term for the sequencing or patterning associated with the culture's basic parameters as characterized in American advertising. The stereotyped Madison Avenue Organization Advertising man—*buy now, pay later* syndrome—is typical seduction: the soft sell. You can own a new home, a new car, a new set of furniture —a small down payment, and monthly installments for life.

Integrity group therapy is profound only if the short-term gain or reward is bypassed by the person identified as the patient. The alcoholic *must not* take the first drink. He is never more than one drink away from a drunk. Berne (1964) describes the alcoholic game as both wet and dry. The short-term gain for the dry alcoholic is linked to his helping the wet alcoholic. The game is the same; only the roles change.

These ideas about patterns of behavior and the process of self-authentication connect the culture's parameters and the power of radical honesty. The fact that many persons are unable to be radically honest with themselves is evidence of the magnitude of the impact of the basic pattern in the lives of members of the American culture. Group methods for learning how to learn radical honesty still continue to evolve as self-help therapeutic groups. The ultimate goal is to make each community of persons a self-help group. This might lead to again making group a way of life as originally intended in family groups.

Reunion: Interpersonal Process

Radical honesty is the ultimate form of self-disclosure. Even I can believe me when being radically honest. Trust is possible both of self and of other persons. The culture approves even though it seems not to be the thing to do. Games do not replace authenticity. Games may fog up or obscure the rational meaning of uninhibited emotion. If civilization is possible only because each of us may learn to throttle impulse, perhaps the rules we use to achieve control of behavior are proper subjects for group. Being polite and following the "thing to do" may lead to good gamesmanship but obscure authenticity. Self-authentication must become a central function of interpersonal interaction process. In group, the rules may be changed long enough to impose a formula that initiates the conditions essential for a given person to confirm an authentic self. We assume that one authentic human person can provide the setting in which others may learn to express behavior that is more than an accommodation of the thing to do. Intimate reunion is then possible through the interpersonal process within a group.

The process is the primer level in a group for learning to read behavior, especially, my own behavior. The more advanced levels occur when one learns to read the other person's behavior. One works from the self-conscious first person singular (I) toward the other person. The process contains a constant and a variable. The self-conscious I is a constant; the other person's behavior is a variable. The constant is an assumption and is therefore subject to error. However, it is an improvement over available alternatives because each alternative produces two or more variables and no constant. It is difficult if not impossible to verify, validate, or confirm variables by any reality test, except to return to the primer level.

The reality test consists of the process of comparing my perception with your perception in the here-and-now happening. My concept of what is happening now rests on my ability to verify it with and through other persons in the same life-event. First person singular is the self-conscious I mentioned above.

Every formula used to guide interaction in a group counseling or group therapy setting will have built-in rules and parameters (limits) to regulate the process, including reality testing at a self-conscious level. The leader or convener provides the model to be used in the group. The method of sharing the formula varies with the style and bias of the sharer. However, there is a typical style for each major type of group. For example, Stoller (1968 a, b, c) includes in a definition for marathon group therapy: setting, contract, ground rules, leader responsibilities, and follow-up, in addition to the formula for interaction. The method is complete when every member is able to comply with the limits.

Self-Respect

Respect for self is crucial. The paradox of introspection may deny forever the possible objective treatment of the subject. Distortion, comprehension, usefulness, and reliability are words to describe some concerns that become central to the individual whenever he deals with information about himself. The criteria for judging self-respect in American culture is complicated by what Robert Theobald (1970) has called "lying." The American culture is based on it and has made telling "truth" an obsolete concept. For the individual, the truth in feedback from others may be, at best, consensus based on lying. Group is complicated as a form of social interaction because of the elaborate formula required to insure some measure of truth. When truth escapes detection a tragic form of ambivalence becomes typical, and sometimes lethal (Packer, 1970).

Self-respect is in some jeopardy in a culture where the lie is the only truth, and where the criteria for valid confirmation of self-perceptions must come out of equally uncertain other selves. However, group as a concept of valid interaction with authentic other persons continues to offer us the only available alternative through the model of self-help. If we return to rely on the professional authority figure, the question of truth reappears. Similarly, the family is confronted in modern society with the questioned authenticity of peer groups and avalanches of unsorted information. The self-help model offers the powerful healing of community as reported by Mowrer (1968) about the early Christians. Self-help for restoring self-respect may be the only way.*

Experience: Existence in a Group

London (1969) thinks the family group has lost power over the full development of children because the peer-group structure in American society has become so prevalent as a source of life style and basic values. Bettelheim (1969) has been studying the Israeli kibbutzim which have a fifty-year history as an active alternative to child rearing in a nuclear family. Not all authorities agree with Bettleheim's claim that the kibbutzim are superior to the family as child-rearing agent group. A kibbutz uses the child's peer group. He thinks it is good because the incidence of mental and emotional disorder is decreased over populations reared in more traditional family groups. Bronfenbrenner (1969) thinks the price is too high. He points to flat affect and reduced ability in kibbutz-reared adults to invest strong intimate emotions in anyone. The repressions of sex and other emotions usually freely expressed outside the confines of a powerful peer group is thought to lead to rigid and inflexible adults.

The groups used to rear children have remained largely a form of family group. The kibbutz is still classed as a limited experiment. Already some claims are made that improvements are entirely clearly established. However, equally viable authorities disagree while using

*The charlatans of the contemporary group movement won't like this.

the very same data. Because group is central to the concept of the kibbutz and the family unit, the continued debate about two different child-rearing methods should prove to be important. Exist in a group and you will create an experience. Perhaps the unique quality of the experience for each of us will preclude any chance for consensus in a given group.

The Hidden Dimension of Culture

The hidden dimension is the common, shared cultural parameters which make up the patterns of behavior observed in the individual in a given life event. The family group sets the pattern for each child by the way life is organized and lived out over the period from birth to adulthood.

The use of space or territory in the home is an example. The family defines the spaces (usually rooms) by encouraging some behavior and discouraging other behavior in a given room at a given time of day, day of week, or week of the year. In a given culture these patterns are very similar from one family to another in a common neighborhood. Behavior is tightly associated with the definitions given to each room. Living rooms are public to all members of the group in a given family. Friends may come and share the living space under restricting rules. However, if stress is added someone may retreat to *his* room. Entry into someone's bedroom or den may require permission. Frequently children will say no to a parent's request for entry. Immediately upon being reassured by the parent's behavior, that of withdrawing quietly, the parent will be vocally solicited to enter and subsequently made to feel very welcome. What happens? Simply a test to ascertain if the parent *really* believes and adheres to the territorial boundries.

Without going into detail, the idea here is to alert the reader to the primary message system (Hall, 1959) and the implications for behavior learned in a family. Sleep is another hidden dimension and must be studied as a part of the family use of space. The vulnerability of the person during sleep has influenced established patterns for the family to such an extent that one might speak of the sociology of sleep. In the study of family behavior, sleep is a major shared activity (Fullmer, 1969 d).

Summary

The task in understanding the concept of group is linked to a culture parameter that sets patterns of behavior for each individual. The individual creates his experience in the context provided by a group. The result may lead toward either intimacy or alienation.

The self-disclosing concepts refer to other persons and to self, first person singular. Even avenues and behaviors used for self-disclosing are tied to the culture parameters. Change of behavior may be seen as a transition or dislocation depending on whether the result is more intimacy or more alienation.

Self-respect is the central concern in all group formulas for interaction. The person is found creating his own experience in the reunion or interpersonal process. The relationship, and how it is perceived by the behaver, bring all of the learning-how-to-learn ideas into focus.

Suggested Additional Readings

Honigmann, J. J., 1967. *Personality In Culture.* New York: Harper & Row, Publishers.
   The anthropologist can help the student of human behavior see the relationships between human organization and the personality development of individuals. Honigmann's book is an important contribution to the student's understanding of the role and meaning of groups.
Hsu, F. L. K. (ed.), 1961. *Psychological Anthropology: Approaches to Culture and Personality.* Homewood, Ill.: The Dorsey Press, Inc.
   This book is especially helpful if the student is unfamiliar with the relationship between culture and human behavior. Other cultures are used by anthropologists to explain how the influence of patterns, rules, and parameters shape the behavior of the individual member of the culture. Language is but one symbol-minded system. Dance, music, art forms, and many artifacts express meanings distinct to a given culture. The nonverbal and contextual cues are very significant in all communication in every culture.
Kaplan, Bert (ed.), 1961. *Studying Personality Cross-Culturally.* New York: Harper & Row, Publishers.
   The collection of readings give the student a broad exposure to the forces in culture and how these forces get inculcated. The complex systems of social beliefs and the behavior to express meanings based upon the culture values may be too much to attempt in an abstract. This book will help the student begin to comprehend some of the forces in any culture social system and their relationships to personality development.
Moore, L., 1969. "A Developmental Approach to Group Counseling with Seventh Graders," *School Counselor,* 16 (4) 274–276 (March).
   This article gives an example of how to set up groups in a school. Group counseling is an addition to individual counseling. The decision to be in a group was voluntary with all seventh-graders given the opportunity to join. Orientation sessions, a questionnaire (to find out what they wanted to find out about), and organization by type, sex, and size were provided.

5

Group Models: Reactive-Proactive Psychology

The group models used in recent development of group counseling and group therapy have grown out of a recognition of the increasing importance of a "systems" concept. A lesser importance is being attached to the individual models of man as an autonomous being away from his community or survival group. There is a vital concern for training groups to add the meaning necessary to confirm a viable self-identity in the here-and-now of contemporary society.

There are two major theoretical divisions recognized because of their influence in psychological thought. One is reactive psychology, the view of man as a reactor to stimuli from internal and external sources in his environment. The second is active psychology, the view of man as an active seeker, generating stimuli as well as responding to stimuli. The latter or active psychology, is based on the observed behavior in its most primitive form, autonomous activity (Allport, 1961; Hebb, 1955). Bertalanffy (1968) claims that general system theory has been a third theoretical construct to be embraced by psychology. General system theory seeks to deal directly with the processes within and among the diversity of variables, contingencies, and individual units that make up the total organization or whole. The difference between systems theory and psychological theory is a difference between parts and wholes. Do the laws governing the parts hold for the whole? In many cases, no—which brings forth the next question, Do new laws govern the unifying processes of the organization of the *whole?* In many cases, yes. When general system theory is combined with psychological theory, a new method of studying group and individual behavior emerges. This is what is meant by finding principles that hold in different systems when the component parts or elements vary. Out of these principles has been derived a way of studying behavior in group. (See Chapter 6 for a discussion of invariance.)

The evidence for the idea or theory came out of the empirical study of family groups in counseling. It was discovered by Fullmer and Bernard (1968) that when one more person is added to a family group, the whole system changes. If an entire family is put together with a second family, similar change seemed to happen. The counselors or consultants, added in pairs, could expect similarly changed conditions. General system theory expresses a similar expectation. Because all the parts are affected by each other part in a complex interdependence, if one part is added (thus changed), all other parts are expected to change. This forms the basis of a family group treatment strategy—whenever one person changes his behavior all other *significant* persons in the family change relationship. The professional task continues to be a search for the nature and direction of change through monitoring the behavior coming out of the new relationships and comparing it with the prior behavior. The context of behavior is as important as the individual acting out of it.

Reactive Psychology

Reactive psychology sees man as a machine or robot responding to an externally programed schedule of stimuli (Murray, 1962). Murray has satirized ignoring the creative and hope generating behavior in man. Robot psychology has a long history and is still around and well (Matson, 1964). An industrial society can use the model of man as machine to be manipulated by advertising in social, political, and economic terms. Henry (1963) points up the similarity between principles of economic man and the principles of academic psychology.

According to reactive psychology, if people wanted to be emotionally healthy all society had to do was reduce tensions and stress. Manipulation of psychological satiation does *not* lead to eradicating mental dysfunction. The affluent society is hung up on nearly every neurosis from sex to drugs. The behavioristic results were not the same as predicted. For example, during periods of great stress, like wars, the increase of tension and stress seems to reduce the incidence of mental disorganization. A leading contemporary economist, Walter Heller (1970), is reported to have said that the consumer satiation level is showing signs of affecting economic predictions. The affluent society seems to lead to more disturbed behavior in man. The result is contrary to expectation according to Bertalanffy (1968), who argues that the reactive-psychology model does not explain the major portion of human behavior in *groups* or *systems*. It should be pointed out that, within a given context, behavior can be observed to respond to the principles of reinforcement. This fact has need of being integrated into the proactive psychology models. The dichotomy is mainly for differentiation of philosophical-commercial points of view and the humanistic viewpoints.

Pragmatic and empirical considerations bring us back to technique in group counseling and group psychotherapy. If only behavior modification schedules are employed in a group, the behavior changes (over time) cannot be accounted for, except as specific frequency counts reflect the new behaviors. If there is a change in the level of organization in the group or system, it cannot be accounted for by such frequency counts. When the group, as a system, is seen as a molar concept, then the general system theory idea of the steady state of disequilibrium in an open system can be used. This takes us beyond technique and leads into the process frequently reported but rarely explained, called *learning to learn*.

An Open System

The learning-to-learn phenomenon is much like the steady state of an open system. The person keeps tensions dispersed through spontaneous activity and advances toward higher and more complex levels of organization. Like levels of knowledge, the levels of organization build up in complex orders, each level serves as an explanation to help one understand the lesser level. This spiral progression toward increasing complex organization and integration of more and more knowledge seems to characterize both the open system and the learning-to-learn phenomenon. Techniques and formulas in group tend to activate this process without identifying the forces and relative power inherent to the procedure.

The forces in the procedure expressed in spontaneous activity are the consequence of the most primitive form of behavior, namely, autonomous activity (Bertalanffy, 1968; also Carmichael, 1954; Schiller, 1957; Hebb, 1949).

Active or proactive psychology is based on the premise of autonomous activity. The organism seeks actively to maintain disequilibrium in order to have a tension and stress potential. Mental dysfunction is associated with the behavior an individual exhibits when he is headed for greater and greater degrees of homeostasis functioning in psychological and biological systems (Frankl, 1959; Arieti, 1965; Menninger et al., 1963).

Learning to learn leads in the direction of greater degrees of heterostasis, i.e., the steady state of an open system—disequilibrium. The group acts to open up the individual. To open up, an individual moves from homeostasis toward heterostasis. Tension and stress become immediate consequences to the spontaneous activity engaged in by the individual within the group. The members in the group learn to release stimuli in response to an increasing intensity in the mobilization of affect. Simultaneously, the nature of the group's organization changes toward a higher order of complex integration of meaning and symbol. The group develops a private code, sometimes called a *restricted code* because only the group members can use it. The code is a shorthand form of complex symbolic signaling. Meaning is shared through the communication process. The experience for an outsider is one of being without meaning in the midst of the group's communication process. This is the nearest an outsider can get to direct experience of the complex learning-to-learn phenomenon. The members experience the learning to learn phenomenon in the group. The experience is one of ever-increasing frequency of verifiable meaning in increasing abstract levels of integration of symbolic meanings. The efficiency and the sheer speed of communication give the impression to the outsider of being instantaneous. This is shockingly disarming to an outsider. The effect on the behavior of an outsider is not unlike the cultural shock experienced when one changes from one culture to another. Peace Corps volunteers sometimes experience cultural shock in reverse when they return home after two years in a new group or culture. The phenomenon is similar in each case (Benedict, 1934–1946).

Learning to learn is a fourth-level abstraction, experienced by most persons out of conscious awareness at a level that may sometimes be called *intuitive*. If direct experience in behavior is first-level, abstraction begins with second level, or verbalization. Third-level abstraction is a belief about second- and first-level meanings or relationships. Third-level assumptions (abstractions) are exceptionally difficult to change. The person must achieve fourth-level abstraction before understanding of third level can begin. It is entirely possible to assume the third-level assumptions are sound. This process is what Bateson (1942) called deutero-learning.

Deutero-learning is an idea that claims the individual learns to punctuate the life events by imposing a redundant structure of sequences and contexts upon the relationship variables in behavior. The idea seems to exclude specific concern for content variables per se, and consider them only as sequence relates to context in terms of patterns within the whole group or system of behavior. Learning to learn is one way of saying that exposure to particular experiences increases the efficacy for learning new behavior in another context. Speed and efficiency seem to increase as the individual gains more and more experiences. In group, the learning-to-learn idea is incorporated in the formula for interaction. The formula is the set of rules and patterns of response enclosed in the guidelines and phrasings, or ways of speaking. The formula is given to the group by the leader. The leader is usually more experienced than other persons in the group. A self-help group may be an exception. However, self-help groups usually have several members with experience in varying amounts. This leads to a style of sharing the leadership role of providing a formula during the interaction within the group. The net effect is similar whether self-help or leader-imposed; the formula sets the limits of potential interaction and sets in motion the learning-to-learn phenomenon.

Proactive Psychology

Theory is essential to guide all group practice and research. Strategies are for finding answers to the questions raised about group practice in counseling and psychotherapy. Proactive psychology is based upon principles that define man as an active and seeking human being instead of a robot. Man's behavior is a response to external conditions and internal disequilibrium created in the relationships he maintains. Response is not just a reaction to stimuli. Response is a modification process implying choice. Reaction is deterministic, implying nonchoice. The contrast between proactive and reactive psychology can be seen in the different strategies for group technique. Reactive organisms require a specific program to follow. Proactive process is a design for evolving a specific program. Menninger et al. (1958), Frankl (1959), and Maslow and Rogers each contributes to the understanding and use of the humanistic proactive psychology theory as a way of explaining behavior.

Interactional Model for Group Counseling

Watzlawick et al. (1967) described a system-oriented interactional model used at the Palo Alto (California) Mental Research Institute. The theory has close kinship with general system theory, namely that idea about the whole being governed by laws and rules different from the laws and rules governing the parts which combine to make up the whole.

The application and study of family group therapy was based upon communication in an interaction model. One major contribution came out of their study of family interaction in those cases which produced one or more schizophrenic children. The results were described as *double-bind* communication. In the double bind, the two persons are locked in. Neither can escape the intense relationship because of strong survival needs. This context creates the impossible paradox of causing a message to have *two* mutually exclusive and contradictory injunctions. The injunctions must be obeyed or disobeyed. However, it is impossible to do either without violating the other. Obey is to disobey and disobey is to obey, as long as one stays locked in to the relationship.

The theory of the double bind has remained a significant contribution even though in some regards it is controversial. The issue seems to be over the claim that anyone caught in a double bind for a significant period of time will show the symptoms of schizophrenia. This pathogenicity issue remains controversial. We are concerned more with the viable concept of the double bind and other forms of paradoxical communication, especially as these relate to group counseling and therapy. For example, the injunction "I command you to be spontaneous" yields confused results because there is a contradiction imposed by the command "Be spontaneous." It is a contradiction and a true paradox. It is impossible to obey a command and be spontaneous at the same time. The variable of most consequence for a person in a double bind is to be able to keep a command of his own subjective reality and not give it up to claim a relationship or maintain one, because to maintain the relationship would distort his perception of his own subjective reality.

Appropriate Behavior

The theory of the double-bind brings us to the vantage point in learning to read behavior which can let us see that a pathogenic context can elicit or induce appropriate behavior that, in itself, is viewed as pathogenic (Watzlawick, Beavin, and Jackson, 1967). Interaction models for group counseling and group psychotherapy permit the creation of appropriate *contexts* for behavior as well as appropriate *behavior* per se. This connects the basic theory set forth in previous chapters with the culture foundations as defined in terms of context parameters for behavior in a given social system.

There are two major subjects of study in group counseling based on the above concepts: (1) the person or behaver; and (2) the context in which the behavior occurs. The author's theory of behavior is based on the idea that behavior arises from a relationship and is an expression of meaning experienced by the behaver. The *relationship* is a *context.* Group counseling is concerned with creating contexts (relationship), out of which new behavior may come.

The Context of Behavior

The interaction model permits a working system for study of the *behaver* and the *context* or relationships as subjects. Because these two subjects of study occur together, they are operationally inseparable.

The context and relationship are like identical twins; they are separate but similar in appearance, especially when seen separately. The context of behavior sets the relationship on the cultural parameter level. The person-to-person level may be redefined or refined by the participants. Time, as a variable, may also alter the relationship. Context retains more stability. For example, a marathon group may meet for a weekend at a private home. The context is altered for the period of time needed to complete the sessions. Relationships among ten to twelve people are permitted to develop in the context of a home for a predetermined period. Following the marathon's close, the home becomes its usual context. Changing the rules in a given context is common procedure in most group counseling and group therapy. Encounter groups and other forms of sensitivity- and awareness-training groups frequently change rules for a given context and proceed with techniques to hasten the redefinition of relationships among the group members. This is another example of the power of *permission*. The culture rules are reestablished at the point of adjournment.

The proactive psychology professionals call the above process "facilitation." The reactive psychology professionals call the above process "manipulation."

There is another harmonic which should be noted in passing. The people most concerned with group process as a religious experience have evolved it since World War II. It was apparent that religion was coming into some group processes, especially during the latter part of the 1960's. Scientology began as a group process and moved through a period of redefinition from dianetics to "church." There are some who believe the group-community concept is the wave of the future in religion. Mowrer (1968) has reported the use of group-community process by early Christians under the term "exomologesis," a form of self-disclosure that was successful in restoring (healing) self-respect.

The Formal Social System

When a group is brought into being, the formal rules of the culture always apply to the social system established. It should be noted that a group can be any set of people who share some common characteristic (or variable) which identifies a linking together in a defined relationship.

The formal social system is provided by the culture and is shared by all persons in a given culture. Hall (1959) claims that compared to oriental cultures, American culture has a minimum of formal social rules. The overwhelming fact in American culture is simply that almost all rules are *informal.* The remainder are technical.

Formal culture rules are verbalized, may be written, and are shared by everyone. The variations one can experience within the culture are caused by another fact. The different social and economic classes and castes have evolved their own formal culture "uniquenesses." During the late 1960's black Americans made some major changes in their formal culture. Hall (1959) says that culture rules change from informal and technical to formal. When the rules become formal, the people take them for "granted" (e.g., "Doesn't everybody?") because formal rules are taught by admonition and by precept. You can observe formal rules being taught in a family whenever the mother tells the child to do a specific thing and gives no alternative. "Do it this way," says mother. When you hear such an exchange, you are observing the teaching of formal culture rules.

Black Americans changed some informal rules—"Uncle Tom" and "accommodation"—to formal admonitions about black Americans. "Black is beautiful" is one example. The point here is that to change a culture rule it must be made technical. Technical culture rules are very specific—e.g., time. Time is measured in milliseconds in computer speeds. This is one example of technical time. The revolution of the 1960's, for black America, achieved some changes from informal to technical to formal culture rules. The trial of the Chicago Seven is another event to document the changes in rules and the reestablishment process for new rules.

The individual may go through a change in his formal culture by joining a particular "group." The group redefines the culture rules for the members. A new biology (physical comfort) is achieved and new behavior becomes possible for the person. It is not different from the way a culture changes rules from one level to another. However, the person may accomplish major changes in much shorter time periods.

We should differentiate for the student of group counseling and group psychotherapy, between the above change in culture rules or levels, and personality adjustment for the neurotic or psychotic person. The literature on "group" has not clearly differentiated between the healthy person and the neurotic. The psychotic has been given much attention and probably needs no expanded discussion here. Group work described above can be used with healthy personalities for growth and development of more differentness. The neurotic needs to receive some remedial and corrective work before he can tolerate the open arena of "group." The neurotic will need a protective cover for a time until resolution of his irrational fears can subside. (The reader may wish to refer to the concept of competence in Chapter 3.)

Informal Social System

The informal social system consists of all the culture rules not classed as formal or technical. Informal culture rules are learned by example while observing models. Models are other people, usually older; however, they may be younger or peers. The best example in American culture is how we learn sex rules. These are almost entirely informal culture rules (Hall, 1959). During the 1960's there was a nation-wide effort to program sex-education materials by classroom television. The uproar against it lasted for many months. No one seemed to realize that making technical the informal rules of sex might be almost no change at all for the youngster, except for one important fact—that children already had sex knowledge but could not confirm it because the knowledge was neither technical nor formal. The best the children could do was to check another person's opinion, because the informal culture rules are largely out of conscious awareness. These same conditions have led to the exotic and even morbid fascination with nude marathon groups. The body tactile groups have shared in the same milieu. The results seem less significant than the curious fascination for the process of changing informal culture rules in a given group for a brief interval.

The group models used to exploit simple culture-rules changes should be carefully observed. Some charlatans could move into the "group" arena and become major con men. The task seems to be for us to achieve enough understanding of the culture rules at all levels to know the difference between legitimate and illegitimate use of group models to change behavior in a given person or group. The question of manipulation or facilitation should be answered in the affirmative. The crucial concern is whether the manipulation is sanctioned by a group or whether the members are unaware of the forces being employed.

Informal social system rules are the major portion of guiding principles in American culture. This creates a rich field for plowing the emotions of individuals—with permission, of course.

The modes for teaching seem to be closely tied in with the three levels of culture—formal, informal, and technical. Formal culture or social system is taught by precept. Admonishment is the mode of communication. Informal culture or social system is taught by model and example: "Watch me." "Follow along and 'see' what I do." Modeling can be systematically planned for any specific behavior. Because the learner needs the permissive milieu to try to apply his new knowledge by himself, the entire process looks much more like the learner "caught on" instead of having been taught. Most of the current generation of counselors were taught or "caught on" in this *informal* mode.

Technical culture or social system is taught directly from specific facts or data gathered from systematic study of the process to be learned. Hall (1959) gives the example of skiing to illustrate the difference between learning by informal means of watching someone else, and technical means based on facts sorted as components and patterns from films of expert skiers, then taught directly as specific steps to be learned in sequence.

Technical Social System

The technical social system is the level of culture where data becomes significant. Most of schooling and on-the-job training may be described as the systematic transfer of technical data. Translating knowledge of human behavior from the informal level to the technical level is the realm of behavior science. The process of systematic data gathering, analyzing, and reporting is research. Evaluation is also a part of the technical level of culture or human organization. We have learned to translate the isolates and sets of behavior from the informal (out-of-awareness) to the technical level of factual information. In counseling and group theory, the translation is just beginning. It will take many years to translate what we have learned at the informal culture level to the technical level. Kagan (1967) and his colleagues at Michigan State University started this procedure in 1962, under what they called IPR (Interpersonal Process Recall). It was the systematic use of video and a debriefing program that could yield specific facts about participants in the counseling process. The success over some five years led to development of a new instruction method in the medical school. Medical students learn to diagnose internal physical conditions in patients by interviewing the "coached" patient (actor) before a video system. The replay is analyzed and compared with the actor's presenting symptoms (Kagan, 1970). This is an example of the use of technical knowledge about a formerly "informal" subject. A similar application to counselor education and teacher education could happen with present knowledge.

Hall (1959) points to one more item of information to be kept in mind when we move from the formal to the informal to the technical: Science is thought of as largely technical. However, it contains some formal systems, i.e., methodology. No one may think to question it, and thus take it for granted. The fact that what becomes technical and subsequently widely accepted, may become formalized as a new formal social system. Apparently this is the progression of culture change—from informal to technical to formal. Investigators will no doubt discover their own systems do progress from flexible informal to rigid formal, while being largely technical.

Culture and the Beehive

Culture is the term used to define the organization of human behavior at the most basic and general levels. Groups are organized in direct relationship to the culture patterns defining relationships. Here is the simple metaphor: the Beehive. The order and pattern of behavior is specialized to such a degree that one can see the interdependent patterns in operation. Culture, for man, is a similar pattern in operation, except for the obvious exaggerations.

"Tightness" of organization may be desirable if one wishes to achieve efficient operation. Certainly, the beehive is one good example of the above. However, the human group seems to be less responsive to tight order in the division of labor, yet it is necessary to strike a balance between too much structure and order and too much ambiguity. Group counseling and group therapy began with very "tight" organization. Psychotherapists and counselors were rigorously prepared under intense supervision. More recent trends bring new concepts of practice and preparation into the arena of group work. Marathon, sensitivity, and awareness training may lead to an independent practitioner following his brief exposure to training. Frequently the person is a fully qualified professional before exposure to the new method. When the social responsibility safeguards are assured, the matter of rigorous control of training is usually evident.

A Technical System from an Informal Method

One of the greatest needs in group counseling is the need for an adequate means to evaluate the relation between *input* and *outcome*. Group work, in the mass, has no standardized criterion measures (Gazda and Larsen, 1968). There has been no systematic method for comparing event A in group 2 with event B in group 1 (Hall, 1959). The reason for the reluctance surrounding group-work measurement and evaluation stems, I postulate, from the informal mode we have used to practice group. As was mentioned earlier in this chapter, the informal social system way of teaching has held sway in group work from its beginning. The informal mode is not verbal but is largely an undifferentiated mass of content and process. The informal mode is mainly a style of living defined in abstract constructs and sample protocols. In this sense, group counseling and everyday living share a common mode, only the name "group counseling" is different. In milieu therapy, living and therapy are the same. (Kaneohe, Hawaii, State Mental Hospital currently uses a milieu treatment plan for adolescents. *Everyone* having anything to do with that ward is present for every decision.) A school and a classroom are something like a milieu living arena. The context is a shared living style governed by an informal and thus largely unverbalized set of rules. Only a violation can be noted. This is one reason children sometimes say, "You always correct my errors, never praise my correctness." Partly, too, we are dealing with that segment of the social system which is "taken for granted" and which everyone knows. To make it technical —to verbalize its isolates, sets and patterns—may be viewed by you, the reader, as a violation. As we proceed, you will know.

Step 1 is to get a recording of the behavior. Group counseling is recorded on videotape. The tape may be rerun. This constitutes replication by exact reproduction. The data source must be complete and be a permanent reference to return to again and again. Have we violated anything in your awareness? Frequently, persons think videotaping is a violation. The response to this is to reassure everyone that enough practice and exposure with the media will be experienced to allow each participant the opportunity to become safe enough to be spontaneous. Spontaneity is the criterion of authentic behavior. Now if you are continuing to question "Yes, but," please read on. What is being said to you here is a violation of your *informal* culture. Video recording of group counseling is done only with written permission of each participant and/or his legal guardian. As we proceed, we will speak of "comfort level." Comfort level is the measure of differentness you are experiencing. The informal mode has only biological comfort as a feedback source. The world of entertainment manipulates intricate techniques to program the audience comfort levels. I am not an entertainer, but group work is frequently exciting and enjoyable in an *entertained* sense. The informal mode is like that. Discovering something for yourself, even though you already know it at the informal level, is stimulating. Here is the entire basis of encounter and sensitivity group experience. The act of bringing to conscious awareness, the connection of a feeling (comfort level) and the life event I am in at this moment, is the happening. Living becomes a role—*do it now*—as contrasted to a goal, a role for tomorrow or a vague future.

A second step in the process is to analyze the behavior on the

videotapes. The analysis will yield the isolates, sets, and patterns pro-
mised by Hall (1959). Once the behavior is translated from informal to
technical level, the mode of teaching can shift from informal to technical. After the counselor has learned the technical knowledge about
group counseling he can proceed to develop his own style. That is, he
moves back into the informal level to operate. Otherwise the counselor
will be perceived as phony, plastic, unauthentic. The mystique that is
a combination of all the isolates, sets, and patterns of behavior is the
informal level we learn to recognize as being genuine, authentic, and
sincere as a person or as a counselor. The techniques we use in group
counseling take us from the behavior itself at the informal level, through
the analysis or verbalizing what is the happening (technical), back
through a biology of feelings (comfort level), to the informal level again.
All authentic behavior happens at the informal level. Teaching is a
technical level mode. One can shift freely from one level to another.

Techniques in Group Encounter

Group encounter has developed rapidly in recent years. Many of
the techniques were developed by Moreno (1946a, 1958) in his use of
psychodrama and sociodrama. The techniques were extended to new
group arenas, especially encounter groups. Some of the more exotic
forms of encounter group may use techniques of nonverbal character,
including nudity and physical touching, to mention a couple. Techniques cover a wide range from videotape to the swimming pool. If they
are combined, you will have either pornography or art, depending upon
the projections from the eye of the beholder.

Ohlsen (1970, p. 240) states that group counseling needs to measure
outcomes compared to inputs in terms of participants and life conditions. To do this we must first analyze what happens in each setting as
each technique is applied. The first task has been to get a valid analysis.
Kagan et al. (1967, 1968, 1970) gave five years to IPR (Interpersonal
Process Recall) research on videotape. The major outcome is the fact
that valid analysis of interpersonal interaction is possible. Furthermore,
one can specify the behavior he wants to develop, it can be put into
technical terms, simulated on video under supervision, learned at the
technical level and put into practice at the informal level of group
method. Valid analysis of replicable specific interpersonal encounters
has produced the capability to directly test any behavior in a real-life
situation by a rigorous method of simulation. The possibility to directly
teach a new behavior to a student is also included. Kagan et al. (1967)
discovered that considerable time is required initially in order to get the

counselors and counselees comfortable enough with the equipment and context to become spontaneous. Following achievement of spontaneity, the data may be collected by videotape. From the isolates, sets, and patterns of behavior identified it is possible to specify a particular behavior for simulation technique. Simulation of interpersonal interaction requires one person to be acting out a role. The only major difference between this technique, as technical model for teaching, and the natural occurrence schedule of waiting for one to come along, is the convenience. Before we learned how to analyze and then duplicate specific behavior, it was necessary to wait for each type to come along. Simulation permits a near duplication of the real thing, much like the simulation trainers for airplane pilots—at least so far as producing duplicate conditions is possible.

It will be difficult to detail every point important to the students' understanding of the technical system of analysis of behavior in group counseling. Nonverbal and random behavior seem to be especially remote for accurate and vivid description. I may have to settle for much less than desired because I'm no Shakespeare, as you may have already concluded. However, even verbal behavior needs to be observed in context to be understood. But on videotape enough of the behavior components are preserved to permit analysis. Therefore, the analysis method may be described in relation to a protocol. The following typescript is the verbal interaction from a ten-minute videotape clip made in a counselor education group counseling simulation session.

Three sixth-grade boys were trained to present specific problems to teams of two counselors. The sessions were recorded for later video playback. This videotape clip has been entitled "The Squealer." See if you can tell why as you read through it. The boys became affectionately known as the "mini-mob." They were hired and paid for their work. When counselors asked about the efficacy of paying the pupils, we were reminded of the stipends the counselors were receiving. The use of coached clients and simulation is very exciting and useful for counselor education supervision in group counseling practicum settings. It permits a specific focus. Counselors are told ahead of time that the group is a coached client group.

The Squealer

COUNSELOR I: You three boys have been sent to the office to the counselor. What seems to be the problem? *(looking at Allen)* Mark?
ALLEN: Mark's over there.
COUNSELOR I: Pardon? Oh, Mark . . .

MARK: We were fighting.

PHIL: We were fighting because me and Mark wrote dirty things on the blackboard, and Alan happened to squeal on us.

MARK: Dirty squealer!

PHIL: And we beat him up in the schoolyard.

COUNSELOR I: You said that he squealed on you because you were writing nasty things on the what—on the walls?

PHIL: On the blackboard.

COUNSELOR I: Uh-huh.

MARK: We were going to erase them.

COUNSELOR II: Why write them in the first place ? *(Pause)* Did you get some pleasure out of writing them?

MARK: Not really.

COUNSELOR II: Then what was the purpose? *(Long pause)*

PHIL: I guess because we were mad at something and we just had to write it down.

COUNSELOR II: By writing something dirty on the blackboard did that help relieve you of being mad? *(Pause)*

MARK: Yes.

COUNSELOR II: How? *(Pause)*

MARK: Just got out our anxieties. *(Pause)*

COUNSELOR II: You really think this helped you?

PHIL: *(Sigh)* The thing we're here for is 'cause we were fighting.

COUNSELOR II: That's right. But there was a reason you were fighting and it all started when you started writing something on the board. So for what purpose did you write on the board?

MARK: We just answered that question.

COUNSELOR II: But do you really think it helped you?

MARK: In some ways.

COUNSELOR I: How?

MARK: Well, like we could have really gotten mad and gone out and beat up somebody else.

ALAN: Yeah, so just go and beat up me, huh?

MARK: Yeah. *(Commotion)*

COUNSELOR I: Fellas . . .

PHIL: You told on us!

MARK: If he hadn't told on us, nobody else would have.

ALAN: Can you prove that?

MARK: Yeah!

COUNSELOR I: Okay, okay, So here Alan thought he was going to be a good citizen and report you in. So you beat him up. *(Pause)* So you did two things wrong today, right? First, you took your anger in school . . . out of school. Secondly, you beat him up. *(Pause)* Okay, before we tackle this problem of how we can resolve this, what could you have done to alleviate your anger, you know, aside from writing on the walls? You came to school angry, you know. Could you have done other things to somewhat relieve this anxiety that you had *(pause)* in a more constructive way?

PHIL: I guess we could have talked to somebody.

COUNSELOR I: Okay. You could have talked to somebody. What else? *(Pause—whistle, throat clearing)*

COUNSELOR I: What else? *(Pause)*

MARK: That's all I can think of.

ALAN: We could not come to school.

COUNSELOR I: Okay. Alan says you could have stayed home.

MARK: Yeah, but . . . we like our classes . . .

COUNSELOR I: Uh-huh.

PHIL: Yeah.

MARK: Most of them.

COUNSELOR I: So you were actually were caught, all caught in a trap, and you, you were angry, ah. One possibility was you could have stayed at home, right? But then, you like, you like your class so much you decided to come to school. Let's see, when you came to school, you took your frustrations out, you see, directed at the school so I don't quite understand what you mean you like, ah, school. The school means more than teachers, you see. It also means respect for the buildings, respect for the students, and so forth, you see. I like your idea, excuse, I like your idea about talking to somebody.

COUNSELOR II: Didn't it ever occur to you that you might offend someone by writing these things on the board?

PHIL: Yeah. We were planning to erase them when we went out of the room.

COUNSELOR II: Nobody was in the room?

PHIL: No, we were planning to erase it.

MARK: Except him.

ALAN: Yeah. They wrote in big letters like three feet tall, two feet wide. Someone just comes in the room, you know, and sees me sitting there and they send me to the office for, uh, not telling.

MARK: How can they do that?

ALAN: Well . . .

MARK: You didn't do anything.

COUNSELOR II: That's right. He didn't do anything. He was just being a good citizen and reporting what he should report. As far as I'm concerned, he's clear of this. It's you two guys.

PHIL: What would you do if your best friend squealed on you?

COUNSELOR II: He wasn't squealing. He was doing what he was supposed to do. You shouldn't have done it in the first place. *(Pause—sighing)* If you see an automobile accident, because you call the police to report it, that's not squealing. There's quite a difference. *(Pause—throat clearing)* I still don't think we've got to the bottom of this as to just why you felt the need to write something on the board that wasn't supposed to be there.

PHIL: Because we were mad at someone at home or something at home and we just came to school and were so mad we just happened to write these words on the board.

COUNSELOR II: Did you think of the consequences if you did get caught?

PHIL: No.

MARK: That might be.

COUNSELOR II: Then was it worth it?

MARK: Not really.

COUNSELOR I: You know you were wrong, then. Now I think that . . . if this should happen again what do think you would do? *(Long pause)*

COUNSELOR I: Do you have somebody you can confide with in school . . . to talk about this problem?

PHIL: Yes.

COUNSELOR I: Who!

PHIL: Each other.

COUNSELOR I: The children?

PHIL: Each other.

COUNSELOR I: Each other? Do you have a favorite teacher you can talk with?

PHIL: No.

COUNSELOR I: No? What about the counselor? *(Short pause)*

PHIL: I didn't think of talking to him. *(Pause—throat clearing)*

COUNSELOR I: How bad did they beat you up, Alan?

ALAN: They broke my glasses.

COUNSELOR I: What do you mean broke your glasses, they . . .

ALAN: They broke this arm, so I had to tape 'em.

MARK: You dropped it.

ALAN: Did not!

MARK: You did. *(Commotion)*

COUNSELOR II: Wait, wait . . . wait, just a minute. How did he come to drop them? Did you, ah, did he have them in his hand? Was this after you started fighting? *(Pause)* All right, then, he wouldn't have dropped them if you hadn't been fighting with him. *(Pause)* Can you wear them like that now?

ALAN: Yeah.

COUNSELOR I: Your mother will question you on that, Alan.

ALAN: Yeah, uh-huh.

Counselor I: You're prepared to pay for the damage here?

PHIL: Yeah.

MARK: Yes.

COUNSELOR I: I think, uh. *(Pause)* I'll talk to all of your parents about the incident, you know. I'll have to inform them because he did get hurt. You did get hurt didn't you?

ALAN: Uh-huh.

COUNSELOR I: Where?

ALAN: In my head.

COUNSELOR I: In your head. I'll have to talk to his mom about his glasses and your parents will have to pay for this, okay? I think it is only fair.

COUNSELOR II: I certainly hope that, uh, next time you will think in a little bit more constructive way of taking care of your anger.

PHIL: Haven't you ever been . . .

COUNSELOR II: Now . . .

PHIL: Haven't you ever done anything like this?

COUNSELOR II: Yes, I'm sure we all have, but that's part of growing up and I hope that the next time, you will know more what to do. Our door is open. We'd much rather see you come in here with something that you want to discuss than be pulled in on a problem.

COUNSELOR I: I think the important thing here is that you have become aware that whatever you did was wrong. I'm sure this wasn't the first time that you, ah, vent your anger at something like this, ah, in this destructive way. But if you become aware that this was wrong that you did, and, ah, next time, you know, you would do it in a more constructive way. I think this is the important thing. Everybody makes mistakes. This is no question, but it's how much a person learns from his mistakes that is the key to this thing.

COUNSELOR II: Well, the main thing is you know you did something wrong. Think of the consequences next time. And you are going to call . . . the parents?

COUNSELOR I: I will call the parents, yes.

COUNSELOR II: Real fine.

Discussion on Simulation

Counselors I and II had been informed only that the group had been coached. The counselors had to find the problem and deal with it in the ten minutes. Several things became immediately apparent. This situation is artificial. The behavior each person brings into an artificial situation is his own and therefore "real" behavior. The counselors did just that. Each counselor seemed to violate his own culture values in response to squealing. The specific here is the equating of reporting an automobile accident and reporting a peer for chalkboard graffitti. The latter "squeal" destroys the trust and safety for survival in a peer group. Another example of a specific behavior that seems in violation of culture rules is the one about citizenship. Is good citizenship equated with informing on a friend when the violation does not threaten anyone's physical safety? If squealing is a good thing, then perhaps it is OK for the counselors to tell the boys' parents—or is it? What do you think?

Second Simulation Group Counseling Example

The previous simulation protocol has been presented to provide a sample videotape record of behavior for analysis. We discussed the content and some obvious specific behavior. The second videotape script was made some five weeks later than the first tape. Some obvious changes are apparent. These changes are due to technical-level interventions, e.g., "You talk too much on tape one—try to reduce your input." This is accomplished in tape two. However, the technical teaching for what to do when you stop the informal level things you did do seems to be missing. During a subsequent period of ten more weeks it is possible to build in the new counselor behavior by systematic simulation of technical level data taken from informal level protocols.

The second tapescript deals with a conflict over money. The culture rules are very strict. The counselors stay very nearly clear of all the conflicts they might meet from the same mini-mob. The young boys had been practicing for more than six weeks when this tape was made. The mini-mob had become spontaneous in the simulation session.

The Missing-Money Caper

COUNSELOR I: Well, boys do you know why you're in here today?
MARK: Yeah.
COUNSELOR I: Phil?
PHIL: Uh-huh.
COUNSELOR I: You want to talk about it? Phil?
PHIL: Not really.
COUNSELOR I: How about you, Alan?
ALAN: There's nothing to talk about.
COUNSELOR I: There seems to be some discrepancy in, uh, the trea-

surer's book. Something to do with money, and I guess you know that Mrs. Lyons did, ah, refer you to us and perhaps you can offer some help to us in trying to rectify this, uh, discrepancy.

ALAN: You use big words. I don't understand you.

COUNSELOR I: I'm sorry, uh, what word didn't you understand, *rectify!*

ALAN: I don't know.

COUNSELOR I: Rectify is, to me anyway, means to correct this situation.

MARK: What he wants to know is why you stole it.

PHIL: We didn't steal it.

ALAN: Stole what?

PHIL: We didn't steal it. It's our money.

MARK: So now I have to make up the difference.

PHIL: It's our money.

COUNSELOR I: What do you mean, "It's our money?"

MARK: You stealer!

PHIL: It's our money so we just took our money back out.

COUNSELOR I: This money you're talking about is in the treasury that you had to pay?

ALAN: Yeah.

COUNSELOR I: But you took it out.

ALAN: Yeah.

PHIL: We were forced to pay.

COUNSELOR I: What is the money for?

ALAN: Ray, the janitor.

MARK: Get him a gift because he's retiring. (*Pause*—sigh)

ALAN: You don't know Ray, do you? *(Pause)* You don't . . .

COUNSELOR I: No.

ALAN: Well, he's about five, three; five, three—about 45 and he's Japanese.

COUNSELOR II: And what has this got to do with the problem?

ALAN: And he's really mean, he's really mean. And he's always trying to get us for something. Just Phil and I.

MARK: 'Cause you tease him.

ALAN: No, we don't tease him. He's always chasing us with the rake.

MARK: So, if you didn't tease him he wouldn't do it.

ALAN: Oh, let us tease him. It's not going to hurt him.

COUNSELOR II: So you all contributed to the fund and then you decided you didn't want to. Is that right?

PHIL: We didn't contribute. We were forced to put money in.

ALAN: Yeah. Blackmail!

COUNSELOR I: What do you mean forced? What do you mean?

COUNSELOR II: How do you mean blackmail?

PHIL: Our teacher said. *(Other voices talking)*

COUNSELOR II: One at a time.

ALAN: If you don't put in the money you can't go on the school picnic and that's blackmail.

COUNSELOR II: So you put the money in and then you took it out again.

MARK: Yeah. We then voted.

PHIL: Yeah. Some vote. Wow!

ALAN: Three people wanted it.

COUNSELOR I: Mark, did you feel the same way as they did?

MARK: No.

PHIL: What? Don't you feel that we were forced to put it in.

MARK: No, they took a vote and now you're going to take your money out, and I have to pay it.

ALAN: What vote? What vote? We didn't vote, we didn't vote. Three people voted, you know.

MARK: Oh, don't exaggerate.

COUNSELOR II: How . . . Wait. How many are in the class?

PHIL: Thirty.

COUNSELOR II: And only three people voted?

PHIL: No, only twenty voted.

COUNSELOR I: So you feel that you have been railroaded into paying this thing.

ALAN: Yeah.

COUNSELOR I: Did you have a choice not to pay.

ALAN: No. *(Pause)* Oh yes, if you don't pay you don't go on the school picnic . . . class picnic.

COUNSELOR I: But you did pay?

COUNSELOR II: Who decided that now?

ALAN: The teacher.

PHIL: The teacher.

COUNSELOR I: So you did pay.

ALAN: Yes, And I needed my quarter *(pause)* and so I couldn't get it any other way and so I really don't like Ray so I just took it.

COUNSELOR I: So this is pilfering then.

ALAN: Sort of.

COUNSELOR I: But that's down right . . . That's . . . That's pilfering, right?

ALAN: So?

COUNSELOR I: When you come down to it. Do you see this as, ah . . .

PHIL: It's our money.

COUNSELOR I: Do you see this as wrong?

PHIL: No.

COUNSELOR I: Nothing wrong? *(Commotion)*

ALAN: We took out as much as we put in.

PHIL: It's our money. We took it out and we were forced to put it in and so we just took it out.

MARK: And now I have to pay it.

PHIL: So what?

M ARK: I don't want to pay seventy-five cents, I don't want to pay it. *(Whispering)* Seventy-five cents.

ALAN: Yeah.

COUNSELOR II: Why did you need your quarter back so desperately just then?

ALAN: I was buying a radio and I have exactly enough, tax and all. And then this stupid thing comes up. You know with the teacher? So I'm a quarter short now and there's no way home that I can earn the money.

MARK: So?

COUNSELOR I: What did you, what did you pay in the first place?

Phil and ALAN: A quarter.

COUNSELOR I: No, but why?

PHIL and ALAN: 'Cause we were forced to.

COUNSELOR I: Okay, but you committed yourself then, but you said you had a choice.

ALAN: No, but we would have, uh, she said that she would, uh, give us bad grades, if we don't.

PHIL: Why don't you just admit it? Why don't you just admit it; it's blackmail.

COUNSELOR I: It's blackmail to you?

PHIL: Yeah, to everyone in the class. If you don't do this, you don't get this.

ALAN: It's like I've got your kid. If you don't pay me a certain amount of money, I'm going to kill him.

COUNSELOR I: Apparently, you don't like things to be done in that fashion.

PHIL: Would you?

COUNSELOR I: No. But I certainly would try to you know, do something about it. What could you have done?

PHIL: Get our money back so we get 'em.

MARK: Pay 'im. You're the only kids who don't like Ray, anyway.

PHIL: So what's that?

MARK: So. It's only fifty cents, I think.

ALAN: Don't have fifty cents.

COUNSELOR II: And the teacher has told you you will make it up although she knows that you took your money back.

ALAN: I don't think she knew it. *(Commotion)*

COUNSELOR II: You don't think she knew you took your money back?

PHIL: I don't know.

COUNSELOR I: You know the terms that you use to describe this teacher—she blackmails you, she's forcing you, she's going to beat it out of you. Apparently you don't have a very good picture of this teacher, do you?

ALAN: Not quite.

PHIL: I don't either.

C OUNSELOR I: You really do? And you feel this is part of why you're taking the money away.

ALAN: No, she wouldn't let me.

COUNSELOR II: Have you tried?

Phil: She won't do anything. We've tried how many . . .

COUNSELOR II: Have you tried?

PHIL: Yeah, we've tried.

ALAN: I haven't. Maybe he has.

COUNSELOR II: Well, would you describe the incident where you really tried and were not successful.

PHIL: What's that got to do with it?

COUNSELOR I: Well. . . .

PHIL: I said I tried and it didn't work out. I'm not going to describe it. *(Pause)* I'd rather not tell.

COUNSELOR I: Keep it a secret from us?

PHIL: It's something that I wouldn't want to tell.

COUNSELOR I: Does it threaten you to tell?

ALAN: It makes me feel like a . . . he tells you maybe he overhears you, and then he blackmails him for fifty cents.

COUNSELOR II: Where did all this scheme of blackmail come from that seems to be your favorite word here?

PHIL: Okay. Maybe that's our favorite word, but we don't do it—the teacher does it.

COUNSELOR II: Have you mentioned to the teacher how you feel about this?

PHIL: She doesn't care how we feel.

MARK: I don't blame the teacher for wanting to take a collection. Ray helps her all the time.

PHIL: Some collection.

ALAN: Yeah.

PHIL: If she wanted a present so bad, why didn't she buy it herself? She forced us to do it.

MARK: Yeah. But now I have to pay yours.

ALAN: Who cares.

MARK: So you took the difference.

PHIL: So why don't you go up to her and tell her that if she wants a present so badly that you (the teacher) pay for the seventy-five cents.

COUNSELOR II: Now why do you feel that you have to make this up?

MARK: Well, if there's a difference, any money that's missing, the treasurer has to make it up.

COUNSELOR II: Even though the teacher is aware of where it went?

MARK: I think so.

ALAN: You accepted the responsibilities. *(Talking all at once)*

MARK: Yes.

PHIL: If you knew . . .

COUNSELOR II: I don't think you have anything to worry about. If the teacher knows who took it, she's not going to make you make it up.

PHIL: 'Cause we're not going to pay for it.

COUNSELOR I: How do you feel about not being able to go on the class picnic?

ALAN: Really, I don't care.

PHIL: I don't care, right now. It's our money.

COUNSELOR I: How do you feel about somebody having to pay for you?

PHIL: Pay for us, huh?

COUNSELOR I: In other words.

PHIL: Let her pay for us. We don't want the present in the first place.

COUNSELOR I: You don't think much of Mark, do you?

PHIL: Mark's just like a little. . . .

ALAN: Crybaby.

PHIL: Dumb Mark.

ALAN: You touch him and he goes "aaaah." He screams and everybody hears him, you know, all the way across the campus. They hear him scream, you know.

MARK: Awh.

PHIL: They think you're dying, you know. You stub your toe and you act like you're going to die.

COUNSELOR I: So Mark is really (   ). Do you think you have anything nice to say about him?

Comment on Simulation

The goal in simulation of group counseling was to achieve a measure of self-disclosure for the counselors in training. Seeing oneself in a contrived circumstance can be as revealing as necessary to gain a perspective on the impact *my* behavior is having on *you*.

The mini-mob members were accomplished, coached clients. The contrived circumstances quickly are converted to real-life adventures by the boys' spontaneous acting out. The counselors were able to demonstrate a new pattern of response quite different from their first encounter where the counselors actually contradicted their own values. Spontaneity is achieved in simulation at the point where the coached clients begin to "play themselves." After spontaneous behavior appears, simulation is identical with real-life behavior. It is real-life because I am playing myself. My response is a contrived circumstance *is* my real behavior! This fact has been important to research functions as well as training in group skills. Research designs require the capability for replication. Simulation is a possible method for replicating behavior.

Summary

The models used in group counseling have come largely from the proactive or interactive psychology theory base. The reactive psychology forms the base for behavior therapy. Behavior therapy has gained considerable notice in the recent past. There is no question that behavior therapy seems to work well on monads. Dyads, triads, and larger groups need a broader-based theory to explain the interrelatedness of behavior along a network of human persons, especially in groups.

Learning to learn is the key concept in the material of this chapter. The attempt to glimpse the connection between the culture's massive conditioning of biology and behavior rules used in human organizations seems to lie at the heart of the effort. The reason it gets easier to learn as one learns more, seems to be tied to another overriding variable. That variable could be the common conditioning or learning model in the culture.

The interaction model takes in to account the context of behavior, appropriate behavior and competence to behave—all at once. The intrapsychic model of counseling and therapy seems to be limited for group work. Family group therapy gave rise to the double-bind theory of communication. Paradox and conflict seem to be generated by interaction as easily as resolution, perhaps more easily sometimes. We do know how to put these paradoxes into technical terms whenever they are encountered in the informal culture context.

The formal social system, informal social system, and technical social system are examples of levels of culture with specific rules governing behavior in each mode. Group work has been done largely in the informal mode, with little or no verbal specification at the technical level. The technical level of behavior is necessary if teaching group behavior skills ever is to lead beyond the "watch me" stage of modeling.

Simulation is possible because specific data in group behavior can be identified and replicated on videotape. Some examples were presented to show the verbal interaction. Analysis of group behavior is complex but can be specified at the technical level from recorded samples of actual informal mode group behavior.

Suggested Additional Readings

Cuban, Larry, 1969. "Teacher and Community," *Harvard Educational Review.* 39 (2) 253–272 (Spring).
  Narrow views of the functions of teaching and unrealistic training of teachers cause the gulfs between school and community. Cuban wants teaching to include instruction, curriculum development, and community involvement. He advises more personal contact between schools and community in an effort to resolve problems of dealing with children. He sees the role of the teacher as being both social reformer and teacher, with emphasis on the latter. The community must become an extension of the classroom. The teacher will be a "middleman" to connect people with services and build relationships.

Edinger, Lois V., and Ole, Sand, 1969. "Schools for the 70's and Beyond," *Today's Education*, 58(6) 74–75 (September).
  According to these authors schooling and education are not synonymous. Schools must learn to work with other educational institutions other than the school. In the future, technology will free teachers from their role as fact dispenser. The teacher will become a diagnostician and catalytic agent who facilitates learning but does not provide all the answers. More emphasis will be on individual needs and strengths.

Maslow, Abraham H., 1968. "Some Educational Implications of the Humanistic Psychologies," *Harvard Educational Review*, 38(4) 685–695 (Fall).
  Maslow says that there are two kinds of learning: culturally determined (extrinsic) and learning about self (our "specieshood and biological idiosyncracy"). The teacher who facilitates learning about self is receptive, but not a lecturer or reinforcer. The teacher must accept a person as he is and help him to capitalize on his potential by learning about his true self. A nonthreatening environment and a concern for the learner are important. Maslow sees the possibility of using "peak experiences" as intrinsic rewards or goals in education.

Pharis, William, John C. Walden, and Lloyd D. Robinson, 1969. "Educational Decision Making," *Today's Education.* 58(7) 52–54 (October).
  Educational decision making in the 1970's will resemble that of state and federal governments. Societal decisions will be made at higher levels (state capitals or Washington, D.C.). Decisions will be influenced by a wider range of people, but the actual decision will be made at higher levels.

Schmuck, Richard A., 1968. "Helping Teachers Improve Classroom Group Processes," *Journal of Applied Behavior Science*, 4(4) 401–434 (December).
  Three strategies for enhancing teacher capabilities were tried in an effort to help the teachers improve classroom group processes. The goal was to bring

teachers to the realization that modification of their own behaviors could improve informal group processes. The projects tried were a teacher development lab, the use of psychological consultants who met with teachers in small groups, an organizational-processes development lab aimed at improving interpersonal relationships, communication and group norms. Approach 1 and 3 facilitated changes, but the intervention of consultants alone did not appear to change actual teacher behavior.

Shane, Harold G., and June G. Shane, 1969. "Forecast for the 70's," *Today's Education*, 58(1) 29–34 (January).

The role and responsibilities of teacher will change. Teachers will become "learning clinicians" in an effort to maximize individual psychosocial development. Each resource person (teacher) will be well informed on a subject such as counseling, media, languages, systems analysis, game theory, or individual needs analysis. New faculties will include culture analysts, media specialists, information-input specialists, biochemical therapist/pharmacists, early childhood specialists, developmental specialists, and community contact personnel.

6

Revolution in Group: Interventions, Simulation, Spontaneity and Technique

The 1970's seem destined to be an heir to the revolution in group that began around the late 1920's and moved from home room guidance in the school (McKown, 1934) to the Western Behavioral Sciences Institute at La Jolla, California, in scope and model (Farson, 1968). The differences in form are legion and readily apparent. Groups may be classrooms filled with students monitored by a teacher, or a small collection of persons encountering one another, and even an individual encountering self, while arranged in the group, at a table, at poolside, or on a carpet in an enclosed room or space. I choose the two groups, described in *form* or *format* above, as the extremes of what constitutes the range of group variations on an *invariant* substance of principle of culture underlying the full spectrum of group organization (APGA, 1970; Rogers, 1968).

For several years I worked with groups of eleventh-graders in several different states—from Hawaii to Pennsylvania and from Louisiana to South Dakota. I could *always* depend on one variable in the seventeen-year-old's behavior. Each of them could reproduce my behavior in leading a group, following only *one* trial. All they had to do was participate with me in a group for up to thirty minutes.

In order to achieve this level or consistent pattern in behavior among widely separated (geographically) individuals, there would need to be a major constant or *invariant* in their respective backgrounds. It seemed to me that the cultural parameters or rules each of us holds in common in a given culture provide the way to account for the phenomenon.

Invariance comes in the cultural parameters of behavior. Variance is the behavior of a given behaver in a given context of culture. This last statement defines "group" as a culture determined phenomenon. Group is, as a concept, governed by principles of invariance (Thayer, 1967; Foa, 1967; Corsini, 1957).

In actual group encounter the multitude of details may obscure the common cultural principles that set the patterns and systems of behavior in group.

The concept of culture as a social system that operates on invariance principles means that the group may be understood on the basis of these principles no matter what the details of relationships and operations actually are. For example, we have known for many years that the studies done in industry have shown positive results, even when no study was going on—only the belief that a study was making something special of the group of production workers and their relationships, increased production. Fiedler (1950 a and b) discovered a similar principle of invariance in relationships factors related to change in patients who were treated by different therapeutic interventions from different treatment systems. Relationship itself is considered the invariant because something in the culture operates in common with each psychotherapy system. The common principle seems to be with relationship on a person-to-person basis. Behavior therapy focuses on the treatment intervention program of rewards and sequencing of reinforcements. However, most behavior-therapy practitioners insist upon selection in two variables. One is the case itself. They tend to ignore relationship factors because the variables cannot be validated. The point we are making here is simply that relationship may be a unitary variable and therefore an invariant of the culture. No intervention can be initiated without encountering relationship definitions in the context of the behavior. The research in family counseling (Fullmer, 1970a) is conclusive only at the level of relationship. Like communication, there is no such thing as *no relationship*. There is always communication, it is a question of what is being communicated (Shockley, 1967). Similarly, relationship always exists: it is a question of what is the definition of the relationship. When the intervention is a relationship, the family redefines prior and existing relationships. This leads to the concern for access to other persons. Access to others seems central in the class organization of society and the classroom organization in a school. Group counseling has been one means of gaining access to others at many levels within social organizations.

Interventions

All group counseling should be aimed at producing specific skills. Some skills are broad-gauged, others are extremely narrow. For example, a counselor may wish to know how to begin a group for the first time in a new school setting. The skills the counselor needs include how to advertise or announce the happening. A friend in Portland, Oregon, puts out a brochure announcing the coming events with time and place. He gets a group from the general public by this means because he has something about which to do training. Psychodrama is his special skill. The persons interested sign up, convene, and train with him. The key point is the message that defines the special skill or task to be learned in the group.

The school is a restricted environment for group methods. First, the classroom and teacher constitute a group. The students form peer groups, and the faculty is another set of groups. The first two above—classroom and student peer groups—cannot be invaded. They must decide whether the counselor may enter. Permission is the prerequisite to intervention on most every life situation.

The counselor may ask permission to join any group. The counselor may ask the group to do a task for him. These two interventions combined—permission and request to perform a useful task—have never failed to provide the necessary conditions for intervention for this writer. I presume these interventions would fail if for any reason I permitted the exploitation of a group by using some "hidden agenda" ploy. Authenticity, genuineness, openness, and sincerity are absolute requirements. Permit no spuriousness, no plastics, no phony moves to discredit or cast doubt on the motives behind the purposes of the group(s).

Perhaps the ultimate intervention in group resides with the *authority* to convene a group for whatever purpose seems agreeable to the participants. In school counseling or community agency work, the reason may be more specific because the potential range of group tasks is greatly restricted by the scope and concern within the social institution. Authority is used to include the social heirarchy and the concept of knowledge and wisdom. The authority of knowing is the most important.

The action taken to call a meeting is the authority central to intervention. To get people involved with a task is the method. The task may be any action the group may wish to commit their energies to carrying through. For example, the decision to commit one's energy to self-improvement would qualify as a task. However, the more specific the delimitation the more realistic is the opportunity to show results. The group may undertake the task of learning the formula for leading sensitivity groups. The leader begins the group in the usual way. The informal mode of "Watch what I do" holds for this activity. The technical discussion of the content of the formula might go like this:

- Each person will speak only for and about himself (first person singular).
- Each person will respond to each other person only in terms of what "I" hear "you" saying is. (Again paraphrase in first person singular.)
- Interpretations and judgments of others must be strongly discouraged. If they are expressed or implied, the leader should request a cutoff in communication.
- The phrasing of comments becomes ritualistic in style and content. The form resembles the restricted code of a group that has been intact for a long time.
- Strict time limits are imposed for the scheduled operation of a group.

More specific technical description of the formula is possible whenever a particular life event and a particular individual are designated within the dynamic ongoing group. If the five rules set forth above are followed in a sensitivity-group action, the results will be similar to every other group that convenes and follows these rules. Beyond these specific guidelines, the culture rules or parameters act as limit setters for guiding individual behavior in a group. The culture rules are examples of invariance principles which create similar results through specifically divergent means or processes. To go back all of the way to the beginning and then map the forces that shape and delimit behavior in a group, it is necessary to decide what one can accept as the base line. I use the culture rules or parameters which are invariant so far as behavior within a given culture context is concerned. Every new idea must be sorted through each significant person's own perception of what constitutes competent behavior within a given context.

An idea may serve as an intervention in group. Ideas may get people involved with each other. The idea may become a *cause* to be defended, promoted, and exploited. Involving people in a group task is frequently achieved by having volunteer membership. You have to *want* to join. Any intervention is in the form required to involve people in a coordinated effort toward the resolution of a specific task.

The idea is in some way the task for redefining the reality of a given group on the basis of each person's notion or perception of the reality defined by culture rules or parameters in a given context. The fact of behavior in response to an idea is not too difficult to explain. But if the behaver is embarrassed because of the informal culture rule against overt display of the idea, the life event may require expert handling. One way to know when an informal culture rule is being broken is simply to note the level of anxiety among the group members. The behavior is biological and usually is not verbalized. Technical culture rules are easily challenged because they are written down and easily verbalized.

Methods of Exploiting a Group

The word *exploit* is meant to convey a positive utilization of a human resource. The exploitation of a group may have multiple positive and productive results. Before a group can move toward productivity, the need for solid purposes exists. A solid purpose is any one that will get people to involve a commitment to a task. The methods of primary importance include turning over to a group the responsibility, accountability, resources, and final decisions about whatever task the group is to do. The main idea is that group members find useful and meaningful satisfactions in carrying through when methods of exploitation are favorable.

Natural groups in the society are examples of the culture social system's human organization design for exploiting human resources. Contrived groups are similar in organization to natural groups. A family is a natural group with many complex levels of organization. The day-to-day social living functions of a family resemble many social peer groups. However, the social peer group may not be a procreation group like the family.

Training Participants in Group

It is perhaps axiomatic to claim the obvious necessity to help persons learn the skills of group membership and leadership. In addition to group members and leaders, there are contributors, volunteers, and special persons with special skills who can make helpful contributions for the training of participants in group. Most training groups do a brief technical orientation session and move quickly into an informal mode of "Watch what I do." Process groups are strictly "informal" in mode and style. Process groups are those in which the central task is one of creating change in the behavior or understanding of behavior in the participants themselves. To change behavior it is necessary to alter the individual's system of beliefs. Sensitivity training, awareness training, and basic encounter groups tend to remain "process" oriented.

The major impact of the process oriented group is found in the exposure to experience within a context controlled by feedback rules designed to create a unique self-disclosure condition. The reinforcement schedules, provided by the impact of self-disclosure in the contrived social system, can be described as systematic desensitization being sought by the researcher or professional practitioner.

Supervision of Activities

Group models are the complex systems used to effect group interventions. In chapter five, we talked about the *reactive* and *proactive* psychology theory bases for group models. Reactive psychology is more closely tied in with behavior therapy models of group and individual applications in professional practice (Lazarus, 1968). Proactive psychology is more closely tied in with systems oriented to humanistic models of group and individual applications (Mowrer, 1968).

The chief differences between the two major divisions of applied psychology are to be found in the nomenclature. For example, the behaviorist manipulates, the humanist facilitates. What really is the difference? There are a number of differences. On close examination these differences reduce to words, points of view, degree of general–specific inclusion–exclusion of variables—in brief, the question is whether one is talking at the technical or informal culture levels. The more technical and therefore specific is the language describing behavior and life events, the more likely it is that the behavior-reactive psychology theory is being applied. The more the informal culture mode is indicated by the language (Hall, 1959), the greater is the possibility it is proactive psychology theory being applied. The point is that instead of speaking of the same thing, it is possible to show in practice that the two positions are speaking about different *portions* of the behavior event. The behavior-therapy position focuses in on the specific behavior and its reinforcers. The humanistic-oriented therapy position leaves specific behavior alone and deals with the whole context and relationship portions which are more inclusive and general-systems oriented, and consequently, less specific.

The practical results for research leaves the behaviorists better off at first glance. However, the symptom orientation imposed by the scope of the behavior-therapy model makes concern for the global context out of reach. For instance, the behavior therapists would treat the monad in a group, like a family, without much concern for the effect on the group following the changes in behavior of the identified patient. In the humanistic mode the entire family would be treated together. The changes in one member would be no less important to the network of relationships, but it could be dealt with directly in the group. Eysenck (1965a) has been quite adamant about the lack of evidence to show results of nonbehaviorist-oriented psychotherapy.

The task here is to raise the issue for the student of group counseling and group psychotherapy. There will be no attempt to argue for science or a belief system, because such a discourse would lead away from the central purpose in this text.

If the student can learn about all the theories and systems in psychology, there could be a basis for choosing. However, the professional-practice side of psychology is usually very biased in the direction of one or another specific systems. The theory base is frequently less distinct. In this text, the bias is away from the position of either-or polarization, toward a more lenient or conservative explanation of behavior utilizing the nomenclature most relevant for communication. The global orientations are best served by general system theory. The specific behavior in a particular behavior incident is better served by learning theory nomenclature.

Group models used to effect interventions may be derived from reactive or proactive psychology. The forces manipulated or facilitated in group can be described in technical language if one can learn to verbalize the behavior used in the informal culture (Hall, 1959). Technical language moves toward scientific description and away from the mysticism associated with the informal mode of "Watch what I do," and "You'll catch on." The world of "group" is filled with the informal mode because there is no other way to achieve "spontaneity." Spontaneity is essential for healthy group behavior. Exposure to new behavior is necessary if one-trial learning is to operate. For most persons, "to catch on" is possible only if they get the opportunity to be exposed to the new behavior in a real-life context.

Simulation and Technique

Games have become important vehicles for improving the quality of communication about behavior. Simulation and the techniques in group work may be studied together as complementary constructs. Simulation may itself be a powerful intervention technique to overcome the resistance of the person or persons involved in a group. The game idea may be more acceptable as a means to instruction than the real-life behavior. Rogers (1962) claims some specific factors have been identified with the problems of diffusion of new ideas or innovations. He offers more than fifty characteristics of persons and social systems defined in terms of resistance to innovations and adoption of innovations. There are a number of paradoxical relationships between leaders of groups and adopters of innovations. For example, the leader of a group is usually more conforming to the group norm than is the average member. This may indicate that to get innovations launched it is necessary to have an entire unit of an organization committed to a given task. The task may be the new innovation. By the strategy implied here, a group may become the technique by which simulation of an innovation can be tried out before anyone risks final commitment at a personal or an organizational level. Loughary (1966) sees the man–machine systems technology applicable to education problems primarily by combining "man" systems or social systems and machine-computerized systems. Technique and simulation are compatible with "people" groups and machine systems.

The need seems reasonable to show evidence that goals for specific interventions in education and counseling have been achieved or missed. The expectation is no less true for innovations as for established practice. Kagan (1968) claims that research done at Michigan State University by his group has provided convincing evidence to show that simulation can be used successfully with human behavior whenever the specific product behavior is defined in advance. The idea of simulation has redefined the myth that human-behavior training must rely on random or chance happenings. The new behavior sought can be achieved in considerably less time than is required if only routine events are relied upon. Even in the medical training clinic it is no longer the only alternative to await the appearance of a specific clinical type as a case for study. Kagan (1968) has been simulating the cases by videotape and coached patients. The controls are better because the input is specific. The medical student gets feedback on his own terms with confirmation for the programmed portions and a visual-auditory retake on the informal culture portions. This example carries the hope for new and expanded uses of newer technologies in the handling of specific learning in behavior made complex because of the informal culture mode in which the behavior happens.

The informal mode and "infinite" variety potential in group types and purposes has been increasingly apparent since about 1960. The revolution in the use of informal process groups to train counselors gave rise to a number of types. The purposes were to achieve the informal culture learning so necessary in direct human encounter. It was verbalized in a multitude of ways—the learning to know oneself, become aware of my impact on you, achieving the capacity for empathy (Fullmer and Bernard, 1964). In the early part of the 1960's no one had verbalized beyond the mysticism of outcome or product behavior, to show that process groups work. At one point your author helped hold a national seminar for Directors of all NDEA Counseling Institutes to share this "process group" idea. The meeting was held at Cambridge, Massachusetts, just ahead of the APGA Convention in Boston for 1963.

The major complaint from those who were in informal-process-oriented groups for the first time was, "What is the purpose?" Of course the purpose was left ambiguous too, as a central part of the strategy. We did not have the technical culture verbal descriptions worked out. We were locked in on an informal method. The verbal expressions in the informal mode are very imprecise. "You'll get the hang of it." "Watch me and after a while you'll catch on." This kind of verbalization characterizes the informal mode, where each person is allowed his own variation on the basic design or rule. Mark Hopkins on a log with his student characterizes the informal mode in education. The counselor and his counselee in an ongoing relationship is not new or different; only another variety in the "infinity" of informal culture behavior.

Following the Cambridge meeting of directors, George Pierson (1965) conducted a study of the more than twenty year-long Counseling and Guidance Institutes held during 1963–64 academic school year. His report was published in 1965 by the U.S. Office of Education, Department of Health, Education and Welfare. In the Pierson report we learned that nearly every Institute was using the small process group as a method of instruction. Again, in keeping with the informal culture mode, there was considerable variety among the group models employed. They were not all following a one type *technical* model.

Let me point out another fact about the informal mode. It is important to have the right conditions when teaching by the informal method because the learning is more *caught* than *taught.* "You'll *catch* on" is but one example. The conditions under which something is learned may be even more important than the content being taught in the informal mode. When we become technical or formal, the concern for the attitude concomitants disappears because these "attitudes" are taught too. We have been a long time in moving from the informal mode to the technical mode for instructing in group skills. Kagan (1968) has documented and confirmed that much essential behavior once locked in to the informal mode can be made into technical skills. There will remain the attitude among some persons that a violation of the sanctions of informal culture rules corrupts every technical statement about behavior. The fact is that when we make technical a formerly informal rule or behavior, the informal simply moves to the next level of abstraction. There is no conflict with that theory of knowledge, only an advance in the level of enlightenment. Frequently, in the experience with family group consultation over nearly ten years of empirical testing as a group method of treatment, we were reminded by the redundance of this behavior fact. Change from informal nonverbalized relationship to technical verbalized relationship increased involvement and commitment to the group. An outcome of considerable significance because the expectation according to popular belief (myth) would lead one to forecast the opposite outcome. Again the reader is reminded that a change in the level of abstraction permits explanation of the previous level in technical language (Watzlawick, Beavin, and Jackson, 1967). This fear of knowing and verbalizing seems deeply rooted in the culture's mythology. The belief is that knowledge will corrupt some innocent person but that paradoxically it is all right for a privileged few to have knowledge. The fact is that such myth seeps into the formal and informal social systems of science itself. The entire society may ask if man's technology has not gone too far and now threatens the very life systems of man. Ecology is the "kick" of the 1970's. While we were busy observing primary data the secondary effects built up almost unnoticed. As early as 1965 Danskin, Kennedy, and Friesen (1965) reminded us that human organizations create environments for psychological survival. Technical knowledge about informal behavior will not corrupt, but it will enlighten, enliven, and enhance the probability for survival in human behavior.

Simulation in Specific Tasks

The technique of simulation is useful whenever a specific task or skill in interpersonal behavior is to be learned. The simple forms of simulation in group counseling happen whenever a role-playing situation is used to practice a new behavior. Intentional plan or random accidental incident makes the product no less useful. However, self-conscious plans add to the efficacy of appropriate use of group counseling time.

The long list of psychodrama techniques for self-disclosure make excellent methods for simulation of entire social contexts. The rerun of a past life event is simulated to reveal alternative ways of meeting new and similar life events.

Interviewing may be learned under the controlled conditions of simulation. A computer may be programmed to respond to certain patterns of interaction with a single individual. Tape recorders for sound and video create more useful variations for direct feedback and accurate simulation. Coached clients may be used to handle interviews where information gathering requires inferences based on informal culture behavior. Combinations of media, methods, and techniques seem to be nearly infinite for the creative professional. Combined with behavior-therapy techniques, the research possibilities are enhanced because simulation permits replication—an essential aspect in human behavior research.

Counselor education for group counseling includes both simulated and supervised real-life group experiences. Because each person creates anew, in each life event, the experience he has, the simulated training sequences are essentially the same quality experience as the real-life group. The formula used in each type group can best be taught through simulated experiences. For example, the coached clients in the group may be programmed by formula. The formulas may be identical. This places the counselors in training in a context that permits them to experience the impact of the formula much like counselees in a group. Further, it is possible to replay the videotape many times for supervision purposes. The direct feedback helps the counselor learn to stop doing what he is doing that gets negative reinforcement.

What does one do when he stops doing his usual formula (behavior)? He needs to learn what to do to achieve positive reinforcement.

Initially, many counselors in training do nothing. They adopt the formula of nondirection, permitting the group to run at random. This too is played back for supervision purposes.

The third phase is more complex. It is necessary to provide the simulated models of what "should" be done, in leading a group, without eliminating the spontaneity and infinite variety of behavior so necessary in the informal mode of the culture. We have used simulation to introduce model behavior for each formula. Then it is necessary to begin the long follow-through with real-life groups. The minimum time to achieve safe levels of competence is nearly two years of supervised work. Because the variations in formulas and group types are numerous we do not feel that two years will be sufficient to master competence in more than one major type. There is some expectation that learning the formula variations for one major type of group counseling would enhance the learning to learn capability. Mastery of additional systems should be relatively easier for the accomplished professional unless he becomes a rigid reactionary for one particular type.

The *formula* in group counseling is one of the hybrids made from the combination of selected techniques taken from some two hundred varieties advocated by American psychotherapists and other helping-relationships professionals (Nelson, 1968). We are using the interaction model in this text, but intrapsychic labels sometimes are used to remind the reader of the wide range of nomenclature associated with group counseling. The range is from psychoanalytic unconscious processes, like transference, to the reconditioning procedures of behavior modification, to the permissive self-actualizing procedures of the humanistic mode—and if you keep subdividing you can approach the two hundred varieties referred to above.

By whatever means the formula gets set up, the fact is that a *context* for interaction is formed, complete with people and the rules and norms of social control operating in the group dynamics. The formula is that set of rules, norms, behaviors, and sanctions employed in the group-counseling sessions to maintain social control. The interaction context thus created is the life context within which relationships are defined and experience is created by the individual. Individual human behavior is formed in the group to express the meanings being experienced. This is linked to our theory of group and explains the function of the "formula" in the interaction. There are several other important variables—the territory or place where the group meets, the physical arrangement of the furniture, the decor, and adjacent spaces; the time of day, day or days of the week, and duration of the sessions scheduled; number and characteristics of the group membership, and the stated or understood purpose motivating the behavior in the group—to name only a few of the influential factors operating with the formula. The formula establishes and maintains the pattern of interaction. In family group consultation (Fullmer and Bernard, 1968), the fourth session is most frequently the elapsed time needed to establish the system of speaking. Sequence of speaking—who speaks first, second, who can talk about which subject, topic—and whether there is any hierarchy of subjects by members, plus a host of similar specifics are all reflected in their speech.

The group interaction "system" seems to reflect general open-system characteristics such as disequilibrium, interdependence, and differentiation. The roles necessary to actualize the interaction system in a group must be learned in the group or exist in the membership a priori. Initially, the group's membership will reflect both conditions. Very soon the group should move to a condition in which everyone is learning a new role. Psychotherapists speak of teaching a person how to be a patient. Group counseling might be similar in teaching membership roles in the group. The formula is the means for achieving this condition. Lennard and Bernstein (1969) claim that almost no research has been done on how the roles are taught or learned in group. Our hypothesis is that the formula along with the other variables in the context provide the informal culture model for roles learned from the leader in the early group sessions. The passive and active leaders in group should show about the same time sequence for learning roles by participants, but the frequency and output of leads would be considerably less for the passive leader. Studies of communication in groups tend to support this idea (Lennard and Bernstein, 1969). There are further indications, though certainly in need of further verification, that the *invariant* in all group counseling is the relationship(s) defined by the *context* and the *formula*. Further research, with simulated and replicated context and relationship, is needed for group counseling before any conclusive statements can be made.

Games and Simulation

Dr. Frederick L. Goodman at the University of Michigan (Bayerl, 1970) has developed games to help participants in a variety of natural culture groups find and learn their roles. The major advantage of games comes from the vehicle value of making concrete and specific the material that is usually academic and abstract. Consequently, a street gang or a college official can operate together. Games range from showing what a street gang is concerned about to improving the performance of counselors, parents, and social agency specialists who help others by making explicit the roles information systems play in the behavior or action taken by a given individual. Games have a number of important advantages as simulation techniques. For training and research the invariant of the game makes replication possible. The focus on role is concrete, clear-cut, structured, and unambiguous. Ambiguity in real-life situations tends to be disorganizing. The games technique offers novelty in controlled amounts to aid motivation and the reinforcement schedule. The game-simulation technique affords the participants with what Sartre called the "power of circumstances" over their experience. Simply stated, they may exercise their freedom and choose to quit. Real-life does not always permit this choice or freedom; one may be required to remain engaged until the cycle achieves closure. Games offer the potential for each participant to develop his own game designed to replicate an essential environment in which he lives. In an age of discontinuity (Drucker, 1969) it may be necessary to help people learn to learn by this simple social group device. Managing the almost infinite variation in informal culture requires a technical conversion system. Games play that way. Who knows—the helping hand may strike again (Fullmer, 1964b).

Games are more versatile than a sophisticated psychotherapeutic system like psychodrama. However, the dramatic results are similar in the realm of self-disclosure and the revealing of interdependent relationships between a life condition and a person's action. The game-simulation technique is safe to use on most populations. As educational material, games rank high in those areas of subject matter made complex by multiple variables which remain largely ambiguous and abstract, such as human interaction in counseling. An activity that deals with information exchange systems can be used in games design, method and interventions. Almost any social agency, school, or family has in it the potential life situations where information systems have powerful effects on the behavior of the participants.

The technique of games permits exposure to wide differentness without the requirement for each person to lay on the line, his own commitments on an a priori basis.

Group Models Sampler

Multiple types of group counseling, therapy, and training have evolved to date. The 1970's seem destined to exploit the human group movement in many ways inside and outside the school. The family has been actively engaged in groups for counseling and consultation. (Fullmer, 1970b). Business and industry began long ago and continue to use group methods for training and development (Gibb, 1968). The community has responded by using groups for personal information and improvement. Mowrer (1968) has reported the ancient history behind the survival value in group for religious and psychological experience. Rogers (1968) continues to move away from the monad psychotherapy models toward the general group models for *facilitation* of learning and being. The remedial and corrective reconstruction of personality has been laid aside. The encounter group has emerged with its many varieties of sensitivity and awareness. Marathon groups seem to be the most accurate attempt to simulate a full-time, continuous simulation of real-life encounter. Other examples range from Synanon games to venture groups. Synanon is a hard-hitting confrontation battle of words between two persons, supervised by a referee. Venture groups are self-help groups convened by members of the same community for self-personal development and information exchange. These two models may be near the poles of differentness in the contemporary group revolution. Synanon game is for the rehabilitation of the addicted. The intervention is powerful; however, like most group models, Synanon required volunteer participation. Again, permission is the key to access in group. Venture groups have a similar requirement for admission, but the intervention is by verbal formula bolstered by nonverbal exercises.

In the silent in-between models of group counseling and group therapy lies the majority of professional practice. There are nearly as many styles of group as there are leaders. The "Meccas" for group began at Bethel, Maine, and spread to the Esalen, California, Big Sur country. Each major type of group has its own Mecca. Many extension centers pop up around the country. The work done has wide appeal and seems to maintain significant controversy around major questions. The evaluation is waiting to get done. Perhaps the careful study needed will be started before the public trust is lost to the revolution in group (Beymer, 1970). The great potential in confrontation groups needs to be capitalized more fully in educational organizations. Business and industry have a history of nearly thirty years with training groups, and the newer forms have been widely exploited (Bradford, Gibb, and Benne, 1964).

The confrontation used in immediate therapy reported by Corsini (1952) is an example of a group method designed to change behavior on a short-term basis. This seems to be similar to the idea reported earlier in this text that postulates an invariant in the relationship based on the culture parameters. Consequently, when a given relationship definition is achieved the behavior changes in response to that life condition. The relationship is seen as the invariant because of the culture norm for the particular relationship. The rebirth phenomenon and spontaneous cure seem likely examples of the results that relationship as an invariant could effect. Again, the systematic study of the invariant principles in culture and behavior has been largely overlooked. Product research misses the definitive study of cause to mobilize their energy in comparing probability expectations and observed reality.

Mowrer (1968) explains the forces behind the healing of self-respect through the group use of a thorough process of self-disclosure. The relationships resulting from self-disclosure bring the culture-invariant principles into the group as healing forces. The product of such confrontation is the restoration of the person to full membership in the community.

Rogers (1968) thinks the important experience for the human person is to have an intense real relationship with another human person. Intimacy is the highest order of relationship. Here we see the use of words that may mean the same as Mowrer's concept of community: a feeling and commitment, a oneness of being and identity (Corsini, 1957, 1965).

Behavior modification and behavior counseling works on specific behaviors with reconditioning procedures and schedules of operant conditioning reinforcement. The central idea seems to be that a group can carry on relationships if no major handicaps exist in any member's behavior repertoire. The reliance is placed, by implication, on the culture's invariant principles. Whether or not this final point is true, the specific value of behavior modification techniques is well established for those behaviors that can be reinforced under controlled conditions.

Cognitive information systems for rational living probably attract more adherents than any other type group procedure. Language does make it possible to exchange information through cognitive-verbal means. There are examples of behavior like that of the alcoholic or smoker who knows at the cognitive level that drinking or smoking should be stopped, but the alcoholic continues to drink and the smoker continues to smoke. This merely reflects a recognition that some behavior is not controlled by cognitive means alone (Blachly, 1969). Any self-defeating behavior that will respond to a rational-cognitive technique should be so managed (Ellis, 1970).

Summary

The revolution in group has been looked at in terms of the multitude of models, types, styles, and purposes we have created to solve problems in communication among persons who work together, live together, or play together, so they may better learn to use groups. The group counseling and group therapy models are used to change behavior. Training groups come in for more widely diversified uses than any other type of group model. Business, industry, and community groups use training-group models. Educational uses of training groups have come more recently to be employed with entire school systems (Harrison, 1970).

Interventions used in group have been described and discussed in relation to the several group models. Confrontation of self by others is one form of intervention mentioned in most of the literature on group. I think that confrontation of *self* by *oneself* is the most significant and powerful potential in group experience. The intervention most likely to set up the possibility of self-confrontation is self-disclosure. Self-disclosure to others is something we cannot *not* do. But self-disclosure to *oneself* is an elusive isolate in behavior. The group is necessary if the person is to have any reality check or validation in his self-disclosure.

The primary techniques for self-disclosure involve replication of reality through the technique of simulation. The psychodrama roles simulate a reality while creating a new reality. I am the one doing the behavior in this artificial drama. My behavior *is real.*

Games have been slow to emerge. However, the recent trend in simulation beings games to a more important function among educational materials in group work. Games help simplify the complex information systems the way simulation in airplane pilot training and submarine handling replicate a real situation. Games are important tools for research because controlled data gathering and replicated experience can be maintained.

Simulation and techniques used to teach and learn specific tasks in group work have developed to high levels of sophistication (Kagan, 1968). Videotape is one feedback system used in simulation training.

Videotape replay is a technique for creating self-disclosure experiences.

The formula for managing a group varies with the theory and applied model selected for use. Different systems were discussed. Behavior modification, rational and cognitive information exchange, the intense-relationship encounter groups, and various training models were presented in terms of interventions and technique. Because of the informal culture mode, the actual behavior for leading and participating in a given group model must be learned in actual encounter within the group. Technical culture mode permits us a language and a cognitive encounter. However, one's biological comfort is only learned in a group.

Suggested Additional Readings

Gendlin, Eugene T., and John Beebc, III, 1968. "An Experiential Approach to Group Therapy," *Journal of Research and Development in Education,* I (2) 19–29 (Winter).
　　This article list some of the ground rules for group safeguards. Also included is a brief description of experiential group phases from that of alienation to interaction. Emphasis is on person-to-person contact, honesty of feelings and action, listening to others, confidentiality and participation of all. This article provides a good explanation of the purpose and process of group therapy for the beginner.
Hewer, Vivian H., 1968. "Group Counseling," *Vocational Guidance Quarterly,* 16 (4) 250–257 (June).
　　Hewer reviews the advantages of group counseling to compensate for ever-expanding case loads and the deficiency of trained personnel, in addition to being more effective than individual counseling. She discusses the sources of various group-counseling models. These included personality theory, trait and factor theory, and self-theory. This article reviews selected research on group through 1967 in the areas of information-seeking behavior (Krumboltz and Thoreson), test interpretation (E. Wayne Wright, Folds, and Gazda), achievement (W. J. Chestnut, Gilbreath), and vocational choice (Caltron, Hoyt, Hewer).
Ingils, C. R., 1968. "Group Dynamics—Boon or Bane," *Personnel and Guidance Journal,* 46 (8) 744–747 (April).
　　Elements of true group characteristics and their effects and implications for education are discussed. Many educators assume that group dynamics is an effective way of developing interaction between people. But Ingils contends that groups as they are now being conducted are ineffectual because of the lack of knowledge on the part of leaders and its effect on group members. Most groups of people brought together to interact don't have the elements essential to "good" groups: (1) shared common attitudes, (2) aspiration to membership (3) ability to select and reject members from the group. Often group members are influenced to conform to a group norm in an effort to be more fully accepted as a member. Ingils sees these as all disadvantages for group, but hopes the movement will improve.
McWhinney, William H., 1968. "Synthesizing a Social Interaction Model," *Sociometry,* 31 (3) 229–244 (September).

Models of social interaction in small informal groups is formulated from Homan's model of social interaction, Festinger's model of response to pressure, and Simon's Berlitz learning model. The new model is expressed in mathematical form. It is related to position and direction of group movement in three dimensions (affect, activity, and difference). This article illustrates the tedious process involved in the investigation of a complex group phenomenon.

Newsweek, May 12, 1969. "The Group: Joy on Thursday." 91 104–106.

Describes some of the more sensational aspects of the group movement along with its rationale according to Maslow, Bindrim, Sampson, Dr. Clifford Sager and others.

Paris, Norman M., 1968. "T-grouping: A Helping Movement." *Phi Delta Kappan,* 49 (8) 458–459 (April).

Paris describes some basic ground rules, procedures, and phases of T-groups and discusses the utilization of natural or already existing groups. The movement is expanding because people are becoming convinced of its benefits. The author believes educators should not maintain static approaches to education, but should investigate new changes. T-group provides positive learning experience.

7

Groups as Information Systems

Contemporary society has been characterized by its information systems. Mass media and advanced mechanical information storage and retrieval systems cause the interval between demand and supply of known facts to approach zero. Exploding technology brings problems and affluence for some people and poverty, joblessness, and alienation for others. Our concern here is simply to recognize the impact of modern technology, especially the influence on information systems.

Information is available in massive volume. It all comes with equal weight, no sorting, no priority loading. This creates a condition that may be unique to our history. The fact that information is not evaluated before it pours out of whichever system produces it, requires us to develop some means to evaluate information. One of the means for evaluating information is the group. In a sense, group becomes an information system in its own function. In an age of information, the task of sorting, grading, and judging information is the individual's personal social problem. Group is an increasingly important source for evaluation of information because the traditional evaluators and authorities we depended upon as sources have become largely impotent.*

Sources of Information

The source of information is the primary criterion for evaluating reliability and validity of the content. The data gathered by the cultural anthropologist is no better than the quality of his informant. The priso-

*"Technology in Guidance," a special issue of the APGA *Personnel and Guidance Journal,* 49(3)171-262 (November 1970), brings to the reader the current level of development for computer-assisted guidance and counseling programs and prospects for information systems. The promise is clearly positive if the human group can respond.

ner's dilemma is a problem of never having any firsthand information about the "outside." The "reliable source" reference is used in news reporting to authenticate the information in the report.

Group is a way of evaluating information any one member may have. Group is a way to *generate* new information, thus becoming a *source.* The membership in the group limits the character of the information to be generated. The individual is always in the position of choosing and evaluating the information he will use. The complex information systems in American culture have brought into being the networks of counseling or helping agencies staffed by professional-level practitioners. School counselors, social welfare workers, psychologists, psychiatrists, employment counselors—even presidents of the United States—employ "counselors" to evaluate information in particularly important and difficult areas—that is, disadvantaged people, poverty, welfare, health, education, and the like. Some of these become part of the formal structure of government, such as urban affairs and transportation. The connections linking information systems and human behavior are much too extensive for coverage here. What I want to do is draw attention to the general problem area defined by the relationship between information and behavior in a given individual. It is known, for example, that the mere fact of having information does not always result in new behavior. The life conditions defining the relationship factors may be such that the person cannot or will not act in response to logical rational facts. Also, we all share the awareness that given an experience or encounter in life, each of us forms his unique perceptions of the reality of the event (Fullmer and Bernard, 1971).

Subjective reality is viewed as unreliable by most any standard of science. It is this subjective reality on which each of us acts in normal life events. Information may affect behavior, but the source of the information is almost always a power influence on behavior. The reasons may be due to some basic principles mentioned by Hall (1959) and Watzlawick et al. (1967). (See also Chapter 9 on social power and the power of a model in changing personal behaviors.)

Some Basic Principles

The behavior of an individual is in response to a specific relationship definition. To understand the meaning of the message it is necessary to disregard the content communicated and look for the relationship pattern, which is not obvious. The principle: The individual's pattern of behavior is revealed in the redundancy of relationship definitions within the context of a given group (Hall, 1959, p. 96).

The content of messages exchanged between persons is found to be zero in relation to defining the nature and quality of their relative (relationship) status and the roles or functions each may engage. In brief, what persons say is zero, the "way" persons say something is everything, so far as our ability to observe existing relationship definitions is concerned (Watzlawick, et al., 1967).

The principles that guide group action and operate as invariants seem to be culture-based. The principles that influence behavior seem to be variant and seem to be more closely related to the *content* of information—that is, the messages. The meanings or relationships process seem to operate more like invariants.

A Frame of Reference for Group As Information System

The receptionist announced, "The group is waiting." Announced or spontaneous, group is usually awaiting us somewhere all of the time. I work with families in groups of two or more. Frequently my work encompasses other clusters of individuals. Groups of adults encountering themselves, children in play, or youth in counseling, constitute some of the familiar forms of human organization engaged in—under the rubric of group. Why "group"? Because there is no tool so pervasive for shaping human behavior. Let us begin to share some of my learning and experience of the past decade. I want to share ideas on a personal subject at a personal level. Aware of the object-subject dichotomy, like the mind that studies itself, the only success may be to lead you into the paradox of accounting only to yourself—minus significant others, for the usual reality check or validation.

To survive, an organism needs organic substances for metabolic vegetation and competent information about the natural and social-psychological environment. In a civilized society, the individual needs are usually learned in a family group. The family provides the two necessities for survival from birth to young adult. Almost no one in civilized cultures has any direct encounter with these two basics during childhood because we do not require our children to gather food. Primitive tribes do require children to gather food, fuel, and other substances. We are admonished to trust our providers. Have faith in your parents, Uncle Sam, Big Brother, the church, police—or any one of the myriad of *providers.* Survival is lived out in the formative years of childhood as a quest for pleasure and learning—all direct play. Direct encounter with vital survival realities has been carefully programmed into safety and, consequently, impotence. Almost no one operates on first-level knowledge. Trust is a first priority, if one is to escape the prisoner's dilemma—no firsthand information.*

Culture is a system for human organization (E. B. Tylor, 1871–1924). Primitive or civilized, the cultures of mankind seem to share one concept of groups—the family. Mead and Heyman (1965) claim over 460 identified cultures in the world use some form of the family group model. They also point up the recorded failures of cultures that discontinued the family. The family group model is one complex unit in a system for human organization, called culture. Culture may be difficult to define to everyone's satisfaction, but I find it useful to think of it as a system of organized meanings and symbols. The components of the system, complete with the blueprint of its operation and interrelationships, are the foundations of every human organization in a given culture. Group is no exception. The operations manual for American culture is published in the family. Each of us has an original edition with one of its infinite variations.

There seems to be no simple way to explain a complex concept like culture. Because group is a concept closely parallel to culture, it is, likewise, complex. Hall (1959, p. 35) claims culture cannot be taught but must be learned in company with someone who is living it. Group is similar to culture. You may learn about group, but living through group, a temporal dimension, you can learn group. The informal and technical culture modes for living are involved with the above behavior. Group, like culture, is a form of communication. Behavior forms in group to communicate the meanings of experience. Each person does his own thing. Group is organized to replicate the basic encounters among persons in a given culture.

Each group is specialized and selective in what is included or excluded. The family, for example, is the most inclusive group because it replicates the socialization necessary in a given culture. The family is also the most exclusive group because to belong to you, you must be *born* into it, or you must have formed it by marriage. Membership is a very crucial phenomenon in all groups.

Family Groups: Foundation for Human Organization

The family group is the basic model for learning the culture. The family has the potential for replicating the culture in microcosm. The human person is the first level in community organization. The task of

---

*There are sixteen levels of community. We are nearer, in terms of communication, the further removed physically or geographically the communities really are. For example, our neighbor dies and we do not know it; the Queen of England has indigestion and we *do* know it.

providing a structure to guarantee his complete freedom of choice may be impossible. However, certain minimums can be maintained. First, the individual must be able to isolate himself. A room of one's own will provide space defined as territory to be invaded only with permission. The power in permission is with the foundation of choice. The biological unit has no sanctity without the power contained in permission to maintain the first level of community, namely the individual. The family sets the pattern in motion by the way it teaches the child to respect the sanctity of the biological unit in its life space or simply, room to live—a womb with a view.

The family group is the basic biosocial community (second level after the single individual—a biological unit). Levels of community form the organization of a culture. The individual has his own level (biological unit), and he ranges among other levels of community. The range represents the social-cultural limits of a given individual. His level of acculturation defines his socialization limits. The individual will encounter only those levels of community he has learned to master. His behavior competence sets limits for his biosocial encounters. All of the knowledge and skill implied as necessary to behave with competence in any level of community is initially dependent upon the quality of learning achieved in the family group. Because the family socialization influence is so powerful, the other agents of socialization in the social system—the school or church—only amplify what is already there. The peer group has power chiefly because it amplifies the family pattern of socialization. At the same time it extends from the home into the wider community. Because the peer groups have mobility between family and community, peer groups are the second most important agents of socialization.

The family is the foundation for social and cultural organization. A person can participate in the levels of community (peer groups, school groups, etc.) only as a result of the behavior competence he achieves initially in the family. The individual's ceiling is critically set in the family—therefore it is basic. The individual's socialization continues to be modified throughout his lifetime. The belief system used in the family sets the limits on information systems managed by a given individual. The system of beliefs the individual uses evaluates the sources of information.

In order to modify the individual's system of beliefs it is usually necessary to achieve the level of authority he experienced in his family group. This requires a group for him to participate in, over time. The length of time may vary with the evaluation the individual places on the group as a source. In turn, the evaluation depends upon the membership in the group, the leader, and the *formula* used to manage the group. The formula will usually contain all of the information and imply or explicitly express the core values, beliefs, and sanctioned behavior.*

Nuclear Family Organization

We live in the nuclear age. The social structure of the family may have arrived before the physical atom-nuclear phenomenon became household jargon. Try the metaphor of one nucleus consisting of a positive and a negative charge (father and mother), encircled by electrons (children) orbiting and accelerating until they spin off to form new nuclei. The model is a complete biosocial unit with the absolute minimum of full-time commitment. Efficiency for mobility is achieved in the nuclear family. Economic unity is gained if increasing income and credit are combined effectively. The ideal in the model for nuclear family is the basic socialization level of community in our culture. The nuclear-family model does permit maximum freedom of movement with minimum energy. One may encounter thousands of other people and remain secure in his obligations to a family. However, the person may be tempted to form taboo alliances with other persons. The nuclear-family model provides a cover for such illicit affairs. The same efficiency as witnessed above is maintained. The sanctions of the biosocial unit with maximum freedom of movement may remain intact.

Critics of the nuclear family point to this vulnerability expressed by the individual who exploits the model for personal reasons. High mobility restricts the numbers of persons able to relocate vocationally, socially, and economically unless the extended family is uncommonly affluent like the Kennedys, Fords, and Rockefellers. The ease of breaking the taboo of exclusive biological sex relationship in nuclear marriage contracts is due in part to the freedom of movement. However, we note the lesson of the communal (tribal) existence of some hippie cults which report the necessity of exclusive sex contracts between adult partners because free love and promiscuity in sex have led to emotional disorganization for some members. Similar reports come from mainland American groups and European communes. Order in social systems seems necessary for individual human personality to function normally. Disorganization of personality and dysfunction in behavior are frequently

---

*To be able not to overstate anything, it is here recognized that exceptions do occur. Once in some infrequent (rare) ratio, a person rises above his family. This can happen when he learns about group and becomes involved. Group is the only arena that can extend the task of family and continue to create learning environments throughout a lifetime.

found to be linked to social chaos. Social chaos seems to follow information that conflicts with prevailing beliefs.

Group Without End

The model of man leads to a model of behavior. Unlike the psychology of man as the intrapsychic isolate, we use a psychology of man as the interactor. Interaction is the baseline characteristic in every group. By studying the interaction pattern we can relate it to the culture harness that sets the limits, guidelines, parameters, patterns, and styles for interaction in a given group in a given place at a given time. These baselines can be traced from the behavior of representative samples from any culture (Hall, 1959). The pattern of behavior in a given culture sets the reinforcement schedules for specific behavior in specific contexts for specific individuals in specific roles. Rediscovering and detailing these schedules of reinforcement are comparable to rediscovering the wheel (the wheel of culture). There is some difference due to changing conditions and environment parameters in the culture—war, urbanization, massive overpopulation, poverty, affluence, educated electorate, and the like.

The technological revolution gets the blame for dislocating large segments of population which in turn changes many practices and values. The index of change is seen in such traditions as the status of women, attitudes toward sexuality, and the revolution in attitudes on human rights (London, 1969). The changes have placed the primary group (the family) outside the experiences necessary to guide behavior of the young. Peer groups are important expanded sources of standards of behavior in such matters as taste and style in life. The declining posture reduces the power and prestige of the primary group (family). This may permit the individual to shift his identity to a new group or community. If this new identity-reinforcing group is outside the nuclear family or extended family, the individual could be in any one of the secondary groups that exist in the social system. If the individual cannot maintain minimum required behavior standards, he may become an isolate. The tragic consequences for nonparticipation are not the central concern in this text. Models of treatment groups help the withdrawn and the overassertive learn competent behavior. Here we are talking about the "natural groups" found at every level of society. Groups form in endless sequence in the social system. These groups are an intricate part of the organized structure of the society. Groups form naturally, spontaneously, and may be established by self-conscious intent.

Group As an Information System

Once formed, a group begins to shape the behavior of each new member. The formula is what does it. The formula, described earlier as the way of talking and defining limits in a group, also sets the stage for manipulating or facilitating behavior. Techniques become part of the formula as the group life extends itself to four or more sessions.

In group, the members give permission to be confronted with the expectations from the group. The expectations are aimed at changing behavior and establishing a standard or norm to be expected in the behavior of each member (*Life*, 1970). Even in drug addiction there are the roles to maintain the network from user to contact to supplier. The group is defined from the "pot party," which is a collection of people, to heroin addicts who need supplies through the network but do not meet or collect together with others in one geographic place.

The example I use to give the student a look at the power of a group has been selected because the history of this group is relatively brief (since World War II). Also, it is significant as a group because it evolved into a church in somewhat less than twenty years. This example is one of the really systematic methods for utilizing the group to organize the life style of its members and to create a community.

The evaluation of the group is omitted. I do not wish to judge whether anyone should or should not join or remain in such a group. The material used here was gathered more than ten years ago, before the group incorporated as a church—the Church of Scientology. The origin of scientology began with Ronald L. Hubbard. Hubbard (1951) published a book on dianetics. As church history the history has been brief, but the organization of a group into a community and sustaining the group or community over time, is not new (Mowrer, 1968).

The theory of group stated in Chapter 3 in the present text claims that all human behavior comes out of the *relationship*. Later in the text the relationship is defined as an invariant, at any given moment in a life event. The *definition of the relationship* is achieved instantaneously by each person. The definition is in terms of *context* as perceived by the person. Therefore the response to the context is the behavior we can observe. The response behavior is an expression by the person to create an experience to accept or redefine the relationship. Reference to the theory and assumptions may assist the reader to link up the subsequent material.

The following material was taken in four interviews over about five weeks during a supervised counseling practicum. The counselor was a young man who had never head of Scientology. The client was a young lady age 18 who had had about ten months' exposure to the Scientology group. The interviews follow with edited copy to assure anonymity of persons and location. There are Scientology groups in most major cities of the United States. (What follows is part of a data-collecting process and should be distinguished from a counseling process.)

First Interview

A (COUNSELOR):   Good afternoon, my name is Mr. Jones.

B (COUNSELEE):   I'm Sumi, Sumi Smith.

A: I wonder if you would tell me about yourself and what brings you here?

B: I used to be unable to talk to other people. Whenever I did, it was a very painful experience for me. Until my sixteenth birthday the whole world was a frightening place, sometimes. Then my father introduced me to Mr. Oliver at the counseling center.

A: How long ago was it?

B: Almost a year ago.

A: So in one year you came to be as assertive and competent as you now appear to be.

B: Oh, yes. The changes have been really great, especially in the last six months.

A: How do you account for such a successful experience?

B: Well, I go to this group. It is called Scientology. You haven't heard of this group?

A: You mean a group where you can go and . . .

B: Yes. Well, . . .

A: No—no I haven't.

B: I'm not sure of all the details, but Scientology was started by Mr. Hubbard.* It's a national group, maybe even international. Anyway, you go and the processes begin.

A: Processes? Please, go on.

B: The first group process is with one other person, called an *auditor.* This person processes you as a *preclear.* The process is a *run* of different *commands.* Doing the commands removes the *engrams.*
     Engrams are things from the past you're hung up on. Past life events accumulate to inhibit present life actions. Processing takes the *charge* off the inhibiting past events. The result frees you so that you're not hung up anymore. This should make you a better human being, generally speaking.

*Ron L. Hubbard was the founder of the Church of Scientology.

A: Can you tell me how you came to be a member of a Scientology group?

B: Yes, it was my father who had known some people in it. Before, about 1950, there was another group called *dianetics.* Scientology came out of it, I think. I'm not too sure, but my father knew someone. Anyhow, last year Mr. Oliver, the top brain, I don't know his title, is head of the Center here. He is a doctor of Scientology. He came over and talked with me. I've been going regularly since that time, mostly to *co-audit* classes. They have had me do some *regular processing* too.

A: What is the difference in regular processing and co-auditing?

B: Co-audit is a do-it-yourself with one other person. They give us a little instruction and then we take turns processing each other. Regular processing is done by a *certified public auditor.* This person has gone to a scientology school and earned a certificate. I think these schools are in Washington, D.C., Phoenix, Arizona, and Los Angeles, California. Anyway, the certified public auditor knows everything there is to know about co-auditing. The auditor is guided by the preclear in choosing the processes to be run. I'm going to learn to be an auditor.

A: Scientology has been responsible for a big change in your attitudes, is that right?

B: Yes.

A: How do you see your contribution to your changing values and behavior?

B: I did it all myself. There is no other way in Scientology. The auditor can guide me and take off the main *charge,* then slowly working until the *terminal* is *clear.* The process makes you more intelligent and changes your personality.

Comment

At this point the person involved in Scientology groups has related how and why the association is a good thing for her, Miss Smith. The credibility, for Miss Smith, is established. The reader may see the terminology as too obvious. For our purposes the nomenclature is important as reference points in the discussion of how a group recruits new members and how the person relates to the group expectations and group norms.

The interview between the counselor Mr. Jones and Miss Smith serves only as a vehicle for gathering descriptive statements about how the Scientology group works. Other groups work in similar ways, except that the nomenclature is less graphic.

Miss Smith was a loner. She was like many shy guys and bashful bunnies. Uncertain she could measure up, the group gave her a *safe* place with a carefully planned development schedule to use to overcome or change behavior.

First, the authority of Mr. Oliver was established. The father certified him to Sumi. Sumi was brought into a dyad first, then put through a series of experiences where only the positive and successful assertive attempts to interact were reinforced. The power of *time* and *supportive* others helped to *shape* her behavior toward confidence and competence.

Second, the group remained more nearly a natural type consisting of brief encounters with one member at a time. The group had multiple levels of status and authority figures consisting of father, the leader, Mr. Oliver, and the co-auditor who is usually a peer, in Sumi's case, a peer of the opposite sex.

Third, the process and procedures set up a controlled expectation schedule that very carefully protected the idea of its being under Sumi's exclusive domain. The process is credible to Sumi because the language (nomenclature) is mastered one step at a time. Sumi reproduced the sequence with the counselor during the four interviews. The process moves from the simple toward the complex. The simple is the co-audit with a young man Sumi's own age. This peer group model coupled with the formula (the way of talking with each other), is expected to give a high frequency of success. Each new idea to explain behavior is linked to an act of behavior. In this systematic way, a system of beliefs evolves for each participant. The group procedure is not unlike other groups whether contrived or natural in origin. The significant result is the idea that, "I did it myself." Motivation depends upon the person linking the do-it-myself idea, and a specific behavior act to confirm it. Sumi had this in the form of *before* and *after* joining the group. Before, she was a loner. After, she could talk with anyone.

The *formula* of a group is the complex of procedures, rules, and beliefs used in the interaction within the group. Scientology is particularly well adapted to show the formula at work. As we continue to relate the account of Sumi's experiences, keep in mind that a group becomes a community (either a newly created community—or joined in with an existing community). It needs a method for each member to use in relating his story and interacting with others in response to it. Usually the interaction is informal, but it can be made technical. The formula in Scientology changes to technical, the usual informal cultural interaction. The process is actually a simulated real-life experience. As we say about role-playing, it is artificial, but the participant's behavior is real in response to the artificial life event. So *behavior is always real* is an assumption made here.

Second Interview

A: Last time you talked about some inhibiting factors in your behavior. I wonder if you could tell me more about them?

B: Mother, that is my real mother, that was inhibiting, and isn't *flat* yet. It is no big thing now. At the beginning, I hated her. She was not even a human being. However, they run the main people in your life before *anything* else. The charge is off and my attitude has changed. Any injury or any person who has done things against you in this life or past lives, can be inhibiting. Any big *engrams* cause problems.

A: Was your mother the heaviest charge?

B: You may find this difficult to believe, but past lives were the times I had a lot to do with her. Her *thetan** and my *thetan*—you maybe can't believe this, but your *thetan* gets new bodies as it goes through time. A *thetan* is a sort of a soul. Well, anyway, our *thetans* were mixed up in past lives and we had to *run* these off, but it isn't flat yet.

Comment

The above material seems to be the way Scientology accounts for the present conditions in life. The effect is to remove the past from any viable influence on the present. The present—here-and-now—is free from the hang-ups. Behavior is free and open, even competent, following practice.

Subsequent interviews brought out a description of how the *formula* for group works in Scientology. The system of beliefs is woven into the interaction in the group and the community of believers. Unexplained concepts become part of the mystical or informal culture.

Third Interview

A: I'm really interested in having you tell me about the things you gained from Scientology group participation.

B: Oh, I, um, I more things, I mean, I know what I can do, more cognition of my abilities and I gained a lot of things that, well, in your past life you picked up a lot of things, you know, and through certain incidents, lots of times, you put an *automatic withhold* on it, or something like that. I've taken some of these withholds off and, I mean, I can do, I think I can probably accomplish just about anything that I try, you know, within reason, of course. I could invent something, I suppose, but, I don't know, nothing like that. I just . . .

*A *theta body* is the soul or life force in a person (Hubbard, 1951).

A: Do you feel that you could have been successful undergoing certain beneficial personality changes, ah, without the aid of the Scientology group?

B: Mm, I don't, that's pretty, that's kind of a mess. I still don't know —yes, but I'm getting towards clear. I'm working on it.

A: You say you're a mess?

B: My *bank* is controlling me. I'm not controlling myself.

A: Ah . . .

B: Your bank, your *reactive bank.*

A: Could you explain that to me?

B: Well, it's part of you that—to you that's your mind that that, ah, I don't know quite how to explain it cause I have never had it explained to me in so many words but . . . There's a part of you that is the part that does the withholding, the automatic withholding, the part that, ah, that makes you dislike dogs or makes you dislike certain, or makes you think you dislike certain things, makes you not able to do things, and when you clean this *bank* up, then you are you. I mean, you know, and I don't know quite how to . . .

Comment

"I mean, you know, . . ." is an example of informal culture mode communication. Meaning and understanding required that "we" share common antecedent experiences. Of course, here the counselor does not share a common antecedent experience with Sumi, so she says accurately, "I don't know quite how to . . ." and trails off open-ended —no closure. The counselor immediately salvages the conversation by focusing on something Sumi can explain. The immediate effect on Sumi is one of confusion—for a brief exchange. "Add to it? Oh, in my situation or in other people's situation?"

The interaction is an example of what happens when the experience goes beyond the technical language and becomes carried into the informal nonexplicit language. Informal culture language is nonverbal.

A: As you keep learning or keep experiencing new things you add to this bank?

B: Add to it? Oh, in my situation or in other people's situation?

A: Well, in any situation as a person just lives he experiences, doesn't he? (B: Oh, yes.) Do these tend sometimes—it's not just a proposition of withdrawal from this bank but also (B: Yes.) sometimes a deposit—

B: Yes, you pick up all kinds of *engrams.* If you scratch your finger and it goes down in your bank.

A: Well, do you ever arrive at a position where your account is balanced, so to speak . . .

B: How do you mean, balanced?

A: So that you have cleared your account.

B: You mean so that . . .

A: Your bank is empty.

B: Oh, when, when you reach clear.

A: Is this the possible objective?

B: Oh, yes, there are clears. There are some, they're becoming more and more. There were a couple of them giving lectures up at near . . . this last weekend; there out at the . . . I haven't actually met any
—

A: You've never talked to one—a clear?

B: Ah, Mr. _____, was in . . . this past winter, but I didn't go to see him.

A: Well, then, a person who is cleared as rapidly as his bank accumulates, ah, it withholds—is always in a clear position.

B: Oh, yuh, well, he knows how to handle the situation, no I mean, you have different, more abilities. You have perfect control of your self, your body, other things, too.

A: And, when you say you're a mess, then, you're referring to the fact that you're conscious, that you're rather large (B: Yuh.). How do you explain the fact that even though this is true you're ah, your bank is large, you still feel that you're beginning to be able to do anything at the present time?

B: Oh, I've been getting rid of a lot of the big things and a lot of the things, you know, things that really are right on top right now and, I mean, well, I've just been working at it and getting better and more towards my goal . . . that's just the way it works. I haven't made a thorough study of it yet, I'm still in the process of reaching original theory. I haven't started—my father made me read it once, but when someone makes you read something, you know, it's no good.

A: Did your father make you join this organization?

B: Oh, no, I didn't join it, it isn't actually . . . I don't have a membership card, or anything like that, I just, um, he introduced me to Mr. _____, head of the center, in _____, and, for awhile, it wasn't. I went, I didn't want to but, I didn't want to quite tell him that so I would do it because that I kind of have this idea that you should obey your parents and not—kind of would, I mean, it's kind of a good idea to. He figured that this would be good for me so I figured, well, it took me a long time, well, February, before I, well, we quit in the beginning of December and Mr. _____ went back to Washington and he came back in February and then well, I've seen some of the results and it took quite awhile for me to believe something —see it but didn't believe it somehow so—

Comment

Again there is difficulty explaining the recruitment, orientation and joining of a group. *Join* as a concept is rejected. But Sumi goes regularly twice a week for nearly a year. This speaks loudly, yet the belief Sumi is expressing has some idea of autonomy in it. Sumi then goes into the idea of outcomes. The things she experienced did work. Taking her description of her prior condition, we can certainly confirm that whatever happened, she is able to act with competent behavior in the counseling sessions.

A: And, now, these results come from you out of session and so forth. How often do you have these?

B: Well, I have been going to co-audit at least two nights a week for an hour and twenty minutes. You process someone else and then, um, this summer I'm going to be trading off with a boy over there and right now I'm processing him and then as soon as we clear it, the terminal he's on now, well, then he'll process me for awhile. It evens up.

A: Could you give me an example of some of the things you do now, ah, you and this boy who is doing the co-auditing. (B: Oh.) Types of discussion . . .

B: Oh, this is regular auditing now. We're not doing co-audit right now, but he has problems with social girls so, ah, the best way to clear this terminal is to be getting him so that he can help a social girl in any way. Be able to help the social girl not to have to go out in helping, but so he feels that he can go out and help any social girl in any way.

A: What is a social girl?

B: Well, this is something that bothers him. He describes it as a female type—humanoid type—female-humanoid type, usually of the upper class, always of the upper class, usually of the aristocrats, you know, the society type who believes in every little mannerism and everything, and so we're running this out, helping or not helping, and this is the latest process and works the fastest. There were some older ones that I really don't know too much about because when dianetics was started, they had them and it just took hours and hours to clear a *terminal* and now it's a lot faster.

A: A terminal, now, when you speak of the word terminal—

B: Is like, for instance, social girl is the terminal he is working on now. Ah, anything can be a terminal.

A: Well, you know, last time you mentioned the term *crash*—it's something of an important terminal that you'd have to clear off. What is the difference between these two things? I mean, ah, is a terminal an obstacle in someone's path?

B: Well, a terminal is something you can communicate to, for, or about,
toward or about, I mean, a rock can be a terminal or it doesn't have
to be living or, right now, most of the big terminals are living. They
clear off the people terminals usually first. Those are usually the
worst aberrations on people.

Comment

The explanation is given almost as if it were memorized. The example here is to show the way a group formula includes ways of saying
things—even quotes.

A: Do you have any people terminals right now?
B: Yes, I'm working on an aberrated mother.
A: Well, can you explain that to me?
B: An aberrated mother is well, not quite insane, but she's kind of, you
know, a mother doesn't have to be the mother of a child or one who
is carrying a child and she is one who doesn't take any responsibility
quite for anything and she really wound up on some terminal—an
aberrated person is wound up on something, usually one specific
thing.
A: Do you think your mother is wound up on something specific?
B: Oh, my own mother is aberrated on a lot of things. Everybody is
aberrated to a certain degree, but some people are really aberrated,
but I'm just doing generally an aberrated mother, and not a specific
one. I find that general terminals clear faster than specific terminals.

Comment

The formula is a way of forming beliefs in the group. The new
beliefs are then shared in the community of others. The unknown is
explained and the explanation is made to appear credible by the group
norm.

A: And then, if you were trying to clear off your own mother, this
would have been an aberrated one, whereas you are working on an
aberrated . . .
B: Umm-hmm. And this can be one that you have manufactured, or
one that you have known, or one that you know in this life, or just
many possibilities. You have to decide these things.
A: Are most of the people in this group about your age or . . .
B: No, it's just—my little brother was going time after time—well, he
just started in February, and he's still in the position I was in last

December, well, he's kind of got the idea that he's a pretty bad mess and this other boy and myself and the rest of them are much older, there aren't too many right now in co-audit. We got some more last night.

A: Do you ever work with older people?

B: Well, in fact, one man I was working with, it really bothered him because he couldn't do the command because I was the age of his daughter and it kind of bothered him. Things like that we usually make adjustments for, but it doesn't make any difference to the people who process it.

Comment

The low key handling of a transference relationship is a way of gaining time and to permit the formula to work. The use of suggestions and some avoidance techniques make a condition referred to as "... we usually make adjustments for ..."

In the interaction following, you can read the paradox-type statements which Sumi makes when asked directly about specific beliefs. The paradox is followed by confused words reflecting the inability to explain the informal or mystical behavior. The formula is not usually required to carry an explanation for paradox. The charismatic leader gets members of the group to take on faith any mystical paradox.

A: Are there a limited number of *thetans* that can occur in an individual? Can this just be indeterminant, really?

B: A *thetan* is the real you, a *thetan* just wears the body—a *thetan* can wear more than one body. He can handle, control more than one body at a time. Most of them, a long time ago, I can't remember exactly—fifty trillion years back—you know, way back, it wasn't at all unusual for *thetans* to have five, maybe six bodies at a time and then they put this over—this withhold deal on it, on controlling it, because one *thetan* was controlling five bodies and they got out of control and so he figured he had better not control more than one body any more—but they can—there are a lot of things they can do, there are a lot of abilities that they've got, I guess.

A: Well, what is, say, the lifetime of a *thetan*?

B: Lifetime?

A: It's infinity?

B: Yeah, some of them go insane once in awhile—that's what ghosts are.

A: You mean all ghosts?

Comment

The formula carries on into mystical material. The system of beliefs take on dogmatic dimensions to keep the source of certainty credible.

B: A ghost is an insane *thetan*. Actually, I mean, most people don't believe in ghosts, but that's what it is. But, *thetan*, you start out a long, long time ago, I've been back several billion years to a past life in another universe, even, well, I remember it. All these things are in your memory bank and you can bring them to the surface.

A: Can you give me an example of something you've remembered or recalled from a million or more years?

B: Well, this one life back there I was—we were running situations of people where I had control of people and lost control and this is why I aberrate on something anyway, but there was a hill and there were a bunch of older men that were controlling all the other people in two towns so that they would do certain specific things—it was sort of a—oh, I really don't know, I never did decide, I think it was some kind of an experiment that someone on another planet was working at it, and it was sort of a hidden underground thing, anyway, they gave me an *implant* in my mind that I wasn't supposed to do anything, but just keep these people from doing certain things, going certain places, and supposed to put in their mind that they were only supposed to do certain things, of course, at that time phaeton had all these abilities.

A: How do you measure this time element involved? How do you know how far back this went? What gives you this time?

B: Well, we had an E-meter which is quite similar to a lie detector and the preclear holds the cans and the auditor checks it and the auditor asks the preclear questions and it works just like a lie detector.

A: And then by certain impulse, you measure how.

B: Well, no. He asks me, was this in A.D. or B.C. and then somehow by snapping a finger, he asks me, give me a date and the preclear can say, oh, billions of years, and the auditor says, was this billions of years ago, and if he gets a rise then, ah, he gets it down more specific and then down to the exact second and quarter of a second; however, seconds are divided into.

A: Tenths, I think, tenths of hundreds?

B: Yeah, well, you can get them down, way down. And to the exact moment that anything happened.

Comment

Certainty and fantasy come close to being unified. The formula holds a sequence which is punctuated by E-meter readings and leader's statements. Sumi did not really think the counselor would believe as she did.

A: Sumi, can you tell me where this is taking you or leading you? This work with this group? Will you eventually become clear?
B: Oh, yes. I would have liked to do it this summer, there isn't enough time right now.
A: Do you think you can accomplish this by next summer?
B: Oh, yeah.
A: Then what happens after this occurs? Do you then have to continue any of these processes to remain clear?
B: Oh, no.
A: Then once you have reached this goal, next summer (B: Well . . .) or whenever, then you would not avail yourself of this group?
B: Well, usually people who go that far become interested in the work and go into it as a business or just to help people.

Comment

The formula comes full circle. The recruitment process makes it possible to be a contributing member of the group. The member knows he can help others because he has just followed the formula to his own success. Sumi knew she could handle the task of helping another person because she had done it *with* others from the beginning.

A: Is this what you plan on doing?
B: Oh, I thought I might get an auditor's certificate, but that's a ways yet. I might become more interested in it. I might want to go that far back.
A: You say you're more interested in it now?
B: Oh, yes, but I'm not interested enough to get a doctor's degree in it.
A: Then there are other things that you'd like to do outside of . . .
B: You can do a lot of things at the same time.
A: You mentioned that you, ah, have never met a clear. These people, then, who are working with you in _____ . . . are themselves not clear?
B: Not yet. I mean we're all working on it.
A: What's the longest anybody has worked in becoming clear?
B: Oh, I don't know. Ah, Mr. _____ has been in Scientology for awhile,

but I don't know I know ... and I are trading on each other and that way there's the cost (A: Is down) no cost at all. Between the two of us.

A: Have you had anything done in this group that has cost some money?

B: Oh, yuh, co-audit, and he, Mr. _____ wants to audit me one of these days and straighten a couple of things out but that's ...

A: What are some of the things you think you would like to plan outside of your environment?

B: Well, I have always been kind of and I think I've found out, kind of been, kind of, ah, leery, sort of, ah, sort of, I mean, I don't know, it's kind of hard to explain, today we ran into something and then there's, there's other things. I don't know any specifics usually check on the E-meter and those with the most charge you take off first.

A: You say you reran sessions with some member of this group or not.

B: Well, sometimes when you're auditing and I was processing ... and I just ran into an incident about the eighteenth century, nineteenth century, 1800's ...

A: You mean after two years ...

B: Yes, that may be one reason why.

A: And you can recall these things clearly?

B: Oh, yes ... process what part of that picture you can confront or what responsibility can you take to what incident to bring it out and, after you're not sure, it can be checked on the E-meter.

A: Then, um, these things that happen to you—weren't they millions of years ago or in the nineteenth century can directly affect your behaviors now?

B: Oh, yuh, all these things in your bank, they don't go away with your body, they stay with you and—

A: Well, what happens to the, did you say, the bank and everything else (B: Well?) when the body that you now have perishes?

B: Sometimes they just float around other times, other times they go right to another body. If they're forced out sometimes they, um ... in things like other living things like flowers and in trees and once in a while they get stuck in animals and they get forced out of the body by immense (A: A lot.) a lot of pain or ... and ... lots of times if the body is buried in tombs so that the body itself won't decay things keep their tension of these things and better not to leave the bodies, but better to burn them (A: Yes.). I mean things like this and usually they'll be floating around for awhile.

Comment

The group has provided a complete system of beliefs supported by the group and its community. The key is the relationships maintained with Sumi. Sumi follows the formula and the belief system but these elements have become secondary to the relationships Sumi can develop and maintain, in front of the group.

A: When, did you have a session yesterday (B: Yes.) Ah, you mentioned that you were going to discuss . . . did you at all?

B: Uh, no, I haven't talked to Mr. _____ about it yet. He's got preclears, too, and he's busy every day of the week. He never takes any time off. I haven't talked to him about . . . but I'm going, I'm planning on going for about two years.

A: Well, of course, your college which you seem to have a fairly good idea of staying in the state (B: Yuh.) which limits it down quite a bit, too. Ah, also, ah, you know what with all the types of schools you want to go to like state schools where the tuition is lower . . .

B: Well, I wouldn't want to go to a religious school because, and there, well, there's religious schools and state schools and what else is there—private (A: Private.) yuh, and there . . .

A: Why not a religious school?

B: Well, it might sound funny, but I don't believe in any religion because I haven't decided about God yet and that I have to decide and it wouldn't do for me to go to a religious school, where everybody goes to church every Sunday and youth classes every Wednesday or something like that and not participate in them . . .

A: You say you haven't decided about God yet, Sumi. Is this because of the conflicts with some of the principles of religion as opposed to some of the principles of scientology?

B: Well, yuh, I kind of outrule religion as they have it in the Bible. I mean they have this book that Dr. _____ has written up because he didn't like the . . . religion, I'm talking about . . . religion, I hope this doesn't, ah, bother you at all and they have a book and it says that great prophets wrote it (spoof), see, I have to see things and maybe they were there, but God is something else, ah, God was or this, I'm not sure of, this isn't quite. . . . God was the original *thetan, the* original *thetan,* and then at one time *thetans* were one and they did things as a group and then they individualized and this is when they began losing their abilities, declining, actually.

A: According to that, then, these *thetans* will continue to lose their abilities?

B: No, it isn't that. There's lots of things that we haven't figured out yet, I mean . . . and I should ask Mr. _____ about some things, but he's so busy that on things that aren't really that important right now I can wait.

A: Is Mr. _____ the only individual that you can discuss these things with—your father . . .

B: Oh, yes, I could. He knows me. He's been in it, but I've never been religious because from the beginning when we were little he had to change churches about every year. He thought it would be a good idea for us to get a look at all the religions and decide for ourselves instead of forcing one religion on us, and so—

A: In order for you to discuss this type of thing intelligently a person would, ah, let's see now . . . as you and I were discussing these things that are puzzling you, I would have to have, then, in your estimation a much broader concept of Scientology?

B: Yes, and Mr. _____ has the latest bulletin, so far, he gets the latest data from Washington as it comes out and from other major centers. He gets some usually after I do. I get to read the bulletin before he does because he isn't over there as much as I am.

A: Do you, ah, do you regard all of this information given to you by a scientologist as truthful merely because the information is given to you?

B: Oh, no, wait a minute—not . . . processes. They say this process works better and I say "okay" and I use it and it works out okay and Mr. _____ knows what he's doing and they know what they're doing and I go along. Of course, if I find something that I don't agree with, then I discuss it or find out more about it and so either I see their way or I don't.

A: But you say that you're the type of person that has to see things?

B: More or less. (A: I mean . . .) I can believe some of the things . . .

A: Yuh, but I mean you have to be given certain concrete proof. (B: Yes.) Well, if these *thetans* and things are very difficult because they're highly intangible, aren't they? (B: Uh-huh.),—how do you accept them fully?

B: It took me a long time.

A: Yes, even though, but what took you a long time? What took place during this long time that (B: Well.) makes you accept them now?

B: Processing. I mean when I got into the past life then I started believing it more or less because just—I finally decided that so and so and so and so and that and that and that must be true. I just added the things up and you accept things like that and there's some things that you can doubt easily and there's some things, like some people who can doubt God, you know, it's just, well, you learn to accept it like some people accept God.

Comment

The process through which Sumi passed had the apparent result of changing her belief system in some significant ways. The point is made repeatedly in the previous interaction that an authority figure at the Center was able to prescribe the formula and the new belief system seemed to emerge from the continuing experiences in the group and the community. The informal culture mode continued as the interviews move toward recruiting the counselor to come into the group or community. The example stops before the recruiting scenes.

A: Ah, (B: I don't quite doubt it, you know . . .) I'd like to ask you another question regarding . . . Now, people who are not versed in Scientology and who have not been audited or processed and yet seem to be fairly well adjusted and successful people, how do you explain or how have they reached a fairly flat or clear situation outside of this realm, been exposed to this knowledge?

B: Their bank isn't aʂ much in control of them as some people's banks are. (A: You mean . . .) Some people take longer to decline than others, I mean, different people work different ways, however some people go down and they just retain more of their abilities or they just, ah, kind of not gotten away from these factors that push you down.

A: Sumi, if you were to pick out one event of your lives that has been the most dramatic thing, what would you arrive with?

B: I cannot say. I mean, because single, I mean, it's just a combination of things. There's no worst thing, I mean, I can't measure . . .

A: What are some of the things, though, that have happened to you throughout your life that has had a noticeable effect on, ah, you mentioned, for instance, that in talking with . . . (B: No.) he's this other . . .

B: Yes, he's a boy that goes to . . .

A: Well, I'm talking with . . . now about the social you say that it stimulates you. Other—(B: Well.) these whole processes are especially stimulating to the auditors (B: Um, that's right.) and you mentioned that this was to you—you had now been . . .

B: He put on a valence, a valence is an identity that people wear, you know, and it just kind of flashed over him and I couldn't look at him, but I had to and we stimulated this and we worked this out afterwards.

A: Would you care to explain this more fully to me?

B: You mean this incident?

A: Well, just everything in general you've said you say you've put on this valence. What was the valence you say . . .

B: I don't know. It reminds me in about the 1800's, I was going to be married and he didn't come to the wedding, the guy that I was supposed to marry, you know, he looked so much like him or reminded me of him so much, kind of, and he had noticed that something was wrong, I mean, he had more experience in auditing than I had cause he's had it quite a while longer and if he hadn't noticed that something was wrong, I probably wouldn't have ever said anything about it and I would just stayed there because that's something I would kind of like to keep. I haven't decided to take responsibility for it and let it go and probably do something about it after this session is over to be able to run me down. I can look at him and, it—

A: Then, this valence that he assumes is permanent. It's not just transitory . . .

B: Oh, no, it's just one of the things that he gave me after the command it was there and it was gone, I mean, it didn't last very long, these things come and go. You have permanent ones and this is one, I guess, he picked up somewhere else—dropped.

A: But, you date (B: Hm?) you date, do you?

B: Once in a while, well, see, like I said before, I don't know about boys and this might be one thing because after this I've decided that, all of a sudden, that's what they are, I'd better keep away from them, automatic withhold, you see, (A: Uh-hum.) and this I kept with me and so it's better that I run this out and get rid of it, but I have, oh, I go out once in a while.

A: Well, are there other things that have happened that, ah, would affect your relationships with boys that you probably would not like to date?

B: Oh, there probably are, but I haven't run across them yet when I get on to that terminal . . .

A: I have an appointment at four, but I would like to talk with you some more.

B: We still haven't talked about college very much now.

A: When would like to make it?

B: Well, you, you suggest some time you think.

A: How about next Tuesday? That would be the twenty-seventh at two or three.

B: As late as I can then I can just work up to that time and then quit and I can come on over here.

A: Fine. Do you work daily, is that . . .

B: Yuh, we have been, we're going to for the rest of the summer except weekends _____'s got to on weekends.

A: How about three next Tuesday? You bite your fingernails.
B: Oh, I can—I do sometimes lately I have been because, ah, _____ bites his.
B: Yes.
A: Why do you do this?
B: I think I'm trying to, ah, I don't know (A: Well, if I . . .), oh, I can let it go, I let it go when I want to.
A: You mean you don't like to bite your fingernails but you bit them because _____ does?
B: Oh, I feel like it or I don't have anything else to do. I mean let them go if I want to.
A: Would you bite them, let's say, like you normally bite them if I bit my fingernails—(No, no, no.) could you explain the difference between _____ and myself?
B: I think there's something back there about him, see, he may have been this guy that stood me up, you see, (A: Well . . .) and, um, grr —, I won't, he really shouldn't be the one processing me, but he should then I can get it out and if he does I won't tell him and it's kind of . . . I'm going tomorrow. He says he's going to finish this off.
A: So you will come in, then a week from today?
B: Yuh.
A: At three.

Comment

What does all of this mean? The contradictions within our culture seem to intensify the confusion within the individual person, especially the adolescent. The transition from childhood to adult status does not come easily, even when all social systems work in their ideal way. As the adolescent grows or moves against the pressures of his own energy to create a life style of his own, he finds frustration because the avenues leading to adult status are largely abstract. Direct expression of feelings and deeds is suppressed to make room for dependence and compliance. The concrete experience for the adolescent to share directly in the sources of power and unmask the authority or god of control constitutes the heart of the rite of passage. In primitive societies, rite of passage is done. In civilized societies, it is castrated and made impotent and nameless by making authority abstract (the system—the establishment, the man), them and us—separation without identification leads to alienation. When we want to separate the adolescent from his childhood, we actually see him separated from his own identity, his own society. The connections between him and his culture remain abstract and largely undefined. Instead, we need to help the adolescent find definition in an identity connected to each of us in direct and concrete experience. The peer group achieves this condition in some degree. However, the legitimate status of adolescent peer-group encounters is any attempt to confirm a value or validate a reality. The disconfirmation of manhood drives boys from school and parents toward violence and silly jester behavior. Some wonder that boys and girls alike seek to encounter some power with mystical forces like drugs and nicotine.

What experiences can help the youth assume the self-confirming role of adulthood? Sumi found power in her group. The formula of the group interaction gave her a sanctified peer group in which she could assume some of the power that formerly oppressed her. Whether you are Freudian, Biblical, behavioristic, existential, or something else, the pragmatic and/or empirical fact is Sumi became an equal and assumed her adult role. The group provides the vehicle she had not found before. Whether one agrees or disagrees with the basic tenents of Scientology is of no matter here. I am concerned if the reader can be helped to grasp the understanding of conditions in our culture. In the Sumi-Scientology example, I try to share the idea behind my theory of group and extend it to a practical application. The magic of sharing the system of beliefs I operate is no less frustrating than to be a youth and try to become an adult. The group provides an arena where youth can share directly with others. They can teach the smaller children, counsel with other adolescents, and even consult with adults (parents, officials)—all in the activities organized and sanctioned by the group. The community of love and concern which is created by Sumi's group is at least one prototype, one way we can operate. I have used family consultation and self-help groups to achieve similar "communities," to achieve the arena for sharing power, identity, and direct action in a group's social system. The control of behavior in a group is connected to the information system. The group is an information system because it generates beliefs and controls access to information through the formula for interaction. The group is an information system because it processes external information and controls the flow of, and access to, information.

Summary

In this chapter group is analyzed as if it were an information system. The idea is to get the reader to look at the patterns of interaction and see the information flow. From this vantage point the counselor or group leader is able to find the rules used by the group. Because there is usually a hierarchy of rules in each group, it is impossible to generalize from any one level of experience to any other level of experience in this same group. The reason is that the rules change as one moves from one level to the next.

Group as information system has a long history because it is an integral part of the organization model used by the culture. Discovering group is like rediscovering the wheel. Similarly, the reinforcement principles used in the culture may be manipulated in a group or community. Behavior therapy works when applied to group because of these invariants in the culture rules or reinforcement principles.

Information systems are organized groups. The concept of freedom and organization may apply to control of information. The way a group achieves order is linked to the flow of information in the group. "Who talks to whom about what, when" comes to mean that only certain people have information. The ideal may be to have order and freedom. Frequently in group the strategy is to have freedom first and then order. This rarely comes off because freedom needs limits to define it. Otherwise, information flow gets ambiguous. When this happens, the need is to meet and clarify the relationships among members. Who can act? What are the procedures? These and many other questions reduce the efficiency and effectiveness of a group. Freedom without order is anarchy. If we have order and no freedom the issue is quite different. Only information from the head source can flow. Groups may be seen in this way if one is interested in the outcome of group action. However, the usual way of analyzing the members' dynamics might dwell more on roles. Analysis of information flow will give a picture of the group in terms of power, behavior control, and behavior change.

The extensive example taken from actual conseling is used to give a student an orientation about the formula for interacting in a group. Scientology seemed unique for this task because of its special nomenclature. The young lady did change her behavior during her experiences in the group. The relative status of the leader, informal mode, mysticism, and technical language have many implications for the strategies used in a group to control information flow.

8

Research in Group Counseling

Group-counseling research is in its infancy. Only one study was reported by Gazda and Larsen (1968), p. 128 as early as 1938. Through the 1940's and 1950's only a very few studies were reported. The majority of these studies appeared in 1959. Since 1960, there has been a steady rise in the frequency of studies reported. In 1970 the literature is viable and growing. Skinner (1965) wrote as early as 1965 that teachers fail because education has neglected method. In the absence of method, teachers use noncorporal means to gain social control. Social control is equated with learning or may be considered a necessary prerequisite to teaching. Noncorporal methods range from ridicule to ostracism. The central task for group counseling would appear to be the establishment of a *method* for analysis of group *process* and group *product.* Without a viable research program, no magic will save group counseling from the fate of teaching —becoming a case for maintaining the form through faith. The use of group counseling for establishing religious communities has already happened. (See previous chapter—note the Church of Scientology.)

Without method, teaching became equated with covering the material. This is a case for *form* without *substance.* The group movement has shown signs of using the form of process for its own sake. The experience of a group may be sufficiently rewarding to justify the commitment of time, energy, and man-hours. Group counseling is required to accumulate evidence to support the claim that it, indeed, is a productive method. Some research reports clearly follow the method in *form,* but miss the substantive elements in the process. The value of evidence is evaluated by rigorous methology—and productivity. If the group process does not produce results, the critics of group counseling may be correct. Unique concerns bring us to confront the paradox of group process—productivity and rigorous methodology.

There are four essentially different types of group counseling considered in this text. First is *therapeutic counseling.* Group psychotherapy is aimed at changing the behavior of one or more members of a group through a process imposed over time. Second is the *educational growth and development group counseling.* The counseling process and consultation intervention utilize the same forces of modeling used in natural groups like the family. Similarly, the influence of values, new behavior, and information has changed conditions for access for every person in the social system. Third is the *training group.* This type is most widely utilized for commercial purposes. Schools and educational organizations have come to use training group only comparatively recently. Business, industry, and government agencies used the group to increase efficiency and productivity of teams of people since the 1940's. Newer forms of training group include sensitivity, awareness, encounter, marathon, and body-tactile groups. Fourth is the *reconditioning and reinforcement types* built around behavior-therapy techniques. This type has the advantage of being specific within a given context. It has the crippling disadvantage of being too limiting in scope to deal with more than one variable in a milieu of variables and invariants. The complex nature of research problems with group counseling will not go away. The Hawthorne and halo effects are great enough to cause concern for any results reported from research done without ample control groups. The skills necessary to effectively employ the interventions presents the second major difficulty in replication of most group research reported. Individual counseling has been known for the subtle characteristic of the counselor. It is no less so for group counseling.

Finally, for our purposes, it must be kept in the forefront of all group work that the variables we study may not be significant variables. Invariant principles seem to operate in human behavior. The design for controls on the systematic taking of data may be a significant treatment strategy. Only by adequate and appropriate control groups will we begin to get conclusive results. Field trials for all outcomes are advised to carefully validate the research findings.

Research Designs

Gazda and Larsen (1968) reported their study of published research on group counseling in the *Journal of Research and Development in Education.* They gave four general classes of research design models. A fifth category was used to cover survey and descriptive studies. Another special category was used to cover studies of group process. No report on group dynamics was mentioned by Gazda and Larsen.*

The major research design models used were classified as Preexperimental Designs, True-Experimental Designs, Quasi-Experimental Designs, and Correlational and Ex-Post Facto Designs (Campbell and Stanley, 1963). The research models applicable to each of these major designs are included under each major design with the number of studies so classified.

For the purposes of this appraisal, the research design models are defined as follows:

Preexperimental Designs

One-Shot Case Study. This is a study in which a carefully studied single instance is compared with remembered or observed events. The inferences made are based on general expectations of what the behavior might have been had the treatment not occurred. The total absence of a control group and posttest observations are significant characteristics of this type study. (Two such studies were among those abstracted.)

One-Group Pretest-Posttest Design. This is a design in which both a pre and a postobservation measure is used in the absence of a control group. (Seven abstracted studies were classified under this model.)

Static-Group Comparison. This design uses only posttreatment observations and the comparison is made between a group which has experienced the treatment and one which has not. Randomization techniques are not employed in group selection. The purpose of the comparison is to establish the effect of the treatment. (Two studies were classified as Static Group Comparison.)

True-Experimental Designs

Pretest-Posttest Control Group Design. This design describes a model in which equivalent groups, as determined by randomization procedures, are used in the experiment. It incorporates many experimental and statistical variations into its model and offers control for all sources of internal validity, and for some but not for all sources of external variation. (Fifty-nine studies were classified under the Pretest-Posttest Control Group Design and its several variations.)

Solomon Four-Group Design. The high rank of this design in the hierarchy of research designs is attributable to its explicit consideration of factors influencing external validity. Since this design did not occur in the studies reviewed, the reader is referred to Campbell and Stanley (1963) for further description.

Posttest-Only Control Group Design. This is a design which employs group randomization and which controls for testing as the main

*G. M. Gazda and M. J. Larsen, "A Comprehensive Appraisal of Group and Multiple Counseling Research," *Journal of Research and Development in Education,* Vol. 1, No. 2 (1968), pp. 62–64, 57–132.

effect but does not yield a measure of these effects. This design is internally valid, offers some external validity and has numerous variations. It is preferable to the Pretest-Posttest Control Group Design when genuine randomness of assignment is assured. However, more powerful statistical tests are available for the Pretest-Posttest Control Group design. The availability of pretest scores in the Pretest-Posttest Control Group design allows for the examination of interaction effects and for the more thorough generalization of the results. (Three studies were classified as Posttest-Only Group Design.)

Quasi-Experimental Designs

Equivalent Material Design. This is a design in which groups which have received equivalent materials (treatments) purported to have enduring effects are compared with groups which have received different content (treatments). The sampling of materials is deemed essential to validity and any degree of proof of the treatment. (One study fit this classification or research model.)

Nonequivalent Control Group Design. Both experimental and control groups have been administered a pretest and a posttest in this design. The groups of subjects used do not have preexperimental sampling equivalence, but consist of naturally assembled groups which are available, such as classroom. In this design the treatment is randomly assigned and is under the control of the experimenter. Since many internal and external validity threats are controlled for in this design (Campbell and Stanley, 1963), it is meaningful for use when the employment of True Experimental Designs is impossible. Analysis of covariance is considered to be particularly applicable to this design (Five studies were classified as fitting this design.)

Separate Sample Pretest-Posttest (No Control) Design. This design is applicable for use in situations where it is impossible to randomly separate subgroups for different experimental treatments and a type of experimental control is exercised by the random assignment of the time which subjects are to be observed. This design affords representative sampling of populations which have been specified prior to the experiments. (Two studies were classified as fitting this model.)

Other Designs

Descriptive-One Group Pretest-Posttest Study. This is a design or study which uses verbal description, rather than statistical procedures, to describe the differences observed between pretest and posttest scores for a single group of subjects. (Three of the abstracted studies were classified as fitting into this design.)

Descriptive-Simple Survey. This type of design or study describes the subject's responses and reactions after his exposure to the treatment. This type study cannot control for the direction of memory bias and the distortions which may have occurred. (Five studies were classified as fitting this model.)

Process Studies

The Process Study. This is a study which attempts to describe and /or explain what is happening in and during the treatment. This "ongoing behavior" is the purpose of study. (Thirteen studies were classified as process studies.)

Summary—Experimental Designs

The summary of research or experimental designs is encouraging. Approximately 70 percent of the outcome studies were classified as "True Experimental Designs," which, among other things, means that some form of control groups was employed.

Longitudinal Study of Groups

There have been some studies of groups that are not classed as group counseling but have characteristics helpful to the student of group. The anthropologist studies an entire culture. The sociologist studies the groups or groupings within a culture. The psychologist studies individual and group behavior. Because he fails to account for what culture invariants do to his data, his study is frequently disappointing. As an author and long-term group researcher, I have some things to suggest to any student headed for group counseling research.

Task I: The researcher must understand the process the group uses on its own. Every group has a life based upon the cultural parameters and rules unique to it. These forces operate anyway. The processes used by a group will influence any intervention and subsequently any outcomes.

Task II: The researcher should identify the cultural parameters in each group study. Groups matched for subordinate variables do not meet the rigorous test for cultural parameter.

Task III: Base-line data require test of time. Only a longitudinal study can yield the necessary results. The task includes the discovery of what would happen anyway—the self-healing qualities in a group.

Task IV: The researcher must keep the natural groups and the contrived groups separated in practice and in controlled studies. The family is a natural group; the peer group is also a natural group. Neither one is influenced by external interventions nearly as much as by internal "intraventions." Contrived groups used for brief encounters in group counseling practice or research are really not groups (in the natural sense) but represent a kind of *external* intervention.

Self-Fulfilling Prophecy

Group-counseling research is a frequent victim of self-fulfilling prophecy because the researcher gives the expectations for behavior to the group which accommodates the wishes of a significant outsider.

The work done with families brings out the impact one more, or one less, person has in a family group. The leader or counselor in a group counseling study *will* have an impact. The amount and direction of the impact, as well as its nature, are all that remains to be made explicit. In therapy groups it is the behavior outcome that counts. In behavior therapy it is the elimination of maladaptive behavior that counts.

To avoid this criterion of doomsday in group counseling research, the researcher *must* provide for two major variables. First, the process used by the group on its own. This process is based on the cultural parameters. Second, the effect of new knowledge and/or information passed into the group.

The assumption underlying the above points is that one major difference in group is the difference in the information they command and the system for using it. The study of group is seen to require two major parts: (1) the complete description of the process, and (2) the complete evaluation of the product or outcome. Without rigorous controls, group counseling research can become a case of self-fulfilling prophecy.

Process Designs

Process designs for the study of group counseling present a paradox between purpose and outcome. The process may be accurately described and carefully coordinated in the activity of the group or groups. But the gap between process and outcome remains abstract, even mystical. The variables are too many and their relationships to specific behaviors too ambiguous. At best, process studies become a structured faith if one is trying to meet the rigorous tests of data and research design.

Process designs can be useful to describe a group and its style and patterns of living. At the very broad and obvious levels of inference, it is possible to see that participant behavior is changed after exposure to the group. The example of Sumi in Scientology is such a case. Her behavior was changed, but from the description given there is no way to know what forces created the difference. Indeed, there seems to be no way to prove, by evidence, that what happened to Sumi would not have been accomplished anyway. The frustration remains, even though the experience of group counseling continues to yield results. The question to raise is whether any particular process is better. The experience of this author indicates that the answer is not Yes or No, but Whether? Whether there is a process or not seems to make a difference. The particular *kind* of group counseling process seems secondary to whether there is a process. The evidence reported in the literature indicates that the person of the counselor is the major influence (Fiedler, 1950 a and b; Glasser, 1970; Rogers, 1951, 1959). The research results on relationship variables have been largely inconclusive. Process designs used to measure relationship variables cannot match the apparent precision of content or product designs. This leaves the process variables in the "black box" category, something like the human mind whenever it studies itself. We can only observe the inputs-outputs (techniques-products), and largely disregard what goes on inside (process) (Watzlawick et al., 1967).

In recent studies Engebretson and Fullmer (1970) have begun what is designed to go into the invariants of the culture influencing the context that defines the relationship between a dyad in a given group at a given time under specific conditions. The initial results have confirmed the assumptions to an encouraging degree. We think that it is possible to measure specific variables that have the effect of setting the definitions of relationships because the culture definitions are invariant. Engebretson and Fullmer (1970) found that different culture groups of subjects had significant differences in a variable like interaction distance. But within a given culture only relationship differences affected the distances. The useful point is that different cultures have different social distance indexes, but within a culture the distances are invariant for a given relationship at a given time. Therefore, relationship in any given moment may be treated as an invariant. The research design must give a measure of interaction distance and a description of the subjects plus a description of the group and its purpose. From these data it is possible to predict the relationship definition of the moment the measures are taken in a given life event. The big gain is that each study can be replicated by other researchers (Engebretson, 1970).

In the attempt to test the reasons why process or relationship variables behaved the way they seem to, the central assumption we have made is that the culture rules and parameters operate in all human encounters.

The criteria used by a given individual to define the relationship between himself and another person are *invariant*. The criteria may be treated as *determinants* of behavior. One such criterion is social distance—the positioning of the body in juxtaposition with the other person. The relative positions are defined by culture rules. Violations of these rules are no less definitive in meaning for participants' relationships. This seems to hold whether the territory is defined physically or verbally. Verbal symbolic abstraction is equated with physical positioning of one's body.

The "black box" analogy seems to be useful in describing process because most individuals assume (or behave as if they believed) that the culture rules are invariant. Hall (1959) has claimed that most cultures have a similar impact because the rules for behavior have become so familiar that they are largely out of awareness until violated. This is particularly true for the informal culture rules which constitute most of American culture behavior. The analysis problem explained by Hall (1959, p. 107) is that when working with cultural data it is impossible to be precise on more than one level of culture at one time. The natural (or cultural) order observed in behavior might lead one to think that precise analysis of precise data would be routine. The relationship or process level is not just one level but a complex multiple-level series of abstractions. As such, indeterminacy seems a reasonable description of the condition. However, studies of mother love show the significance of close interpersonal distance and tactile communication if a human infant is to grow and develop in a healthy way. We may be precise on the level of social distance but in no way can we claim more than general patterns at the relationships level.

Process Groups and Process Designs

The powerful fascination for the varieties of group sensitivity, encounter, marathon, and body-tactile process groups may be found in what Hall (1959) explained as informal culture learning. The basic vehicle for informal culture learning is the *model.* A model can be used only if physical contiguity can be maintained. The example used to explain this idea is how we Americans learn sex. Many people refuse to believe research reports on sex behavior because the reporter was not "there" when the behavior happened. Now the conditions are such that a new team of researchers have published results of technical studies of male-female sexual intercourse. The findings indicate that large portions of the population of adult males and females do *not* know how to achieve orgasm in the heterosexual act of intercourse (Masters and Johnson, 1970). It might seem that informal learning in a complex culture has failed to provide adequate models or exposure to the models (Gunther, 1968). Groups form around the idea of exposure to tactile body therapy, nude marathon, or other body-awareness experiences. For contrast to process designs the reader is encouraged to read Eysenck (1965 a and b). He gives eight major conclusions about the comparison of process-oriented psychotherapy and no treatment except normal exposure to usual groups. Without question he is convinced that process oriented psychotherapy is of limited value. Eysenck thinks modern learning theory is sufficient to supply the basis of a reconditioning therapy that does show results. The outcome orientation is the predominant concern of the professional practitioner. The research orientation seeks a method to probe the depths of process. Techniques to manipulate behavior are abundant. It is possible to view the culture patterns of rules and parameters as a massive reward-and-punishment contingency schedule. The challenge, in research on process or relationship, lies in the possibility of making explicit significant and specific informal culture behavior isolates, sets, and patterns. In complex groups like the family we might become capable of measuring specific variables to use in predicting the behavior of a particular child in a given life event, such as a school classroom with a particular teacher.

Process designs for research in group counseling do not enjoy the record of success in producing evidence of a clear-cut and definitive nature that many relationships oriented counselors have expected. Partly it is a research design problem. It is also a problem of extremely complex levels, somewhat indeterminant, like culture itself.

Product Design

The ultimate pragmatic test of any empirical variable is to measure the product. The outcome in group counseling is usually a changed condition. The change in behavior following treatment in group counseling is changed from what the beginning behavior was. The measures range from direct observation of others to the responses to items on instruments designed to measure changes in attitudes, values, knowledge facts, and other personality variables.

Product designs are most frequently used in group-counseling research for what are perhaps obvious reasons. The expenditure of time and money in school, clinic, industry, business, and government, should stand some test for evaluation (Dickson and Roethlisberger, 1966). The rationale is simple and direct. The method selected may have those same properties, at least on the surface. Some recently reported findings in a national study of innovations to education sponsored by the Kettering Foundation and evaluated with financial assistance from the U.S. Office of Education may be significant to our discussion of the product design (Bernard and Huckins, 1968).

The extant finding was the idea about process. It did not seem to matter what innovation was used. The significant thing was the process set in motion that affected the relationships within a staff—made them special. The "Hawthorne" effect (caused because of the impact of a changed situation) was found to be similar in studies done on the relative productivity of groups of workers in industry. *The process set in motion is more important than the specific innovation.* Product designs may be subject to forces beyond those controlled for, in the usual group-counseling studies. The safeguards against contamination of data should include enough control groups to cover the Hawthorne effect (Dickson, 1945) of being told, "you are special because you are being studied." Such a simple thing as showing a set of test items to a group will change the behavior in that group. Process variables do operate all of the time, anyway. Controls are necessary if product designs are to be expected to yield definitive results. Group counseling is especially vulnerable because of the intensive emotional character associated with the enterprise. The "Rosenthal" effect (caused by the impact of changed expectations) must be controlled for in all group research.

Control-Group Designs

The use of experimental design to model the studies in group counseling is a hopeful trend. Early reports failed to show the quality of definitive findings hoped for by many of us. It is a recognized problem in most educational research efforts, that not only the designs and models used in the method, but the methodology itself is too primitive to answer the complex questions. Edmund W. Gordon (1970) has pointed up the problem we have in *conceptualization* of the condition called *disadvantaged.* We need *to know* when we are studying the right problem and answering the right question. Of course, no research design can tell us what we should investigate. If we want to evaluate group counseling, the right effort would seem to be to study the products by direct comparisons between groups given the experimental treatment and groups not receiving anything different from the usual fare. This is the essence of control-group designs. How to accomplish uncontaminated results is quite another problem.

Purpose of the research study may range from the testing of a technique for intervention to an infinite variety of comparisons within and between groups on almost any variable conceivable. For practical reasons the economy of time is a delimiting force. Many studies of group counseling are part of the doctoral dissertation program in a given institution. The ongoing longitudinal study of group counseling must be sustained to be of any particular validity. Specific control group studies may be carried on within the framework of a long-term purpose.

The skills to work with group counseling must be learned before systematic studies are feasible. The research skills can be learned concomitantly if an ongoing laboratory on group counseling exists. It took almost ten years to develop the skills essential to the research efforts undertaken in family consultation and family group counseling. Other group-counseling research will be done with school populations, families of court delinquent cases, disadvantaged populations, multiple and cross-cultural populations (in Hawaii), and the drug population. The purpose will range from initial base-line and definitive studies of each group to the rigorous control group experiment with forming new behavior. The promise of process research (relationship manipulation) is the possibility of adding relationship variables to behavior therapy research. We could combine the new research studies with what we know in the behaviorist conditioning studies. The control-group deisgns would test the findings from the relationships studies. It may be anticipated, with some favorable degree of probability, that we could demonstrate the assumption that once new behavior is formed by a person in a relationship it is shaped by subsequent life events in the way demonstrated in operant and instrumental conditioning studies. The group in this sense becomes a shaper of behavior by conscious intent instead of by random chance happenings.

Significantly, our early attempts have been very encouraging. The case of Sammy Suzuki is a recent example. His case and a summary of family, school, and community agencies coordinated treatment plan appears in a later chapter. Briefly, the story is a Japanese Dibs (Axline, 1964).

Selected Examples of Studies Using Control-Group Designs

Bilovsky, McMasters, Shorr, and Singer (1953) reported a control-group study comparing group and individual counseling treatment to find if there was any significant difference in the realism of vocational choice for twelfth-grade boys following counseling. No statistically significant difference was found between those receiving individual counseling and those receiving group counseling. An F ratio was used to analyze the posttests. Groups were matched by age, grade, and, of course, sex. The outcomes were almost identical across groups, measured by counselor judgment, observation, a three-point scale to rate *realism* of vocational choice, and case folders plus a final individual interview to get current objectives for each boy.

The stage of development for measuring subjective variables like vocational choice has not improved much (Dickson and Roethlisberger,

1946). The range and nature of the world of work have continued to change, except for the most structured professions. Even here the diversity of specialization continues to proliferate.

Individual or group counseling should equate on results whenever compared, if the counselors are professionally competent. Of course the issue is mostly academic because individual counseling is appropriate to the treatment methods usually associated with it. Likewise, group counseling is appropriate to the treatment methods usually associated with it. There is some overlap. To be involved with controversy over the question of whether to use individual or group counseling is considered by this author to be a misuse of resources. The purpose of group-individual comparison may have been appropriate when Bilovsky, et al. (1953) carried out their study. In the 1970's we need to be concerned with other issues, such as whether what we are doing in group counseling is effective or not effective (Woodyard, 1970).

Stan Caplan's study (1957) stands as an example of good control-group design in group counseling. He measured outcomes to test the effectiveness of technique (group counseling) on self-concept, school achievement, and personal behavior. Significant results were achieved on congruence and citizenship variables. No significant change in group occurred. Groups were matched by age, intelligence-test scores, school record, and sex. Pretest–posttest and control group design was used with a carefully defined set of statistical tests. Ten weekly group counseling sessions were used. The subjects ranged in age from 12 years to 15 years. A Q-sort instrument was employed to measure change in congruence and citizenship variables.

The Caplan (1957) study met the test of the control-group design, but whether the treatment method or the items on the pretest Q-sort "caused" the changes we cannot tell. The process variables remain the property of assumptions. The achievement as reflected in grades did not change. However, the nature of grades and the multiplicity of variables unaccounted for make a difficult package to interpret. One interesting contrast on the above discussion of teacher grades is reported by Spielberger et al. (1962). Using an Adlerian group-counseling treatment method including both parents and teachers, significant changes in grade-point averages were achieved with fifth-grade underachievers. Note the inclusion of teachers in the group counseling sessions. This may create positive effects beyond those included in the design.

Ohlsen et al. (1962 a and b) conducted process studies which did not yield statistically significant results. Again, the process design is less well adapted to the rigors of statistical tests than control group studies. As a consequence, there has been little reporting of process design studies in the literature (Gazda and Larsen, 1968).

A study using experimental design with control groups was conducted with cooperation of the Rehabilitation Center of Hawaii and the U.S. Department of Labor. (Fullmer, 1969 b). Four groups were used to test the group-interaction counseling method comparing pretest and posttest data on specific variables believed to be related to employment stability. The product measure was a job (employment). The quality of the product measure was taken from how long a job was held. If the person remained employed for six months, the program of treatment was considered to be successful. Except for one group made up of mentally retarded and illiterate subjects, the results were encouraging. The subjects were taken from the handicapped hard-core unemployed.

The findings were significant in two directions. When a process method of unstructured personal interaction or sensitivity treatment was used, only two out of twelve persons gained employment. When a more powerful structured program was used in a second group, half the group dropped out. The half (another six persons) who stayed in the program produced only one employed member. The two groups which produced the most success in stabilizing employed members (20 out of 24), were the groups where the program was carefully combined and balanced with process methods and structured inputs.

The groups were made up of subjects from the same sample. It would be very misleading to claim the subjects could be considered matched in their characteristics due to the uniqueness of physical handicaps ranging from blinded to paraplegia. There were mental-hospital resident cases, mentally retardees, illiterates, and others with multiple medical, psychological, and social personal handicaps. The sample of subjects were not homogeneous except as handicapped unemployed. Each group was given six weeks of intensive group counseling, two hours per session, three days each week. Some subjects were in a condition to really benefit by the program. Others were less able to use the help. No claim can be made that the design yielded conclusive results if you want to separate treatment effects responsible for any specific outcome.

Stoller (1968 c) reports the use of videotape replay as a device to focus the feedback to each participant in group counseling. The purpose has multiple specific interventions. The method has been tested subsequently (Stoller, 1970). Kagan et al. (1965) carried out five years of careful research on videotape feedback in counseling. The evidence clearly supports the idea about behavior change for the counselor and the counselee. The Kagan (1968) work led to the systematic development and use of stimulation, discussed earlier in this text. Simulation technique involved groups as teams who coordinated the efforts to reproduce the conditions being simulated. Stoller has focused on group. However, both Kagan and Stoller have shown something to validate the assumption the present writer makes about group. You focus on each individual subject in the group on recall or feedback. The group is the vehicle and creates the context. The context of behavior is tied into the culture parameters. The group members are the vehicles for carrying the culture parameters. In Hawaii it is easy to find examples to demonstrate and replicate the above condition. The East-West Center at the University of Hawaii enrolls up to half of the approximately 1,400 foreign students. Among the foreign students it is possible to convene a group from any one of several countries and show the contrast in context the different cultural parameters provide. Of course, behavior goes on with apparent ease in each social system. It is a simple and direct matter to place one individual in each of two different culturally constituted group—thus showing biosocially (as with boy-girl distinctions) that there is a difference in context.

The major advantage videotape gives to group counseling is the shift from *random* incidence to *control* of what is focused on. Guided reflection strikes evidence on the *self* that might be ignored or overlooked in the normal stream of interaction events. Impact on others and other impact on the self form useful data in group interaction in a group-counseling session. Control group designs evaluated by product and compared across individual and group in IPR (Interpersonal Process Recall with Videotape) (Kagan, 1968) provides the base-line data to develop programs of interpersonal and interaction instruction for relationship and process variables in medical education. Kagan uses videotape to simulate the problem of diagnosis for internal medicine students in the Medical School at Michigan State University. The claim is made that we now know how to create the simulated training program to produce most kinds of behavior, if the behavior can be operationally described in terms of specific behavioral skills.

The precision of behavioral technology and the science of prediction go ahead of practice. This is understandable due to the nature of the issues which form one of the important professional debates in the field of group counseling. The contrast with practice in school counseling in Hawaii was revealed in a study conducted by the counselor education group at the University of Hawaii. Engebretson et al. (1970) found that almost no group counseling was done by school counselors in Hawaii. The average percentage of time spent counseling was reported as:

Individual one-to-one	21
Group counseling	6
Parent consultation	6

The way counselors say they are spending their time does not support the idea that utilization of newer technology and more assertive methods of group counseling will soon become an active part of the school counseling program in Hawaii. This program highlights a central problem in bridging between research discoveries and applied practices. One area of the newer technologies is applied to in-service education of counselors. Or perhaps if the knowledge we claim really exists, the application of the knowledge should be its own best explanation of what interventions to employ. This paradox is the same as the one cited earlier in chapter 1, where the claim is: that a problem population must heal itself. The cultural wisdom expressed as "Physician, heal thyself" is a similar paradox.

Behavioral-Group Counseling

Model reinforcement in group counseling with elementary school children was reported by Hansen et al. (1969). Behavioral-group counseling has been particularly adaptable to the control-group–product-research design. The specific delimits fit the operational context with more precision than process oriented methods. In the Hansen et al. study, socially successful models (children) representing the desired behaviors were more conducive to changing social behavior in others than were either counselors or other students. The assumption supported by the findings is that behavioral counseling can help solve personal-social problems.

Research in group counseling has had a brief history. Contributing to this fact is the relative recency of group counseling as a distinct method. Allen (1931) has been credited with the earliest use of the term *group counseling* in print in the United States. The thirty to sixty years given by selected authors as the history of a group treatment method clearly indicates the limited potential for a build-up of a research body that would yield definitive results in all areas of practice. Group counseling is but one of many forms of group work. Group psychotherapy (Corsini, 1957) and psychodrama (Moreno, 1966) cover another portion of the professional practice of group. Psychodrama is unchallenged as the originator of many group techniques employed in sensitivity and awareness encounter-type groups. Like most other methods, the practice is confined to the institution in which it developed. This characteristic is still with us. Group counseling stays in schools and certain community agencies. Group psychotherapy stays in the psychological and/ or psychiatric clinic, and psychodrama is frequently kept in its theater of operation. Leon Fine, of the University of Oregon Medical School, Portland, has a program built around psychodrama which he uses in the psychiatric clinic and in the community with encounter groups. His techniques are particularly well suited to control group and/or process designs.

The late Don Jackson led the Palo Alto, California, group at the Mental Research Institute through several years of research on family group (Jackson, 1965). Their work established the idea that a group lives through its shared characteristics and behavior is closely related to its pattern of interaction.

My own work with the family group has confirmed parallel finding with several other investigators. McGregor et al. (1964) reported a study on families that was done to test a new technique for clinic treatment. The major assumption was that each family group has a self-rehabilitative power in its group. If this can be activated, positive behavior consequences can be predicted. They found a measure of success except with the families of schizophrenics. The assumption of self-rehabilitative power seems closely aligned with the process idea discussed earlier—namely, if something can initiate a new process in a group, that group will become more productive.

In the introduction of a translation of A. S. Makarenko's handbook for Russian parents, Bronfenbrenner (1967) wrote that character education was at the center of Makarenko's work. Contrast this with a similar time in American family development—1935–1970, and you will find the focus has been mostly on health—physical and mental. Character education has been left to broader socialization agencies. Makarenko got into his life work following the revolution in Russia. Bands of youth roamed Russia in groups. They lived as displaced persons without any link-up with the community. The bands of youth became a great threat because they looted and killed as scavenger mobs to gain a living. Makarenko was commissioned to round up these youths and put them into concentration camps. He then instituted a system of socialization and acculturation, using group methods. His work produced success and formed the basis of his book published in 1936. Bronfenbrenner said the handbook had gone through some twelve editions. Socialization and acculturation through group processes led to the focus on character education. The serious student is referred to Makarenko if more than this cursory report is of interest.

Criterion Measures in Group Counseling

Research designs take care of the methodology and the internal processes for data. The research design cannot improve on the criterion measure. In group-counseling research, only one criterion measure is of any importance: Did the behavior change? This criterion is so pervasive and frequently so obvious that a temptation emerges to not be too concerned about which variables account for what part of the change. A tender trap forms in group-counseling research because of the massive problems encountered by the investigator.

The major suggestion is to choose a more specific criterion measure that is less general in scope than *gross* behavior change. The behavior and learning-theory studies achieve specificity of criterion measures by defining behavior change around some specific adaptive behavior related to a particular life event like interpersonal assertive behavior, study habits, and desensitization of a habit (Varenhorst, 1969). The gains in control of variables is surrendered to the other horn of the dilemma. Namely, the narrowly delimited scope of the context contained in the experiment. The problem is akin to statistical significance when the investigator must choose between type I and type II error.

Criterion measures dependent on indirect outcomes such as improved grades will become less and less useful. The direct observation of behavior change will become dominant. Process-oriented groups are prone to gross behavior change. The behavior change is observable in marathon, sensitivity, and body-awareness groups. The concern for specific connections between criterion measures, treatment variables, and specific behaviors in specific subjects usually fades away before the impact of the new behavior.

The criterion measures used in group psychotherapy are similar to criterion measures used in family consultation. Behavior change comes from changed relationships. Relationships are assumed to be invariant. The paradox is pseudo because of the way our language (nomenclature) works. It appears in the above statements that behavior change and relationship change happen on the same level of abstraction. Not so, because behavior comes out of relationship. Relationship change and relationship as an invariant is an open conflict. The conflict is only apparent if you equate relationship in every context. Mother-son relationship is such an example. The son may be six months old or twenty-six years old. Still, there is the mother-son relationship, but context and time have redefined it many times. The mother-son relationship is invariant—at one level of abstraction after 25½ years the relationship is still mother-son. The additional relationships definitions are the result of the diversity of redefinitions, thus the multiple levels of abstraction erase the paradox. Behavior change is the criterion of group psychotherapy in family consultation and group counseling. The behavior change is the group behavior that is associated with a broad repertoire of responses to meet a diversity of relationships.

Behavior therapy and behavior counseling use criteria of less breadth and scope when compared with the relationships therapies. A specific behavioral objective could be the elimination of a maladaptive behavior. The objective could be the acquisition of a new behavior

(Hansen et al., 1969). Modeling the new behavior is one example used in behavior therapy and behavior counseling which is closely related to the relationship therapy and counseling criterion. Modeling behavior is a way of learning the informal culture behavior. Because informal behavior mode is learned *only* by being with others who exhibit the behavior (Hall, 1959), the systematic exposure of one subject to one or more other *models* will have a predictable outcome. Modeling behavior is like the method in all groups for behavior modification. Each person learns to talk all by himself, largely through modeling. Once the person begins to talk or make sounds, the child learns to connect behavior to certain sounds. The reinforcement schedules are built into the behavior of the group. In no other example is it more apparent that discovery of group, modeling reinforcement principles, and conditioning are much like having rediscovered the culture wheel. The hub of a group turns on spokes of reinforcement and conditioning connected with behavior at the rim. The design or pattern of the tread leaves a trace behind it in the sands of time. Values and attitudes are contained in the quality of the materials used to build the wheel. The entire enterprise turns on a cultural race bearing the history of a group.

Summary

The aim in this chapter was to bring together the designs and rationale essential for research in group counseling. The problems associated with research on group seem to be legion. Process-research designs have a history of failure to show results that may be easily replicated. Control-group designs have a somewhat better record. There remain problems of Hawthorne and Rosenthal effects, plus many others, including the logistics of preventing contamination of data taken in group experiments.

The behaviorists have the edge on research-design problem solution. However, relationships research designs more nearly approximate group conditions in the culture. Specific criterion measures create a more easily manipulated experimental context. The variable affecting the change may be outside the experiment. The multiple levels of abstraction make complex, even the most simple experiment.

Some value may come from research on the culture "invariants." Group-counseling research may always confront the problem of merely rediscovering the wheel, the culture wheel.

9

Empirical Knowing Through Research in Group Counseling

How do you know? How do I find out? What is it we know? What is it we do not know? The fine line separating fact and fiction is an empirical test. All would be well if the empirical test of a theory or proposition could yield definitive results. The result is frequently complicated by uncertain "facts" and many new fictions. The reason seems simple enough. C. Gilbert Wrenn (1969), in a lecture to University of Hawaii students, explained the fact this way: When the balloon of knowledge expands, the perimeter of ignorance increases as the area of the balloon surface is enlarged. The more we know, the more I know there is more I do not know. The first proposition is the paradox of knowing.

1. Proposition of knowledge and ignorance:

The more new knowledge we discover, the more ignorance is exposed to our awareness. The ratio seems to be in favor of ignorance. The conflict is between the paradox created by knowing with ignorance, and the finite human mind demanding closure. Closure gives an illusion of certainty. Most of us seem to need a source of certainty. The age of science tries to give us a sense of certainty through data. The research design and its rationale frequently have a better "fit" on the investigator's bias than on the reality being tested, observed, measured, and evaluated. Objective data may lead to new subjective realities.

2. Proposition: *Practice precedes theory.* The development of knowledge in group counseling has been based on practice and theory. The research studies have reflected the influence of the major schools of psychology. However, close examination reveals the presence of a technique or method of application existing first. Then an investigator evolves the theory to test the results (products) he observed (Schein, 1965). The pragmatic nature of group counseling may explain the pattern of development so apparently characteristic of theory and practice.

In sequence, research designs seem to have developed later in response to questions concerned with conducting group counseling and group psychotherapy (Truax, 1966).

3.   Proposition: *Culture rules and parameters are invariant within each culture.* Hall (1959) claims the culture is a *silent language.* The culture is a communications system that is connected to the human organizations in the social system. The human group is regulated by the rules of the culture shared and held in common by the members of the group. I frequently get reminded of the reality presented above whenever a group is assembled at the University of Hawaii because foreign students are usually present. A group-counseling session operates at the lowest common denominator of common culture within the group. Foreign students from dramatically different cultures become extremely helpful in our counselor education experiences in group counseling. I have a built-in object lesson on proposition 3, because each foreign student member of a group confronts us anew with the task of finding the least common denominator. Second and third year foreign students are able to detail the rules, parameters, and behaviors in both cultures. The synthesis leads to more understanding on the part of both (all) cultures represented.

4.   Proposition: *Social and economic class or caste differences within the American culture operate as cultural differences in group and individual behavior.*

The culturally different and the disadvantaged populations in America have been the target of poverty programs during the past decade. Sharp differences in values, attitudes, rules, and behavior have received attention from the professional who attempted to change behavior of the poor. Gordon (1970) clearly relates the complex nature of cultural differences. Zigler (1970) has detailed some of the value and attitude differences between the classes. The question of whether separate classes of population, from upper-upper to lower-lower, can be considered as different cultures, remains controversial. The point I want to make is: Behavior is different in the different socioeconomic strata. The reason behavior is different seems to be closely related to the values and attitudes held by the individual member of a group. Group norms are set by the group membership. It seems reasonable to assume that an individual joins a group because of the norm it supports or because he wants to acquire the behavior sanctioned by the group (Sherif and Sherif, 1964).

The schools of the 1960's attempted to treat cultural diversity among students by compensatory programs in and out of schools. No major attempt to change the *substance* of the school or its personnel gained much visibility. The hope in the 1970's is to gain reforms in the school program which will change the substance and the personnel to accommodate the cultural diversity among students, even to treasure it (Fullmer and Bernard, 1971). The concept of a classroom must be expanded to include "community." The use of group counseling, consultation and prototypes yet to be developed will be commonplace according to Fantini (1970). The major issue in Fantini's comment has to do with whether we continue to try to fit the child to the school or focus on expanding the school program to redefine the *form* and *substance* of what the school can accommodate. What we know about human behavior and group procedures should be useful when teachers, parents, students and counselors evolve the action implicit in a self-help model of group counseling (Fullmer, 1971).

5. Proposition: *Self-disclosure and self-discovery are necessary prerequisites to behavior change.* Psychodrama is a method for simulating life in a group. The powerful techniques developed in psychodrama include:

Life rehearsal	Doubling
Dream rehearsal	Role reversal
(Daydreams and nocturnal)	Soliloquy
Warm-up activities	Interpretation (director)
Spontaneous improvisation	Auxillary ego (world)
Therapeutic community	Projection (future)
Mirroring	

Other ways of confronting and creating illusion may be used to get the person to change his perception and behavior (Moreno, 1923, 1946 a and b). Psychodrama and sociodrama introduced by Moreno gave the entire role-playing enterprise the theory (role theory) and a method. Some of the more important techniques for self-disclosure and self-discovery are listed above. Creative adaptations continue to appear in psychodrama and in the newer encounter type groups (see Chapter 10).

Mowrer (1968) describes the healing forces in group therapy and group counseling. He claims that hearing *me* speak the truth about *me* in the presence of others significant to *me* is what heals me. The treatment *I* receive from others does not heal me. Mowrer puts the entire healing power into the forces of an unconditional and "total" *self-disclosure.* The elimination of the *secret* is the goal. Mowrer comes down hard on the artificial group of strangers contrived to give opportunities to practice "honest" self-disclosure and "candid" confrontation of oneself with others. If we combine the Moreno and Mowrer contributions to what we know, there is an answer to the question of whether introspection or empirical testing should dominate the method of science in studying behavior. It is that we should strive to get the benefits of the best of both worlds—namely, test the hypotheses from introspection by empirical experiments replicated to assure valid results.

My own idea is summarized by saying that introspection is a simple paradox and that self-disclosure is a sacred paradox. Disclosure of me to myself is extremely difficult without the validating feedback from significant others. The simpler paradox of introspection gets to be a more convenient and much safer refuge. Radical honesty is what is necessary to achieve self-disclosure. Children frequently charm each other and adults with their capability for radical honesty. We know that it is not the expert leader of a group that achieves the healing condition in a group. Any group—family, work, play, contrived—that achieves a climate of radical honesty will be helpful to its members. Self-help groups, family groups, and groups in the community have the greatest potential power to modify life conditions so the individual can achieve the necessary prerequisites for behavior change. In leader dominated groups, the leader must achieve full membership status—and paradoxically lose his leadership (life) or leader status and become a member in the group—before unconditional self-disclosure is possible for *every* member. Eastern religions attempt to achieve self-disclosure (wisdom) through meditation (introspection). Western religions attempt to achieve *community in group* (the kingdom), through group interaction and self-disclosure (Mowrer, 1968). (See also Scientology in Chapter 7.)

6.   Proposition: *In attaining knowledge—whether derived from the humanities, the creative arts, or science, we employ a logic for discovering the "unknown," and we create a* logic *for the newly "known"* (Popper, 1958).

Every intervention employed to modify the behavior of myself or another human being, posits some specific model of man. Contract psychology as explained by Pratt and Tooley (1964) is explained as a modern model of man. They look at the sample of available models to choose from and select *contractual transactions.* Synanon House and its various replications (Bierer, 1962) employ a contractual method of reciprocal role contracts. The central assumption is the obvious claim that each of us can be operationally defined through his contractual transactions. Other models of man include: trial-and-error empiricism, the distortions of reductionism, models derived from modern learning theories, information theories including communications, cybernation, and general-system theory; dynamic systems such as homeostatic, heterostatic, or behaviorism like that of B. F. Skinner; psychoanalytic theories; existential theories, individual theories, and more. All of these models including the *social contract* conceptualization, impose a logic on both the discovery and the discovered. My point is to alert the student to seek clarification of his own "logic" as a scientist and as a practitioner.

7.   Proposition: *A personal subjective value choice can set in motion scientific inquiry, the results of which deny the existence of a thing called subjective choice.* This apparent paradox in scientific inquiry rests close to the heart of Rogers' (1961) question about science and specifically, B. F. Skinner's (1948) *Walden Two* fiction. The "logic" may fit either way. However, we are reminded that levels of abstraction shift over time and good may become bad, and vice versa. The example of foreign aid to India in the early 1950's seemed good. The fact that millions more people will starve in the 1970's because of increased population directly related to available food in the 1950's (Drucker, 1968) places the subjective morality question in a similar paradox with the one on science and Mr. Skinner. My point is for any student who searches for certainty. The source may be sound when you begin. Beyond a beginning, the surveilance must be carefully exercised to assure your "logic" will hold in any one time and place. To achieve the perspective I have, it is necessary to get outside of a particular scientific endeavor. Like a paradox, the value and purpose in a subjective choice lie outside of the contradictions at another level of abstraction.

8.   Proposition: *Sensory deprivation will create abnormal behavior responses in most normal human subjects.* Beston, Heron, and Scott (1954) reported the discovery that sensory deprivation can produce psychotic type hallucinations and even bizarre ideation. The experience seemed too dangerous to pursue to any final disposition. The findings do show how normal and healthy human subjects react to being isolated from the usual sounds, temperatures, and rhythms associated with daily living. Sleep deprivation is another powerful form of behavior control.

Prediction and control of human behavior are the apparent goals of behavioral scientists. However, the problems created for us may be that no one seriously studies the ultimate implication of a *controlled* culture (Rogers, 1961). The idea that contemporary culture is controlling each of us seems endurable because we believe no one is in *direct* control of any *one* else. It is a "popular" myth with most persons I have known. The age-old question of *means–ends* comes into the center of concern. If we can agree on the end product, can we then justify the means? The other horn of the value dilemma is: If we have the means, can we justify the end? Physics gives us the means to release the power of the atom. Biochemistry gives us the means to achieve zero population growth. The obvious problems involve a question of behavior control, yours and mine.

I want the reader to realize that science can give us the means to achieve almost any *end.* The decision to choose an *end* is a subjective value judgment, outside the endeavor of science. So I am as concerned with how knowledge gets put to use as I am with the production of knowledge. The best hope I see available to us is the human group.

9. Proposition: *Attitudes in man can be influenced through manipulation of concurrent symbols when the fact is kept out of his awareness or at a subliminal level.*

Hall (1959) has shown the three major categories of culture to be formal, informal and technical. Formal culture and technical culture are verbalized and are learned mainly in conscious awareness in verbal symbols. Informal culture is not verbalized and except when violated by someone is largely out of conscious awareness. Smith, Spence, and Klein (1959) demonstrated the possibility that we can be influenced by verbal stimuli without being consciously aware of the happening. Their experiment was designed to see if words flashed on a screen for extremely short intervals so that they were "unseen" at conscious levels could effect changes in the way a neutral portrait's expression is perceived. The subjects viewed the expressionless portrait as changing toward anger or happiness, depending on which word (anger–happy) was flashed on the screen. Rogers (1961) selected the above study to show how the behavioral sciences could control individual behavior without the subject being aware of it. He listed five additional ways behavior could be controlled without the conscious permission of the subject.

The ethical issues connected with subliminal stimulation continue to be controversial. Again I refer the reader to the question of valuing. The naive hope that no one will use the knowledge we have to control you and me is not enough to prevent it. Some group counselors make no excuses for using manipulative interventions (Fullmer and Bernard, 1964). Many of the contemporary group methods make a great fetish of the act of free choice (permission), even while being totally controlled within the life of the group. (See Chapter 7.)

Safeguards against the invasion of privacy exist in the statutes of the professions and most institutions. However, the reader is reminded that political groups in some countries have violated the personal-social ethic in the name of the State during the past forty years. There are indications that large proportions of the world's society live under some form of privacy invasion.

10. Proposition: *Behavior and attitudes in a subject (person) can be influenced to change in a specific direction by having a model who demonstrates the behavior expressing the particular values involved.*

There is little doubt that at the broad culture level, every child learns his language, behavior, and values from those persons close to him during his initial years following birth. But when we begin to say that a particular behavior, attitude, or value can be "set in" by a technique, you may begin to question it. Imprinting, imitation, and modeling have been clearly established phenomena, each representing its own level of complex learning. Imprinting is the most primitive autonomous response. Classical conditioning is the simple learning from the manipulation of stimuli and responses. Instrumental learning based on reinforcement principles, and its major branch, operant conditioning, fit into the priority sequence of flexibility and complexity leading to the maximum of flexibility in behavior—imitation and modeling (Walker, 1967). Modeling is a basic phenomenon. The characteristics of the model and the relationships between the subject (person) and the model have a controlling effect on the outcomes. Just being in the presence of a model will not alter behavior or attitudes. (See propositions 17 and 18.)

In group counseling, family consultation, and individual counseling and psychotherapy the relationship between the counselor and the counselee long has been considered the key to treatment and behavior change (Wolff, 1952; Mowrer, 1953; Mowrer, 1968). My own idea about the culture invariants and the relationship may lead to more research findings concerning the forces that make the change in behavior. Even though we have learned to facilitate and/or manipulate the milieu in which relationships happen, we move to mysticism in trying to account for a reason the behavior changed—or did not change—in a particular subject.

11.   Proposition: *Behavior can be changed through the biochemical manipulation of subjects.*

Drugs and other chemicals are used to tranquilize or stimulate behavior in humans. We will not attempt a comprehensive coverage of the medical use of drugs to quiet the mentally ill or energize the depressed. Neither will we cover the illicit use of drugs by youth and adults. Drug addiction, glue sniffing, and paint sniffing are examples of existing practices that can and do change behavior (Wikler, 1961).

12.   Proposition: *Seduction, in drug dependency, sex, alcoholism, and smoking, is characterized by short-term reward followed by long-term penalty.*

Paul Blachly (1969), a psychiatrist at the University of Oregon Medical School has traced the patterns of reinforcement on short-term rewards and long-term punishment for a number of addictive behaviors. Blachly has drawn the "addictive cycle" to explain the complex concepts about drug dependency (Blachly, 1970).

What we know about drugs and how to cope with drug dependency is extremely limited. We do know about the "seductive" pattern of hustle, reward, and punishment. Because *people* seem to be drug substitutes, the group-counseling efforts continue. My students continue group and family counseling at the Waikiki Drug Clinic. They tell me that many public agency professionals avoid more than nominal contact with persons who have drug-dependency histories because of the poor prognosis for successful treatment. Perhaps as a society we are developing a tolerance for drugs?

13.   Proposition: *We know that counseling, whether group or individual, requires the counselor to* interrupt *what is happening: to* intervene and *take some new action; and to* influence *the direction of the changed behavior.*

Fullmer and Bernard (1964) first set forth the three "I's" of counseling in the hope that professional counselors could cease the apologetic climate in the counseling service and the counseling literature. This chapter's set of propositions present further evidence of change in the way we can now report about counseling. The point on intervention is by no means moot. Many of my colleagues would consider the point on intervention to be controversial. The Masters and Johnson (1970) studies of sexual behavior has led to an intervention to save marriages through sex counseling. The success reported indicates the three "I's" have an application potential for saving sexually incompatible marriages.

Behavior group counseling uses a number of specific interventions. Each plan to structure the environment and each frequency in the reinforcement schedule constitute direct intervention. Influence comes in the format of preselected goals in the treatment strategy.

14.   Proposition: *We know that intellectual functions and emotional conditions are of a piece.* To speak of cognitive and affective processes as separate entities limits the potential for generalization of research findings beyond the experiment itself.

Cognitive theory usually omits any concern for the affective conditions which do have an impact on intellectual functioning. Piaget (Hall, E. 1970) has studied the development of cognitive processes with a kind of subjective behaviorism. Theories of intelligence fail to help explain the behavior encountered with a child who doesn't learn school subjects. Learning theory has remained narrow-gauged, focusing on subject matter acquisition.

15.   Proposition: *Learning Processes.*

(a)   Conditioning is the simplest form of learning. Pavlov (1927) is generally recognized as one of the first to report on classical conditioning. The process is the stimulus-response model. Conditioning is process of learning where a given response to stimulus A is transferred to stimulus B. Now stimulus B elicits the response.

Conditioning is more complex learning than is instinct or imprinting. But conditioning is not as complex as instrumental learning which requires the consideration of reinforcement principles.

Learning is defined as the change in behavior observed in the performance which cannot be explained by nonlearning growth. Learning refers to the organism, not to changes in the context or milieu. The changes that take place in the organism (conditioning) (learning) are not explained by learning theory and remain largely mystical. By carefully controlling the stimulus situation, the experimenter can manipulate the subject. The rigorous test requires that the changes in behavior are due to changes in the subject, not changes in the external stimulus (Walker, 1967).

(b)   Reinforcement principles govern what is kept or discarded from all that is learned (experienced). If there is such a thing as a culture wheel, the axle is reinforcement. The human group encompasses the portion of the culture represented in its members. To a large degree, the group remains the control over what gets which kind of reinforcement. Therefore, if we speak of a culture wheel the hub would contain the reinforcement schedule. The metaphor loses something if we try to explain unique and creative individual behavior as the different tread designs or tired infinity. In a more expansive moment I might try for more than a tired wheel-and-axle paradigm. Let it suffice to say that without reinforcement there would be no *selection* in learning.

(c)   Instrumental learning is the *selection* of the response that works (is instrumental) in achieving the goal (the response with the most reinforcement power).

If we combine instrumental learning and logic, we have selective thinking. This notion may describe the scientist more closely than it describes his method.

Conditioning and selection are two concepts essential to understanding where we are in the development of knowledge about man and how he learns. What happens inside man when learning occurs is left largely in a state of mysticism. The technology to observe and count trials gave us the understanding of processes for manipulating the subject (organism). You should keep in mind the fact that learning theory is still quite primitive. For example, there is no explanation for the phenomenon reported by Pavlov (1927) sometimes called "experimental neurosis." We need to know much more about what goes on *inside* the organism before we can claim nonprimitive sophistication.

(d)   Operant conditioning is the manipulation of the subject by the investigator through reinforcement of the subject's response.

Operant learning is the application of reinforcement to a response *selected* by the experimenter from the repertoire of the subject. No concern is given about why the reward is reinforcing, nor what stimulus situation elicited the response. The behavior is selected and given positive reinforcement. The reinforced behavior tends to be continued.

Operant learning or conditioning is an extension of instrumental learning. Skinner (1951) used operant learning to develop his research with birds.

16.   Proposition: *Attitudes and Values.*

(a)   People tend to select and join groups with norms which agree with their own attitudes, values, and opinions. They cut off communication with persons holding divergent and contradictory views (Watson, 1960).

At first blush the proposition seems too obvious. Why try to accentuate the obvious? Because we have found that Americans are particularly unaware of any culture differences among themselves and others. Hall (1959) notes the extent of exaggerated ethnocentricity among Americans. We noted in family counseling that individual members would treat a particular "other" family member as though his different behavior disqualified him as a person. There is usually a reluctance to consider that the other person has a unique "culture," and should be valued in his own context. The extent of prejudice, racism, and national origin identity among Americans may be due to the multiple ethnic, racial, and national origins or backgrounds of all of us, except the Indian. The above is a speculation based on Hawaii experiences where origins are more recent. Ethnocentricity exaggerated brings to us charges of being "ugly" Americans.

Diversity in American schools and society remains more of an "ideal" than a "reality." (Fantini, 1970; Bronfenbrenner, 1970). The role of peer groups and reference groups in socialization was studied by Sherif and Sherif (1964) and the findings supported the proposition stated above. Individuals tend to join the group that expressed the values *held* by the individual. Individuals joined a group because it supported values and expressed attitudes the individual wanted to *acquire.* Both motives were found frequently in sufficient proportions of the sampled groups to be regarded as significant knowledge.

Abercrombie (1960) reported that her studies indicated there was almost zero relationship between behavior of medical students in the clinic and their behavior in solving their personal problems. In her attempts to bridge this gap and get the students to transfer their problem-solving skills from clinic to home and neighborhood, she found the selective perception used by every individual prevented transfer.

(b)   We remember the new information which confirms and validates previously held attitudes. We tend to forget information that is counter to our attitudes and values.

The first time I watched the film "Twelve Angry Men" I found myself shifting from *guilty* to *not guilty* with shocking frequency. When I watched the film as a study of group dynamics the entire focus shifted to the forces controlling the perception of each juror. Many random thoughts seemed more relevent when I reflected on the "drama" of twelve men, angry. Does our system of justice really hang on such tenuous stability? But then, eleven men changed their vote! What stability? It was a case of selective perception. Each juror changed his vote when he realized the reason for his original perception of *guilty.*

The second film to document the above proposition is "The Eye of the Beholder." The purpose of the film is to show how perception of social conditions is affected by the beholder's projection. The viewer is not required to work so hard as in the "Angry Men" film to get the full impact of the film's message.

17.   Proposition: *The power person A has over person B's opinion rests with the perception person B has of the relative social power of person A.*

There is little question in my thinking about the *leader* or *reinforcer* role in the social system of a human group. I feel uncertain whether or not the behavior observed in a given group can be accounted for by one of the learning-theory models. The operant paradigm seems to work whenever the behavior to be shaped is made contingent upon a re- sponse-reinforcement sequence. In group counseling the leader or counselor may dispense rewards. Behavior counseling uses this para- digm. But let us back up one step in the sequence of events which established the group in question. In largely a verbal-conditioning model of group counseling, why should the leader (counselor or ther- apist) be seen as *the* reinforcer? To account for an answer, French (1956) set forth his formal theory of social power. [The similarity of French's social power paradigm and Bandura's (1964) attributes of suc- cessful social learning models, is nearly identical.] (See proposition 18 below.)

The counselor reading my words may ask what happened to those high-sounding phrases in the counseling literature, such as: work only with permission, counsel those who come in voluntarily, get a good interpersonal relationship, and so on. Notice that I use some symbols like Dr. or Professor, and if we were to meet I would try very "naturally" to maintain the culturally sanctioned *image* of those symbols. The editor of this volume said to me, "I will read the manuscript with the mind set that you are the expert." According to French, an expert is someone you perceive as having superior knowledge or information. I see the editor of this volume as an expert. Phil can now mediate rewards and punish- ment through the editorial comments he sends to me. Phil also has legitimate power as I see him, because the publisher gave him the right to prescribe my behavior. I like Phil and I work diligently to behave so Phil will like me. This is attraction power. If I can write well enough to get my point clearly stated, maybe we can all be beautiful people.

In order to summarize French's types of power and the attributes of Bandara et al. following proposition 18, the two sets of information are presented together in the following table.

Alternatives to Group Ways to Rule a Human Organization

Types	Social Power Bases	Successful Social Models' Attributes	Power Bases of Cultural Symbols
Legitimate	My belief that the other person has a right to prescribe my behavior.	High status-prestigeful	My belief that ideally I shall be like the other person.
Expert	My perception that the other person has superior knowledge or information.	Competent	I should learn from him because he does everything well.
Attraction	I like the other person.	Attractive	I like to be with you because it fits the cultural symbols.
Reward	The other person can mediate my rewards.	Rewarding	My rewards come with being in your hands.
Coercive	The other person can mediate my punishment.	Powerful	I am without an alternative. I must follow your lead.

Exhibit 1.   A direct comparison of terms used to describe types of social power and attributes of successful models.

18.   Proposition: *Power in a successful model for personal and social behavior rests with the perception of the model as having the following characteristics: attractive, competent, rewarding, powerful, high status, and prestigeful.*

As mentioned above, the similarity between the types of social power and the attributes of a successful social model, are very interesting. One study reported by Bandura, Ross, and Ross (1963) found that models who dispense rewards were more powerful (in French's terms) than were models who consumed rewards. The issue seems clear enough when the research findings bear out the assumptions so consistently. At the general level of characteristics, the power to influence behavior change becomes a self-fulfilling philosophy rather than a controlled expression in science. From the statements of Walker (1967), the most flexibility in the learning paradigm comes with modeling and imitating—on a scale beginning with instinct, imprinting, and classical conditioning, moving through instrumental conditioning (learning) and especially the operant paradigm, to modeling and imitating. A problem encountered with the learning paradigm is brought up in modeling. The control of specific stimulus— response links become speculative because the cultural context and individual subject's history define the reinforcement contingencies. Studies of communication within information systems show the fact that a subordinate in a hierarchial system will select information to give to his superior. Information selected will be that information which most enhances the subordinate's chances for promotion. If we tie this information system to the social power—social model concepts—many interesting hypotheses can be generated, i.e., does the subordinate "learn" his behavior from his model, the superior? It "fits" the findings reported by Bandura et al. (1963) that the most powerful models were the ones that dispense rewards.

19.   Proposition: *Group Relations* (Havighurst, 1970).

(a)   People learn from each other in a group. Students learn more from each other than they learn from a teacher. Professor James Coleman (May 13, 1970) was reported by the news media making the latter statement (above) before the United States Senate's Labor and Education Committee. Coleman was testifying on behalf of children who lack equal opportunity to learn because they go to schools where everyone is just about alike. The argument is supported by previous propositions: Diversity enhances the probability of exposure to models ranging in characteristics more nearly representative of the culture. Coleman (1966) found in a national survey that children from poverty learned more in school when placed with children from middle-income families. The achievement in school subjects for middle-income students was not affected in any negative way on the variables measured.

People learn from each other in a family group. The fundamental importance of the human group for basic socialization through membership in a family has been repeatedly reconfirmed in my counseling experiences with families. The intervention by a counselor in any group must be aimed at the improvement of those functions performed by the human group resulting in socialization learning. This learning is not necessarily like the narrower scope of learning school subjects. However, counselors, teachers, and parents may wish to keep in mind that instruction in school subjects in classroom groups, carries socialization learning opportunities. The learning climate of a school is controlled through the opportunities for socialization experiences in the human groups within the school (Coleman, 1966).

(b)   New material is learned more easily from one of my own group than from a stranger. All of the propositions on group relations share mutually inclusive statements of explanation and expansion. There are several axiomatic statements in the list. Proposition (19b) is one that seems axiomatic.

Some additional reasons in support of this proposition include the tendency of a group to develop a private or restricted code of its own. The communications mechanics become more efficient because of the shorthand nature of a restricted code. Another factor enhancing a group's interpersonal learning climate is the existence of established interpersonal relationships. In a new group, these relationships are defined for the first time before anything can happen. A stranger in an established group encounters similar *new* relationship definitions before information can pass within the system.

(c)   Peer consensus is a powerful force in the social dynamics of a group.

Conformity behavior may be defined as the product of forces in the group which have altered the behavior in the direction of a group norm. Evidence is under continuing study to determine if the peer-group, work-group, and family-group structure and pattern in Japan can account for their relatively low death rate from heart attacks (arteriosclerotic and degenerative heart disease). The rate among males in the United States was approximately five times higher in 1960–61, according to Dr. Scott Matsumoto, Associate Professor of Public Health, University of Hawaii. The two variables in the health picture are fats in the diet and emotional stress. Peer-group consensus seems central in the Japanese strategy for stress reduction. Among his peers the Japanese man may express any emotion openly without subsequent guilt. Let us take as an example tenderness and the expression of it between two males. The Japanese males may express openly, to each other, what each feels. Two American males are more likely to be embarrassed and ill at ease or even awkward, perhaps unable to express tenderness at all.

Peer groups have great potential for Americans if we can learn to use them to our advantage.

(d)   A group member is most uncomfortable when he stands alone in disagreement with his peers.

Proposition 20 deals with one outcome based on the fact that when a person is in conflict with the "will of the group," he frequently is outside his usual sources of certainty—namely, confirmation from others in his group. The condition in question here is by no means new or unusual knowledge to the student of human behavior. However, when a person has not had a close personal relationship with another human being, he is able to stand alone. The condition is usually called *autistic.* Ginott (1961) points out that through a confidential relationship, over time, it is possible to establish the need in the child to respond to group expectations and norms.

The idea I want the reader to know about is how widely used (in

American society) is the group pressure to conform. Is it any wonder that individual courage to stand alone is highly prized in the same society? Remember, however that anyone untouched by group social pressure may be behaving in a pathological manner.

(e) Leadership is not a general ability.

The power of a leader is like the power source of a successful social model. Because the characteristics change from one life situation to another, the likelihood of some *one* person having leadership characteristics for all situations is highly improbable. Frequently in family consultation we encounter a man who leads a corporation but cannot lead his son or family. I once had a superior in higher education who could not lead people. Like the Peter principle, the promotion of a person successful at one level in a human organization does not assure success at the next higher level. Fortunately for higher education, there is fairly rapid turnover among administrators—even college presidents.

Leadership can be trained and developed. The task in a group is to get leadership talent organized around tasks appropriate to particular talent. Every human organization utilizes some leadership functions. Styles of leadership vary within organizations and also, different organizations require different styles. The leader of a platoon and the leader of a national moratorium against War, may share many similar leadership characteristics.

20. Proposition: *The tendency in man to conform to the expectations of his group's norm is powerful enough to get him to reverse the evidence of his own experience.*

With the exception of autism discussed above in Proposition 19d, any of us would probably give way to the belief of the peer group if pressure to conform were exercised. Crutchfield (1955) reported research which left little doubt that if I am led to believe everyone in my "group" holds a certain belief—I will agree (conform) even when the evidence of my own senses contradicts the group held belief. The belief system of a society of humans is maintained largely because of this tendency to support the myths held in common by the group or community. The phenomenon also seems to account for the fact that every culture, society, group and individual behaves in such a way as to produce self-fulfilling prophecies. The products of such prophecy then becomes the evidence to support the belief system. A cycle or pattern of action will lead persons to support all manner of groups.

Professional ethics require us to keep within the range of experiences we can reasonably agree are therapeutic, enlightening, or entertaining. Development of the individual is our goal. Groups can be used for exploitation.

21. Proposition: *Social Class-Caste Stratification:*

(a) Persons choose their best friends from homes of the same socioeconomic class or caste as they perceive to be their own (Havighurst and Neugarten, 1962).

Early studies by Havighurst indicated clearly the class structure in American society. More recent evidence of racism and ethnic class-caste systems cut across the neighborhoods of American cities. Neighborhood schools have retained the patterns of segregation by socioeconomic status, education, affluence, and poverty. Race takes different patterns but the separation is no less evident. The South, the Northern and Eastern cities, and Hawaii all have the American problem of separation, alienation, instead of the rich potential of diversity. Mixing races may be easier than getting poverty and middle-income people together.

James Coleman testified before the United States Senate on May 13, 1970 that diversity in enrollment was the course for American public schools. Bus the children across the neighborhood boundries. The children will develop peer groups with membership from different races and different socioeconomic levels. Whether or not the school can achieve this integration remains to be seen. Hopefully, it can. Desegregation may be accomplished without the long-term benefits of social integration, unless counselors and teachers can help children understand the American dilemma on social integration. Because of what we know about how people pick their friends, it should be anticipated that teachers, counselors, and parents are likely to pick their friends from socioeconomic classes comparable to their perception of their own.

Group counseling may have much to offer to this task of resocialization of the adults before leading groups to socialize the young. Adults model their behavior. Whenever they model their behavior they also model their values and attitudes. The process of integration will begin to happen as soon as children play together and achieve peer status in the same school classroom.

(b)   A person will internalize the evaluation of himself which he perceives from peers, superiors, and subordinates.

In school, the superior-subordinate status goes with older and younger children. In the human organizations of adults we can begin with the family. All human organizations have a corporate structure (hierarchy). The child begins to internalize an evaluation of his "worth" at home. Then he goes to school. The teacher carries on with smiles, frowns, and grades. The long-term effect is permanent for all practical purposes.

Puffer (1913, pp. 22-23) published in his book *Vocational Guidance*, a story of the animal's school. His story has long epitomized the folly of the human's school. All of the animals had differences. Some could fly, others could swim, and still others could walk and run. The duck became a dropout because he could not pass walking. The eagle failed climbing, though when permitted to use his own way of getting to the top of the tree, he broke all records. Even though the eagle could get higher than anyone in the class, the performance was counted a demerit because he had *not* done it according to the curriculum's prescribed course of study. The school valedictorian was an abnormal eel who proved he could walk, run, climb, swim and even fly a little. The eel was valedictorian because he passed all of the courses with an average of less than human schools use. The idiotic nature of what we do in the name of education should not be done to animals.

Group counseling can be used to create an example of positive and helpful evaluation for each child or adult. The counselor will have a long and arduous task to achieve a turnabout on long-embedded practices and beliefs about grades and put-downs. I saw recently (1970) a case where the school had achieved the outstanding "success" with a teen-age boy. It reminded me how far we are in our efforts to make eagles climb trees and ducks walk, much less run. Symbolic stories almost sixty years old serve to remind me of the continuing error in trying to make everyone the same. Please, could we make the school fit the child? Let eagles fly and ducks swim—please?

22.   Proposition: *Group Communication:*

(a)   Group communication is both verbal and nonverbal behavior.

Watzlawick, Beavin, and Jackson (1967) speak of the impossibility of not communicating. In a similar vein, Thayer (1967) has talked of the continuum of communications. Mahl, Danet, and Norton (1959) studied the nonverbal behavior of many subjects. The major assumption was that *expressive aspects* of one's behavior "fits" the personality characteristics. Freud thought anyone with eyes and ears can see and hear the secrets of mortals. Hall (1959) calls behavior a language. The evidence is so plentiful that no one need be unenlightened about what each of us participates in every day. The major influence on behavior from outside the person is the context. The context in which behavior happens inevitably effects the character and meaning of the behavior. Gestalt psychologists call the phenomenon the "membership character" of a given behavior under any one of several sets of conditions (contexts).

The concluding summary for the proposition is that group communication is verbal, nonverbal and *contextual* in make-up.

(b)   In a group, there is *always* communication.

When I step into a new group for the first time, it is rare not to interrupt the action completely. The silence is a form of instant communication alerting each member to a new condition.

From the phenomena of self-fulfilling prophecies to total ambiguity, a group always has some behavior response to the life condition, even if *no one knows* the meaning of the message. Watzlawick et al. (1967) claim that physiological symptoms frequently are found to have a meaning—message communication from, "I don't feel good" to hysterical blindness.

I want the reader to know that one may not always know what was communicated in a group, but you can rest assured that some message, some communication is present all of the time. The task of a counselor is to find out what was communicated. The behavior may be the only indication one can get. I find I can *read* behavior as a language, only when I'm fully familiar with the subculture and on an intimate basis (relationship) with the group.

(c) The verbal–nonverbal messages control the meaning of communication.

(d) Verbal messages are mainly *content* defining.

(e) Nonverbal messages are mainly *relationship* defining.

Here is a package of what is known. Whether or not you can learn to read the behavior, let me state some of the obvious and usual signals associated with most communication.

Verbal content can be analyzed by semantic and/or linguistic methods. I think most persons have small difficulty with messages so far as verbal content goes.

Nonverbal messages have no content, no concrete symbol I can take to an external standard like a dictionary. I must interpret the tone of voice, gross body posture, and double-bind paradox created by two messages simultaneously, each in mutual contradiction to the other — one of which is verbal and the other nonverbal!

(f) Group communication is a major source for individual identity confirmation.

Who am I? What am I? How am I? How are you? Who are you? What are you? How are we doing? What are we doing? Why are we doing it? Why don't you ask your own questions?

In the popular book, *The Naked Ape* (Morris, 1967), a clever question is implied by stating that mating or pair-formation leads to imprinting for sights, sounds, smells, and touch (tactile)—which leads to symbolic meanings in the sex role. Also explained is the same concept using popular people language. The "one and only!" romantic love is like the hole in the doughnut—"without you, I would be nothing." No matter how you think or which game you choose, the question of *identity* is still with us. We know that a group is going to put social pressure on each member to conform to the group norm. The deviant who chooses not to comply is left out. The belief system in the group may confirm his individual identity in any case. *The group will confirm its own belief system.* Each individual may use the group as a resource for confirming his personal identity. Communication is implied because of why "I choose" a group—to do what I want to do, or to acquire behavior I want to acquire because the group has it.

(g)   Communication in a group tends to be outside the conscious awareness of most persons in a given group.

Hall (1959) divides culture into formal, technical, and informal categories for rules, parameters and personal or group behavior. The formal culture rules are taught by the mother to the child by admonishment and precept. No alternative to behavior is given. Mother says to her child, "Do it this way." Child responds, "Why, Mommy?" Mother responds to the child, "Because this is the way we do it." Again and again the mother will permit no exceptions. The child goes to school. The teacher does exactly the same formal teaching. The school and home match, culturewise.

Technical culture is seen in the definitive description of a behavior or event based on precise rules, measures or parameters. The operations manual for a jet aircraft will give specific directions for the pilot to follow.

The technical and formal culture behavior is largely a conscious and cognitive function. The third category is informal culture. The informal culture rules are largely out of conscious awareness except when they are violated in our presence. We are instantly conscious of violations, yet we cannot give explicit directions to another person. The conversation goes like this, "You should do it this way—watch me." The way we learn informal culture rules and behavior is to be around a model who does the behavior in context. We have learned to simulate most interpersonal encounters by using group counseling as the vehicle. However, the task is not easy because you and I do not give up our cultural conditioning painlessly.

A group of scientists can be observed using a newer formal system based on empirical fact instead of the older formal system based on folk beliefs, like the Kahuna of Hawaii. The formal, informal and technical belief systems are "technically" serving a similar purpose, much of which is outside the conscious awareness of the persons involved.

Sullivan (1947) explained that the unconscious aspects of one's behavior or personality are not hidden to anyone except the individual himself. The out-of-awareness idea is significant because the explanation Sullivan gave opened up the interpersonal process in group to a phenomenon for study. I can see you seeing me. You can see me seeing you. I cannot see me, save through feedback from you. The formula works so well it is disarming initially. There are numerous methods for employing the formula for self-disclosure. The *Gestalt Institute of Washington,* Charles R. Walsmith, Director, provides one example. The training in self-disclosure and self-awareness is economical and for most persons rewarding in breaking through the mysticism of out-of-awareness communication (Elliott, 1970).

Summary

The following summary is the list of propositions discussed in this chapter as what we *know* that we can empirically demonstrate through blind trial and error or replicated designs to simulate reality in a social context. The list is by no means exhaustive. I hope to have a representative sample of what is known that is important to *group* and group counseling.

Propositions Summary

1. Knowledge and ignorance are closely related.
2. Practice precedes theory in professional model building.
3. Culture rules and parameters are invariant within cultures.
4. Social-economic class or caste differences within the American culture operate as cultural differences in group and individual behavior.
5. Self-disclosure and self-discovery are necessary prerequisites to behavior change.
6. In aquiring knowledge, whether derived from the humanities, the creative arts, or science, we employ a *logic* for discovering the "unknown" and we create a *logic* for the newly discovered "known."
7. A personal subjective value choice can set in motion a scientific inquiry, the results of which deny the existence of a thing called subjective choice.
8. Sensory deprivation will create abnormal behavior responses in most normal human subjects.
9. Attitudes in man can be influenced through manipulation of concurrent symbols when the fact is kept out of his awareness or at a subliminal level.
10. Behavior and attitudes in a subject can be influenced to change in a specific direction by having a model demonstrate the behavior expressing the particular values involved.
11. Behavior can be changed through the biochemical manipulation of a subject.
12. Seduction, in drug dependency, sex, alcoholism, and smoking, is characterized by short-term reward followed by long-term penalty.
13. We know that counseling, whether group or individual, re-

quires the counselor to *interrupt* what is happening, to *intervene* and take some new action, and to *influence* the direction of the changed behavior.

14. We know that intellectual functions and emotional conditions are of a piece. To speak of cognitive and affective processes as separate entities limits the potential for generalization of research findings beyond the experiment itself.

15. Learning processes:

(a) Conditioning is the simplest form of learning.

(b) Reinforcement principles govern what is kept or discarded from all that is learned.

(c) Instrumental learning is the selection of the response that works (is instrumental) in achieving the goal (the response with the most reinforcement power).

(d) Operant conditioning is the manipulation of the subject by the investigator through reinforcement of the subject's response.

16. Attitudes and values:

(a) People tend to select and join groups with norms which agree with their own attitudes, values, and opinions. They cut off communication with persons holding divergent and contradictory views.

(b) We remember the new information which confirms and validates previously held attitudes. We tend to forget information that is counter to our attitudes and values.

17. The power person A has over person B's opinion rests with the perception person B has of the relative social power of person A.

18. Power as a successful model for personal and social behavior, rests with the perception of the model as having the following characteristics: attractive, competent, rewarding, powerful, high-status, and prestigeful.

19. Group relations:

(a) People learn from each other in a group. Students learn more from each other than they learn from a teacher.

(b) New material is learned more easily from one of my own group than from a stranger.

(c) Peer consensus is a powerful force in the social dynamics of a group.

(d) A group member is most uncomfortable when he stands alone in disagreement with his peers.

(e) Leadership is not a general ability.

20. The tendency in man to conform to the expectation of his group's norm is powerful enough to get him to reverse the evidence of his own experience.

21. Social class-caste stratification
(a) Persons choose their best friends from homes of the same socio-economic class or caste as they perceive their own to be.
(b) A person will internalize the evaluation of himself which he perceives from peers, superiors, and subordinates.
22. Group communication:
(a) Group communication is both verbal and nonverbal behavior.
(b) In a group, there is *always* communication.
(c) The verbal–nonverbal messages control the meaning of communication.
(d) Verbal messages are mainly content-defining.
(e) Nonverbal messages are mainly relationship-defining.
(f) Group communication is a major source for individual identity confirmation.
(g) Communication in a group tends to be outside the conscious awareness of most persons in a given group.

This chapter tries to summarize the pertinent knowledge relevant to group counseling. No claim is made that all possible knowledge examples are included here.

Suggested Additional Readings

Corrigan, D., 1969. "Educational Personnel Development: What's Ahead," *Journal of Research and Development in Education,* 2 (3) 3–11 (Spring).
  Present preparation plans for education of personnel necessitates long-range assessment of the future world. Corrigan identifies some changes that will take place and their probable influence on training of education personnel. Explosion of knowledge and the growing emphasis of human interaction will greatly affect the form of the future's educational program. Technology will affect the process of education, especially the use of systems analysis and cybernetics. Creativity will be a must in one's work. Education will need to teach people how to be comfortable and deal with complexity and change. Continuing education and more emphasis on the process of learning will be crucial. Man's importance will not rely so much on the kind of work he does but the kind of life he leads. Education will help people to develop and clarify their values and focus on personal feelings.
Kemp, C. G. 1970. *Foundations of Group Counseling.* New York: McGraw-Hill Book Company.
  The most immediate reason for a recommendation to read Dr. Kemp's book is his use in Chapter 3 of "The Concept of Group." The parallel in verbal expression is one measure of the similarity in direction between his thinking and mine. There are many differences in point of view beyond those surface similarities. The student should find the Kemp book a good source for expansion and extension of what we know about group.
Rogers C. R., 1969. "The Increasing Involvement of the Psychologist in Social Problems: Some Comments Positive and Negative," *Journal of Applied Behavioral Science* 5 (1) 3–9.

Rogers discusses the involvement of the psychologist in the areas of racial problems, reduction of warlike tensions, government, international relationships, education, and alienation because of change. He envisions programmed learning as improving education if the programs are short and used voluntarily and according to the students' needs. The greatest single social problem will be how fast human beings can adapt to change. Rogers says that adaptation to change will not be developed by the use of existing and traditional knowledge and static guidelines. He sees psychology as implementing the humanization of education.

10

Group-Counseling Methods I

Introduction

Group-counseling methods are designed to create relationships of a particular type. The goal is to evolve the *relationship* out of which the identified patient or group member may form new behavior. The type of new behavior should be more adaptive or less maladaptive than the old behavior. Old behavior could include the conditions encountered as action, *reaction*, nonaction. If the person does not act because he does not know an appropriate behavior (action) new behavior can be action replacing nonaction or inaction. Such a condition will require a model appropriate to the subject. The subject person will be black and poor. An appropriate model will be black and *not* poor. The above example is pointing to the prerequisites to achieving relationships that can help create new behavior in one life arena in contemporary society. In Hawaii the counselor may need to be local; in addition he may need to be any one of some eight varieties of national and ethnic backgrounds. The principle is a continuing need to provide models within groups for self-help within problem populations.

The theory I have stated in Chapter 3 claims that behavior forms in the relationship to express a meaning unique to the person. The person forming the behavior does so in the act of creating a new experience. Once the new behavior is formed, it becomes subject to the principles of reinforcement and subsequently to instrumental and classical learning (or conditioning). The following methods of group counseling and group psychotherapy have been evolved to enhance and to create the human relationships in which new behavior can form. In addition, the group provides an intact reinforcement schedule to shape the selection and strengthening of selected behavior(s). Behavior that forms and is not reinforced or given negative reinforcement will atrophy. The group parallels (closely resembles) the culture's community of

177

persons. The group is a concept or model of the culture's social system; therefore behavior formed in a group (and which survives the reinforcement schedule in the group) should transfer to the wider community. New behavior will not succeed in a group with a deviant or different reinforcement schedule. For example, a patient is "cured" in the psychiatric hospital and returns home, yet within a few months the patient is back in the psychiatric ward. Another example common to the school counselor's milieu is the child who is worked with in the isolation of the counselor's office and returns to the classroom. What will happen? He will return for reasons that are probably universal in the helping professions. Namely, *we must work in the context in which the behavior change is to occur*—in the hospital ward, in the school, or in the family groups. Transfer of learned behavior will happen *only* when the group and community are *exactly* parallel. I have found that families which are not parallel to the society's wider community cannot produce behavior in the members that "works" outside the family any more proficiently than it seems to work within the family group.

The wisdom seems to be conventional in contemporary group practice. Take the group concept into the arena where behavior is to be changed. Create the new relationship definitions *within* the context where new behavior is wanted. The professional counselor will need the special skills to use any one of the recognized methods for group counseling intervention. I do not cherish a naive hope that merely convening a group of persons will create any change in behavior. Neither do I believe that having read this text you are ready to lead a group. We all need supervised practice. Perhaps we should have continuing in-service supervision to assure a reasonable safeguard against excesses of any sort. I have found the continuous exposure to supervision by respected colleagues, students, and consultants to be a source of feedback essential to a continuing evaluation (reality check).

The following descriptions of group-counseling methods have been selected to give the reader a preview of major samples in the field of group work. The selected samples are representative of established systems or methods based on recognized theories. The list is not intended to be exhaustive. Further reading is encouraged through the references used to collect the abstracts on each group counseling method.

Psychodrama, Sociodrama and Role Playing

Moreno (1946, 1958, 1951, 1953) has been the founder and prime mover behind the development of psychodrama and sociodrama in the United States. The ultimate goal of psychodrama is the *therapeutic community.* Psychodrama and sociodrama, group psychotherapy and psychopharmacology, together constitute the third revolution in psychiatry. The first revolution followed the unchaining of mental patients and treating them as people instead of demons. The second revolution was the founding of psychoanalysis by Freud and the discovery by Pavlov of conditioning as the simple learning process.

Most of the significant methods and techniques in use in group-counseling and group-encounter practices can be traced back to psychodrama and sociodrama. The remainder can be accounted for on the basis of conditioning, instrumental learning, and psychoanalytic processes. Creative innovations may account for most of the newer group methods in use. The rediscovery by Mowrer (1968) of some community group forces and the techniques to manipulate them brought new understanding of why some established (trial-and-error) discoveries have been effective in changing behavior, reinstating self-respect, and maintaining therapeutic community within groups.

Statement of Theory

Psychodrama is a group-counseling method. It is based on a unique theory called *role theory.* Drama, role, enactment, are concrete forms of expression which instantly reflect the culture parameters for meaning. In contrast with the concept of ego, role is much less mysterious and abstract.

The role theory states that the self emerges from the roles we take in encountering others. The self (personality) exists in action in relation to others within a situation or context *in situ.*

Assumptions about Behavior

The key assumptions about behavior begin with a basic concept about reality. Moreno in psychodrama avoids the academic effete concern with *objective* reality and *subjective* reality. All that matters is that each member, and especially the protagonist, achieves a *spontaneous* expression in his role.

Assumption 1. I am the way I behave. The role one takes is his reality.

Assumption 2. *Tele,* the *uno cum uno* (becoming one) through distance with another person creates a two-way empathy. Two persons, or more, create a unity or oneness leading to shared responsibility, values, and purposes.

Assumption 3. Encounter is direct confrontation and access to the other person in reciprocal interpersonal interaction. Encounter can happen only once and is unique each time, like my concept of experience. It is created new every time it happens. Therefore *the experience —the encounter,* cannot be exchanged by symbolic languages. Encounter is when I meet you and we exchange or transact meanings which each of us comprehends completely in each other's terms. Encounter is two-way empathy.

Assumption 4. Spontaneity is the criterion of a reality experience. Rehearsed role play is a form of gamesmanship. Games are artificial, unreal—even sick sometimes.

Assumption 5. Catharsis and abreaction are essential to group and individual process in group counseling. Mowrer (1968) thinks the *secret* is what disables the individual—not the content of the secret which is usually benign—but the *fact* the secret exists. Catharsis may be the verbal or acting-out way to get secrets disclosed. Once disclosed, the benign character usually dissolves the hang-up.

Assumption 6. Conscious-unconscious-preconscious and coconscious-counconscious, all operate all of the time in each of our behavior patterns. Moreno uses the concept of free association to explain access to unconscious. I think my concept of a culture parameter is an explanation for why two or more people act together simultaneously under identical conditions. They are programmed the same way because of the common culture. In contrast, persons from different cultures in the same group do not experience simultaneous encounter initially. Following many sessions in the life of a group, the shared "culture" of the group does the providing of a common culture, and simultaneous meanings permit encounter among persons with different cultural backgrounds.

Assumption 7. The concept of community is based on the idea that every person in a group is the therapeutic agent of every other person in the same group. Herein lies the heart of the *shared-responsibility concept* in psychodrama. Our work with family counseling, therapy and consultation, reflects the wisdom of the above assumption. We thought of our role as therapists only in terms of working through one or more members of the family group.

Assumption 8. Therapeutic interaction may be helpful or harmful. The role of the leader is assured by this idea. The professional counselor *must* be prepared to be responsible and accountable for deciding when a social relationship shifts from one to the other pole of health. The great share of social interaction is probably in between—benign! The identified patient in a family group is usually an example of how harmful the social interaction may be. Following a successful treatment in family group therapy, we can say the interaction has been converted to a less sick, more healthy outcome.

Assumption 9. Confrontation is the only direct reality test. The group serves to check and balance the interpretation of each member and the leader.

Assumption 10. The verbal model for therapy has some distinct limits. The combining of verbal and nonverbal, acting-out procedures, makes a more complete model for therapy. Exclusive use of a nonverbal model can quickly demonstrate the above idea. Many of the newer innovations to group process depend heavily upon the nonverbal exercises (Gunther, 1968).

Assumption 11. Transactions between two or more persons can happen only after they achieve the status of an encounter—two-way empathy.

Assumption 12. The sociometric principles accurately describe the social-communication dynamics in a group or community.

Group dynamic laws, according to Moreno, are:

(a) Higher group or human organization evolves from the simple group organizations based on continguity and attraction. For example, in a university you bring persons together and they develop and grow toward higher group organization. I think the opposite extreme is self-evident—namely, persons who never meet almost never get married to each other.

(b) Isolates and overchosen persons in a sociogram tend to hold their respective statuses over long time periods in a given formal organization. The principle of *sociodynamic effect* is that whatever holds for an individual also holds for groups insofar as relative status within a society. An example from contemporary groups in America is the subject of a special issue of the *American Personnel and Guidance Journal* (May 1970) entitled "What Guidance for Blacks?"

(c) The forces of rejection and the forces of attraction are balanced in social gravitation. The dynamics are in favor of the attraction forces when the forces of rejection are reduced. When rejection outweighs attraction the rejected person is hindered in carrying forward any plan that requires group support.

(d) Interpersonal networks have social-emotional networks which seem to work as a permanent basis of communication for social-emotional support within an established group. On the surface, life events are always changing. Underneath the kaleidoscopic surface content is a permanent stability on the relationship level. The best example I can share which would be part of almost everybody's experiences is the lover's quarrel. Any third party attempting to enter the conflict of two or more persons from the same group such as a family, lovers, or siblings will be turned upon and rejected. Subsequently, the parties to the conflict may continue their "experiences."

Group dynamics laws are basic to the methods of sociodrama and sociometry. Culture parameters may be used to explain group dynamics. Therefore I think the reader will find both Moreno's and Hall's (1959) ideas helpful in expanding awareness of group counseling potential.

Blajan-Marcus (1970) points out the diverse uses of psychodrama under four major categories. Psychodrama may be used as therapy with one or more hospitalized patients. Here it fits the clinic and goes beyond the other psychotherapies in depth and in communications forms. It goes beyond language into nonverbal and body languages (symbolism). Psychodrama may be used for group training of individual therapists, counselors, and group leaders. This technique involves both subjective and objective feedback. Psychodrama may be used as social therapy or sociodrama. Sociodrama is group therapy or group counseling and may be used to resolve conflicts and to clarify issues. Psychodrama may be used to conduct education and recreation. Learning and spontaneity problems may be solved through psychodramatic techniques.

Treatment Formula

The treatment formula used to manipulate the forces to change behavior in the group participants in psychodrama and sociodrama centers in the dynamics of simulated real-life action called *drama.* The instruments of psychodrama method include the director, the group of participants, the identified patient, the audience, and the stage.

The director knows all of the rules and acts in the mode of a magician. The group of participants supply all of the roles needed to complete all aspects and dimensions of the life event in the social setting. No distinction is made between fantasy and reality. Self-disclosure, self-presentation, and self-perception become central purposes in the attempt to create spontaneous expression in the process of enactment.

The target person, called an *identified patient* or *protagonist,* is the one who sets up the drama by supplying the life event complete with roles to be cast in the enactment. The audience and the stage complete the setting.

Goals, Purposes, End Results

The goal is to simulate reality through the medium of play. Play is a concept throught to be linked to spontaneous cure in therapeutic terms. The central purpose is to replicate a real-life context and rehearse the new behavior to be used for creating new roles for oneself in other groups. The end result is to establish higher levels of group cohesiveness. The belief is carried to an ultimate aim to establish a therapeutic society, a natural expansion from a therapeutic community.

Interventions

Interventions in psychodrama consist of the basic techniques used to create the relationships out of which new behavior will come. New behavior forms in a relationship. The techniques make up a method for creating new relationships among the participants. Specific techniques include:

Role playing (i.e., soliloquy, doubling, role reversal, life rehearsal, future projection)

Mirror technique

Self-realization

Self-presentation

Psychodramatic presentations—hallucinations, fantasy dreams (day or nocturnal), real-life events (past-future), auxiliary world

Warm-up techniques

Spontaneous improvisation

Therapeutic community

Audience feedback

Lecture—directions from the director

Tactile body contact, nonverbal exercises

The techniques included in the above list are representative of the major interventions for creating new relationships. Psychodrama has set the pace for effective group techniques. Moreno claims that psychodrama extends beyond other group psychotherapy methods. The trend of the past decade has been toward adapting many of Moreno's ideas to newer forms of group intervention. I want to remind the reader of the importance of psychodrama techniques. These techniques for self-disclosure and life rehearsal simulate reality more effectively than most other methods.

Leader's Role

The director in psychodrama is the central figure. Only the director knows the rules. The rules are necessary to bring the self-disclosure essential to creating new relationships. A director in psychodrama operates in the mode of a magician.

The qualifications to become a director are difficult to acquire for at least two reasons. First, the number of certified psychodrama centers remains few. Second, the magician is effective at plying his skills, and is therefore equally effective in discouraging students from attempting to duplicate the master magician. I have remarked to one friend skilled in psychodrama that the method by any other name would probably be most frequently used in counseling. Now that the shift is away from benign, permissive, and nonauthoritarian leaders in group work, the chances are much more favorable for psychodrama and sociodrama.

Group and Member Roles

Every individual is a therapeutic agent for every other individual in the group. The group role is to create the most useful grouping of individuals to promote sharing of responsibility and enhance cohesiveness. The group must achieve a feeling of oneness, the choice emotional climate for *encounter* or two-way empathy. New roles are learned in the encounter with only one other individual.

This concept of encounter is similar to my idea about how behavior is changed, but differs because I do think there is more to the process than the desirable condition created in two-way empathy (encounter). Behavior change comes from new behavior. New behavior forms in a relationship in which *each* individual finds it necessary to express *new* meaning. The experience is created, anew, every time the relationship is defined differently. The encounter is an intermediate step in a complex process of confirming the redefined relationship. There is such a thing as *pseudoencounter.* Moreno and proponents of the newer group methods emphasizing encounter have largely missed this fact. The small child is the best example I know. The narcissism of the child combined with his uninhibited openness create the emotional climate for encounter. Because the child will be unconcerned with maintaining his end of the interpersonal *contract* beyond the duration of the encounter, the pseudoencounter occurs. Another variation in pseudoencounter may occur when one acquires a pet animal, especially a cat. The aloofness of the cat is far more fascinating precisely because of the ability to be open and uninhibited in dropping the relationship anytime the cat is so inclined. Whenever a group is convened on a terminal contract the hopes of achieving genuine, long-term encounter are dashed. Repeated sessions are desired by many members of short-term groups because a longer time together enhances the chances for encounter and diminishes the hiatus of pseudoencounter.

Summary of Change

Psychodrama may continue over a long period of time. The group may maintain long-term relationships. Yet *each* episode, each *enactment,* is complete in itself. Closure is achieved in much the way real-life encounters occur. Each life event achieves closure, but the promise of more to come, a lifeline, is constant. *No other group method has the versatility of intermittent reinforcement* at the level of social interaction. The sequence of self-disclosure, self-presentation, and life rehearsal may be used as a spiral to development of higher and more complex new behavior. The entire process can be contained in the enactments of the psychodrama theater and enjoy the safety of a protected environment. Like anything else carried to an extreme, the play may become a game of life.

Moreno has invented the term *tele*—communication over distance between two or more subjects—to explain the dynamics of a group. Tele is to group what transference was to Freudian psychoanalysis, though considerably different concepts with extremely different consequences. Transference in a group is destructive, like one couple pairing off and doing their own thing.

Change is accomplished in psychodrama through tele and encounter. New roles are learned and reinforced by the group. The group is a social system and shapes behavior after it appears in the same way a peer group, family group, or task group would do it in the "square" (real) world.

The rate of change may vary from *never* to instantaneous. The *spontaneous cure* is possible in psychodrama. Most neurotic and psychotic persons require longer to achieve encounter. Most so-called "normal" persons can achieve encounter almost immediately following the creation of the *right* relationship. Psychodrama can be life itself in the ideal form—life as one long moment of truth!

Selection of the Group Members

Psychodrama treats the group process, not the individual person's psyche. As such, the emphasis is upon sociometric measures of individuals—the attraction-rejection of and toward others. Analysis is on the chances for productive interpersonal relationships, tele, and encounter. The person as a modality in isolation is ignored. The level of sophistication necessary to achieve the desired relationships is substantial. However, it does not need to be a stumbling block. Dr. Leon Fine of the University of Oregon Medical School in Portland, Oregon, has been doing psychodrama for several years with intact groups. The staff group at an in-patient facility, the patient group at the Medical School Hospital, or an Institute of counselors in training, may become psychodrama groups. Most any group could attempt psychodrama if a qualified director were available. Psychodrama with families has been found especially useful.

Special Skills

The psychodrama director is a professional level person with a unique array of special skills. The total list of possible skills would make almost anyone think the task is too great to be undertaken as a career plan. However, most skilled psychodrama directors seem to have added these skills to an already impressive array of professional skills. Some hold the medical doctorate, others the doctor of philosophy degree. Many more directors hold masters degrees in an academic field and have acquired psychodrama skills as an adjunct to other applied skills. Others have studied with Moreno, the founder of psychodrama in America. By whatever means one acquires the special skills in psychodrama, the list will probably include the following.

- There is a need for coaching skills—the ability to walk or live through an intimate life event with another person.
- Some level of proficiency is needed in executing the *rules* of psychodrama. The rules must be followed precisely or the creation of an opportunity for spontaneity will not come off.
- Also needed is interpretation and analysis ability for whatever behavior comes up in a session.
- The director must communicate directions in detail with dispatch.
- He must handle the complex flow of emotion without limiting or cutting off communication.
- He must motivate the group to keep on functioning again and again.
- There is no script in psychodrama. The director has the skill to achieve spontaneity.
- The director has the skill to move into and out of the intimate interaction of others.
- He needs the skill to take any role at any moment.
- He must be able to time his actions in tempo with the participants.
- The director should know sociometrics and how to create and use the techniques and instruments, and interpret the data.

Unique Features

Psychodrama and sociodrama have the unique capability to disclose to the person acting his own role and to others—simultaneously—his behavior, values, attitudes, conscious, unconscious, and indeed almost anything about the person that can be revealed by social enactment. The self-disclosure and self-presentation features of psychodrama techniques may reach all interpersonal data. The techniques yield no intrapsychic data.

Encounter is an unique feature. Two-way empathy in genuine encounter is the definition given to intimacy. Alienation or separation is the opposite. Transference (one-way empathy) is discouraged because it alienates members from the group.

Psychodrama and sociodrama require a powerful leader. These are not self-help group phenomena. Herein may lie the greatest handicap, the scarce supply of powerful leaders in a society hooked on nondirective and permissive principles.

Finally, the techniques of psychodrama seem to be the major input in many of the newer methods for group work.

Integrity Therapy: The Practice of Radical Honesty

Mowrer (1968) stated his major thesis supporting integrity therapy as the simple truth about one's behavior and oneself. Simple *elusive* truth is a relative concept, not absolute truth. Relative truth requires a balance between what is perceived by the individual—what is perceived by the significant others to that individual—and what the culture sets up as the rules or parameters defining for us what should be. Mowrer's group counseling process is designed to establish the conditions to create the opportunities for helping an individual achieve *radical honesty* (Mowrer, 1964; Dabrowski, 1964).

Statement of Theory

Integrity therapy is a group-treatment method developed by Mowrer to create the healing relationships needed to reinstate a wayward group member to full status in the group with self-esteem and self-respect intact.

Neurosis and functional psychosis are formed out of the relationship between self and others because of the denial of reality about one's true behavior. Radical honesty with self and others leads to reintegration from alienation.

Assumptions Supporting the Theory. There are a number of assumptions supporting the theory that complete and unabridged self-disclosure is the avenue leading to mental health. A group of two or more persons is considered the essential community for achieving and maintaining self-disclosure (Mowrer, 1966).

- Secrets are sometimes an abuse of privacy.
- Radical honesty is achievable.
- Self-disclosure is a paradox.
- Others, significant others, are essential to resolve the paradox of self-disclosure through feedback.

- Feedback is a reality check (test).
- Psychopathology arises from what we ourselves do, and then hide from ourselves.
- Therapy is a process for authenticating oneself.
- The professional counselor cannot treat and cure anyone. He sets the stage for self-help.
- Self-help is the goal.
- Best therapist or counselor is the one who can set up to help others help themselves.
- Psychopathology is social alienation.
- Psychological health is social intimacy.
- Integrity therapy achieves restoration of self-respect.
- Self-respect is antecedent to mental health.
- Mental health is achieved in authentic human existence.
- Authentic human existence is achieved in a community of significant others.
- One is authentic when self-perceptions match perceptions of him by others.
- Self-authentication is an interpersonal process.
- Reintegration of the personality and person is the central aim of group therapy, social psychiatry and religion.
- Restitution or penance is essential to the process of restoring self-respect.

Treatment Formula

The immutable consequences of "I am the way I behave" brings the Mowrer (1968) concept of group treatment into sharp focus. The group teaches that the way I behave in the world sets a pattern of consequences from what it draws from others. The task in group counseling consists of helping each person find out what his contribution to his own fate really is. The treatment process using the above combination of self-disclosure and confrontation will result in the massing of tensions and the mobilization of affect. Emotions cannot be directly managed, so the task is to manage the tensions. The mangement of tensions cannot occur before the group produces them. Prevention of tension is not a goal in group work. Involvement is the major consequence of tension management. Involvement over time in a group produces access. It is the access we have to significant others that helps us maintain psychological health.

The above abstract of Mowrer (1968) shows the essential elements in creating interpersonal *experience*. Experience is the primary force in the integrity-therapy-treatment system. Experience is the expression of the group member's accountability to the expectations of the group. As with all informal culture modes of behavior, it is necessary to be in the group in order to learn how to conduct the treatment formula of integrity therapy.

Goals of Treatment

The primary purpose of integrity therapy in groups is to help someone learn to help himself. This is accomplished through the experience of meeting the expectations of the group. The group and the therapist share openly all the relevant feelings of each member. Each member tries to achieve full accountability to the expectations of the group for radical honesty and authenticity.

Interventions Used in Treatment

Direct self-confrontation followed by admission of error, wrongdoing, or an unworthy act against some significant other in the member's life is the major intervention used in integrity therapy. The manipulation of a group and the process of interpersonal interaction would take an entire volume to present (Mowrer, 1964). Self-disclosure through confession is the vehicle for achieving intervention. The person needs help in the build-up necessary to achieve self-confrontation. The formula in treatment is designed to bring about the necessary conditions for authentic self-disclosure.

Leader's Role

The leader must do what he expects members of the group to do, namely, self-disclose in a radically honest and authentic way. Qualifications necessary to achieve the quality of leadership required are a paradox. Mowrer (1968) thinks the professional role is not necessary. If people can achieve the intervention discussed above by themselves without a leader, the results would be the same. I think we need to understand that most groups and most people will need a lot of training before they achieve the level of honesty, authenticity, and skill antecedent to living the way Mowrer (1968) thinks we can. The leader role for the group counselor is to achieve and then to practice these skills. The skills and the formula conducted by the leader have many parallel functions with family consultation. We have found families can learn to "do it themselves" on a self-help basis if we take the time to help them learn how to be successful group members.

Member's Role and Group's Role

Support and encouragement rank high for group feedback and member contributions to integrity therapy. The leader does the interpretation of the behavior in terms of the formula used by Mowrer (1964) in integrity therapy. Integrity is the key word in all interpretation. The aim is to move each *member* in the group toward the realization that *what I say about myself* to the other group members, *significant others,* is what is important. What *others say to me* is of little consequence to changing my behavior.

The member's role is to speak the truth. The group's role is to provide the significant others. To become significant, a group member will have developed a relationship or will have come into the group with a relationship with the confessing member. According to Mowrer (1968), confessing the radical truth to strangers has a poor record for healing the wayward, neurotic, and psychotic. Counselors in school and agency settings may find they are able to set up self-help programs with families, peer groups, and some contrived groups, based upon Mowrer's claim that it is not the professional specialist but the *member* himself who heals a sick soul. The group provides the motivation for change and supplies feedback.

Change in Behavior

How change is accomplished in integrity therapy has some unique historical background. Mowrer (1968) tells about the early Christians and their use of a deep and thorough form of self-disclosure called *exomologesis.* First, a wayward member confessed to one or two group members. Next, the process was repeated to a group from the community of *believers.* Finally, a public confession to the entire community (congregation) completed the self-disclosure. The response from the one or two individuals, the group, and the community shared a common theme—support, deep respect for his courage to speak the truth about himself, and love and rejoicing for his rebirth of desirable virtues. But reinstatement was not automatic. Forgiveness for wayward behavior required penance. When the restitution was completed over a period of *time* then he could be fully restored to the community, his *self-respect* intact.

The significance of this last point—keeping his *self-respect intact*—has been missing from most all of Western man's attempts to rehabilitate the wayward felon, the sinner, the mentally ill, or whatever label we use to categorize the behaver as out-of-community because of his maladaptive behavior. I point to this historically important discovery of Mowrer's as the keystone in all systems of counseling and therapy used to change behavior. Namely, if the behavior can be changed without mutilating self-respect, the system of counseling or therapy may be evaluated in more positive terms. There are several group-counseling systems using techniques and methods that permit the conditions for public self-disclosure to happen. The Adlerian family counseling centers practice a method of public community sharing similar to the confessional described by Mowrer. We have used the open system of group in our group family consultation program. Many of the newer group methods are employed to promote growth in personal behavior, e.g., the late Perls' Gestalt Institutes, encounter groups, venture groups, Synanon, and marathon groups, to name but a few. I do not wish to imply that all of the above methods achieve the rigorous conditions defined by Mowrer, but to the extent we do achieve the criteria of self-disclosure, significant other, restitution, time and restoration of self-respect, we have succeeded.

Rate of change is dependent upon the person's ability to accept the blame for his own action. To become responsible for my behavior and accountable to the *group expectations* for my behavior constitutes the major criteria for the antecedents to behavior change. The *rate* of change may vary from *instant cure* to a lifetime. Some of us never change our behavior. Some of us change immediately. Others change following various amounts of time. The major point is: Whenever the conditions for change are met, the behavior will change quite quickly depending upon the period of time needed to complete the penance of restitution.

Selection of the Group

The members of a group in integrity therapy should be persons ready to accept the criteria for change in behavior described in the previous section. They should understand the conditions may be painful and should contract to stay in the group all the way to termination. Integrity therapy is not a situation one should run away from in midcourse. The member should stay in the group until self-respect is restored.

Special Techniques

Special skills include the leader's ability to self-disclose. The model presented by the leader will be followed by each member. In addition, many special techniques are used in integrity therapy. Some of them are included here to give the reader an idea about similarities and differences with other group-counseling methods.

Initially, the leader gives a verbal explanation of how the group will work. Each member has an idea about what is expected from him and what may happen to him and others in the group.

Feedback comes from group members. Each member talks in turn. Process is usually restricted to verbal interaction. Nonverbal exercises can be suggested and used.

Each member is encouraged to confess the truth about his behavior. A period of relaxation is used after confession.

Confession is made in a sequence, first to the therapist (leader) and then to the group, followed by confession to the significant other(s). The process is similar to exomologesis described earlier.

Unique Features

The unique feature of integrity therapy is the strength given to self-help group models and methods. Here is a system built around the central premise that people need only people. The cultural beliefs which persist and separate person from person are seen as the major barriers to mental health. Access to significant others and candid openness would eliminate secrets and nourish authentic encounter with one another. Mowrer and Moreno come together in goals for a therapeutic society consisting of therapeutic communities. They seem to differ only in whether a professional leader is necessary. That seems to me to be a minor point. For me the major point revolves around whether or not people can discover some of the culture's basic errors about interpersonal relations and then learn to correct these errors in their own behavior. Most group-counseling methods are aimed at this problem. I might be even more optimistic about the future of society if I could find success in achieving the above goal in my own department at the university! The forces that separate us in our society sometimes present us with an awesome challenge.

System of Group Counseling—Adlerian Teleoanalytic Method

The Adlerian individual psychology came from the work of Alfred Adler. Adler, Jung, and Freud are names associated with the three main branches of psychoanalytic theory and practice. Jung developed *analytic* psychology, but has not become prominent in group-counseling work. Freudian psychoanalysis is discussed in Chapter 11. Adlerian individual psychology became the basis of Rudolph Dreikurs' (1968) approach to group counseling in what came to be known as Adlerian teleoanalytic family counseling. Many prominent authorities have studied with Dr. Dreikurs and continue to develop centers for parent education in child rearing methods. Dreikurs, Corsini, Lowe, and Sonstegard

(1959) are among the better-known leaders of Adlerian family counseling. Sonstegard (1970) has written an important statement of rationale for school counselors.

During the 1950's and 1960's the method was more controversial than it is in the 1970's. Part of the change in climate of positive regard toward Adlerian family counseling was a growing recognition of the importance of the basic premises and child-rearing practices claimed by Dreikurs et al. (1959). My own exposure to Adlerian family counseling began in 1955. Over the past fifteen years, I have come to understand and actively support the goals and purposes in Adlerian family counseling. It is particularly important for parent education in child-rearing practices. Dreikurs and Soltz (1964) go so far as to claim American parents do not know how to raise children, an ability achieved by most other living organisms. However, the Harlows (1962) did show us that parent skills could be lost in one generation.

The controversial aspects of the Adlerian family counseling approach seem to come from the directive nature of the techniques for control of the child's behavior. Dreikurs and Grey (1968) show how the natural or logical consequences become the reinforcement schedule of the child whenever he acts. To merely allow the child to experience the logical consequences is enough correction. No other intervention is necessary, they claim. The cultural parameters are assumed to be in operation to produce the logical consequences. Some parents have to learn how to behave in the family group in order to produce the logical consequences. In fact, they need to learn the behavior to produce the culture's parameters. Children raised in the 1940's and 1950's were exposed to the cult of permissiveness. The chances for learning how limits are set in the human organization were missed. Such parents are destroyed by powerful children. Adlerian family counseling can help them learn to set and maintain limits for the children. The children can then experience logical consequences.

The Adlerian Method

The method has four major divisions. Each is a phase of the group-counseling practice. The phases are by no means mutually exclusive nor are they sequential. Relationships, analysis, interpretation, and reeducation are the four main phases (Sonstegard, 1970).

Relationship is defined as a cooperative venture. The counselor must achieve the calibre of relationship needed to achieve the counseling task. Individual and group counseling are essentially the same where the relationship phase is concerned. A group creates more opportunities for cooperative relationships to develop. The group exerts more social

pressure for conformity to social norms or parameters. The counselor is
the interpreter of norms for the group.

The premise is that the counselor uses his relationship to influence
the values, attitudes, and behavior needs of the members of the group.
The formula for achieving the fulfillment of the premise on relationship
goes as follows:

The leader of Adlerian family counseling sessions does not relinquish direct control of the process. Questions are asked to gather information. The information is interpreted and feedback is given directly
in the attitude of interrogation, admonition, and precept. The method
is in the same model as used by a mother teaching the formal culture
to her child (Hall, 1959). No exception is permitted. However, explanations are given frequently to enhance the reeducation value of the
encounters. The relationship is kept complementary with the counselor
one-up on the counselee or group member. The subordinated status of
the group members places the leader-counselor in the position of hand-
ing verbal instructions to them. The instructions include directions
about how to think, what to think, and how to act. The formula carries
the method through all four phases. The formula defines and redefines
the relationships between the counselor and the group members. The
group-counseling process is seen as an educational milieu primarily for
character education for both parent and child.

Analysis is like diagnosis in other group-counseling methods. The
counselor investigates the family in terms of each person in it. Usually
the counselor begins with the identified patient (or the one referred for
treatment). A complete history of the person's life experiences is gathered together, because the Adlerian method believes early formative
years have a lasting effect on present behavior. In addition to the history
a contemporary view is important. The counselor wants to know what
his style of life is. How does the counselee see himself? Rehabilitation
depends upon a complete analysis of all of the previous relationships
which formed his present character and personality. The analysis is a
way of seeing the social system of the person in relation to each other
person in the family group and to the culture parameters for behavior.

Life style is seen as a product of the placement in the family constel-
lation. The order of birth is given significance because the social milieu
for each child is unique due to each additional sibling in the family
group. The only child lives in a different world from the eldest of five
or six siblings. The middle-child syndrome is recognized for yielding
distinctive behavior not found in other placements in the family con-
stellation. The parents are the major power source in behavior in the
family. The counselor looks carefully at the parts and the whole family
unit. This preparation is for gathering the background to be used to

interpret the meaning of the person's early childhood memories. What conclusions were drawn by the counselee about early childhood experiences? The recall of early events in your life will reveal a pattern consistent with every other recollection because you tend to forget everything that is in contradiction with your pattern of conclusions. These conclusions are similar to the system of beliefs I use to explain the individual social system or the group norm or the cultural parameters of beliefs. The analysis technique the Adlerians use gains access to the source of these beliefs. Many times it is discovered the person has beliefs which are in error based on early experience and bias. These are confronted by the counselor and challenged as false or erroneous. Selective perception operates over time to produce the unique subjective experience for each of us. The Adlerian principle of a "will to power" may be the individual's attempt to impose his subjective perceptions into the group.

There are probably no techniques in any other group-counseling method more useful to a counselor whenever the need is to understand the source and system of beliefs of a counselee or a group of persons.

Interpretation is continuous and simultaneous in the interview sessions for either individual or group. Interpretations influence subsequent disclosures. There is a possibility that the counselor will risk self-fulfilling prophecy dynamics unless he is a skilled professional. The interpretation is shared in the group. The family group, the peer group, and the school milieu contribute material to support the interpretations. The focus is on the goals the person wants to achieve. This strategy avoids the quicksand of current feelings about how things are going. The built-in reorientation or reeducation overlaps in this phase. Much of the teaching in Adlerian family counseling comes during interpretations and the development of each interpretation by the group.

The action the person takes is considered important. Almost no significance is attached to the "why" of his behavior. The goal or purpose the action is trying to achieve is considered very important. My way of sharing the idea behind the action-purpose focus is simply: The person can tell you what he has done, how he did it and for what purpose or immediate or long-term goal he was trying to achieve. No one can tell me *why* he behaves. Because "the why" is unobservable, I cannot verify it by confirmation or validation. Each human being has a "private logic" which is influential in his thinking and belief systems. Each person needs to be helped to understand his private logic.

Insight has no dependence on emotion. Emotions are unessential to Adlerian family counseling. The interpretations are given in terms of the person's basic premise. This is his life style. The person is *never* told what to do. He is told what the purposes are for his behavior. Freedom comes in the choice of alternatives the person makes. He may choose to remain as he is. He may choose to change.

Reeducation goes on during all phases of Adlerian family counseling. The reeducation or reorientation process is the heart of the Adlerian group method. Reorientation is considered essential in Frankl's logotherapy. The premise is that depth understanding of purposes for behavior is necessary to sustained behavior change. Permanence of change is a concern in most group-counseling methods because any of us can play a game for sustained periods without permanent change.

Reeducation is based on a technique for confrontation with the goals and purposes of the person's own behavior. Intentions are the key to motivations for specific behavior. The counselee gains insight and understands the power he has to decide for himself what behavior he will choose to employ. The wisdom of self-direction becomes the prime motivation for the person.

Unique Features

Adlerian family counseling is unique in several respects. The group counseling method is safe to use in a public hearing type of setting. Every session becomes a training session for all participants. The lack of abuse of privacy creates one of the best teaching-learning arenas of any method now in use for group counseling. Our society is afraid of revealing deficiencies of individuals in public because of the heavy stress on competition. The courage to self-disclose in the open setting is deeply rewarding even though, initially, painful. The cultural myth is false. Radical honesty is rewarding, not punishing, on impact.

The authority of the counselor and the style of interpretation was unique until the emergence of Albert Ellis and his system of therapy. The analyst has no peer. The Adlerians have a complete system for parent education in child rearing. The method is of limited value for families with children twelve years or older.

Summary

Chapter 10 has been the first of three chapters to describe existing group-counseling methods and how they relate to one another and to the theory I present in Chapter 3. Chapter 11 continues the outline presentation of some more of the major group-counseling methods. A single volume cannot presume to exhaust the possibilities for group counseling. We can present a unified thesis about how group counseling can change behavior. This goal is a limited one. However, the need for direct supervised experience to learn a given group-counseling method cannot be abridged in a textbook. The attempt is to remove some of the mystic veil from the arena of group counseling.

Moreno and Mowrer represent the most basic forces in their respective systems. Moreno's psychodrama has given the world of group its primary techniques. Mowrer has given group counseling a primary function essential to healthy behavior. Neither psychodrama, sociodrama, nor integrity therapy has found the universal method to counter the forces of separation and alienation in our culture.

Adlerian counseling is the group method for use with families and school settings. Most Family Education Centers organized by Adlerians operate under their own board of directors. I serve on such a board for Dr. Raymond Corsini and Dr. Harold Kozuma in Honolulu. The Family Education Centers of Hawaii have family counseling centers to help parents learn how to manage children.

Suggested Additional Readings

Dinkmeyer, D., 1970. "Developmental Group Counseling," *Elementary School Guidance and Counseling.* 4(4) 267–272 (May).
> Developmental group counseling is in some way a response to therapy and remedial and corrective emphases. The author wishes to encourage others to experiment with groups in counseling aimed at helping children grow through their normal developmental stages.

Friedlander, Frank, 1968. "A Comparative Study of Consulting Processes and Group Development," *Journal of Applied Behavioral Science,* 4(4) 377–400 (December).
> In a study concerning consultant processes, the author found that use of an internal consultant group could facilitate data gathering and action taken by clients or consultants. Increased knowledge of an ongoing group stimulates more appropriate group procedures. The transfer of group learning to the outside world is implemented by increased knowledge of the group. The consultant encourages confrontation, feedback, and use of resources in groups to implement diagnosis and change.

McWhirter, J. Jeffries, 1969. "Group Counseling with Transfer Students," *School Counselor,* 16(4) 300–302 (March).
> The article illustrates how to develop group counseling to help transfer students. Loss of peer group leads to difficulty adjusting to social situations with adolescents. To counteract this, school psychologists met with groups in a consultation role. Their goals were to develop a situation in which students could learn more about themselves, to provide a place to express feelings and find acceptance, and to answer individual questions about the school.

Miller, Norman, 1969. "The Ineffectiveness of Punishment Power in Group Interaction," *Sociometry,* 32(1) 24–41 (March).
> Individuals rely on their ability to inflict reward and punishment in order to

influence others. Effectiveness of the communication of these is important. Miller's study looks at effectiveness of social (reward, punishment) power in group interaction. He found that those with greatest social power were best able to communicate reward rather than punishment. Those who have the greatest reward power are more likely to receive rewards in turn.

11

Group-Counseling Methods II

This chapter is a continuation of the material of Chapter 10, which covers psychodrama, the provider of basic techniques in all group counseling, and Mowrer's integrity therapy, which provides the basic explanation of why group counseling can change behavior.

The continuation of the discussion of the systems of group counseling should help the reader become more familiar with the range of methods available in the field. Also, I hope to show how each method uses the techniques from psychodrama, or modifications of psychodrama techniques, in the formula employed by the method. Further, I expect to show how each formula and its method reconstitute the basic explanations given by Mowrer. Because our evidence indicates what Fiedler (1950a) found to be true—namely, the methods of psychotherapy have about the same level of success, depending upon the level of sophistication of the therapist. The indications are that something other than the formula of a particular method of group counseling creates the forces that change behavior. I claim it is the interpersonal relationship definition. Moreno and Mowrer point toward a similar basic reason. Moreno's *encounter* is a two-way empathy. Mowrer's radical honesty— to hear oneself speak the truth—is achieved only in a profound relationship. The techniques involved to create the opportunities for the necessary antecedent interpersonal and interdependent relationships, must be basically parallel in all methods. The differences are in the way the techniques are employed. Some methods use only one or two techniques as Mowrer appears to do. Other methods employ a wide range of techniques to bring about changed behavior. The reader may wish to review the things we know and the theory statement of Chapters 3 and 9. The emphasis will be upon the method. The following abstracts will be cursive, and the reader is encouraged to expand his reading about any one method he finds interesting. The verbal model of communication has many limitations. One of these seems to be an inability to transact the skills and other behavior to the reader necessary to carry on any of the methods abstracted in the text. The informal culture mode requires the direct encounter by each person who would become a professional practitioner in group counseling (Montagu, 1970). There is much to learn. The aim here is to help you along the way.

Group Psychoanalysis

The psychoanalytic method of treatment applied to group counseling is an attempt to shift from the historical reference of classical psychoanalysis to an emphasis on the here-and-now behavior of an individual in a group. I do not choose to battle about the nuances of psychoanalysis. My purpose is to acquaint the reader with the unique features of one of the more influential methods for treating neurotics. Moreno claims his development of psychodrama is an extension of the principles of psychoanalysis. For this reason the background of the reader can better be served by including a brief abstract on psychoanalytic group method.

The Method

There are multiple "schools" of psychoanalytic thought. Basic theoretical differences are recognized within the community of disciples of Freudian psychoanalysis. Like Jung and Adler, some may have founded "schools" of their own. The techniques employed are similar enough to provide a common framework for the group method. The techniques are employed in the group based on here-and-now behavior instead of being based on historical data supplied by the patient. Beyond the emphasis, the interaction may shift to past events in the group members' lives.

Statement of the Theory

The behavior of a person is due to unconscious processes motivated by past experiences. The past experiences must be relived and changed in order to change the person's behavior. Psychoanalysis is a method. Multiple theories may be stated on the basis of the method (Alexander, 1963).

The *intrapsychic* model of human behavior faces some problems when one tries to apply the techniques in an *interaction* model. Watzlawick, Beavin, and Jackson (1967) point out the contrast between the intrapsychic model of psychoanalysis and the interaction model or communication model they employed in the study and treatment of families with one or more schizophrenics among its members. Watzlawick et al. (1967) discuss the effects on treatment of human behavior using the one-up complementarity between analyst and patient. The assumption they make is that therapy ends whenever the patient figures out (gets insight) that the analysis could go on forever with the therapist (analyst) always being one-up. Otherwise the patient will always be faced with a paradox. If I say I'm getting well I'm resisting by escaping into health. If I think I'm getting worse I'm resisting but encouraged because the problem will be revealed and analyzed. The therapeutic double bind* is a paradox within a paradox. Most all psychotherapies use one. Psychoanalysis has one too. Group psychoanalysis is no exception. It works this way. Once the person has joined a group the voluntary nature of the relationship changes to a compulsory one. The complex group situation places the patient in a relationship he cannot escape from unless he changes. Of course, the assumption is that he will change if he stays in the situation. Is it any wonder why many persons are reluctant to enter therapeutic relationships? To be entirely fair, I should mention the therapist's problem posed by the patient who comes to group counseling communicating verbally, "Help me!" but nonverbally, "I will not let you help me!" Who said double-binding was one-way?

The unconscious is a problem in communication in group psychoanalysis because if the group member doesn't accept an interpretation given by the analyst he can claim it is beyond the person's conscious awareness. If the person speaks of his own unconscious the analyst may call it nonsense. Here are some of the communication or interaction-model comments about the complementary relationships used in the intrapsychic model for explaining behavior.

Psychoanalysis applied to groups is a dynamically oriented theory and method. Psychodynamics have a depth dimension with the conscious level on the surface. The preconscious is just out of awareness, but can be recalled by the individual. The unconscious is the remainder and covers most of the past experiences not recalled and out of conscious awareness. The id–life energy, the ego–the self; and the superego, the conscience make up the personality structure. Ego psychology emphasizes mastery functions of the personality. Whether or not you see behavior based on deep-seated personality factors, the use of group interaction requires that some faith be placed with the person's perceptual organization, such as ego psychologists claim. Montagu (1970) points up six facets of personality: perception, physical functions, social relations, memory or imitation, manipulative skill, and intelligence. A

---

*Therapeutic double bind is based on the double-bind theory of schizophrenia advanced by Bateson and Jackson in the 1950's (Watzlawick et al., 1967, pp. 212–213).

synthesis of all of these facets yields a development index. A group will test behavior, as well as the underlying assumptions.

Assumptions Supporting the Method

The assumptions supporting the use of psychoanalysis in groups go beyond the assumptions underlying the more traditional dyadic model of analyst-patient. Foremost among the assumptions are:

- Interpretation of behavior based on intrapsychic model concepts is applicable in an interpersonal group context.
- Psychoanalytic techniques applied in a group context, change behavior in the members of the group.
- Each case requires a special strategy for successful treatment.
- Supportive therapy should be supplied until a thorough diagnosis is possible.
- Free association is the psychoanalytic technique for achieving spontaneity.
- Spontaneity is the direct access to the personality, especially the preconscious and the unconscious.
- Transference is the reenactment of the neurosis. The irrational material is rerun and projected onto the therapist.
- Countertransference is transference by the therapist toward the patient. A unique double bind happens when the analyst interrupts his spontaneous feedback and monitors a contrived attitude toward the patient.
- Interpretation is aimed at resolving the transference (and countertransference) relationship between analyst and patient. His reasons for behaving pass from his unconscious to his conscious levels of personality.
- Conscious level material is subject to logical control of behavior. This idea is similar to Hall's (1959) notion about the *informal culture* being out of awareness until violated, and the *formal culture* being fully conscious.
- Interpretation is mainly a process of pointing out what the patient's resistance is directed against. Resistance is very closely aligned with the *relationship* concept set forth by Watzlawick et al. (1967).
- Dreams can be analyzed to reveal unconscious material.
- Dreams are an enactment of wishes that cannot be brought into the conscious awareness of the patient, spontaneously.
- The group provides several parameters for treatment not found in the one-to-one arena. Multiple reactivity, hierarchial and peer vectors (authority and peer relationships), intra-inter communica-

tion, shifting attention, alternating roles, and forced interaction (Wolf and Schwartz, 1962).

- Not everyone should be permitted to enter into group psychoanalysis.
- Changes in behavior may result from the group experience, but it is mainly due to the intervention by psychoanalytic techniques.

It may seem possible to find an almost unlimited set of assumptions to include in this list. However, my attempt is to include the chief assumptions to try to show something of the parameters and interventions in group psychoanalysis. Because my bias will probably show anyway, it should perhaps be said that techniques provide the vehicles for therapeutic encounter. Any set of techniques will provide some therapy. The real reason for change is in the relationship generated in the group. The techniques merely make a happening and thus add or detract interest and motivation to the process.

Treatment Formula in Group Psychoanalysis

The leader or analyst uses intervention strategies designed to manipulate forces thought to be therapeutic. The enrollment into group involves the initial set of interventions. Intervention begins before the group meets.

Selection of the group is a major intervention. Each participant must negotiate a contract with the analyst. Up to ten persons may join a group. This limit creates a kind of exclusiveness for being selected. The participant must accept the leader's authority over him and the group. The hierarchial relationship is clearly defined. A peer relationship will become evident when the group begins.

Many categories of persons, ranging from heart-disease patients to psychotics, should be excluded from group psychoanalysis. This condition will assure the creation of suitably congenial groups. Once the group has been selected, the process of treatment begins.

The leader (analyst) is in charge. Because he is the authority figure in the group, he is expected to supply answers to everyone's problems. This expectation sets up the first major treatment intervention. The analyst puts the group member (patient) in charge. The intervention is the first of a series of paradoxes where the patient is told to be spontaneous or that whatever perception the patient reports the analyst *interprets* it. The intervention strategy manipulates the forces of the therapeutic double bind. The formula, in treatment, is to have the analyst stay one-up on the patient and the group.

Goals of Treatment

The goal of psychoanalysis is the resolution of the patient's neurotic hang-ups. The process of therapy in group psychoanalysis consists of working through the resistances, exposing the pathological ideas, and generally changing from irrational wishes to rational reality-oriented action and thought associations.

Nothing is said about more adaptive behavior replacing poorly adjusted behavior. The assumption clearly leads to a belief in more adaptive behavior. If neurotic behavior is exposed to the light of reason, you then expect the behavior to change and to show evidence of better adjustment. I think there is a major flaw in the logic here. The experience with families has shown us the fact that in the absence of adaptive behavior there is almost always a gap in the knowledge repertoire of the family. *They do not know how to behave differently.* To remove their maladaptive behavior is an act of placing them in limbo. They do not know what to do until they are taught (or able to learn) new behavior or are placed in a group with new models where new behavior may be "caught."

The key to changed behavior is the new model practicing more adaptive behavior. The explanation of *how change comes about* in psychoanalytic group therapy is under serious question in light of what we know.

Rational change in behavior is tied to the rate of resolution of resistances and the change from neurotic to rational ideation. The more neurotic, the longer it takes to change behavior.

Unique features include the hierarchial relationship between the leader (analyst) and the group. The authority relationship imposes a state of *dependence* upon the group members. The double bind is imposed as another unique feature. If I accept the dependence, I'm regressing to infantile behavior. If I resist the authority of the leader, it is because I cannot accept authority. There being no other choice, what do I do?

Strengths, Limitations and Modifications

The chief strength in the psychoanalytic group process is the high level of professional preparation required for the analyst to qualify as a group leader. Many of the newer formats for group counseling do not require the rigorous training maintained by psychoanalysts. There is no cop-out accepted here that by definition we can separate *therapy* and *counseling* and therefore shave off much rigorous training required to assure professional competence. If there is a danger in the group-counseling movement today, it is resident in the underprepared *leaders* of groups.

Another factor that group psychoanalysis has may be counted as a strength or limitation depending on your bias and the task the group is to perform. It is the selection of members for the group. Many cannot participate because of the restrictions imposed by most therapists.

Modifications of psychoanalytic method have been progressing for many years. Sullivan (1953) gave one major insight with his interpersonal theory of psychiatry which makes group psychoanalysis a viable concept. It was the idea that each person has a composite of behavior patterns called *dynamisms*. These are largely hidden from the individual but are immediately apparent to others. In a group, the feedback about my behavior from others would be mostly a reflection of these unseen behavior patterns of mine; the process of conscious awareness is greatly enhanced. I have choices where before I was a victim in the interpersonal arena. Sullivan's work was never completed due to his untimely death, so we do not have a method of group work directly from him.

Psychoanalysis in groups has a limited application to school counseling for some quite obvious reasons. Teachers and parents may be able to afford to purchase such therapy for themselves. Other methods are more adaptable to the school arena. The clinic, hospital and private practitioners will undoubtedly continue to employ the theory, techniques, and method.

Existential, Experiential, Logotherapy

Group counseling using existential approaches would require many more pages of text than I plan to devote here. It is necessary to select one example and present an abstract of it—logotherapy.

Viktor Frankl presented his theory and practice of logotherapy in more than a dozen volumes. I will try to present only some of the method and the major ideas contributed to group counseling by Frankl's work. During World War II Frankl was a prisoner in German concentration camps. The experiences with deprivation, persecution, and degradation form a powerful influence in the concepts of logotherapy, Frankl's approach to existential psychotherapy.

The View of Man

Man is, in essence, whatever he is powerful enough to create in himself. He is his existence—his existential self. Essence is an abstraction; existence is concrete. I am the way I behave. But until the life situation comes along to test my behavior, I am resigned to speculate with my potentialities. Frankl thinks he has faced the life situations in concentration camps that let him see his potential. I find the ideas Frankl bases on those experiences the most exciting in the field of group counseling. The task of producing the life situations in group counseling to test the potentials of me or someone else may be beyond the current level of skill. It might even be foolish, supposing we had the skill to do it. The fact is that no volcano will erupt. The experience that reveals my potentials is very benign and extremely humbling, but safe. The myth is in the culture to protect you and me from seeing the truth—the limits (not limitless) of our potential. The myths form the mystique surrounding groups to protect the reality of limited potential. Groups form a vital function in our human organization. If each person who joins a peer group had to share the bare reality of the group's existence in place of the myths of values shared by that group's members, who would join a group?

Group counseling in the existential approaches can be seen to have two main purposes. The capability of revealing to you the potentials you do have, and the capability of helping you learn new behavior to utilize such potentials, are the purposes. The contrast of this idea and other purposes of other psychotherapies must be the greatest difference in the entire field of psychotherapy. From meaninglessness (existential vacuum) to fulfillment in self-actualizing and self-perpetuating behavior, man is in charge of his destiny. The philosophy of man's existence as a pragmatic set of consequences leaves with man the choice of how it is going to be. Frankl's theory of neurosis claims that it does not arise from conflicts among values (moral conflicts), and therefore is basically spiritual, not mental or physical. However you choose to believe, the fact of group remains the same. According to Frankl, man is *not* always in charge of his context, his environment, or milieu; but man is *always* in charge of how he reacts to the life context he finds himself in, whether or not he likes it. The method follows that only man—you—me-other—can be responsible for what *I* do. I must ultimately accept accountability for what choices I make. Once accountability is accomplished, therapy ends. Logotherapy is one method for achieving the above conditions (Frankl, 1955, 1962).

Man can survive most any trauma if he can find meaning in his existence. Without hope, man perishes.

Statement of Theory for Group

Existential group psychotherapy and counseling is based on the assumption that the group is a piece of the whole world. The group is a segment of the world, a microcosm (Hora, 1968). The theory further assumes that behavior learned in a group will transfer to the future life of the behaver. The theory is an idea about the group and its existence rather than a theory about behavior and an individual. The goal is to get the person to understand his particular way of being-in-his world, how it affects others, and in turn, how it affects him.

The group of up to ten members has the size characteristics of an extended family. The family group produces behavior that can last a lifetime. Therefore the family group model is the most powerful model for group psychotherapy.

I would say that to the degree it is possible to match the group and cultural parameters on the relationship dimensions of contract commitment, loyalty, intimacy, or heterogeneity there is the possibility of success in existential group counseling. The technology of existential group counseling is very primitive. The method is almost a *no-method*, no-system approach. Except for logotherapy, the above seems to hold.

Assumptions Supporting Existential Approaches

The assumptions are important to the understanding of any method of psychotherapy and counseling. Existential approaches have even more concern with assumptions. Assumptions are dynamisms. Sullivan (1954) in the psychoanalytic interpersonal theory and method used the concept to explain how each of us integrates with other human beings. Sullivan saw man as an operating self—a composite of behavior patterns called *dynamisms*. Assumptions are like behavior patterns in influencing our behavior. If I am in a group, I want to *be like* everyone else in most all the external protocol. I don't wish to be too different. Assumptions are acquired from the group-culture experience, operate as concepts based on the past, and are used to interpret the present and the future. This means assumptions are usually in conflict with reality at some level all of the time. Existential group counseling assumes the person making assumptions has his thinking (cognition) impaired, and that he is in some degree of disharmony with the world. The dilemma of any man dependent upon assumptions is a kind of double-bind paradox. Therefore it is assumed in order better to confront reality as existence, a pragmatic here-and-now. The tendency in man to apply assumptions may rest with his need for certainty and permanence. If thought is limited by the assumptions made, then no transcendence or healing can occur in existential terms (Hora, 1968). Consequently, if we abandon assumptions from past experience and go with the concept of transcendence, what happens? We have a quick look at the method or the nearest existential approaches come to a method of therapy. The change is in the way we cognize reality. We are no longer stuck with or limited to dichotomies, polarities, and multiplicities characteristic of assumptions. The resolution of the problem is seen to be in the transcendence of it. Going beyond the problem and going outside the limits of assumption in paradoxical double-binding have striking similarities in the dynamics of behavior which follow. For example, I have faced a problem that could not be compromised without doing violence to my self-concept as long as I held to the assumptions defining life as a win-lose dualism. Anxiety departed from my existence the moment I could step beyond the assumptions. I didn't win and I didn't lose, but I could accept the reality with humility because the pride was based on the discarded assumptions. I may become even more of a phenomenologist, except I may have difficulty with the assumptions!

Goals of Treatment

Existential group counseling tries to transcend the thinking based on cause and effect because knowing the cause of my behavior will not change it, or heal it. Healing is the mystery, and I can offer no more reasonable explanation than the abstraction of transcendence. Tele—the teleoanalytic form in Adlerian group counseling and the tele of Moreno's psychodrama—have no more substance than to postulate, predict the future, or describe the past. What is reality *now?* is the question at the very center of the existential stage. Knowing about myself in terms of assumptions is no help. Knowing myself is a help. *Know thyself* is an admonishment from the cultural wisdoms. I find it is the real goal of treatment in existential group counseling. I am left with the wish *to know how* to achieve the goal. Perhaps the answer is to transcend the question and no answer is necessary.

Hora (1968) mentions some eleven transcendence phenomena at the heart of existential group therapy. Frankl (1962) sums up the goal as a search for meaning. I have less difficulty with Frankl's goal concept. The shift to a discussion of logotherapy may yield more structure to follow in trying to find out what existential psychotherapy in groups will look like in action.

The Method of Logotherapy

Logotherapy was developed by Frankl as a method of analyzing existence. His terminology reflects his early studies under Freud. Existential therapy proceeds toward the spiritual, and logotherapy moves out from the spiritual. Existential analysis is a kind of diagnosis, and logotherapy is an actual treatment strategy. I do not wish to belabor the gnat of difference, only the fact of logotherapy as a method is the important point for us here. Spiritual refers to a reason for being, a meaning in life, which gives meaning to each life event. A sick spirit is seen as reflecting a meaningless existence. Frankl goes so far with his idea that he claims a man who has a meaningful existence can survive any trauma short of death itself. If death is inevitable and beyond his control, a man can at least choose how he will die. He is free to choose the attitude he will have to remain an organized (meaningful) personality to the very end. The method of logotherapy and the philosophy of life and the nature of man are highly integrated phenomena. Suffering is the task a man cannot escape. Suffering is unique for each man. Hope for the future provides the will to life; to give up is to die. The way a man meets his fate defines the meaning life has for him. The opportunities are always present even in the concentration camp, where physical existence was completely controlled.

The nature of man is derived from the unity of three phenomena: physical, mental (psychological), and spiritual. The spiritual (meaning) side of man is the guiding conscience of his existence. Man is motivated by a will-to-meaning. This principle is quite unique when compared to the Freudian pleasure principle or the Adlerian will-to-power.

In summary, the basic goal in logotherapy method is to achieve a sense of meaning for the suffering the patient is experiencing. Symptoms are symbols of the meaning for existence and therefore become bearable. The method is unique among psychotherapies in the fact that no *removal* of symptoms is attempted. Likewise, no *removal* of deep-seated *causes* of the symptoms is attempted.

There is no intention here to cover all of the concepts in logotherapy method. The reader is encouraged to go directly to Frankl's writing for more complete study. Group counseling goes beyond the scope of many theories and methods designed originally to explain individual (relationship) phenomena. In my work with family consultation, I found a need for some conceptualization of behavior beyond the simple seeking of pleasure or power. I found it is possible to remove symptoms only to see them return or manifest anew at another level in a previously symptom-free arena of life.

Logotherapy treats the spiritual dimension of man—the meaning of existence. Psychotherapy treats the mind, the psychological dimension of man. In the logotherapy method there is no real separation of mind and spirit. The goal is to get the person to assume responsibility for his behavior. The *freedom* and *responsibility* idea is a central issue in logotherapy and existential therapies. I would go beyond freedom and responsibility to include *accountability.* Accountability to the expectations of the group is the central concept in my theory and practice of group counseling. I combine Mowrer's concepts mentioned in Chapter 10, and Moreno's ideas, add Frankl's "will-to-meaning," and I can see some hope for future understanding of human behavior.

Techniques and the Treatment Formula

Frankl adds a third category to the diagnostic categories of psychoanalytic psychothreapies. The three categories in Logotherapy diagnosis are:

1. Somatogenic—the physical, the psychoses
2. Psychogenic—the mind, the neuroses
3. Noögenic—the spirit, a noögenic neurosis

The diagnoses are never based upon just one category. The idea is that one category is primary and therefore bears the label. Logotherapy treats the spiritual and the existential or human nature of man. The person has potential and the immediate concern is to bring out these latent values. Behavior becomes the object of treatment. Behavior is concrete and can be observed. The contrast with a Freudian goal to make the unconscious conscious is obvious. There is no need to probe a person's secrets.

The treatment formula is a direct attack upon the stupidity of unrealistic assumptions in a person's thinking. The formula has the therapist discover whether the patient sees himself as a *victim* of his destiny. The value or meaning in life is based on the attitude one takes. For example, life is not for pleasure and happiness, because these are consequences of behavior events, not primary goals. Life is existence; death is not existence. The matter of consequence is *how* one exists. Because human life is finite, it will not last forever, so a person must act now. Life is action and cannot be put off.

The nonchoices are crucial to the logotherapy treatment formula. Nonchoices require acceptance. This is what Frankl calls the *attitudinal value.* Because of attitudinal values, life can have meaning to the end of life.

Techniques in logotherapy assume that a simple change in behavior is no change at all, because soon the patient will regress to previous habits and behave the same as before. This is the essential difference between logotherapy and behavior therapy. There is the belief in logotherapy that a change in attitude toward previously neurotic behavior will change the orientation of the person's values in such a way as to sustain change in behavior. Techniques are aimed at reorientation of the person's values, his meaning in life. The ability to *reorient* a person is the therapeutic effect in logotherapy. Reorientation is possible because the human being has the unusual capacity to detach himself from his world or from himself and view his life condition as if it were an object. The dynamics of treatment are based on the assumption that the patient does not need to consciously accept the idea, so that there is no need to debate it with the patient.

The first specific technique of logotherapy is *dereflection*. Dereflection is the simple technique of ignoring the difficult condition or conflict. Success depends upon the ability of the patient to direct attention to positive alternatives and act out on other potential meanings. The technique is to ignore anything beyond your control and become aware of the positive alternatives to act on in order to create or develop new opportunities.

The second technique of logotherapy is *paradoxical intention*. Here the process becomes one in which the preson decides what behavior is troublesome and proceeds to wish for it to happen. As I mentioned earlier when discussing paradoxes in double binds, the effect of prescribing the behavior to be avoided sets up a complex therapy. "Be spontaneous" is a familiar example. I use it to give students a direct experience with a simple paradox. It is impossible to be spontaneous on command because the admonition destroys the meaning of spontaneity. You can try it, with safety, to experience directly the basic dynamic concerned in paradoxical intention. The dynamics in behavior controlled by paradox places the behaver in the position of being engaged in right passivity only if he can bypass wrong passivity. Likewise, dereflection replaces wrong activity with right activity.*

Dereflection and paradoxical intention are complex techniques because the aim is to change a depth phenomenon called *reorientation*. On the surface, the interventions resemble behavioral counseling or behavior therapy. The apparent similarity between dereflection and desensitization is one example. Verbal conditioning seems central to logotherapy because the therapy is conducted through the verbal model. However, logotherapy escapes to abstraction when the discussion moves from the behavior to its explanation. This seems to characterize one controversial issue in the contemporary debate about counseling methods and the strategies for choosing and employing

---

*Ellis, A., 1962. *Reason and Emotion in Psychotherapy.* New York: Lyle Stuart, Inc. Ellis (1962) has built a complete system of counseling and psychotherapy around the paradox created by *prescribing the symptom* through the use of the method of *prestige-suggestion* under the label of Rational-Emotive psychotherapy. The treatment leads the patient to *expect* his behavior to change because he will do as he is admonished to do. The self-fulfilling prophecy is created by the dereflection (ignoring present behavior) and paradoxical intention (prescribing a double-bind) between existing behavior and prescribed behavior. The dynamics of behavior in a small group using logotherapy methods or Ellis' Rational-Emotive treatment are not unlike what Wolpe (1969) uses in his substitution of more adaptive behavior for more certain unadaptive behavior.

techniques. Behavioral counseling (Krumboltz and Thoresen, 1969) is based on the premise that we should use any technique that works. Trial-and-error empiricism is justified if the ends (new behavior) fit the purposes. The active intervention defines the scope of similarity between behavior therapy and logotherapy. I agree with the active intervention posture (Fullmer and Bernard, 1964). In practice, I like to combine the consortium of techniques in behavioral counseling with the theory and rationale of logotherapy. The strategy does fit the theory I set forth in Chapter 3. Logotherapy provides the technique for creating the conditions for encouraging new behavior to form. Behavior therapy provides a systematic methodology for shaping it (once it is formed). This bypasses one of the major complaints about the operant conditioning method application in counseling. Operant conditioning is dependent upon the *chance* appearance of a new behavior. Logotherapy techniques improve the odds (probability) in favor of controlling the appearance of a new behavior. The formula in group counseling incorporates some of the techniques of logotherapy by the way a group and the leader define the rules for interacting. The formula for interacting has a built-in schedule of reinforcement, whether or not it is described.

Strengths, Limitations, and Modifications

Frankl has made some profound contributions to the field of therapy and counseling. If the desensitization and extinction schedules of reinforcement employed in behavior therapy really are dependent upon a changed attitude, then Frankl's (1962) contribution of attitudinal values is profound. Attitudinal values give meaning to life all the way to death. Ungersman (1961) thinks Frankl's contributions to the field of psychotherapy transcends the contributions of most other authorities.

There is an urgency about counseling in the 1970's reflected in the search for methods that seem to work. The criteria for defining what works and why it works, and what are the long-term and short-term consequences, remind me of Blachly's (1969) seduction in the drug-dependencies syndrome. If we are faced, because of the pathology in society, with the task of finding answers to questions even if the question must be reduced to a very limited scope before an answer is found, I fear the creation of a professional St. Vitus' dance. Logotherapy is a method to avoid the limitations of oversimplification. This complexity may be a limitation when we face the task of training counselors to use the techniques and understand the theory behind logotherapy.

The major modification I have found useful is to employ the techniques of logotherapy but stay clear of the verbal model. Hall (1959) points out the effect of behavior in the informal, formal, and technical culture modes. The connection is striking. If the behavior skill is learned, the group may employ paradox in nonverbal models too. The group may use a psychodrama technique to create a paradox in the nonverbal model by simply asking a member to *show* the group through reenactment of a given life event. Such an exposure will surface all of the hidden agendas involved in producing the conflict. The modification employs active intervention techniques necessary to create the conditions for change in behavior. The premise I use is that any action will lead to redefinition of relationships out of which new behavior may form.

Unique Feature

The unique feature in logotherapy is the explanation it holds for behavior. Meaning and understanding are abstractions, like freedom and responsibility. There is some uniqueness in the life experiences of Frankl. He seems to have lived almost all the way to death and returned to share his experiences. The essential mysticism to cover some logical explanation for what we do not know may be excused as another attempt to avoid fatalism and meaninglessness. We do know some things from logotherapy. How might we use paradoxical intention?

System of Group Counseling
Behavioral Group Counseling

Behavior therapy is new enough to have become recognized as a viable system on which to base group counseling method. Eysenck (1970) writes on "Behavior Therapy and its Critics" in the journal of *Behavior Therapy and Experimental Psychiatry.* The editorial board reads like a Who's Who in behavioral counseling and therapy. The method of behavior therapy and/or counseling is by no means unitary. The diversity of techniques and the absence of a unifying theory have led critics to claim it is only a pragmatic exploitation of any technique that seems to work, on the short-term. The removal of a symptom or the "cure" of an alcoholic seem to be brashly lumped together.

There is some defense of the system of behavioral counseling if we keep in mind the recent efforts to get the modern learning principles introduced into the classroom learning, the counselor's office, the social worker's repertoire, the special and exceptional handicapped-student education movement, the mental hospital, and the prison. In the rush, a literature evolved showing the results of systematic research studies of the techniques in action. "Tell me what behavior you want and I'll produce it" became the party line in behaviorism. Some critics like Ivey (1969) think the scope of behavioral counseling is too narrow. Hosford (1969) is in favor of using behavioral counseling. Sorenson (1969) thinks the Hosford presentation of three viewpoints on behavioral counseling is more broad than most theories of counseling. My point in this brief abstract on behavioral group counseling is to alert the student to a promising new development in group work. I wish to make certain the student is alerted to the strong rush of feeling supporting the thinking and the acting of the proponents of behavior psychology (behaviorism) from Watson to Skinner to Hosford. Oversell, like overkill, threatens our loss of a promising *active*-oriented method for counseling before there has been time to get off the polarization (taking sides) infantilism. In recent years I moved away from those against behavioral group counseling because the idea became important in two respects in terms of the research I have been doing. Like Sorenson, I wanted to substitute rigorous research for myth, faith, and superstitution in counseling practice. The reader is being reminded that the "disciples" in the "behavioral revolution" are no less faithful in pushing the attention of all of us toward a new *myth*. However, my lucid moments bring me back to the topic at hand.

First is the need in counseling practice for a direct intervention method. Fullmer and Bernard (1964) published the three I's of counseling—Interrupt, Intervene, and Influence (the behavior of the counselee). The *active* counselor is desired over the *passive* counselor.

Second is a more profound reason for using the behavioral counselor's ideas. Form, the connection between the culture's conditioning and reinforcement schedule, and the behavioral theory and practices match exceedingly well because they are each a piece of the whole. Earlier I mentioned that behavioral group counseling had rediscovered the culture wheel. I meant that what the culture uses in human groups to shape behavior can be simulated in contrived groups. The portion of behaviorism I find useful is the contingency concept and the manipulative principles which, in effect, give a method to the cultural rules and parameters in a group.

The call for specific, observable, and replicated behavior is of some interest. The urge to be scientific in *form* rather than *substance* has no appeal to me. The science of behavior I am interested in is a substance that might take any form. I think the reader should know my bias is somewhat tempered by a disappointment in the proponents of behavioral group counseling for not having developed a unified theory to give substance to the method. Hosford (1969) lends some support to the above lament when he points out in his "rejoinder" that, in practice, it is the technique not the theory that takes precedence. Theory is important too, but not as necessary as a technique that works.

If a technique works, the behavioral counselor sees no need or purpose served by such inferences as *why* a technique works. Critics of behavioral counseling point to the fact that behavior changed by direct manipulation will regress to the earlier pattern as soon as the manipulative force is removed. Change in behavior is discussed under a subsequent paragraph. We mean that a technique works whenever the behavior changes. There is probably no method of counseling that can guarantee permanent change.

The Method

The method in behavior group counseling is primarily a direct attempt to manipulate the environment. The manipulation of an environment covers a broad range of possible specific events in human behavior, from adding one person—a counselor to a group like the family—to the operant conditioning of a specific behavior response in a given individual. Indeed, any stimulus or any response may become the focus. The stimulus-response paradigm is limited by complex behavior because the response becomes the stimulus, and vice versa. Theoretically, the question is always in the middle of a behavior event. You should assume it was learned sometime in the past and proceed because all that is important is the behavior exhibited *now*. "I am the way I behave," is a premise of behavioral group counseling.

The method is contingent upon several major assumptions. Some of the assumptions are:

- Variables that control behavior may be manipulated.
- Manipulation of the variables affecting human behavior will cure a neurosis not create a neurosis.
- Simple learning is the same as classical conditioning as demonstrated by Pavlov.
- Humans learn maladaptive behavior and relearn adaptive behavior by pairing response and reward.
- Neurosis or conditioned fear is learned.
- Most behavior is learned.
- Man develops the capability to mediate his responses. Unlike animals and birds, man can invent new behavior responses.
- Whatever is real behavior is observable behavior.
- Only behavior that is operationally defined and measured by some form of quantified system is of use in behavioral counseling.
- Inappropriate (deviant) behavior and appropriate behavior are learned in the same way.

- The culture parameters or rules determine whether a given behavior is appropriate or inappropriate.
- Desensitization is a process capable of nullifying inappropriate behavior.
- Normal behavior and abnormal behavior are definitions dependent upon the culture's criteria for normal-abnormal (Ullmann and Krasner, 1969).
- Symptom treatment is better strategy than treatment of internal (mystical) causes.
- Objective phenomena are the necessary bases for treating psychotic or neurotic behavior.
- Mental illness is a sick myth (Szasz, 1965).
- Bad habits, maladaptive, inappropriate behavior descriptions are better for use in treatment than abstract nomenclature steeped in mystery.
- Observable behavior is necessary to meet the requirements for research.
- Symptom substitution is impossible (Bandura, 1969).
- Social modeling may enhance the learning of behavior, particularly in cases of gross deficits in behavior.
- Vicarious experience in learning from a model is as potent as direct experience in learning.
- Imitation is the primary force in social modeling.
- Social modeling and imitation may be achieved through symbolic models.

The Goals of Treatment—Changes in Behavior

The key idea in behavioral-group counseling is the fact that, when a new behavior replaces a previous behavior, the entire milieu is changed. My contribution to behavioral-group counseling is indirect because the theory I stated in Chapter 3 is based on the observed behavior changes in family groups whenever *one* member changes his behavior. Watzlawick, Beavin, and Jackson (1967) reported similar evidence from their work with family therapy.

The reason one person has so much impact is based on what the behaviorist defines as the *reward and response schedules*. If one person changes one behavior, every other behavior must respond to a different stimulus. New behavior responses must be learned to cope with a new life situation.

The obvious nature of the above has become the substance of what I mean by saying that interpersonal relationships are redefined by each change in a behavior by each participant. Relationship is an abstract term, but it can be broken up into observable and measurable variables such as social distance (Engebretson, 1970).

Formula and Behavior Change

The formula employed in behavioral-group counseling leads to the phenomenon of self-fulfilling hypotheses by getting the group members to behave in the ways expected by the leader or counselor. A difference does exist in the techniques employed in the formula. The behaviorist uses direct verbal statements to signal the intentions for group-member responses. The group member follows the directions given by the counselor. The counselee tries to respond appropriately in terms of what is expected in the group. The similarity between counselor reinforcement through selective attention and encouraging or discouraging comments is no less a form of verbal conditioning in evocative than in behavior modification formulas. The formula is a schedule for reinforcing behavior desired and ignoring (dereflection) of behavior not desired.

The shaping forces of desensitization schedules of reinforcement are built into the formulas of most group methods and operate whenever behavior *not* desired is practiced by a group member. Assertive behavior is taught by behavioral-group counseling method by employing desensitization techniques (Lazarus, 1968). Desensitization techniques may contribute to the strengthening or weakening of a particular behavior response. The instructions or guidelines given to the group by the leader set up the milieu for manipulation of rewards and responses in systematic ways. Behavior change will come more quickly if the target behavior to be changed is highly specific and operationally defined.

Selection of the Group

Not everyone can profit from behavioral-group counseling. Lazarus (1968) explains the nature of the roles for leader and members. The roles change with the specific nature of the problem being treated. Group members should fit the requirements of the techniques to be employed. Desensitization requires the group give permission for leader-member encounters. Assertive training is mostly a group function with the leader in the background.

The purpose the group is to achieve has a bearing in the selection of participants. There is an opportunity to match persons who have the gross behavior characteristics someone wishes to acquire with the person who wants to learn the behavior. Social modeling makes imitation possible with little more than arrangement to have the persons in the same group. For example, Bandura, Ross and Ross (1961) found that if someone is shy and wishes to acquire more assertive behavior, an aggressive male would be the best model for almost anyone to imitate.

Strengths, Limitations and Modifications

The brash recognition of social modeling and imitation for modifying behavior in group counseling has given a language to a dynamic of most group methods. This strength, coupled with systematic desensitization techniques, makes a potentially powerful new set of approaches to counseling.

The claim by Hosford (1969) is for the profession to recognize a new set of principles and techniques based on *scientific* research. Yet no attempt is made to claim a perfect unity between treatment and cure. The idea of diagnosis is changed to identify goals and specify treatment and evaluate whether or not the goals are achieved. It is a neat formula. Perhaps more professionals should employ it.

The chief limitation seems to be the zest and brashness of the new converts to behavioral-group counseling. There is a tendency to exaggerate and *oversell* the method. The need to be scientific sometimes overshadows the required amount of humility when reporting research studies from a relatively narrow segment of behavioral phenomena (Alper and Kranzler, 1970).

The modifications in behavioral-group counseling a given professional counselor would expect are no doubt dependent upon the philosophical orientation he subscribes to as a basis for the application of theory. If there is a strong emphasis on freedom and responsibility as in existential group counseling, the response to behavioral-group counseling will probably be negative. If there is a strong orientation toward authority domination of the counseling process as in Adlerian group counseling, the response to behavioral-group counseling will probably be more positive. The issue in many instances seems to depend upon the view of man and the nature of behavior subscribed to by the professional. It seems to me that the empirical, trial-and-error, expedient approach used in behavioral-group counseling may be as logically defended as any other approach.

Summary

There can be no complete synthesis for all the methods of group counseling presented here and in Chapter 10. A systesis of the forces manipulated in changing behavior can be achieved. The techniques and the skills to carry on the method seem to be different in nomenclature and stated goal but highly similar in effect. The reason for similarity in effect of a set of techniques rests with the forces being manipulated and the scope of behavior designated as the target for change.

The philosophy underlying the system of psychology that spawns a given method has become less important in group counseling when consideration is given to *outcomes* instead of *process* as the central emphasis. Outcomes may be another level of synthesis for the group-counseling method. The question of whether a technique has scientific verification and the ability to be replicated is important. Behavioral-group counseling proponents have made this test a prime criterion in their work. Frankl and other existentialists spread their blanket of theory and practice with the emphasis upon the ultimate human freedom principles: "I have the power to decide, ultimately, how I will behave."

Psychoanalysis has been influential in the thinking of depth psychologists. The iceberg phenomenon of human behavior holds sway. "Why become concerned with what we can only know by inference?" ask the behaviorists. "Why not deal with what we can observe?" The attempt here is to introduce the student to existing concepts. The more complete coverage of the methods should be taken up in additional reading from the writings of authorities in the respective fields.

Suggested Additional Readings

Hansen, James C., Thomas M. Niland, and Leonard P. Zani, 1969. "Model Reinforcement in Group Counseling of Elementary School Children," *Personnel and Guidance Journal*, 47(8) 741–744 (April).
   A study of groups was conducted to ascertain the effectiveness of models (representing desired behaviors) in changing less desirable behaviors. The authors found that models in group counseling help in the learning of appropriate social behavior. The more socially successful models are more conducive to change in others than either counselors or other low sociometric students. The authors felt their study verifies Krumboltz and Thoreson's (1964, 1967) hypothesis that behavioral counseling can help solve personal problems.
Johnson, Robert L., 1969. "Game Theory and Short-Term Group Counseling," *Personnel and Guidance Journal*, 47(8) 758–761 (April).
   This article contains a description of game theory (Berne, *Games People Play*, 1964), coupled with the advantages and disadvantages as used with prisoners in a Navy brig (unmotivated counselees). Most of the group's members felt that games provide a good description of their behavior, especially self-defeating ones. Games present less threat, allay anxiety by structuring group meetings. The authors thus feel that game theory works well with short-term groups also.
Mayer, G. Roy, Terrence M. Rohen, and Dan A. Whitley, 1969. "Group Counseling with Children: A Cognitive-Behavioral Application," *Journal of Counseling Psychology*, 16(2) 142–149.

Aspects of social learning and cognitive dissonance theory were utilized in counseling with group of elementary children, in an attempt to see if a change in attitudes or behavior occurred. Counselors purposely manipulated circumstances to create dissonance. Often increased group interaction increases dissonance. The authors conclude that changes in counselee behavior and attitudes can result through application of the two theories. Attitudinal and behavioral changes must be simultaneous for maximum growth. Group counseling provides a good environment for creating dissonance because there are present a variety of divergent attitudes and behaviors to model. Group provides sources of reinforcement which facilitate behavioral change.

Tose, D. J., C. Swanson, and P. McLean, 1970. "Group Counseling with Nonverbalizing Elementary School Children," *Elementary School Guidance and Counseling,* 4(4) 260–266 (May).

The primary emphasis has shifted toward prevention of disorders in emotional and behavioral variables of elementary aged children. School counseling has become more important at the elementary school level. The study reported here found that it is possible to increase the verbal responses in previously nonverbalizing youngsters by using social reinforcement through counselor's verbal responses. Many more studies are needed to validate the efficacy of behavioral group counseling. The student may wish to try some controlled-group group counseling similar to the type conducted by Tose et al.

12

Contemporary Group Methods

by Darold E. Engebretson

In 1947, in Bethel, Maine, a new form of group was inaugurated under the auspices of the National Training Laboratories (NTL) Institute for Applied Behavioral Science. The emphasis of the movement was on education and training in contrast to earlier forms of group which were oriented to psychotherapy. In the ensuing quarter-century this movement has generated diverse forms which attempt to help individuals develop more satisfying patterns of interpersonal communication, become more sensitive to themselves and others, and develop more awareness of their impact on others.

This chapter begins with an overview of sensitivity training, to be followed by a greater in-depth examination of some of its more prevalent forms: the T-group, the encounter group, and the marathon, sensory awareness, and video simulation groups or methods.

Sensitivity Training

Lakin (1969) offers "experiential learning" as an appropriate designation for this form of group interaction where the focus is on the individual, interaction patterns and the group process. While the form of sensitivity training varies as a function of leader type, time devoted to group interaction and context, the group members are essentially healthy people* who desire a higher level of functioning and greater interpersonal satisfaction. A laboratory in human relationships would caption the purpose of this enterprise.

*A recent study by Olcl and Snow (1970) questions the validity of this assumption as they found striking similarities between volunteers for sensitivity groups and persons seeking counseling.

Theory Basis

Since practice characteristically precedes theory, it is not unexpected that sensitivity training would follow this sequence. While attempting to establish a theoretical framework, this movement has appropriated such diverse elements as fantasy trips via psychoanalysis, role theory from psychodrama, gestalt principles of perception, group dynamics à la sociometry, learning theory as derived from the laboratory and the classroom, an existentialistic view of man, and management practices from the "marketplace."

While Gibb and Gibb (1969) and Forer (1969a and b) set forth the genesis of a theoretical base, this text offers additional criteria for establishing a functional theory of group.

The position taken in this text stresses the importance of culture and while many of the advocates of sensitivity training acknowledge the shaping effect of culture upon the individual there is, nevertheless, a general failure to appreciate the extent to which cultural parameters delineate the form and occurrence of behavior within each of the various forms of group. For Rakstis (1970), the goal of sensitivity training is the development of honesty, trust and freedom; however, such outcomes are attained only as the individual follows the interaction rules prescribed by the leader and the group. (See the *formula* in Chapter 7.) Such is the pervasiveness of cultural parameters, within the group as well as without.

In the following sections an attempt will be made to delineate some of the differences among selected variations of sensitivity training and to interpret these forms in light of the basic premises set forth in this text.

T-group

The core of sensitivity training is the T (training)-group which is also an experience-base type of learning situation (Paris, 1968). Meeting in a small group environment the T-group operates on the assumption that understanding of oneself and others can best be accomplished through the sharing of perceptions, of self and others, feelings and reactions. This is to be accomplished in the here-and-now. Out of this learning how to learn experience comes the knowledge of self and the dynamics of group interaction which, hopefully, each individual will be able to incorporate in his ordinary life setting to enhance his level of communication skill, increase his ability to help others and to increase the creative productivity of the groups in which he may participate, social or business.

Assumptions about Behavior (Learning)

T-groups basically are learning laboratories and the approach utilized in a given group will be a function of the learning theory of the trainer who is leading the group. Clear lines of demarcation are not in evidence, but there are five fundamental positions which characterize the assumptions of most trainers (Schein and Bennis, 1965).

1. Using Blake's "dilemma-invention-experimentation-feedback" model, learning occurs through problem identification and discovering a resolution by shaping responses through group feedback.
2. Learning occurs as the individual becomes emotionally able to explore his own feelings and attend to similar responses of other group members.
3. Learning occurs as the individual experiences relationship definition through the process of modeling the authentic and congruent behavior of the trainer.
4. Learning occurs as the individual becomes sensitive to and cognizant of the process of gathering data about himself and the group analyzing and interpreting them in the here-and-now—in a phrase, learning how to learn.
5. Learning occurs as unconscious material is surfaced. This is accomplished in the process of group feedback in interaction with the discloser.

Treatment Formula

While a great deal of latitude prevails, T-groups are generally small (10–15 people), unstructured learning situations. Although a leader is present his role is initially limited to stating the purpose of the sessions, i.e., increasing sensitivity to self and others, and then adopting a passive stance. In this ambiguous setting frustration and hostility are usually generated as the group members begin to cope with this nonauthoritarian climate. As members participate their actions and reactions become the data for analysis. In this process focused feedback is the principal tool. The familiar (meeting in a group) becomes strange (no appointed leader); the certain (role definition) becomes ambiguous (Do I lead or follow?); and reality (my self-perception) is disconfirmed (Is *that* how he sees me?).

After the original dilemma (how to get started) has been resolved other such "problems" are created in the ongoing interaction or they are created by the trainer. As the cycle continues, greater sensitivity is the desired goal.

The above sequence is the agenda even though the time format of the laboratory may vary from three hours, a mini-lab, to a two-week training schedule. It should also be noted that the sequencing is consistent whether in a T-group where the primary focus is on the organization or in a training laboratory where personal development is emphasized.

Openness and straightforwardness are the acceptable behaviors during this interaction, and the leader may serve as such a model, especially at the beginning of the laboratory.

Goals of Treatment

For Schein and Bennis (1965) T-group experiences aid the individual in gaining a more authentic self-knowledge, an increased understanding of the processes that facilitate as well as hinder a productive group atmosphere, a greater familiarity with group dynamics, including interpersonal interactions, and greater facility in diagnostic skills in the interpretation of individual, group, and organizational behaviors. Bradford (1964) summarizes the goals as (1) learning how to learn, (2) learning how to give help, and (3) developing effective group membership.

While goals vary as a function of the group's composition, hierarchical ordering of such goals is established in relation to the primary emphasis, i.e., organizational functioning in the T-group and personal development in the training laboratory.

Interventions Used in Treatment

While time is a factor in deciding the number and type of learning experiences offered (a "group" may last three hours, over the weekend, two weeks, or several weeks), the T-group interaction session is basic. Group confrontation centered on a "dilemma" is fundamental in this schema. Lecture materials may also be presented to further the understanding of theory. Paired interviews are common (Kemp, 1970c) and multiple role playing followed by rebuttal may also be used (Whitman, 1964). Most sessions will also include demonstrations and opportunities for role rehearsals (Stock, 1964).

The goal is to provide such experiences that facilitate self-awareness, awareness of others, and how these two factors contribute to group effectiveness.

Leader's Role

Whether the leader is called a process observer (Thomas, 1968) or a trainer (Benne, 1964) he has the dubious task of being a democratic authoritarian. Actually, the trainer is not considered a group member (Bradford, 1964), although he can facilitate movement in the beginning by consciously serving as a model for self-disclosing (Culbert, 1968a). Benne (1964) offers the most descriptive definition of the leader as an ambiguous authority figure who serves as a projection screen for the group members.

Throughout the sessions the trainer has the responsibility of helping members examine the group process, clarifying, interpreting and offering suggestions (Kemp, 1970a), while encouraging the data flow (Bradford, 1964). This latter function includes the lecture and visual aid materials that may be utilized. While the here-and-now is of central concern, the trainer facilitates a shift into the there-and-then arena by assisting the group members in applying what they are learning to the job situations they will face after the group has terminated.

Among the sensitivity groups, the T-groups which are affiliated with NTL have high professional standards for their trainers. Advanced degrees plus supervised training are normative.

Member's Role and Group's Role

One of the assumptions of T-grouping is that a democratic group is a viable, productive, and satisfying experience (Kemp, 1970b). Business, education and other professional titles are not respected within the group.

While group members are to provide feedback no pretense of total honesty is made (Paris, 1968). Since education, not therapy, is the goal, group members can readily provide the psychological security necessary for mutual awareness training.

Change in Behavior

Stock (1964) reports that many research programs indicate change for 60–75 percent of those who participate in T-groups. She suggests caution in interpreting these figures as self-reports are generally the data source.

Among the variables appearing to have a functional relationship to change are level of anxiety, degree of tolerance for dissonance, degree of perceived threat, emotional climate of the group, and expectancy set at the beginning of the group.

Ongoing research concentrates in two areas of inquiry: specific techniques such as feedback, and testing specific phases of learning theory which have been utilized in T-groups. The reader is referred to Chapter 8 for an alternate approach to the study of group.

Rate of Change

Campbell and Dunnette's (1968) review of the literature on T-group research indicated that out of 37 studies of outcomes, 23 used internal criteria, i.e., measures which were related to the content and process of the training. However, research on the more important criterion of job performance is equivocal. Miles (1965), for example, found only a moderate relationship (.55) between changes as reported by trainers and observable changes on-the-job. If, therefore, internal criteria continue to be the prevailing measures, rate of change will be an esoteric exercise.

Special Techniques

While concern for feelings predominate in most forms of sensitivity training, in T-group the cognitive input (lectures, explanation of theory, visual aids) is an additional feature which helps to create a more balanced program. With this exception, T-group utilizes confrontation and feedback which are the major tools in the other sensitivity-group forms.

In recent years videotaping is often included and experimentation with instrumented T-groups (Bradford et al., 1964) has evolved. This latter innovation is a trainerless structure which uses programmed materials.

Unique Features: Pro and Con

On the positive side of the ledger, T-groups have the largest body of research of any group form. This thoroughness is also reflected in the professional training which NTL certified trainers must acquire. Also impressive is the dedication to democratic societal ideals—for the individual, the group, and the organization. While these positive attributes are notable, there are other factors which are vital to the development of a group approach which will produce significant and perduring behavior changes. First of all, the lack of theory is delimiting; however, the advocates of T-group are aware of this deficiency and are engaged in attempts to rectify this condition.

Questions concerning transfer of training, however, cannot be glossed over so lightly. As noted by Eitington (1968), the T-group and the work environment are vastly different and the respective models are not mutually interchangeable. Schein and Bennis (1965) in their discussion of psychological safety within the group note some of the differences between the group and work scenes. First, the group members work together according to the T-group formula in the training program for relatively long periods of time; second, the culture or climate within the group is more supportive; and third, all group members know that the training program is of limited duration.

Basic in this text is the concept that each context (culture) has its parameters (formula or rules) which delimit the behaviors appropriate to that setting. As Ohlsen (1970) suggests, role expectations are generally met by the assigned individual(s). Simply stated, the rules "at work" and in the T-group are not the same. Therefore, transfer of training has this additional concern. Secondly, as noted by Schein and Bennis (1965), time that trainees spend together in the program is a significant factor in behavior change. This raises a question of procedure—what might happen on-the-job if the T-group training were to be incorporated directly into the work situation with a consultant-trainer, for lack of a more descriptive term, working with the entire group (system) or personnel? Too ambitious? I wonder.

Encounter Groups

Beymer (1970) raises the plea for standardization of nomenclature in the field of group work, noting that the proliferation of labels has created a semantic disaster area. Beginning in 1947, with the National Training Laboratory in Bethel, Maine, there has been a succession of encountering experiences within groups variously tagged sensitivity training, encounter workshop, T-group, or lab group. To add to the confusion the numerous types of groups are utilized in a wide variety of settings including churches, schools, and places of business, as well as in clinics, hospitals, and college counseling centers. While commonalities exist across these groups, in this section the focus is on what Rogers (1967) calls the basic encounter group. Having participated in an intensive one-week workshop in 1950, Rogers began to use this approach in his group work.

As the name implies, this group attempts to create an atmosphere in which people can encounter each other at depths greater than those generally found in usual interactions. Toward that goal a pragmatic approach is taken, i.e., use what seems to work. As Rogers (1967) states, the theoretical concepts employed range across client-centered, Gestalt, Lewinian, and even psychoanalytic theory. Art production and sensory awareness techniques are also utilized at the discretion of the facilitator or trainer (group leader). While its principal deficiency is the lack of an integrative theory, Forer (1969b) makes a notable beginning toward such a goal. (The reader is referred to this source for the author's complete statement.)

Surveying the adherents of this approach, it would seem that twentieth-century man is experiencing existential neurosis (Burton, 1969b) which is manifested in alienation, fear of absorption, and a lack of meaningful interpersonal communication (Haigh, 1967). Auditing man at the feeling level reveals a preponderance of liabilities and unrealized asset potential. Encounter groups, then, are designed to help free the frozen assets through an experience of emotional investments (risks) expecting the return rate to influence the individual's continuation in such a program until he has realized his maximum growth potential.

Assumptions about Behavior

Burton (1969a) describes the encounter group as a microcommunity and later (1969b), suggests that this same group is a significant alteration of the cultural norm. In my words, the behavior of the people is comparable to the larger community, but the subcultural rules (of the encounter group) facilitate a different expression within that group.

Behavior is seen in terms of psychosocial development in that the individual's growth may be aborted, fixated or facilitated, depending on the nature and magnitude of environmental influence. From birth the individual begins to develop a self structure through a process of introjection (Forer, 1969b). This structure is shaped by the perceptions and reinforcements of persons significant to the developing person which are internalized forming the self.

As the person develops, the self structure often congeals prematurely which inhibits the proactive organism rendering the person less willing to take risks, defending against vulnerability, and, in general, closing himself off to experiences that involve change or ambiguity. Fear and defensive behavior result. These consequents are in direct conflict with man's need for self-acceptance and interfere with his attempts to gain social nourishment (Forer, 1969a). Alienation is the result.

Treatment Formula

The encounter group focuses on personal growth rather than healing of the sick (Schutz, 1967). Meeting in groups of 6–12 people the focus is on self-disclosure in terms of both self-revelation and personal perception in feedback. Such disclosure is considered essential if a deep interpersonal relationship is to develop (Culbert, 1968). This process of radical disclosure is called *confrontation* (Rogers, 1967).

While group structure is at a minimum and freedom of expression is encouraged, each group member has knowledge of the rules, i.e., self-disclosure through confrontation, and experiences a reduction in self-esteem should he fail to interact in the prescribed manner (Vosen, 1966). Further, each individual seeks social reinforcement, and this adds an additional impetus toward leveling, or confrontation.

Goals of Treatment

Basic to the individual and the group is the development of trust; this is essential (Gibb, 1965). To complete the tetragram (TORI) of Gibb and Gibb (1969), openness, realization, and interdependence need to be included as goals.

As a consequence of encountering, the following are desired changes: fear altered by trust, lines of communication becoming more open, dependence changing to self-determination and interdependence (Gibb & Gibb, 1969), movement toward realization of potential (Schutz, 1967), heightening of self-awareness (Stoller, 1969), enhancing self-understanding and relating more effectively in everyday life (Rogers, 1967).

Interventions Used in Treatment

While sensory-awareness techniques and experiences (exercises) are often utilized (Schutz, 1967), the primary tool of basic encounter is confrontation (Rogers, 1967). This "leveling" process involves self-revelation for both the discloser and the reactor. Culbert (1968) sets forth important criteria for this type of interaction:

1. Interactants anticipate (predict) reciprocal levels of self-disclosing.
2. The nature and intensity of such self-disclosing is negotiated within the context of a relationship.
3. A relationship evolves norms for its continuation.
4. To be appropriate the self-discloser is guided by the established norms, of which he must be aware.

Rogers (1967) comments that often the behavior changes observed during group encountering do not seem to persist, i.e., continue on when the person resumes his life in the larger community. Culbert (1968b) seems to support the position of this text in asserting that the reason these changes don't continue is that the rules of interaction change from the context of the subculture (encounter group) to those of the society (culture) at large.

As Culbert (1968b) suggests insufficient reality testing is a function of insufficient self-disclosures; however, as stated above, the reality of the group and the reality of the world outside do not have a unitary correlation relationship. Perhaps the confrontation suggested by Mowrer (1964) offers greater hope for man as he seeks to move toward self acceptance and fulfillment.

Leader's Role

The group is convened by a facilitator or trainer who has the task of assisting in the expression of both feelings and thoughts of the members (Rogers, 1967). Since freedom within the group receives high priority the leader does not take the sole responsibility for setting directions or goals; however, as Beymer (1970) asserts, leaders cannot ignore their responsibility for what takes place during these sessions, as some have done. Further, the leader functions as a model independent of his willingness to assume that function.

Jourard (1964) states that there is a curvilinear relationship between self-disclosure and mental health. If we consider the act of self-disclosure to be an invitation to relationship, then Jourard's thesis can be readily understood. For example, to disclose very personal self-knowledge at the beginning of an initial encounter is to invite the other person(s) to reciprocate at the same level, to become intimate. However, if the mental health of the individuals so invited is such that intimacy is threatening, the one who extends the invitation is also perceived as threatening (unsafe). On the other hand, to minimally disclose conveys a message of indifference, i.e., no overture of intimacy. A person in such an act can also be perceived as unsafe because the risk is too great that rejection will result if "I" commit "myself" to someone who is indifferent toward "me." The net result in either circumstance is alienation, a deficiency in mental health. From my experience this is especially important when the group is initially convened. Therefore it would appear that the facilitator should have sufficient professional training and supervised experience to be able to incorporate this understanding into the group process.

Member's Role and Group's Role

Each member of the group has the responsibility for setting the directions and the goals of the group. If successful this will result in a creative amalgamation of personal goals (Gibb and Gibb, 1967). Since a shared goal exists, that of seeking social nourishment, a common dependency is created which provides power for effecting change (Forer, 1969a).

Confrontation and focused feedback assume the greatest measure of each group member's responsibility. These are the formal rules of this subculture, and the informal rules are developed as the encountering proceeds.

Change in Behavior

As a criterion of change Bales (1950) suggests that we consider what occurs between persons rather than attempting to ascertain what is taking place within the individual. The interpersonal model offers more reliable data. With this measure the focus is on observable rather than intervening or subjective variables. Self-acceptance, for example, is only a meaningful change when it is demonstrated in the quality of relationships with others. Spontaneity, Rogers (1967) suggests, is a change that is readily observable. Such behavior is of greater assessment value than any self-report (Zimpfer, 1967).

As Rogers (1967) observed, change is often of short duration; however, the reason for this seems clear: short-term contacts cannot provide the intimacy that requires development over time. Problems are resolved not in momentary intimacies but in long-term relationships. This statement is compatible with the position set forth in this text.

Rate of Change

In addition to the individual variables which influence direction and rate of change, Rogers (1967) underscores two significant factors: *commitment* to relationships and the group's *permission* to engage in facilitative encountering. Both of these factors have a functional relationship to the development of the "we" feeling essential for a change in affective interaction. The degree of peer acceptance (social reinforcement or nourishment) is a more reliable measure of change than the expressed individual evaluation (Zimpfer, 1967).

Selection of the Group

As with most of the group forms mentioned in this chapter, self-selection is the usual entrance procedure. This, however, can lead to the hula-hoop phenomenon of group (Beymer, 1970). To prevent this experience from becoming another fad, it will be necessary to exercise professional judgment and responsibility in the area of screening.

Special Techniques

Leadership style, arena for encountering, and group-member characteristics are tremendously varied, providing an almost unlimited opportunity for the exploration of human diversity in encountering others.

Such diversity, however, makes it difficult to develop meaningful evaluation procedures and precludes assessment of the various techniques which are being utilized.

Strengths and Weakness

In addition to the problems of research mentioned previously, Burton (1969) suggests that this type of group appeals mainly to the middle class, who tend to internalize their problems. This preference predominates for group members as well as for facilitators (leaders). While this phenomenon restricts the application of this group approach, its greatest deficiency lies elsewhere.

Bates' (1968) article on "groupsmanship," while being a humorous discourse, nevertheless clearly illustrates that this subculture has its own rules which govern the form and content of the interactions. If one participates according to these rules, the outcomes are predictable *within this context.* Burton (1969a) also noted that in the framework of the analyst's office the patient generally fulfills the expectations of the therapist. In both of these arenas rules are learned which are context-specific. Generalization to other contexts is then a function of degree of similarity. The "old pro" typifies this stereotype.

As Rogers (1967) has indicated the most significant aspect of the encounter group is its *potency.* To this I utter a loud Amen. Groups are potent. Family and peer groups are awesome on this dimension, and we need to look closely at them to discover the potency therein. It is hoped that this text is a step in that direction.

The Marathon

In 1963, Dr. Lehner of U.C.L.A. conducted a sensitivity laboratory for professionals and business executives which Dr. Frederich Stoller attended. Out of this experience came an appreciation for group interaction which continued beyond the time parameters of traditional forms of group. It was felt that the massed experiences not only changed the quality of the psychotherapeutic approach but also permitted change to occur at a more rapid rate (Stoller, 1968). The "weekend" which characterizes this form has been labeled "accelerated interaction" (Stoller, 1966), a form of marathon group.

Statement of Theory

The proponents of the marathon group claim a view of man which is different from that implied, or stated, by other group theorists. Man need not be understood by self or others, in terms of insight, but rather needs to be reacted to and to become aware of the nature of, including his contribution to, that reaction (Stoller, 1968). The marathon, then, is not a treatment form but an experiential learning unit (Bach, 1966) which makes one-trial learning a possibility (Stoller, 1968). Personal experience in honest self-presentation followed by straightforward feedback (leveling) enables man to dissolve his usual game of role playing, to rely less on his defense structure, to become more willing to risk rejection, and decrease his need to manipulate others for acceptance or self-esteem. The ultimate goals are seen as an appreciation for interdependence and an increased capacity for intimacy (Bach, 1968).

Assumptions about Behavior

Adherents to the marathon approach suggest a reappraisal of man, how he learns, what he needs to learn, and what conditions or experiences enhance this learning. As a basis for this reevaluation, the following assumptions are set forth.

1. Direct experience in the here-and-now is of greater value than a thorough understanding of previous behavior.
2. Each person has a preconceived gestalt for his actions which, in normal social interaction, are ambiguously related to consequent reactions.
3. Learning occurs in whole units, i.e., action, reaction, subsequent reaction.
4. Behavioral patterns become fixed and delimit the individual's repertoire.
5. Incompetent social behavior is a function of the lack of exposure to appropriate models and an incomplete feedback network.
6. Accommodation in personal interaction fosters repressed anger and hostility.
7. What *I* am, *you* see, i.e., the actions you observe is a representative sample of my total behavioral functioning.
8. Defensive behavior acts as a barrier to intimacy.
9. Experience, not time, is the prominent agent for change.
10. Individual perceptions remain distorted without feedback (reality check).
11. Interdependence, rather than autonomy, is basic for man.

Treatment Formula

A recurring theme in this text is that each form of group has its own characteristic or patterned formula which facilitates the members in the establishment and maintenance of the relationship(s) over time. The consistency of such patterning is no less true for the marathon group than for any of the other forms which are reported here.

As a subculture, the marathon group utilizes the technical learning model (Hall, 1959) in an attempt to reach the goal of intimacy concomitant with acceptance of interdependence. The key ingredient is time —*kairos* (quality of time), not *chronos* (linear time). Time is telescoped by means of the explicit rules, i.e., parameters of interaction. By this delineation, the group avoids the trial-and-error method of discovering the reinforcement schedule with which the members operate. A unified system is introduced. In this manner the marathon group is akin to traditional societies wherein the behavioral expectations (and rewards) are at the level of each member's awareness. He does what he has learned (been instructed) to do, and earns rewards according to the self-fulfilling prophecies. The formulae share a common function under both conditions.

Honest self-presentation in the here-and-now is the genesis of intimacy and an experience in interdependency. In reaction to this disclosure, the other members respond to the initiator as a person, and not to the verbal message he conveyed. This in turn prompts a counterreaction of how *I* respond to *you* responding to *me*. Throughout this process, which continues until someone else gains the focus of the group's attention, the participating members have an opportunity, through feedback, to appraise their self-perception as well as to reevaluate their prediction of the others' perception of him.

In this feedback exchange the reality principle operates—that is, the initiator is responsible for maintaining the level of interaction. Since "no holds barred" is the rule of the game, the initiator experiences openly what he generally fails to encounter because of accommodation which is practiced within the larger society. No pretense of "being nice" is acceptable. Such a response is earned as a consequent of appropriate eliciting behaviors, not the goodwill of fellow group members.

Within the group, crises events form the loci for interaction. Initially, the crises evolve out of the concern *I* have for how I will come across to *you*. This massing of tension is seen as essential for movement to occur. Tension continues as *I* await *your* reaction to me. In the movement toward increasing levels of intimacy, tension is always present, motivating the group to continue. Within the larger society one could, and usually does, withdraw. Here, however, one cannot without violating the rules of the subculture. We need not dwell on the repercussions of such action, socially or psychologically.

For Bach (1966), time is an important component in developing the learning climate of the group. By providing Ten Marathon Commandments, Bach (1966) continues a tradition which, though centuries old, had been designed for the same function—provide the cement that adheres social interaction, allowing relationships to develop.

The original Marathon Commandments, through rigid attention to the formula by its adherents, lost sight of the goal of intimacy and interdependency, becoming instead growth-negating, dependency-producing, restrictive, and in want of fulfillment. A later interpreter was necessary to remind them that the formula, apart from its relationship context, could not be functional or therapeutic (relationship development).

While the above sounds apocalyptically ominous, the intent was to underscore the premise that interaction formulas which are contextually incongruent with cultural rules of the larger society may be and often are of debilitating consequences. The Marathon Man who attempts to transport the rules of the group to the society-at-large has the experience which is akin to the Samoan who enters the Hawaiian culture—separation, mistrust, misunderstanding and alienation.

Goals of Treatment

In brief, the goal is not a cure for individual members, but self-exploration by everyone. By establishing an intimate group, the individual has the opportunity to discover the incongruity of self-perceptions and perceptions of others, to become more open, to gain interpersonal closeness and to distinguish intention from actions. Specifically, the following learning tasks are the objectives:

1. To relate *my* actions to their subsequent responses.
2. To appraise *my* goals in terms of present behavior.
3. Through the leveling process, to gain experience in responding as coequal with others.
4. By honest self-presentation and straight feedback, to become safe for continuing interaction (trust).
5. Recognize, cognitively and behaviorally, that honest aggression leads to intimacy, not alienation.
6. By being responsible for my behavior I create opportunities rather than passively accommodating the "natural flow" of life events.
7. Loosening of defensive posture allows for greater available constructive energy to cope more creatively with present situations.

Interventions Used in Treatment

Since the group is to be a microcosm of the world-at-large, it attempts to incorporate similar features. One example is the reliance on *group pressure* wherein all members are coequal and coresponsible for what transpires during the marathon. All group members are to participate in the *leveling* process which is focused feedback to the individual who is telling his "story." In this exchange erroneous self-perceptions and perceptions of others can be altered.

Using common *crises events, my* anxiety in interaction with *you,* the individual experiences change, has the opportunity to experiment and practice in the here-and-now while sharing in the creation of the learning culture of the group (Bach, 1966).

Leader's Role

While the leader is to be coequal with the other members, the role expectancies (a cultural phenomenon which spills over from the larger community) do not allow for this equality. Gluckson (1968), in stressing the importance of the leader, quotes Albert Schweitzer in asserting that modeling by the teacher (leader) is not only of great significance but is his sole function. This seems to be supported by research findings which indicate that the skilled leader facilitates a greater number of peak experiences and is readily modeled by group members (Gurman, 1967).

In the initial contract, agreed upon in advance, the leader's role is clear in that he is the one who specifies the rules of order and makes the major decisions (Stoller, 1968). The skill of the leader will greatly influence the outcome of the marathon session(s).

Member's and Group's Role

In making the original contract to enter the group, the individual has made an initial commitment to change. This begins by initiating honest self-presentation and, in turn, being an active reactor to the self-presentations of others. He further has the coresponsibility of functioning as cotherapist.

The group is charged with two primary functions: provide focused feedback (individual perceptions) to the presenter, a reaction to him as a person, and keeping the imitator honest (leveling). While the group can make decisions as to when to take breaks, etc., it is ultimately the leader who has the final word.

Change in Behavior

While claiming changes, both immediate and long-term, in the ways of communicating and engaging others is made for those who have participated in marathons (Stoller, 1968), another researcher, Weigel (1968), found no differences between counseling and discussion groups, both of which were run under marathon conditions.

The changes which are deemed desirable are:
1. Honest self-presentations and reactions.
2. Increased risk taking in interpersonal relations.
3. Improved ability to utilize aggression.
4. Remaining in encounters without withdrawing.
5. Learning to dissolve role addictions.
6. Increased capacity for intimacy.
It appears that the difficulty to date is the attempt to define more clearly the behavioral and cultural inputs for these categories.

Rate of Change

Members of the marathon group are largely self-selected, which predisposes the group to divergencies in social competencies, degree of intrapersonal difficulty, differing levels in ability to self-reveal, and dissimilar rates in resolution of crises. The literature reveals an 80 percent response rate of positive reactions to this experience; however, the magnitude or duration of the change is not known. It would appear that those entering the group have an expectancy set for what is to be accomplished by the time of termination. Emphasizing this point, Stoller (1968) states that, surprisingly, a sense of closure is regularly attained when termination is eminent.

Stating this another way—within the larger culture the amount of change is a function of the time and opportunity available for that change to occur. For the marathon, it would appear that this cultural phenomenon is functioning assisted by the treatment formula which allows for, rather than demands, change.

Selection of the Group

Self-selection is the usual entrance procedure in which the noviate must convince the leaders of his desire for change (Bach, 1966). Accomplishing this, he then joins with ten to fourteen others for the marathon experience.

Groups may be comprised of students, managers in business, married couples or couples contemplating marriage (Stoller, 1968). Experimentation continues on the benefits of this experience for people from other life situations.

Special Techniques

While not the exclusive domain of the marathon approach, the time factor (24–48 hours) is one of its most distinguishing characteristics. In this block of time, tension is massed, fatigue lowers defenses, and continuously straight feedback (leveling) is demanded. In this setting the accent is on experience, not mere cognition or insight.

Unique Features

In terms of its strengths, the marathon experience attempts to foster personal responsibility for each individual. Insofar as it is successful, on this dimension, this experience approximates the nongroup world. In contrast to the "real" world, the subculture of the group provides straight feedback, which is not common in the interactions that occur beyond its boundaries. Another positive aspect of the marathon group is the opportunity it provides for experimentation with new behaviors. This feature enables the individual to gain, experientially, a better understanding of the relationship between his action and the reaction of others. In recent years this learning has been enhanced by the use of videotape feedback (see section on video simulation).

The limitations of marathon warrant considerable attention by its practitioners. Perhaps the greatest problem is the difference between the rules of marathon and those of the larger community. Specifically, the formula utilized in the marathon does *not* apply for the individuals once they leave this context. In fact, to attempt to use this formula beyond the confines of the group is to invite suspicion, ostracism, and alienation. Also, the marathon tends to develop a symbolism (language) which to the uninitiated is at best mystical. This barrier not only hinders research efforts, but also promotes anti-intellectualism (Beymer, 1970).

Having participated in such groups, I have felt the emotional intensity that can be generated, leading to peak experiences. However, to seek such heightened states as an end in themselves can become a quest akin to that of Ponce de Leon.

Sensory Awareness

In presenting a format for the discussion of the various types of group, it was inevitable that such an approach would coerce a particular system into an apparent straightjacket. Such is the case with sensory awareness, which has been pioneered by Bernard Gunther in his Esalen Institute at Big Sur, California. McMahon and Campbell (1969) in their book *Please Touch* seem to capture the theme of his work by writing that life is to be experienced, celebrated, in each and every life event whenever and wherever it occurs.

It is Gunther's position that contemporary man has lost touch with his basic senses (no pun intended) and therefore is not celebrating life in its fullest. With the advent of Sputnik, man's attention has been focused on cognitive functioning, towards technological improvement and, as a consequence, the "feeling" man has been left behind. Thus Gunther sees a need to reawaken the concern for developing the total organism, man in all his senses, to rediscover the joy of being (Schutz, 1967).

While sensory awareness is without a clear theoretical foundation, it posits a developmental understanding of the gradual insensitization of the senses. To understand this progression, it is necessary to look within the culture and examine it at the formal level of learning (Hall, 1959). Boys, for example, are taught to inhibit the behavioral expression of an emotional response. A mother says to Johnny, a four-year-old, "Big boys don't cry." To Jane, a frolicking nine-year-old climbing a tree, "That's for tomboys!"

Gunther (1968), citing a report by Sidney Jourard on his trip to Europe, comments that there is also a difference in touching, culturally. In Europe, friends touched at the rate of 100 times per hour, while in Midwest United States the frequency dropped to 3. It has been stated that the United States has a noncontact culture. In fact, relationship between dyads has been defined by the physical distance they maintain (Engebretson and Fullmer, 1970). One could speculate that this phenomenon is related to the myth of rugged individualism—remaining apart from and independent of others—but the point being underscored is the lack of concentration on the basic senses which is part of the American cultural expression. It is in this setting that Mr. Gunther sees the need to regain a "feeling individualism."

Assumptions about Behavior

Man is endowed with senses of touch, smell, taste, sight and hearing, but it is known that sensory thresholds and ranges vary according to the culture of the individual. Sensory awareness, then, is a method for reorientating the individual to an earlier life state, prior to the accumulation of cultural influences which shaped, or restricted, the individual's ability to finely discriminate the sensory input. The following assumptions reflect Mr. Gunther's emphasis:
1. Sensory input is culturally integrated (received).
2. Sensory deprivation results in disorientation, disassociation and hallucinations.
3. Sensory stimulation influences rate of growth and the total life process (e.g., marasmus).
4. Man is basically proactive—he seeks stimulation.
5. DIS/ease is the expression of continuous tension.

6. Tension is produced by the individual from within, not from sources outside.
7. Inhibition of the behavioral aspect of emotional responses has been learned in direct experiences (disinhibition also must be learned by direct experience).
8. Spontaneity loss is a function of controlled muscular contractions which results in mistrust of one's organism.
9. Language separates the actor from the action, i.e., "I injured my foot" is different from "I hurt" (experience pain).
10. Tension inhibits man's productivity and creativity.

Treatment Formula

In that sensory awareness is a method for regaining sensory sensitivity, it is not, strictly speaking, a therapeutic form of group; rather it is seen as an adjunct to therapy, education, work, and religious groups. Since man has already developed his verbal and cognitive skills, the accent is on nonverbal forms of intra- and interpersonal communication.

Experiences, i.e., exercises, are programmed for individuals, dyads and/or entire groups; however, the area of concentration is the increase of sensitivity of each individual. Experiencing in a group does not alter this basic goal. Since these experiences occur in a group setting, the usual group pressures operate toward conformity, sharing of experiences, and the like.

Goals of Treatment

In a phrase, the goal is for each person to become a "total organism," fully receiving and appreciating the sensory input in any moment of time. Again, in the words of McMahon and Campbell (1969), to be really *me*, free and fully human.

Rather than training the intellect (making "sense") Sensory Awareness strives to develop the expression of "non-sense," i.e., to reduce excessive thought, to release tension and to promote direct sensory-reality. If successful, the individual is freed from his conditioned states of tension and is then enabled to respond more openly and completely to the immediate tasks which confront him. This state Gunther (1968) has labeled "Optimal Tonus."

Interventions Used in Treatment

Basically the experiences (exercises) are divided into four treatment procedures:

1. Learning to relax.

2. Experiencing—becoming aware that you are the source of the tensions.
3. Identifying the somatic areas of tension, how they are caused and continued.
4. Letting go, which is to fully experience the tension without trying to avoid it (Gunther, 1968).

For the individual the following experiences are to reawaken and stimulate sensitivity:

Tapping
Slapping
Yelling
Arm or leg shaking
Arm or leg lifting
Pillow rock

Also, micro-meditations or mini-sensory experiences:

Orange A-peeling
Hand washing
Cigarette smoking
Sound listening
Use of subordinate hand
One-eyeing
Silent meal
Smellon
Blind shower
Rock experience
A new familiar room
Sense walk

Intimate games for married or engaged couples:

Back talk (nonverbal)
Head knowing
Palm, head and/or arm dance
Foot washing
Foot conversation
Exchange shampoos

Group games:

Slapping, shaking, lifting
Back knowing
Passing in a circle
Blind walk
Under the sheets
Om chant
Bread ceremony
Gunther hero sandwich

Leader's Role

The leader is responsible for issuing the instructions for the experiences (exercises), usually demonstrating (modeling) before the group begins. For the more common experiences, such instructions may be placed on tape. The leader, generally, does not become a group member as he has the task of observing, correcting and assisting those who are participating in the experiencing.

Member's Role and Group Role

During the micro-meditations, focus is on the individual as he seeks to reorient his sensory perception; thus this phase is intrapersonal. The group games accent interpersonal relations and provide opportunities for shared reactions to the experiences. Such sharing provides the basis for whatever group cohesion that develops. Reality checks evolve out of the comparison of these subjective reactions.

The contract which permits group interaction is the individual's assent to participation and sharing. The games are the means.

Change in Behavior

Wolpe (1958) notes that anxiety is the result of conditioning to intrinsically nonthreatening stimuli within one's environment. To cope with the resulting tension, techniques involving relaxation responses, systematic desensitization and respiratory responses were developed. While sensory awareness does not incorporate Wolpe's systematic methodology, comparable techniques have been instituted which are designed to enable the individual to cope more effectively with his tensions.

The lack of a systematic approach precludes acquisition of data necessary to substantiate changes in behavior. However, self-reports by participants would suggest lessening of tensions and increased sensitivity.

Rate of Change

Since the goal of sensory awareness is to increase the depth of sensitivity, the criterion for change is basically a subjective evaluation; thus, empirical evidence would be difficult to establish. Nonverbally, it would be possible to detect a more relaxed state and a greater receptivity for experimentation by a given individual, but to determine differences in rate of change is beyond the present level of competence for this group.

In general, it would be assumed that rate of change would be a function of degree of initial tension(s), amount and type of experiencing (exercises), ability to relax and degree of participation.

Selection of the Group

As in the marathon groups, the members are generally self-selected, although some are referred by therapists who endorse this approach as an adjunct to the continuing treatment program.

While serving on the staff of the Counseling Center at the University of Hawaii, I participated in such experiences which were conducted by a colleague who had visited the Esalen Institute. Additional sessions were held for students and faculty on campus as well. Students reported that some professors in the Art and Communication Departments were also utilizing this method as an adjunct to their classroom presentation.

Special Techniques

While specific experiences (exercises) are presented as a format, there are no restrictions on the type that could be used to enhance direct sensory input. The flexibility and creativity of the leader and/or group are the only limitations. As I write these words I have now begun to monitor the pressure with which I clasp my pen, becoming aware of the tensions involved, experimenting with varying pressures, but I fear that I haven't reached "optimal tonus" due to the self-induced tension of attempting to meet a self-imposed deadline.

Unique Features

Although Gunther uses different symbols to describe his method, I would support his contention that our cultural conditioning affects our sensory reception. This premise is well documented. We have learned to attend to those stimuli which are selectively reinforced in our everyday life.

In contrast to the other systems reviewed in this text, which focus on interpersonal relations, sensory awareness is basically an intrapersonal experience. The formulas of the experiences permit interaction, but it is *my* feelings that are central. Gunther makes no claim for therapy in the traditional sense, and thereby establishes some of the limitations of this method. Subjective experience is an unmeasurable quantity and this restricts empirical verification (research). Still, as McMahon and Campbell (1969) write, life is more than what can be observed by others. Subjective experience is a meaningful part of man's reality too. Touch flesh, touch life, touch love, and be.

Video Simulation

In the field of athletics, it has been known for quite some time that the performer could correct and improve his performance not only through his coach's critique, but also by viewing his actions by means of films (now videotape). In the 1960's this technique has been extended to include classroom behaviors of teachers and students, training of counselors and medical interns, cross-cultural training of Peace Corps volunteers, and focused feedback in group counseling.

Simulation as a technique in learning has been an effective means for helping counseling trainees to differentiate affective and cognitive responses, to develop counselor leads which facilitate client growth (Beaird and Standish, 1964) and to familiarize the trainee with a counselor's role and function (Dunlap, 1968).

Since the focus of this text is on group, the narrative that follows will concentrate on video simulation as utilized within group settings.

Assumptions about Behavior

Kelley (1955) states that prediction and control of behavior are central in man's functioning. These predictions may be based on accurate or inaccurate data of self, others, and the immediate context. Also, control of one's behavior may be accepted or delegated to someone else. Both are choice options which are open to the individual. The predictions which a person makes include the perception of others and once this hypothesis is made the individual proceeds to gather data which will confirm it (Kagan and Krathwohl, 1967).

Stoller (1968b), acknowledging indebtedness to George Herbert Mead's theory of human development, states that self-perception is shaped by and is a function of the attitudes and reactions of significant others, particularly during the formative years. Once formed, maintenance of this image is central for the individual as he attempts to structure his interactions so as to gain confirmation of this image. In usual social interaction, the individual attempts to select others who will reinforce his self-perception. This confirmation process is negotiated indirectly. Direct access to confirmation is characteristic of structured group settings where feedback is one of the "rules of interaction."

As Culbert (1968a) suggests, it takes two to see one—that is, I am not fully aware of my impact upon you unless you so inform me. Video simulation, then, is another method for acquiring this data about self.

Simulation Formula

During group interactions the most important aspect is the group process itself and videotaping is not a replacement form but a technique for enhancing this process. As noted in the other types of group, confrontation and feedback constitute the major effort; the same holds true for videotaping.

With the large amount of data available from a single tape, it is necessary to select the material for replay which has the greatest potential for facilitating growth, individually and collectively. This, as Poling (1968) suggests, is the major advantage of videotaping—the control of focused stimuli and its availability for detailed analysis.

A second decision, with respect to the material to be presented, is when it should be replayed. Should the group process be interrupted? Should it follow termination of the recorded session? In making this decision the criterion is, which method would be most productive in terms of group process?

Another area where video simulation is beneficial is during the production of behaviors which are novel for the group members. Replay at this time enhances learning due to the contiguity of reinforcement and behavior.

Goals of Simulation

As in the other forms of group mentioned in this chapter, increased self-awareness is the desired product. In viewing oneself, and others, nonverbal behaviors may provide increased understanding and may be the most important (Ryan, 1969). Incongruities between intent and action are clarified through feedback and video presents an experience of the all-at-once learning which can have a powerful impact.

In a recent group experience with adolescents, video was utilized after the group had been meeting for several weeks. A 15-year-old girl had dominated the group preventing relationship development and in spite of feedback from the group, she continued her self-defeating behavior. After two focused feedback sessions, this girl began to experiment with other behaviors which led to group reinforcement and ultimately to improved interpersonal relationships within the group.

Interventions Used in Simulation

In traditional forms of therapy, interpretation plays a major role; however, this technique is limited in that the client(s) may perceive the therapist's interpretation (or that of another group member) as biased.

Videotaping, on the other hand, presents the most unbiased feedback. That *is* my behavior!

With multi-cameras it is possible to capture actor as well as reactors to determine sources of incongruities in perception, intent versus action, and process. With the immediacy capability of the equipment, contiguity offers increased validity of reality checks.

Leader's Role

The addition of television equipment requires support personnel whom the group leader(s) needs to train to record the most meaningful data. While the leader may not operate the equipment, he needs to be familiar with its capability.

The leader's role, while similar to those in most groups, differs in that he usually needs a coleader to assist in noting the segments to be replayed and feedback on the appropriateness of the selection (it still requires two to see one; a reality check for the leaders).

Member's Role and Group's Role

The presence of television equipment does not change the roles of the group members; confrontation and feedback are still utilized in the group process. Initially, regression may be noted in the behaviors of the group; however, most people adjust rapidly to the equipment, gaining an appreciation for the relatively unbiased feedback which it provides.

Change in Behavior

Theoretically, knowledge of performance enhances learning in that fewer trials are required to reach criterion measures. If, as suggested by Hall (1959), most learning in our culture occurs at the informal level then, by definition, such learning takes place out of one's awareness. Under this condition most behaviors are the result of nonchoice. Video brings these behaviors to the level of awareness and makes choice a reality, offering the individual greater control of his own behavior and consequently over the reactions to that behavior. Where dissonance or incongruities exist, the individual or group have the opportunity to reexamine perceptions, behaviors and context variables by means of the video playback.

Rate of Change

While research is limited, due to the brief history of this approach, Kagan, et al. (1967) have found that counselor training time can be appreciably shortened by this means. As previously mentioned, feedback from others can always be interpreted as containing the perceiver's bias which necessitates resolution, but with video the feedback is relatively free of such distortion and therefore, more "believable." This should result in a more rapid acceleration of awareness learning and an enhancement of the group process.

Selection of the Group

Self-selection is the usual procedure for groups using video simulation. In most settings, written permission to tape is obtained to protect the confidentiality of the group members.

The group is generally composed of eight to ten persons. The settings vary from therapists in private practice to clinics and hospitals.

Special Techniques

While the video equipment clearly differentiates this group from other forms, the group process is much the same. New techniques will develop as therapists and counselors acquire sufficient skill and experience with this approach. In counselor education, for example, Delaney (1969) suggests that "programmed clients" offer a wider range of experiences for the beginning counselor than live clients. Role playing and role rehearsal should also be improved with this technique.

Unique Features

In every scene of group interaction, the number, intensity, and frequency of stimuli make for an almost impossible task when attempting reconstruction of a given segment. Video replay presents the best available technique for reviewing such moments. By appropriate selection, group members, actors and reactors, individually and collectively, can become more aware of their behavior and the responses which are evoked. Using Hall's terminology (1959), I can observe what I have learned informally, i.e., out of my awareness. What I *felt*, I now *see*.

One word of caution is necessary for the use of videotaping in groups. Prolonged exposure to video playback can become a process of diminishing returns, much like the patient in analysis who needs a few more months to fully understand the nature of his problem. Focused feedback to develop self-awareness, individually and collectively, to call attention to the floundering a group may be experiencing, and to supply performance data in the learning of new behaviors, offers the most productive utilization of this electronic tool.

Summary

This chapter has presented an analysis of some of the group forms which share a common goal of increasing intra- and interpersonal sensitivity. This movement, which began at National Training Laboratories in 1947, has spawned a variety of related offspring. In each form it was noted that an interaction formula exists which defines the necessary role behaviors for establishing relationships within that specific context.

While each group rightfully lays claim to success in reaching designated objectives or goals, it was maintained that short-term encounters cannot provide the intimacy that contemporary man seeks (see Chapter 3, page 44). It was further maintained that each group is akin to a subculture within the context of the larger community. As such, the behaviors learned may not render the group member socially competent once he leaves that environment.

To understand individual and group behavior, the context must always be considered. To do less increases the risk of misunderstanding.

Suggested Additional Readings

Bindrim, Paul, 1969. "Nudity as a Quick Grab for Intimacy in Group Therapy," *Psychology Today*, 3(1) 25–28 (June).
   Bindrim discusses the nude marathons that he has been conducting for several years now. He contends that group nudity hastens the process in which people share their "authentic selves." A high level of trust and voluntary nudity go hand in hand.
Fiebart, Martin S., 1968. "Sensitivity Training: An Analysis of Trainer Intervention and Group Process," *Psychological Reports.* 22(3), Part 1, 829–838 (June).
   The theoretical and practical components basic to sensitivity trainer intervention and influence on group process is discussed. Group process or change is conceived as an ongoing progress through developmental phases. It is necessary to match trainer strategy with each particular phase. According to Fiebart, this is even a more important issue than spontaneity versus manipulation of the counselor.
Haigh, Gerard V., 1968. "A Personal Growth Crisis in Laboratory Training," *Journal of Applied Behavioral Science*, 4(4) 437–452 (December).
   A disturbing incident becomes therapeutic because of the leader not avoiding the emotional distress, his search for meaning of a confused behavior, his support and reassurance from the group and other members' identification with the member's crisis experience. The author assumes that increased knowledge about lab training can be facilitated through study of crisis occurrences in group. The purpose of the study was to discover eventually what aspects of a lab training experience implement perceived personal changes.
Lakin, Martin, 1969. "Some Ethical Issues in Sensitivity Training," *American Psychologist*, 24(10) 923–928 (October).

Sensitivity provides experiential learning about processes and people and is used to study helping relationships in the areas of management, education, community, and family. Ethical issues crop up in setting up a group, in conducting a group and after its termination. Participants have no way of knowing in advance or being able to appraise trainers' intentions. Lakin discusses "seductive" advertising for groups. He criticizes the advent of more directive trainer practices and pressures put on the group members to conform. Members can't really evaluate trainer influences. In the issue of group processes analysis versus personal expressiveness, Lakin favors the focus on group processes. Possible remedies for the ethical dilemma are more awareness of ethical problems, self-monitoring among group members and counselors, standards of professional trainer preparation, creation of a commission (APA) to investigate training practices, and a code of ethics.

Seashore, Charles, James Dimple, and Gloria Kinney, 1969. "Sensitivity Training: Can It Work for the Schools?" *Nation's Schools,* 83(3) 83–87 (March).

The goal of sensitivity training as used in large corporations is organizational development through the improvement of interpersonnel understanding. Group members' experiences are focused to facilitate an understanding and constructive use of group dynamics. Some administrators see sensitivity training involving administrators and teachers as the way to produce significant changes in school.

Shostrom, Everett L., 1968. "Witnessed Group Therapy on Commercial Television," *American Psychologist,* 23(3) 207–209 (March).

Shostrom describes the reactions to a series of group therapy sessions conducted on live television. As the therapist for ten sessions, he points out the significance of psychotherapy in a public setting. Reactions were those of viewers, patients, therapists, and other professionals. Viewer response was favorable; some felt that they too gained insight. Patients coincided in this reaction—they felt that growth was accelerated. The two therapists felt that the feedback and the pressure of a TV audience were instrumental in their improvement as practitioners. Shostrom discusses the rationale for making therapy public. He cites Mowrer and Berne in his argument that revealing one's weaknesses and needs to others openly is a healing force.

Thomas, Donald, 1968. "T-Grouping: The White-Collar Hippie Movement." *Phi Delta Kappan.* 49(8) 458–459 (April).

This author feels that T-group is a faddish innovation which does not significantly facilitate the in-service training of teachers. This conclusion is based on Thomas' study of sensitivity training. He feels that sensitivity training currently is ineffectual—it could be improved for educational purposes if groups become more task-oriented (to solve organizational problems) and evaluative. Thomas sees the idealized goals of T-group as beneficial to teachers and administrators.

13

Family Group Consultation

The purpose of guidance has moved from the focus on the individual to the guiding of social forces creating learning environments for the individual. It is done through the intervention and influence of the informal interpersonal relationships within the person's primary groups.

Background and Development of Family Group Consultation

Family consultation is a recently developed method for counseling with parents, children, teachers, school administrators, and other significant persons important to the learning environments of students. Other professional practitioners, including psychiatrists, pastors, social workers, and juvenile-court counselors have participated in formal training programs to learn how to work with the entire family "all-at-once" in groups.

Family group consultation was begun in the psychiatric outpatient clinic at the University of Oregon Medical School during 1961. The initial goal was to develop a method for counseling the family which could be applied in the school setting by school counselors. The first school testing of family consultation was conducted in April of the initial trial year. The results from the testing were favorable (Fullmer and Bernard, 1964). The trial group, with the initial families, was moved from the Medical School to a continuing education counseling center and carried to termination. Three of the four initial families continued for approximately three years.

A second experimental group was continued for one year (Zwetschke and Grenfell, 1965). School trial groups were conducted on a six-, eight-, and twelve-session terminal contract. The option to reenter family consultation was open for every family. Approximately one in five families return for additional counseling or continue beyond the recommended terminal session following a brief period.

During a decade of development, the method of family group consultation was subjected to many variations in format. Variations range from parent-counselor encounters to one-family–two-counselors sessions, to two or three families and two or three counselors sharing responsibility for the case load; to large group meetings for up to ten parents in a conference. New variations on the basic pattern of one or two families and two counselors meeting together in a classroom continue to emerge. Group counseling provides a safe encounter environment. I encourage counselors to innovate and find a workable model for their school and community.

There were two significant discoveries during the initial development of family group consultation. First was the discovery that a group of families can create an intensive learning environment for training counselors in group procedures. Second was the discovery that a group of families can constitute a powerful treatment arena for modifying behavior of one or more members in a family.

A family is a group too. The power of a family is seen in the learning environment created for members to shape their behavior, form new behavior, and practice for transfer to the world outside the family (Linton, 1936).

The process in a group holds a unique fascination for the counselor in family group consultation. In a family, the group process generates behavior in the members. Family group consultation has led me to consider whether I might reproduce this powerful behavior formation phenomenon in our contrived groups for counseling. To understand what happens in a family it is necessary to look at the cultural framework out of which comes individual behavior (Bennis et al., 1964).

Each family carries on a representative sample of the behavior for a given culture. The family has the power to continue, discontinue, or change the behavior representative of a culture. Anthropologists like Mead and Heyman (1965) tell us that every culture has terminated as a society where the family ceased to be used as a primary group in socialization of the young. Bronfenbrenner (1970) has said that it is *not* necessary for every culture to use the family in the same way. In more than 460 cultures in the world today, some form of the family group is used for procreation and socialization functions. I assume individual behavior comes out of group influences on choice of behavior. The possession and practice of behavior appears to be linked closely to the parameters set in a group by the formula used to control the interaction. In family group consultation I have observed the group influence behavior in individual members. The creation of a learning environment capable of influencing behavior formation is a prime objective of family group consultation. The objective has been incorporated in group-counseling and group-guidance programs in school practice and university counselor education. A second goal is to form and shape competent behaviors in each individual.

We have become less concerned with changing behavior and more concerned with improving the learning environments through direct intervention in family and classroom (Bronfenbrenner, 1967). The purpose of guidance has moved from the focus on the individual to the guiding of social forces creating learning environments for the individual. Treatment of the individual in isolation is frequently a luxury the school can ill afford. Treatment of the individual in his primary groups has shown us more realistic results. Teachers, parents, and students learn the counselors' skills when all participate together, as in a team. The team, as a group, generates new knowledge in a way similar to the process in a healthy family. Like the family, the team can use the information sharing model so highly developed in the school classroom. The information sharing model used in family group consultation, contrived group, and in the healthy family group, is basically concerned with affective learning and conative learning (skill) development.

Outline of Theory Used in Family Group Consultation

The theory outlined here came after the practice of family group consultation had produced positive results. What began as a one-year experiment became a ten-years-plus program. Theory is essential to family consultation because meaningful development requires a conceptual framework to use in testing the method of training and the method of treatment in group counseling. Theory is developed to serve research efforts. The methods will require continuing testing and revision to maintain the purpose of this chapter.

The following two models for information processing serve as a vehicle for conceptualizing the essential difference between learning environments in a classroom and in a family. The family utilizes the *information-transfer model* whenever it is appropriate. In addition, the healthy family has an *information-generating model.* There is a significant difference. The theory to be outlined here is based on the information-generating model.

The individual learns his behavior primarily within the family. The degree of competence manifested by a given person reflects the quality of his family's information-creating model.* The theory includes a

*Information is knowledge once it has been verbalized (generated). Transfer of existing information can happen by teaching methods. Generating information for the first time in a group happens by learning together. In a sense, the group becomes the teacher or more accurately, the learning environment.

concern for the individual's ability to test reality in ways that result in information he can use to effect appropriate behavior (Fullmer, 1968).

The individual's behavior is analyzed to show the pattern of meanings derived from his personal system of beliefs as compared to the cultural system of beliefs. The pattern is taken from the story of a life event in which the individual and his family members have participated. His observations and perceptions of his own behavior are compared to those reported by others. This is the basic interaction process. The process moves from past events to present events. The here-and-now quality of behavior avoids a hang-up with history. Each person reality tests his behavior in the here-and-now. Even as you read this, the model you use is reflected in your thinking and acting out as your systematic characteristic way of responding to stress (Moreno, 1958; Mowrer, 1968). We always have our model of behavior with us. This assumption is the initial point of departure in the family group consultation methods of training and treatment. I take present behavior and ask, "What is happening now?" The chances are that each person in a given life situation or life event will give a *unique* reply. If the answers are all similar, you have an expression of the common cultural learnings for such an event.

Each life situation in a given social system has a pattern or map to follow in acting out the appropriate competent behavior. Children learn the cultural guidelines in family encounters. These are used by the children in encounters with life events outside the home when they are at play, at school, at the shopping center, and elsewhere. For example, language is a way of thinking. Each culture has a way to learn. These ways to learn and to think are essential maps or guides for every person if he is to function competently within a society. Common experiences, common learnings, common wisdoms, common beliefs, and common guides or maps for sequence, timing, and significance in life events give rise to similar answers within a group to the question: "What is happening?" The happening itself is familiar only to the extent that it "fits" the cultural parameters. Small variations appear gross because the expectations are programmed with the meanings in a common culture. The hippie was such a phenomenon in the 1960's. In the 1970's, a militant dissenter gives a "different" type of behavior to achieve a similar impact of "change." The "informal" culture of the hippie has meaning as dissent only within the context of our American "formal" culture. The protest may lose its meaning when the behavior of the "formal" modifies to incorporate its symbols such as long hair on men, beards, and old or multicolored clothes. The militant dissenter may stimulate a rejection response from the society. Expulsion is quite different from incorporation (Hall, 1959).

Information-Transfer Model

Imagine a classroom viewed from the outside. The teacher is standing before a roomful of students. The informed authority is transferring knowledge to less informed subordinates. Parent-child, pastor-parishioner, coach-athlete, employer-employee, and many you could name all give evidence of widespread application of the information transfer model for learning and teaching used in our society.

For transferring existing knowledge, the information-transfer model is very appropriate. In the hands of a master teacher, it is probably the most effective and efficient model available. However, when one is facing a new problem, without precedent, the need is for a model to generate new knowledge. The information-generating model is used for this purpose by the emotionally healthy family (Irish, 1966; Loukes, 1964).

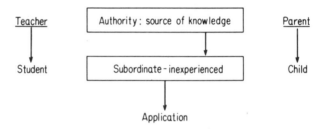

FIG. 1.   Information Transfer Model. Widely used and efficient model for relating existing knowledge to the uninformed. Control is from the powerful to the weak—the authority to the neophyte.

Information-Generating Model

The emotionally healthy family generates new knowledge when a new problem is encountered.* If a source of information is available to the family, it will use the information transfer model. But when no authority is available, the family shares the information it has and comes

---

*An emotionally unhealthy or sick family group can neither use information nor generate any information. Depending on the degree of pathology, the sick family has difficulty using the information it has (Fullmer, 1969).

up with new behavior to meet the need. The information-generating model is not exclusively a family phenomenon. Other groups, highly developed, use the model. Teams in industry and research use an information generating model to solve new problems. The level of commitment or morale of a group is important because it is an expression of the measure of potential available in a group for generating or creating new knowledge. An emotionally healthy family is a powerful group. It is no place for a weakling where members are actively engaged in living out life-and-death quality commitments. The moments, of generating new behavior and practice with new applications of new knowledge, give vent to generous portions of intense emotional expression by each member. To stay in the life situation during stress-filled periods is necessary if one is to influence the forming of new knowledge for any member of the group (Fullmer and Bernard, 1968, 1971).

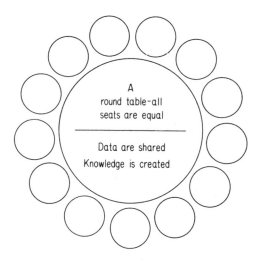

FIG. 2. Information—Generating Model. A family is a group of equals. The corporate structure is part of its organization (roles are assumed by members). Open communication provides the arena for knowledge generating to meet new problems. Control is shared by each participant. Control of self is the goal. "Equals" does not imply sameness in rank, age, or role.

Statement of Theory Used in Family Consultation

Theory

Behavior is formed in an interpersonal relationship encounter. The behavior forms to communicate the personal meaning the experience creates for the individual.

Discussion

The interpersonal interaction context defines the relationship within the group. The individual responds to the relationship definition of him by forming new behavior to communicate his meaning. The individual creates his own experience in each encounter.

The style used by the individual is a characteristic way of responding. The characteristic style of response can be identified by the counselor as a pattern of behavior. The patterns are maintained by the individual as consistent themes which help to keep predictable his behavior in a given situation, because behavior tends to be redundant in redundant life situations. The sets and isolates of behavior patterns may be observed. Observations reveal patterns that are similar within a given culture.

All behavior is given expression in a context of culture. Culture is a set of beliefs expressed through direct action, symbols, and relationships. There are at least two social systems or "cultures" operating in all behavior. The individual system includes a formal cultural system of beliefs and an informal social system of beliefs. To achieve an accurate assessment of meaning, one must learn to read behavior in its subtle shifting from one level to another within a given context. Levels are formal-informal and technical (Hall, 1959). To modify behavior for a family member, it is necessary to modify the reinforcement pattern or schedule within the group. We interrupt the existing pattern by our presence. We intervene through interpersonal relationships and interaction schedules. We influence through our behavior together within the group.

Interpersonal Contract, an Expression of Commitment

To achieve a group with commitment enough to produce the power to form behavior, the group must have a purpose strong enough to enlist a life-and-death commitment from the members. The family has this potential as does a number of other groups in our culture. The platoon in the military and the peer group under extreme stress are two examples. Friendship groups use love, but a buddy system in a platoon of soldiers mainly uses the fear of death. They also employ love. Love is a more lasting and powerful discipline. Love is defined as that force which binds an individual to his group (Montagu, 1970). The source of meaning is a stronger force than sex. Self-esteem is directly derived from meaning. The level of identification with a group is established by the intensity of meaning derived from membership. The intensity of meaning is an expression of how the group gives real meaning to a system of beliefs. This power in a family generates new behavior to communicate the individual's meaning in a new experience.

Loyalty to reason keeps us looking for a more simple explanation of the conditions necessary to generate behavior that is competent and adequate in a functioning person (Bernard and Fullmer, 1969). The family group consultation method has exposed us to the arena where behavior is formed. I have developed a theory based upon the work carried out to date. There are a number of assumptions about behavior and about the group. As the statement of theory in Chapter 3 states, behavior is formed in a relationship as an expression of meaning which comes from the new experience. If the group or someone in the group responds favorably, the behavior may be retained. Retention is contingent upon whether the reinforcement schedule of the group strengthens the probability of continuing the new behavior. The reinforcement schedule of a group does not create new behavior. New behavior will form only out of a direct encounter relationship. A basic assumption is made that the principle of reinforcement is ever present. Negative, neutral, and positive reinforcement may function simultaneously in the same life event at different levels. Primary and secondary reinforcement may be used (Pavlov, 1927; Jensen, 1968).

The patterns of reinforcement maintained in a group are the primary influences on behavior formed in the group. To modify behavior through group process it is necessary to change the patterns of reinforcement through direct intervention. The interruption of present patterns of reinforcement is achieved by adding a counselor team and another family to the group. Interrupt, intervene, and influence are the assumptions supporting all action taken in family group consultation (Fullmer and Bernard, 1964). The assumptions are met if one person in a family can change his behavior response in a recurring life event such as mealtime or bedtime. Most frequent is a significant change in the way one member is treated by a significant other. Examples are: touch the one who is given little or no tactile reinforcement; spend time with the target person and aim to give more love because it is needed; remove the means for secondary gains from behavior by identifying the reinforcing behavior and providing an alternative action, such as having mother remove herself physically from the vicinity of a sibling squabble.

The introduction of new primary reinforcers will not interrupt established behavior where the secondary gains are valued by the person (Blachly, 1969). The alcoholic, for example, cannot be bribed by some attractive primary alternative because the secondary gains have more seductive power. The forces operating in a group may overpower the counselors even when working as a team of two or more. The behavior paradox will continue to confound practitioners, because the power to remain the same is in control. The "yes-but" phenomenon, identified elsewhere as the immaculate exception, remains the same.

The assumptions cover the organic needs of each family member. The biological needs must be met to insure the basic vegetative necessities and safety requirements of the organism for metabolic functions. Competent behavior provides adequate information about the environment to insure social survival.

Paradigm of a Competently Functioning Person

Behavior is a product of the social system of the person. Other persons provide the cultural-social context of each life event. Behavior is used by the individual to communicate his meanings. His meanings are derived from his identity in response to a system of beliefs. His needs are learned in a group and the behavior to meet them is acquired in a personal-social context of meaning (Ginott, 1968). The confirmation or denial of his identity depends upon the evaluation the person ascribes to his behavior and the response from others. Competent individual behavior has a high degree of congruence with the cultural system of beliefs (Linton, 1936). Competent behavior is essentially a social system that is self-fulfilling. The family is healthy when all individuals successfully function with competent behavior (Fullmer, 1964).

Individual behavior is learned in a family group and exported into the social system. The degree of congruence between behavior practiced by the individual, the significant groups in his life, and the cultural-social systems will be manifested in the conflicts encountered by the individual. Groups are essential to provide learning environments to acquire and modify behavior. The family group is the primary source of behavior formation. Peer groups, work groups, and play groups serve to extend and sustain the individual's behavior. Reference groups form a significant and complex influence system affecting behavior.

Alienation results when there is any consistent reversal in the confirmation of the individual's beliefs. This concept is important within groups, such as family, peer, work, and play, but more testing is essential to find if it holds for the community in cases of delinquent behavior (Mowrer, 1968, p. 138). School behavior of a given youngster may be traced to alienation within his family group. We have found this a very useful way of looking at behavior that teachers or parents find objectionable. Family consultation provides an arena for direct intervention to attempt a reversal of the trend toward alienation.

Principles Affecting Family Group Behavior

The informal culture behavior described by Hall (1959) is learned by each person but is not taught by anyone. The informal culture meanings are learned from being with other persons over a period of time. Because informal culture rules are not verbalized, the behavior representing informal culture is regarded as mystical and intuitive. Contrast is evident with the formal culture rules (behavior). Formal culture is taught by the mother by admonishment and precept. No alternative behavior is ever allowed in formal culture behavior. An example is given by the mother when she tells her child to wear clothes and the child protests, "Why, Mommy?" The mother's reply is, "That is the way it is." No exceptions are permitted. If the child violates a formal culture behavior, his life is threatened by the parents' behavior responses through showing grave concern, physical arrest, or some other specific behavior.

The family is a living group. It provides a powerful model for learning and teaching (Mead and Heyman, 1965). The following principles of behavior are derived from systematic observation of families in counseling using the consultation method.

1. *Most of what a person learns and uses to understand the meaning of his existence is not taught.*

At school where a child is found not knowing how to behave in the classroom, it is folly to set out to "teach" him how to behave. He should be put into a group where the behavior he needs to acquire is being put into practice. He will need to spend time together with members of the new group so he can become a participant in the new social system. Group counseling is a useful method as in family group consultation for such a purpose.

2. *The healthy family is a representative example of the model for learning used by a culture.*

The culture is perpetuated through the family's use of its learning model. Bernstein (1964) reports that a family uses restricted codes as part of the form of communication learned by it within a specific social class. The code sensitizes family members to specific meanings within relationships. Neither the code nor the meanings are taught; they are *caught*. This implies that one must be as concerned with the conditions in which learning will occur as one is usually concerned with what is the content of learning. Culkin (1967) gives significance to the idea when he claims a person's most important learning is not taught. Culture, community, and meaning merge in the living group—a family. The school may use family consultation to link up with the family and secure the best of both worlds for the child and his learning purposes.

3.   *It is necessary to comprehend the meaning of a life event in terms of the social system (personality) of the other person.* To understand your behavior, I must comprehend your meanings. The reverse is important for encounter.

Kemp (1967) claims one errs by using his own social system to interpret for other persons the meaning of a life event. The counselors seek the meaning of life events in the family because the task is to understand what is the meaning for each family member. On a person-to-person basis, the counselor learns each family member's concept of himself. From this it is possible to estimate how each member regards others. The system of beliefs used by an individual is one key to his behavior. According to Moreno (1968), encounter is two-way empathy.

4.   *The individual's personality is formed out of the social system of his family.*

Personality is used to mean "social system." Handel (1965) studied whole families and concluded with a similar idea. The child's behavior reflects the character of the family. The way a person behaves is the way he is. Behavior is analyzed (read) for its meaning to the person. Sometimes one must ignore the content of verbal behavior and respond to the relationship definitions, if understanding is to be achieved (Watzlawick et al., 1967).

5.   *Behavior and knowledge get perpetuated on a generation-to-generation basis because of the family social system.* Gaps or voids in the family repertoire of behavior and knowledge also get perpetuated.

Behavior and knowledge newly acquired by a family may be perpetuated from one generation to the next. Family consultation as education is supported by this principle. Behavior and knowledge gaps are identified by maladaptive behavior. The healthy family resolves its conflicts without disorganizing anyone or itself. New knowledge is created and behavior is used because information generating is a key the healthy family commands. What is learned in a healthy family will work when applied in the larger social system outside the family.

6.   *A group creates a life of its own.* The forces that shape the individual's behavior are those that reinforce his sense of con-

trol over his immediate life situation. His behavior forms in relationships which constitute his source of certainty.

The healthy family creates safe environments for each of its members. The family is a living and developing social system for each child. The environment forms as the child grows to adult status. Family group consultation provides the conditions for a partnership between the school and home. The family and the counselors can become a team. As partners with parents, the family pattern of forces may be examined and evaluated. Changes in the reinforcement schedules can be effected. The school environments and the home environments may be shaped into a more complementary set of social systems.

7.   *Each family develops unique characteristics including beliefs, personal meanings, and restricted codes.* Behavior is the communications system used by the individual. It utilizes the unique qualities of his family.

In family group consultation the counselors need to learn to read the sets and isolates of the behavior messages. It is important to distinguish between verbal behavior about messages and meanings and the real happenings. In effect, the condition is similar to the problem one faces in communicating with an alien culture. The symbols, patterns, and guides to meaning are different. The behavior is strong and the problems of decoding (reading) it are total. This is also true with families of the disadvantaged or culturally different. The behavior language must be common to both the counselors and the family members. The helper (caring for persons) needs to comprehend and understand the "language" of the helped (the cared-for person). The individual systems of belief and the shared cultural system of beliefs must be alike. To make the happening a meaningful and useful educational experience, the counselors may need to learn the "new" or "other" culture of the family —on the spot. On-the-spot learning of new knowledge by the counselors shares the conditions of information generating used in the healthy family. The group achieves the capability for knowledge creation if a new "family-life" condition is established. What is shared was not previously known. Learning together with the family and counselors means sharing a system of beliefs as new beliefs and behavior to confirm them emerge.

8.   *The character of a child is formed in his family group by the reinforcement schedules created and maintained by parents, siblings, and significant others.*

Behavior responses, together with the attitudes, values, and beliefs supporting them, are conditioned (learned) habit patterns that may last a lifetime. The way of thinking, feeling, and learning shape the patterns of interaction which characterize the individual. The person-to-person model of family interaction is the prime place for effective intervention in family consultation. The school counselor may gain access to the family arena through a program of family group consultation.

9. *Human beings represent, by symbols, abstract relationships and events.* A concrete behavior act may be a direct expression of a relationship experience.

The essence is found in the report of a behavior event that goes like this: "Wasn't it a touching experience?" Symbolically, one can have a touching experience where no one touches anyone else! "Keep in touch" is heard often. These are simple examples to illustrate the point. Culture is a set of symbolized meanings acted out in time and place with a tempo and a sequence to guide its concrete form. The infinite leeway allows for each other person's being through a complex informal culture. Family consultation works to make the person aware of the culture as a framework of meanings. Symbols may be verbal sounds, nonverbal acts, and noncontextual cues. (The office size may tell you which man is the president.)

The Method in Practice

The Language of Behavior

Family group consultation led to the idea, expressed by Edward Hall (1959), that behavior is a symbolic system of meanings, or silent language. The total verbal, nonverbal, contextual, and noncontextual behavior is needed to derive meaning from the patterns of an individual's social system. The first task in family group consultation is to learn to read (analyze) behavior as language (code). The culture provides the behavior "alphabet." The family is the key to the dictionary of meanings in a culture. Mead and Heyman (1965) claim that if the family is terminated as the socialization group in a culture, the culture also terminates.

Family Group Consultation Sessions

The method is a group-counseling procedure founded upon the assumption that a person's behavior is formed within relationships in a family. The efficacy of family group consultation is well established for training counselors in group counseling (Fullmer and Bernard, 1968). The treatment results have been similar to other group-counseling methods. More research is needed to test the theory and evaluate the practice. The following session by session guide is given with the hope that more school counselors will join in using family group consultation (Fullmer, 1969a).

The purpose of the method is to achieve a group relationship similar to that found in a family when it generates new behavior. To do this, the counselors remain separate from the family. Each family is capable of the quality of interpersonal relationships essential to form new behavior in one of the children or an adult.

Session One. The first session is used for orientation. The family comes into a new and novel situation. There are always two or more counselors. We begin by collecting familiar data necessary to identify each person. "Please, would you tell us about yourself?" "How has it been going, this week?" "Please, tell us more about that?" are some initial questions we have found useful.

We answer any questions raised by the family within our competence. The family is in a novel situation and will respond by using whatever they know. This creates an opportunity to observe the family managing its affairs. The unique conditions will pass quickly. What a family discloses under novel conditions we have found to be very reliable information concerning life in that family. I assume that each of us uses everything we know all of the time. The initial contact is the most productive because everything is revealed symbolically all-at-once.

The formula is expressed in terms like "Speak for yourself," "Speak about yourself," and, "Tell us how you see the other's impact compared with your own." The focus is upon a recent life event. The concern is to have each person tell his story for everyone else to hear. The interaction will reveal the family relationships within it among members (interpersonal) and with external agents. External agents are peer groups, work groups, play groups, counselors, and the other family's members. Information is gathered in this way as long as sessions continue. The cross-validation of each person's story told in first person singular will reveal the family rules about who is allowed to talk about which subjects.

The formula for interaction carries the counselors and family members to common life experiences. Evaluation by each person is revealed in his behavior response. All participants are exposed to the same conditions. The differences in behavior responses serve to focus on individual perceptions of one's self and others. The result is an object lesson in learning how to learn. This shared experience is repeated for each person during each session. The family takes the formula for interacting with them and learns to use it without the supervision of counselors. This is an important developmental task because it helps the family learn to talk with each other. This fact alone will redefine some relationships.

Analysis and interpretation of all data gathered in "group" has an open hearing. Open participation will reveal hidden agendas which in turn must be labeled to identify their content. Interpretation leads to the identification of conflicts within the family and/or between the family and the social system.

Session One should accomplish a complete hearing for family consultation, its purpose and promise. The process for family learning should be clearly defined as, "everyone speaks for himself." The purpose of family consultation is defined as "the identification of conflicts within systems of belief." We are not concerned with solving problems. We are concerned with the identification and clarification and the possible resolution of conflicts.

Each family member responds to the questions, "What issues are before this family?" "In what way are you important to your family?" Each person shares how he sees himself in his family. All family members are encouraged to attend each session. However, we initially work with whatever part of the family is available to meet. Counselors are encouraged to set limits with regard to how they spend their time. Our experience has shown the importance of working with the *entire* family all at once. The absent-member syndrome is always an unknown quality. Working with a piece of a family is no different from other standard treatment methods for single clients or small groups of subjects.

Counselors keep records of the members present in each session. The relationships that appear between the mother and father, the mother, father, and a child, and/or among siblings. Patterns of relationships will emerge from these data. It is possible to learn who controls the family and who controls whom within the family. Who talks for himself? Who talks for others? Who talks for the family?

The interaction sequence of who talks for whom will lead to a look at the *control system* the family uses. Who talks for whom is a criterion for assessment. The family member who is *absent* in a session may have someone speak for him or he may control by withholding his participation.

In addition to the verbal exchange in family consultation, the non-contextual cues such as facial expression, physical activity, autistic disregard of external reality, body posture, and intonation of voice form the multiple levels exposed for the awareness of the counselors. Reading (analyzing) behavior and interpreting meaning within this context become the tasks of counselors. The counselor must have a nearly complete self-awareness concerning his own biases when making interpretations of other people's behavior. The task is always two-sided —my side–your side (my bias–your bias.) We learn to read behavior as a language of messages and meanings. Decoding the messages and meanings can become an impossible task unless you get the family to do it for you.

Session One is when the counselors assess the involvement of each individual in a family group. The assessment is based upon an estimate of interpersonal loyalty, alliances, and personal-interpersonal contracts in subgroups within the family. We form an hypothesis concerning the involvement of each individual in relation to each other individual in the family group. The hypothesis is tested by subsequent events within family consultation sessions as the decoding of behavior continues.

Parents and youngsters meet together in the same room with the counselors. We recommend breaking the group into two parts for part of each session. By dividing the group into two separate meetings it is possible to help children and adults feel freer to discuss their concerns. One goal in family consultation is to help parents and children learn to negotiate their concerns without a mediator. Frequently, the parents have secrets from their children. It is good to know if the children have these same secrets. Children usually protect the parents' myths.

Session Two. The process of discussing basic issues and concerns facing the family members has begun. The counselors act as mediators. The counselors open the session with, "How has it been going?" The lead is brief and general. This will allow the family members an opportunity to determine the topic for the session. "Well, we visited Aunt Sue last Sunday." The happenings while the family was visiting Aunt Sue become the topic. What transpired between them and among them? How did each person feel about his experience? What perceptions are reported by each member concerning each event? What happened before, during, and following the event? What did *I* do? What did each other person do, as *I* see it? From these reports, patterns of behavior will emerge that lead to concepts of what it is like to be a member of the family. The consequences of a given life event become predictable for each member. The counselors can generate hypotheses. Hypotheses are tested over time to establish the validity of the predictions. This is a good reality check on any agenda carried by a counselor. The counselor with an agenda will have a high frequency of self-fulfilling prophecies.

The counselors learn the patterns for interpersonal loyalties, alliances, and contracts used in the family. The dimensions of loyalties, alliances, and personal contracts are checked out with each member of the family. Counselors participate verbally to check out what is said. We want to know: What happens in this family? What is life like? What meanings would I have in such a family?

It is necessary to allow each person the right to take ownership or title to his behavior. Who owns the behavior? is a basic question in family group consultation. Responsibility is with the owner of the behavior. Accountability is whether the behavior has met group expectations for him. Rather than answering any question, the counselor asks the person to talk about behavior alternatives available. He might ask, What ways of behaving are you aware of ? How do you think you *should* act? The group is utilized for discussion. In this way the person listens to others making statements about what they think is possible. Ideas are shared with the person representing other points of view which otherwise might be unavailable. The goal is to give the members of each family practice in reporting about their behavior.

Session Three. Counselors have accepted the reporting of events in terms of other persons. It is essential to use the pronoun "I" rather than *he, she, or it,* as the story is told. We begin by being careful to have each individual speak for himself. The principle is: "Each person must take title to his own behavior." My own behavior is the only behavior over which I have any *direct* control. Each of us shares this truism. The pronoun "I" focuses the report upon the individual telling the story. Counselors discourage parents or siblings from adjusting the story another individual tells. "You can tell your story next—now we want to hear Mark's," is one way we discourage attempts to speak for someone else. The person who is telling the story is encouraged to own (take title to) his perceptions of events. Identical life events are described by each member of the family. The counselors formulate new ideas concerning the pattern of behavior within the family. Individuals within the family consultation setting acquire new experiences together. The experiences they have together become a source of validation. This method of validation is unique to "group." The process is used to teach persons how to *use* help. To *get* help from other persons is another phase of treatment.

The individual begins an evaluation of his own behavior. The families usually establish confidence in the idea of family consultation as a method of learning. Each individual will need to learn the method of feedback. Learning to tell the story of the family is a basic developmental task.

Session Four. Regular attendance at sessions is an indication of how well motivated each individual is. Legitimate reasons for being absent should be accepted. However, the member of a family who is absent most of the time is usually less motivated to get help. Covert concerns should be exposed by the counselors.

Counselors validate and confirm the individual family members' reporting observed during the previous sessions. The counselors then relate to the family members any consistencies and discrepancies so clarification by each person is possible. They ask in first person singular: "I see your behavior this way; I wonder if that is the way others see it?" "Do you see it this way?" The feedback forms the basis for dialogue in family consultation. The person is free to agree, disagree, or clarify the counselor's perception.

The fourth session is the beginning of a new phase. The individual person is encouraged to focus upon himself in relation to other members. This focus is the most complex behavior expected in family consultation. The individual states his perception of the relationship between himself and each other person. The assessment is in terms of a set of values, a way of valuing (a way of thinking), and a system of beliefs. The interaction is particularly difficult because other persons are present. The validity of the story is checked by other family members. *The highest level of achievement in family consultation is when the individual can assess his input, the input of others, analyze accurately the relative meaning for each person involved, and confront himself with discrepancies and consistencies in his own behavior and the behavior of others.* The person is considered able to learn by his own efforts when he can achieve this level and have others confirm his behavior.

Some families and some individuals do not achieve the desired goal. They tend to wander aimlessly. The counselors may introject a question: "We seem to be unable to focus on any one subject today. I wonder what is happening?" What follows may prove more enlightening if the counselors refuse to *wander* with them.

Session Five. The family will be able to use some of the counseling skills learned in family group consultation. The formula for speaking and interacting should be in use. Owning one's perceptions of behavior is important. The usc of first person singular "I" helps to establish ownership. An individual will have learned to focus upon the results of his relationships with other people. The consequences of behavior constitute a significant force operating in a learning-how-to-learn situation. Making the process of learning a consciously aware concern is a step in the direction of achieving successful conditions in family group consultation.

Each person looks at his own behavior. He looks at the behavior of others in response to his behavior. Family consultation should continue for six to twelve sessions. If people want to go longer than twelve sessions, they are encouraged to take a furlough from family consultation and return several weeks later. Sessions should be contracted on a terminal basis when school counselors use family group consultation. Six to eight sessions are adequate for most families in a school setting.

The sender and the receiver of messages in family group consultation constitute the points of evaluation for the feedback systems utilized. Attempts to clarify meaning between the signal sender and the receiver is a check-and-balance system in family consultation. Some attempts to clarify are as follows: "What did you really mean to the other person? How does the other person respond to your meanings? Is there consensus or conflict between the sender and the receiver?"

Specific life events happening within the group during consultation are the basis for the validation procedures. The preception of one person is compared and contrasted with others in terms of the discrepant meanings formed in a particular life experience. Systematically established perceptions and meanings provide a base line for assessment of the similarities and differences experienced by each individual. Clarification of meaning is a basic process in the communication system in family group consultation. Family members learn to use the process by themselves without the counselors as mediators. The transfer of behavior in family group consultation becomes paramount to the success of the method. Family group consultation is complete when the family can actually interact without a mediator. They should be able to handle controversial issues and emotionally loaded material on their own. Most families will achieve success by Session Eight; others will require more time. If they require more than twelve sessions, they may need a different kind of help.

Sessions Six to Twelve. The same procedure is used to continue family group consultation to the terminal session. The identification of conflicts in the family continues as the central theme. We assume that all families encounter conflicts all of the time. Our concern is whether the problems derived from such conflicts actually handicap the family. We also wish to know if any handicap is transferred or spreads to other areas of operation. The healthy family is able to function in all other areas even though a drastic conflict exists in a given area. The less healthy family is incapacitated in *all* areas by a conflict in a given area. Teachers and students seem to carry similar conditions into the classroom. The healthy classroom is one where conflict coexists with productive behavior. The less emotionally healthy classroom is one where everything stops until the conflict is resolved. Our educational system has a goal to create competent behavior. Competent behavior is defined as behavior which is enhancing to the self and/or others. Idea production is compatible with the goals of education and may constitute a significant product of the information-generating model for learning used by the emotionally healthy family.

We want to help the family develop alternative ways of behaving in the significant life encounters. The processes of family consultation are designed to achieve this purpose. The sources of these alternatives are the members of other families and counselors. The family is encouraged to practice new alternatives. Using experimentation, they report the experiences to family consultation and evaluate the results from new behavior. The family decides if the new behavior is something they wish to keep or discard. The "event analysis" procedure continues. What happened before, during, and following the event? Who did what, where, when and to whom? How did it go? Is this the way you want it to be? Does anything stand in your way? What do you see ahead? What help could you use? What might we do here-and-now to help? Summary, evaluation, and planning are sequences in the procedures. The family is encouraged to plan ahead, anticipate events, prepare a strategy, and evaluate the outcomes in terms of their hopes, aspirations, and realities. The reliving of past events serves a purpose in the preparation for anticipating future events. Learning and teaching are part of the all-at-once nature of behavior in a knowledge creating model of the family. The counselors serve an information-transfer function.

We encourage the family to practice at home the process that goes on in family consultation. By the time the terminal session comes up, it is hoped, the family is able to use the method on their own. The method is designed to produce new knowledge to meet new life situations. The information-generation model is unique because it seems to work as well for the individual as for groups. For example, most intelligent people know what should be done in a given life situation; the problem is to do it. The person needs to learn to use the information he has on hand and/or can easily acquire by information transfer.

In family consultation we work with the informal social system of a family. The formal social system or protocol remains intact.

An Exercise to Involve a Group in the Process Used In Family Group Consultation

First: Make a list of words which describe yourself.

I. Who Am I?

(Question No. 1 *must* be thoroughly answered before going to Question No. 2)

1. Name—Self (sex)
     (Sex role in family)

2. Family—significant other(s)

3. Class—Occupation (social roles)

4. Religion

5. Additional adjectives

II. What behavior do I use to confirm Who I am?

(Question No. 2 *must* be thoroughly sorted out before going to Question No. 3)

One must have others to transact with him to accumulate the feedback to confirm his beliefs about Who am I?

The person should be able to competently behave in appropriate ways to confirm (reality test) his identity—in a group—here and now.

III. What new identity am I trying to achieve or become?

In group, we focus upon the I (self) in each of us. As I act out, you (others) react or respond to what happens. The happening becomes the life event to analyze. The life event is sorted out by each group member. The group member participates through *sharing* his sorted-out response with the group. Each one does the same in turn.

The accumulated responses are called *feedback*. The feedback is sorted out by categories of agreement, disagreement, other. "Other" represents the original I (self). This we have called "the immaculate exception." Each of us tends to think of ourselves as exceptions—except *me*, of course.

Guidelines

Continue the *process* and gather the *content* on each group member. (Nothing is ever written down; it may be tape-recorded—video or magnetic sound.)

Allow no external points of reference to replace the focus on *self!* (We tend to think in terms of other persons and things. This aura on *my mystique* must be interrupted.)

Interrupt, Intervene, Influence (Fullmer and Bernard, 1964)

The group (you) must interrupt my mystique because otherwise I am living out my personal *exception*. Yes, but— is the frequent expression of the immaculate exception. The group must intervene. You must keep my focus on you. *We* may gain a consensus but nothing is proven or disproven by such happenings because we can agree on an error or the obvious. The intervention is at the point in our thinking when each of us gives way to an assumption. The assumption is: It is better to allow the person to believe his own mystique than to force him to defend it (his self). Social protocol or etiquette has changed the usual rules regarding the interpersonal contract. Each of us gives permission initially by agreeing with the terms of *group*.

Influence comes from others in a group. The individual retains his power of choice and thus his independence as a person. Few of us can ignore for long the exposure to the sincere expectations of significant others. Except for the person who has never had an adequate interpersonal relationship, we can ignore forever the same conditions from nonsignificant others (Ginott, 1968). Here is the crux of meaning for the quality of our group relationship. I may prefer people who like me, but they may be handicapped in relating to me what might help me most. They may not be able to disappoint me that much. With such friends

I may learn less. For behavior, an enemy may help me learn because he can risk losing our relationship. Herein lies a basic truth in group: In order for me to help you learn about yourself, I must risk losing you as a friend. For me to learn, you must risk losing me as a friend. (A friend is someone to whom I may speak but do not need to answer.) Friends are no help. They only confirm my favorite myths about my identity, behavior, and beliefs. Most of us are not blessed with so many that we can be careless. The healthy family engages its members in a life and death, all or nothing risk taking. The consequence is strong, autonomous, and adequately competent individuals.

What sort of interpersonal relationship do group participants develop?

The Parameters May Be Defined in Categories

Mutual respect	Instead of	Mutual exploitation
"Self" reference	Instead of	"Other" reference
Internal reference	Instead of	External reference
Here-and now-happening	Instead of	There-and-then happening
We share	Instead of	I give-you take (and reverse)
Help—Care game	Instead of	Win-lose game

Discussion

Because we focus on the *self* instead of *other* or *external* phenomena, the reinforcement schedules are significantly modified within the family group. The behavior is the subject matter, just as math or English can be subject matter. We can take behavior out and look at it, or we can simply use behavior—live it. The entire enterprise rests upon the decision of the "self" person to share his own perceptions of himself and permit others to do the same—namely, share their perceptions of themselves (significant). Then the process of feedback to each participant begins. Each one permits each other to share his perceptions of each other one *openly* in the group. There can be no secrets— no special or privileged relationships, no secret societies, or any private contracts. This holds for whatever the individual chooses to share with anyone in the group. Anything any person chooses to keep private and to himself about himself, he is not pressured to share. In fact, each person is encouraged to keep his intimate *reserves* for himself. There may be some things we should not share. This will vary with individuals and with groups as well as time and place. The rules engaged in any group—family, training, play, work, reference, peer—are unique to that group and its "culture" guidelines.

Description of Family Consultation

Family group consultation was new in the 1960's. It has continued to be developed as a method for use in school settings. The method was begun in an effort to find a more productive model to use in schools with children identified as learning and/or behavior problems. Family group consultation is a way of working with the significant persons concerned about a child. Method in family group consultation combines the talents of all the people concerned with the child. A team concept is used to create both a training and treatment environment. The children, parents, teachers, administrators, and specialized personnel form the team to help one or more of the participants. The number of sessions can be adapted to meet the demands. Six to twelve sessions are recommended for minimum results. Some families are capable of getting help during a single session. Other families have had to participate for a year or more.

The school people are the prime movers for convening the family. The school counselor creates a teaching arena in which all persons significant to the child have access to each other. The classroom is a convenient model for teaching and provides an appropriate arena for most families. Learning may result from repeated and continuing dialogue among the significant professional, parents, and children.

Family group consultation is conducted in a classroom atmosphere with one family or up to four families meeting together with two or more counselors. Tables and chairs are used to approximate a family gathering. The session runs for one and one-half to two hours. All significant persons are encouraged to be present. The time to experience *together* over a period of time a variety of life events, forms the basis for subsequent sharing of behavior among the counselors and the family participants. All data are gathered in the all-at-once, here-and-now milieu of the group encounter. Structure is imposed upon the ambiguous mass of the data. The structure is based on the theory described earlier. The projections and interpretations of meaning are kept open to challenge, clarification, confirmation, and validation with each person.

Case Material*

The empirical evidence has accumulated in the form of individual case studies over the past ten years. The majority have been a success as evaluated by visible change to more productive or better adjustive behavior. There are those cases where nothing seemed to happen. The

*Names are changed to hide real identity.

absence of visible change in behavior pattern is evaluated as failure of the method. Families were turned away because no progress was achieved following a reasonable effort during a time trial. The above was more frequent in a family with an identified conflict to which one member, usually parent, would not respond with any alternative behavior. If the reinforcement schedules in the family are not altered, the existing conflicts will continue. Thus the rationale of termination in such cases leaves us with a qualified failure. Frequently, our diagnosis was successful but the treatment method went limp. An example was the family referred by a juvenile court through the 15-year-old son's school counselor. The father, mother, brother (9 years), and the identified case (a 15-year-old boy) came regularly to family consultation. Seventeen sessions were used. The mother had maintained an auxiliary lover for five years. The 15-year-old son had learned of this and had become an acting-out delinquent. The court hoped for a resolution of the basic conflict. The mother steadfastly held to her life situation. The boy increased his delinquent acts. Termination followed the realization the mother would not change her behavior. Recommendation was made to the court to place the 15-year-old boy in a foster home. The one-year follow-up confirmed the recommendation. The boy felt he was the only one in his family who needed help. The delinquent behavior had gone away with the initial placement in a foster home.

A second-type family requires referral to a different treatment arena. The example of a family referred by a summer school principal tells the story in a vivid but tragic fashion. The 16-year-old daughter was running away from home, was emotionally upset at school, and generally giving signals of "crisis." We saw the family three times in the first two days following initial contact. The conditions in the family were lethal. This was confirmed by a verbal report of the father one week later. Less than a year later an automobile accident claimed his life. What conditions created such a crisis?

The daughter learned that her mother and father lived in the same house just so she would have the benefit of a family. For the past dozen years they had not been man and wife in the usual sense. The daughter felt that she was responsible. The emotional intensity was very strong. We called in a psychiatric consultant and made a referral to her.

There are more happy cases to relate. Jack and Jill are such a case. Jack and Jill were fraternal twins adopted at age two. They were about to be 13 years old. There were no other children in the family. Jack and Jill are pseudo names but they represent real youngsters. They were a pair of thieves. They stole everything or anything from their parents and grandparents. Sometimes they would shoplift. The refrigerator had a padlock on it. The dresser drawers were locked. The children were locked out of the home whenever they would be there unsupervised. It took six months to resolve the conflicts. We first demonstrated that Jack and Jill would not steal from everybody. They were selective. We established this by having each one come and spend an entire day with us for two or three days per week. They were treated as partners in our activitites. The youngsters did not steal from us or anyone associated with our activities. We confronted the parents with this knowledge and began the process of helping them learn new behavior to use with the children. That process is a story in itself. We terminated after all need for locks had disappeared. Follow-up phone calls confirmed a successful case.

The case of Jody is typical of a school-phobia problem. She was depressive and remained out of school for one entire year. We do not count this case as a success even though several improvements happened. The chief concern is that the mother and sister never really modified their belief that Jody was just pretending. Jody would improve for sustained periods of several months. The family would interrupt family consultation. The next contact would be several months later— a crisis, Jody was depressed again. We terminated as a last-chance ultimatum to try to interrupt the behavior pattern in the family. We were not successful.

The case of Sally is more positive. She was referred from the Medical School Psychiatric Division for family consultation. The school counselor had referred Sally to the psychiatrist because of withdrawn behavior and decreasing grade-point average. The underachievement in school became acute. We worked with her entire family's cooperation. The case was a success. Sally finished high school and entered college. She became a success in social activities but flunked out after two quarters in college. She returned to summer school and regained admission. Sally succeeded in college the second attempt and graduated with her class. At my last report in mid-1970, Sally was continuing to function competently.

Summary

Family group consultation is a well-established method for treating families in distress over school-related problems. We have continued to use family group consultation as a major laboratory experience in group counseling training. Many of the graduates of our school counselor education program have employed modifications of family group consultation in their school counseling programs. I encourage students to experiment with parent groups and families to improve the possibilities for parent education. I think a group of counselors could make our ideas work for them.

Suggested Additional Readings

Bjerg, Kreston, 1968. "Interplay-Analysis: A Preliminary Report on an Approach to the Problems of Interpersonal Understanding," *Acta Psychologica,* 28(3) 201–243.

Bjerg presents a classification system for interaction. He uses the term "agon" to depict the social interaction context within which resources are used. He then relates this to specific types of interaction and their products (power, love, esteem, reproach, pleasing, entertainment). His conceptualization is intended to clarify descriptions of complex human interaction.

Dunphy, Dexter C., 1968. "Phases, Roles, and Myths in Self-Analytic Groups," *Journal of Applied Behavioral Science,* 4(2) 195–225.

This is a study comparing the development of two groups and the developmental phases and role types characteristic of them. Phases and roles may be the result of development of a group mythology focused on an authority figure and the group. Myths depict the way group members see the leader and other members. Each phase is accompanied by a myth expressing an ideal conception of group relationships.

Ferguson, Charles K., 1968. "Concerning the Nature of Human Systems and the Consultant's Role," *Applied Behavioral Science,* 4(2) 179–193.

The consultant's role is as diagnostician and change agent. He enhances cooperation between subparts and subsystems of human systems. The author describes processes which stimulate the externalizing of disruptive forces, in a move toward collaboration instead of destructive competition.

Walum, Laurel R., 1968. "Group Perception of Threat of Non-Members," *Sociometry,* 31(3) 278–284 (September).

Merton's reference group theory differentiates between different types of "nonmembers" of groups. Two variables affecting membership are eligibility and orientation. Six types of nonmembers are listed—the candidate, the detached person, the potential member, the marginal person, the antagonistic person, and the autonomous person. Nonmembers are sometimes threatening to a group in that they increase tension. This amount of threat is connected to how the group copes with its tension.

14

Cultural Interchange in Family
Consultation: A Case Study

The single case (an N of one) has been used by leading authorities to carry the message and the meaning of the method or system of applied psychology. The case is a family, the target is a boy's behavior. It is very difficult for me to know who has experienced the most change in behavior: the boy, his parents, the teachers at his school, the school's counselor, or the graduate students who started and will finish the three years task. This is written at the halfway point. Eighteen months have elapsed since the beginning of treatment. As the book was published there were about nine months left to go on the three years. The gains recorded to date make the report justified because if we were to stop now (at this writing) the boy would probably be able to complete his education in regular classes.

The most difficult task I face in science is the dissemination of the proper understanding of methods and techniques used in group counseling to bring changes in behavior to the participants. The substance of my career as a teacher "swings like the pendulum do" through the lives of persons who come and who go along the way. Colleagues are an especially important peer group for me. Students come as unleavened mixtures and go as sweet or sour dough, usually never completely baked. The families we encounter, because the centers are a training ground for all participants, seem to fall quickly into the short-term or long-term case categories. The long-term case reported here is typical of the antecedent conditions in such cases. The family had tried almost everything. Nothing seemed to have helped. Probably no other family would permit the extensive interventions necessary to carry out the treatment phases in this case. The cooperative efforts of the family, combined with the persistent efforts of about a dozen persons, brought about the changes in behavior reported on the following pages. Group counseling is the organization of humans into viable producers of environments for others to learn, and in learning, produce new environments for the producers, and consequently, new learning for all.

Some may ask whether this case is the typical case for school counselors to handle. I can say yes, it was for one school counselor—a case she handled by enlisting resources outside the school. The school counselor brought the case to the center. She remained active in the case by attending the weekly sessions with the parents and the boy, and by coordinating the school personnel and classroom placements.

Our Family Consultation Centers charge no fees because graduate students in counseling train there in group work under supervision. During the summer the graduate students working on the case were paid for their services from funds supplied by the parents. During the academic year, any professional service given outside the center or training milieu was paid for by the parents. I am the only person anyone can identify from what is written here. All other names, times, places, and events are disguised to protect the identity of everyone concerned. Those close to the case and those involved in the treatment will be able to identify themselves and others. This is a happy story and we all share in the success.

For the reader, I am concerned that you can begin to understand family group consultation as a method, and group counseling as a versatile tool or vehicle on which one or many persons may learn together any new behavior the culture provides. My skill—or yours—will place the limits on what is accomplished.

The Family

Sammy Suzuki was 9½ years old. He had lived in America for the past five years. The mother is Japanese born, non-English speaking, approximately forty-five years of age. The father is older, maybe fifty-five. For each parent, the current marriage is number two. The mother, a former widow, has a daughter about seventeen years old. The father had a married daughter about thirty years of age.

In family group consultation any person in or near the family group is invited to participate actively in the sessions. The domestic servant lady attended all group counseling sessions. She too spoke only Japanese. I do not speak Japanese. We have an interpreter, a colleague who is doing advanced graduate work.

The family has lived in Honolulu since about 1963. They maintain a home in Japan. The father lives there most of each year. He spends approximately three months in Honolulu each winter. The father was born in California, and lived there until he was about thirty-five. Because he is a citizen of these United States, he wanted his son raised here in the 50th state. The father founded a business in Japan. The business has done well and supports the international addresses of the family. Sammy and his mother make two or three trips a year to Japan. They would spend more time in Japan if we did not require their presence in Honolulu for most of the summer. Sammy speaks two languages, Japanese and English. Japanese was his first language, an important point because he thinks in Japanese. Language is a way of thinking. For example, English tends to polarize our thinking because of the structure of a simple sentence. Every language is not the same in this respect, a minor point.

The family lives at an expensive address and sends the child to a public school away from the home neighborhood on what is called in Honolulu a *district exception.* Sammy goes to and from school on the city bus system. This was begun after one year of treatment to encourage independence and to demonstrate to all the staff, teachers, and parents that Sammy could ride the bus by himself. In both Tokyo and Honolulu during the past year, Sammy has demonstrated his ability to find his way alone.

History

Every case of unique quality comes to us with a history. Remember that Family Consultation was begun in a Psychiatric Clinic of a medical school with cases for which no service could be found. Sammy was a terminal case in the sense that everyone had failed or stopped active treatment. The family seemed resigned to what was painfully obvious; no one wanted to teach Sammy. At age 9½ Sammy had been dropped from more than a dozen schools, private and public. The most recent turndown had come from a national chain of schools that specialize in resident training for mentally retarded and emotionally disturbed children.

Sammy was under the care of a psychiatrist and taking depressant drugs to keep him more docile. The public elementary school had accepted Sammy with the stipulation the family attend the Family Group Consultation Center in a nearby church school facility. It was late in November when we first met Sammy and his mother. We invited the domestic servant to come to subsequent sessions. The school counselor was a graduate student in family group consultation at the University of Hawaii. The center served as the laboratory for each student to work with families under supervision. Sammy and his mother were introduced to our work via the initial interview. Before we began our counseling, Sammy had been accepted into the school and placed in a class for the mentally retarded.

The medical history indicated two very significant facts. (1) The electroencephalograph showed a normal brain-wave pattern. (2) The physical health status of Sammy was well within the normal range for boys his age. Medically speaking, he was OK. Why was he on tranquilizers? Because he was on tranquilizers, we could not see the full range of his reported hyperactivity. With a medical record like this, our psychiatric consultants in Oregon and Hawaii have encouraged us to work without medications so the full impact of our interventions in group counseling can be assessed. We followed the same strategy with Sammy. He was off tranquilizers within three months from our initial contact. No further dependence on medications has been necessary.

What complaints were recorded in the school record? Each time Sammy was refused readmission to a former school or dropped from a current school, he had received statements in his record to justify the professional decisions reached. Sammy does not respond to directions given by the teacher. Sammy does not attend. He was out of school at least as much as he was in school. On paper, Sammy could meet most of the criteria to classify him as an autistic child. Yet he was not autistic. He was a behavior and social control problem at school. At home he had mother and one or two servants to meet his every whim. The mother remained convinced that Sammy had a neurological deficiency, and therefore no one was responsible for Sammy's behavior—especially his mother. Sammy was placed in a special class for MR's with a teacher who speaks both English and Japanese. This is not unusual in Honolulu, where we have many teachers with a Japanese ancestry. We began in the usual way. The family came and the initial session was conducted with several counselors present. We asked my Japanese-speaking colleague to be on the case as a counselor-interpreter. The school counselor presented the case to us by giving a brief verbal introduction. We explained, through the interpreter, how we work. The conditions we set require everyone significant to the case to be present everytime we meet. Exceptions are easily made for good reasons but when the mother came to the second session alone because the boy was asleep at home, we refused to meet with her alone and sent her home. She returned the following week with everyone on board.

The story began to unfold. It seemed each of the schools had required a complete psychological and frequently a psychiatric, neurological, and medical work-up with each new admission application. As a certified psychologist first in Oregon and currently in Hawaii, I know the data were complete and competently recorded. The answer to Sammy's problems must not be in the psychiatric and psychological data. That clue was a big jump for us. We would not need to get reruns on the work completed. The first decision was to study the case carefully and determine whether we could undertake the long task of trying to rehabilitate Sammy. The study period would be six months long. At the end of the spring semester, we would reevaluate and decide the next steps.

The history of Sammy's psychosocial development provided the second major clue to the treatment strategy we would employ. *Sammy had never had a playmate his own age.* He had servants and a mother, and almost anything else he wanted. We used this clue to begin to understand what psychosocial developmental tasks Sammy had missed. Our job became a psychosocial scavenger hunt. What we found out was so gross and overwhelming that we decided Sammy would require a group of age-mates or peers who would tolerate him long enough for Sammy to begin to have models to imitate. A group of bright nine-year-old boys was recruited. Parents were asked to give permission for their sons to participate. Every afternoon for one to two hours after school for six months the "peer group" met with one of the counselors for a play period. During the summer the boys were enrolled in a special summer fun program financed by the family and staffed by two counselors. The first summer program was nine weeks long. The purpose was to provide peer models for Sammy.

In September, ten months after we started, we were able to take measures of his achievement in school subjects and get baseline scores for IQ. The socialization was a success. We were ready for the special tutoring in reading and physical-motor development. The second summer a pair of boys from the original peer group came every day for six weeks to help tutor Sammy and reestablish the social modeling project.

The School

The school is a standard elementary public school including grades K–6. It has special classes for slow learners and mentally retarded. The total enrollment is under 1,000. About 50 percent of the children come from public housing, low-income families of mixed and multiple national and racial origins. The remaining 50 percent come from middle-class homes. The predominant ancestry is Japanese.

The school counselor divides her time between testing and counseling. Through family and teacher consultation, the counselor has learned to expand and extend the counseling services. Resources external to the school in the surrounding community have been mobilized to help with specific problems. We are such a resource at the Family Consultation Center. An example of the cooperative effort in action is that Sammy's teacher attends regularly the family group consultation sessions.

The school district is most cooperative. The central office staff in Special Services welcomes the assistance with difficult cases. The principal gives the support of his office to our combined efforts.

The Special Class

There are eight to twelve children enrolled in the special class. The children are classified mentally retarded. Some of the children are slow learners because they are deprived, disadvantaged, or emotionally disturbed. Whatever the status or label, the children accept Sammy at school and at home. The boys like to go to Sammy's house and spend the night because their homes are modest by contrast to Sammy's affluent apartment in an exclusive neighborhood. When Sammy is invited to spend a night with one of his classmates, he is put in as one of the family of five to eight persons. At dinner, there may be no seconds. The portions served may be limited. In this way Sammy has been exposed to a different way of life.

Sammy is able to do the work in the class. He is particularly adept at math and reading. If his social behavior will continue to improve, Sammy will be placed with the regular class for his grade.

The teacher is a key member of the team. Some of the special tutoring came during the regular class time. Sammy was able to carry his regular in-classroom schedule and meet his tutors by special arrangements.

The Family Group Consultation Counseling Session

Each week during the academic year and during the summer program we all meet with Sammy, his mother, the domestic servant, and the half-sister and the father when either of the latter are resident in the home. The counseling group includes the interpreter, who doubles as supervisor of the case, a psychologist consultant (the author), the school counselor, two graduate students who have been on the case from the start, and any other specialist we employ for specific services such as testing, tutoring, and general assistance. The teacher comes on call, or whenever she has a reason of her own she can sit in on one or more sessions.

The sessions are conducted as evaluation and planning periods. The number of persons in contact with Sammy at any one time may be five or more. We must coordinate each effort and assess the progress to be certain we are not regressing Sammy rather than advancing with him. Initially, the sessions were regular family counseling periods in which we tried to enlist the usual changes in the family. The mother was so ineffective that I told her to just be herself. The cooperative efforts she has maintained by bringing Sammy to our workers wherever they convene whether at the University, a community college, the optometrist's office, or the school, have been remarkable. It is an expression of the high level of motivation to get help for Sammy. Sammy attends all counseling sessions and carefully monitors all communications in English and Japanese. He is quick to point up any discrepancy the interpreter has made in the translation. On several occasions Sammy has been the interpreter because my colleague was unable to attend.

The coordination of the different professional specialists requires direct supervision and continuous evaluation to assure cooperative effort. Competition would destroy our purposes. We know that no one specialty applied in isolation has enough power to do all things for Sammy. We needed many different special services, some educational, others psychological, social, medical, and psychiatric. The services were applied in a sequence based on measured progress and readiness on Sammy's part.

The Peer Group

The peer group consisted of five nine-year-old boys. They met Sammy in pairs on alternate days beginning in January, about six weeks after our initial session. Each boy was asked if he were interested, after clearance from his parents was secured. The Sammy case was explained to each boy who would eventually be with us. Each boy had to help Sammy learn how to be a boy. The task was unique for each boy. They have continued to be involved and three of them are engaged in the summer (second) program at this writing. They take turns inviting Sammy to their homes for overnight visit. Each boy goes to Sammy's house when invited to a party or for an overnight stay. All of the boys have reached age 11 at the time of this report. Two boys from Sammy's class at school were included in the peer group during the first summer program.

The purpose of the peer group is to provide Sammy with social models to imitate. The goal is socialization of Sammy. In the beginning Sammy could actively function with the peer group for only a few minutes before he would complain of fatigue. Gradually, the stamina gain made it possible to have activities for one hour at a time. The first summer program was scheduled for six hours each day, five days each week for nine weeks. By having regular rest periods, Sammy could keep the schedule by summer's end.

The boys were amazed that Sammy could not keep up with them physically. He could not run, jump, climb, kick, throw, catch or bat the ball, or do most of the expected skills for nine-year-olds. Sammy's eye–hand and small-muscle coordination was very poor. He had never manipulated the blocks, pegs, and toys so familiar to the development of such abilities and skills. His mother said they had (always) done the manipulations for him. Sammy did have many toys and games. He also had servants to do the actual work. Sammy still expects the tutor to do any work new to him, expecting to be served.

The peer group began to do what no teacher or adult could hope to do—model every behavior needed. The jungle gym is a convenient example of what Sammy could do. With great effort he could get up one level off the ground. His hands and arms were not strong enough to support him. Sixteen months later Sammy did some balance skills that two of the peer group currently working with him in the second summer program could not do without special instruction and practice from Sammy. Sammy did five full push-ups at one time beginning the second summer program. Prior to this time he could only do "girl" style push-ups (knees touching the floor).

The tutors and supervisors report an increase in competition between Sammy and the peers. Sammy competes with his older sister who came to visit from Japan. Whenever the mother is away the children are congenial. The ruckus begins when the mother comes into the situation. Competition, in the peer group and sibling group, is considered an improvement in Sammy's behavior because he is more frequently successful in the give-and-take of routine encounters. An example came up in the first family consultation session of the second summer program. The peer group boys were there to report on Sammy's behavior. Sammy didn't hesitate to use the information he had about one of the boys in the peer group. "Johnny shi shi in the bed," Sammy said. (Shi shi is Japanese for urinate.) It was a fact that Johnnie found vulnerable because more than a year earlier Johnny went to spend a night with Sammy. At eleven p.m. the maid came in excitement to the mother, "Johnny shi shi the bed!" The mother calmed the maid and did a commendable job of handling the minor crisis. We wondered why Johnny's mother had failed to inform Sammy's mother about Johnny's enuresis. However, Sammy used the fact to his advantage. Johnny and Mark were extremely reluctant to report any negative behavior incidents and found more favorable examples to relate to the group. Following the group session, Sammy went home with Johnny to spend the night, as scheduled.

Eighteen months earlier no such verbal exchange could have happened. Sammy would have been disarmed by his peers. Social pressure created from the report of a teacher or a counselor would have caused distress in Sammy, but the response would most likely have been inappropriate or "junk" behavior. Junk behavior is the use by Sammy of apparently randomly selected behavior, both verbal and nonverbal.

Anger is another example of new learning in the peer group based on imitation of the other boys. Sammy has learned to express anger, act out the stress of it, calm himself, and proceed as usual in appropriate activity—all within a reasonable time period.

The following quotations are taken from the case reports kept by us from the beginning of each new phase in our planned work with Sammy. Each counselor and tutor kept a log each day. The patterns revealed the gaps and voids in Sammy's social-physical-psychological behavior repertoire. There were many behavior acts he could not perform. Our hypothesis was that Sammy had not had exposure to appropriate behavior, and if we arranged to expose Sammy to new behavior he would be able to develop his own appropriate behavior. This was not entirely accurate as reflected in the visual-motor training we have had a specialist conduct for the past six months. Movie film was used to record what Sammy could do at the beginning of the exercises. That is the base-line data. Then periodic records are made. When the film is later spliced together and run in sequence, it is possible to see the contrast (improvement in before-and-after behavior). The following report is based on data collected over a five-month period from January to June, 1969.

> The data were collected at his home, daily peer group sessions and the weekly family group consultation counseling session. . . .Certain patterns began to emerge such as gaps or voids and incompetencies in his social-physical-psychological interactions.
>
> Physically, Sammy is about at the level of a five-year-old boy. In the initial peer-group sessions, the other boys described him as "skinny." Stamina is very low. He cannot do a push-up, a chin-up, or hang by his hands on a jungle gym. Sammy can be actively engaged with the peer group in active play for only two or three minutes before he complains of fatigue. Motor development is below the norm for six-year-old boys. For example, in skills such as running, throwing, jumping, and other eye-hand coordinations, his development appears to be around the five-year-old level, based on the evaluation by a professional physical education consultant (March 1969).
>
> Sammy is emotionally immature. He acts out in apparent random

fashion whenever he cannot cope with the expectations in group play. He uses nonverbal behavior to express his feelings.

Social development is Sammy's most incompetent area. There are so many behaviors missing that Sammy appears to have voids in his behavior repertoire. Sammy has little or no concept of territoriality, property rights, or the meaning of the word "no." His behavior isolates him in the group. He is not safe to play with because he is unpredictable in all situations. Sammy has no apparent social play skills. The only competent area he seems to have is manipulating adults to the extent that they appear helpless.

Physical-motor incompetencies influence the emotional condition in Sammy. He becomes very upset and hostile when he attempts to do the things other children do with ease. He is overwhelmed most of the time in play situations. Sammy is not successful in social relationships with peers because he cannot make the appropriate responses to the simplest social encounters. Sammy's social interactions are impeded by bizarre expression of his emotions. He has little concept of pain and danger. For example, Sammy may push another child when on a stairway or throw rocks at the other children whenever he is overwhelmed by not knowing an appropriate behavior response. Sammy may be accurately described as a misfit, incompetent, and unpredictable boy. Because he has not had peers to play with in the past, Sammy does not know the informal culture signals which cue the behavior in a social interaction group. Parents and servants have always met his every whim. Sammy is in control to the extent that he knows someone will rescue him. (Note that a year after these notes were recorded, a tutor in math reported the same behavior. What Sammy didn't know, he expected the tutor to supply immediately.)

Sammy's physical-motor base line emphasizes a lack of eye-hand–small-muscle coordination. Stamina is absent because only minor movements require great effort and are exhausting. Because Sammy was reared in social isolation (had no playmates) he never developed the skills necessary for social-group play. When he went to school, the other children ostracized him for lack of skills; his protective parents kept him home. As a consequence, by age 9, the gap between Sammy and his age-mates had become an "impossible" barrier for Sammy to handle alone.

February, 1969. After running for two minutes, Sammy was exhausted and panting for air. The sessions for play in the peer group were gradually extended. In two months, the sessions were extended to one hour, and Sammy could remain active the full time. After three months Sammy could keep active for well over two and a half hours.

The base line for jungle gym was to barely hang on to one bar and support his body weight. In six days Sammy could move across three bars, but the blisters on his hands made it quite painful. A month later, hands hardened, Sammy made it across all twelve bars. Sammy showed rapid improvement in running, walking, and throwing. (Catching a ball requires eye-hand and small-muscle coordination. Special instruction was needed. It was given under the direction of a specialist during the second year of treatment.)

The emotional and social functions were handled in the peer group by counselor verbal responses. The strategy was to explain what was happening in each situation. Subsequently, each event was verbalized by Sammy to the counselor or to one of the peer group. The boys in the peer group were encouraged to do the same verbalizing. The results were most encouraging both from the standpoint of the peers' ability to verbalize to Sammy and Sammy's diminished panic responses to new social encounters.

Perhaps the most difficult single task I faced in the Sammy Suzuki case was the student counselors' reluctance to believe Sammy's behavior was an accurate representation of his condition. As they learned to verbalize to Sammy, he returned the verbal behavior and dropped the nonverbal excesses. Within four months from the beginning of treatment, Sammy replaced a sad and indifferent appearance with an active-happy chatter at home and at school.

The social base line was so low we called Sammy's condition, "social illiteracy." Sammy was unable to communicate with peers. He was very effective with adults if we look only at his ability to manipulate them. It took me some ten months to get across to the counselors that Sammy was an expert at manipulating them. When they began to catch him manipulating them, he would verbalize that he was teasing. One example was reported by a counselor who found it very uncomfortable to come into the department chairman's office to get Sammy. Sammy used the behavior for most of a month before the manipulation was exposed.

Sammy has a very short attention span. The erratic pattern of behavior has slowly modified until a recent (June 1970) psychological examiner's report stated, "Sammy can sit and work on a given task for more than one hour at a time."

Testing

The neurological examinations in Sammy's record all confirm the absence of any abnormal brain wave patterns. We did have a follow-up examination by our consulting psychiatrist in March 1969. The report confirmed the earlier impressions and we proceeded under the assumption that Sammy is neurologically sound.

The psychological examinations were conducted in March 1969. No results were obtained due to Sammy's manipulation of the psychological examiner. Sammy responded in Japanese to many of the questions. The examiner did not speak or understand Japanese.

In September 1969 we were able to get a complete set of psychological tests administered. The base lines in mental ability and achievement in reading, spelling and arithmetic were recorded.

Sammy, Age 10 years 5 months (September 1969)

	September 1969	May 1970	September 1970
WISC Verbal IQ	57	70	82
Reading, grade level, Gray Oral	2.7	4.4	4.6
Spelling, grade level, wide range	3.2	3.9	3.5
Arithmetic, grade level, wide range	3.6	3.9	3.9
Reading, grade level, wide-range	3.5	3.9	3.9

In subtests on the Gates-McKillop Reading Diagnostic Test form 2 in Sept. 1969 and 1970, and Form 1, May 1970, showed the following pattern:

Gates-McKillop	September 1969 Form 2	May 1970 Form 1	September 1970 Form 2
Words, untimed	3.6	3.7	3.8
Words, flash	3.7	3.8	3.9
Phrases, flash	5.4	5.4 (perfect score)	5.4
Visual equivalents for sounds			
Initial sounds	16	19 (perfect score)	19
Final sounds	3	14 (perfect score)	14
Vowels (10)	1	6	7
Oral vocabulary	2.3	4.7	4.1
Auditory discrimination	11	12 (14 possible)	12
Auditory blending	0	7 (15 possible)	11
Letter-sound corrspondence	0	25 (26 possible)	26

The test examiner reported marked improvement in behavior during the test administration periods. Sammy could work for more than an hour at a time. He was not easily distracted and wanted to know how well he was doing. These behaviors are in marked contrast to reports of earlier testing where attention and effort were absent.

The visual-motor training had helped improve handwriting. Auditory memory and immediate recall improved from a September 1969 base line of 6 years 3 months, to a February 1970 score of 9 years 6 months. Sammy was better able to follow verbal instructions. He continues to give up if the task is too difficult or new to him.

The Gaps in School Subject Learning

Nearly ten months elapsed before we were able to secure reliable base-line scores from tests administered by qualified professionals not regularly connected to the case. It took that long before Sammy had developed enough socialization ability to comply with the requirements of the testing room. The results reflected the pattern Sammy had acquired from his staccato pattern of school attendance. One early clue to Sammy's intelligence was the fact he spoke two languages. Knowing how to speak a language and knowing *about* a language are by no means the same thing. Sammy was using two languages. He knows how to speak and comprehend in each language. However, he did not know the isolated sounds of either language. Phonics, and even words in isolation, constituted a problem because Sammy didn't know anything *about* either language. Sammy had learned to read in much the same way as most people learn to speak a language. He read words in context with comprehension, but he could not identify many of the same words in isolation. This gap reflected in the test profile of scores. Sammy learned to read by rote memory. He can identify the gestalt of word combinations because that is the way he learned initially. The math tutor reports a similar pattern in arithmetic combinations of numbers. He knows some but others are missed and the relationships are not known. Sammy demands the answers to addition problems, again using the earlier pattern of expecting the servant to rescue him. Learning how to learn has been missed. Sammy cannot use what he knows, put it together with a new problem, and solve for a new answer.

The void of problem solving skill combined with the expectation that a servant will rescue him is the gap the second summer program tried to close. The following summary and recommendations are taken from the May 1970 testing report

Summary.

1. Reading, spelling and arithmetic skills are developing and are at least at the 3.9 grade level.
2. Handwriting is still poor, but much improved over September 1969.
3. Visual skills are still superior to the purely auditory.
4. Context is still the basic approach to reading, but phonics skill is developing and is applied when context is not available.

Recommendations

1. Spelling: Use *Sound and Sense* or some other program that is logically organized and provides application of spelling principles taught.
2. Arithmetic: Sammy needs to learn basic multiplication and division facts. A combined flash-card and practice-sheet approach should work well. Borrowing, fractions, two-digit multiplication, long division, time and linear measurement conversions should be taught step-by-step and practice sheets should be provided.
3. Handwriting: Continue with step-by-step instruction in simple cursive.
4. Reading: Continue with Houghton Mifflin for structural analysis and meaning. Use library books that appeal to him for further enjoyment.

Evaluative Observations

1. Attention: Sammy can work well for periods of over an hour in a one: one situation. He was not distracted in the testing period and seemed to enjoy working. Sammy wanted to start testing as soon as he arrived in the test room, cut his recess short, and invited me to stay for lunch so he could work some more in the afternoon. He gains satisfaction from his work.
2. Approach: Definite limits and expectations are required, but Sammy now also responds to a friendly, supportive approach. At one point he asked how he was doing and indicated that he wanted his teachers and his mother to be pleased. For the first time he seemed to me to be affected by others.

The gaps in Sammy's visual-motor areas were extremely handicapping in social encounters with peer-group and classroom learning. Special exercises were employed under the supervision of an optometrist. The specialist recommended exercises to strengthen eye-hand coordination, gross muscle involvement used in handwriting, balance-beam, tactile and auditory perception skills. Tactile manipulation of objects and lined drawings were used to improve visual skills. The results have been very encouraging. Sammy has improved handwriting and playground skills as a result of the special exercises.

Tutoring

In addition to the regular activities in the special classroom at school, we carried on several tutorial projects designed to amplify and extend Sammy's social-emotional development skills, visual-motor skills, and academic skills. The peer group was the first intervention. The boys were to be models for Sammy. They were also encouraged to verbalize many ideas in the events they shared so that Sammy could learn to use words and other cues to interaction in an interpersonal encounter. The group is a complete learning environment. Socialization was the key goal. High expectations were placed on the peer group. Play group activities and overnight visitations were the vehicles for employing peers. The social-emotional development phase is continuous and varies only in intensity and frequency of contacts. During the academic year 1969–70 social-emotional peer group work was reduced to permit more time for academic tutoring. The visual-motor tutoring also was carried on from November 1969. The second summer program was a combination of all three emphases.

Visual-motor tutoring was carried on through a specialist consultant to direct the special exercises to improve visual-motor skills. During the academic year about five hours each week were used for the exercises. The summer program increased the time to ten hours per week for the six weeks. The peer group participates with Sammy in all of the exercises and academic tutoring in the second summer program. Games for fun are a part of the summer program too.

Academic tutoring is aimed at reading and mathematics. Handwriting is also included. Phonics continue to be worked on until the tutor is reasonably assured Sammy has mastered all of the sounds. Academic tutoring has been carried on in reading and phonics since September 1969.

The schedule for tutoring in academic skills has been carried as a part of the regular school day. Sammy is permitted to come to the University for two hours every morning during the academic year for tutorial. The exercises are carried on after school hours in a room provided at the school Sammy attends. The summer program is carried on at the University from 9 a.m. to 3 p.m. daily.

The Case of Sammy Suzuki

Initial Session

I always try to get the most learning opportunities for graduate students compatible with effective professional practice. The Suzuki family was treated in the same way as other families coming to family group consultation centers. They are seen without too much advanced information in order to provide training in history taking and data collection from a family in a group counseling setting. The school counselor, the classroom teacher, Sammy, and his mother all met with three counselors for the initial session. Verbal communication was always through the interpreter. There was a considerable amount of nonverbal communication. The history of the case was quickly reviewed. The family was given an explanation about our methods of work. We agreed to work on the case for a few sessions until a decision could be made about whether we had any service to offer. We asked if the maid might also come to the sessions.

In the initial session, the family is facing a new and sometimes unfamiliar situation. This makes a good opportunity to watch the family work. Several significant clues were gathered beyond the verbal messages. The first of these is that Sammy kept a close watch on everything being said in both English and Japanese. The emotional climate seemed to be monitored also and Sammy's behavior reflected the levels of stress or intensity brought on by the specific subject being disclosed. The clue was important because it is the first evidence to indicate that Sammy was not autistic. The second clue was derived from observing the mother in her attempts to control Sammy. She was very ineffective and appeared bewildered about whether to take action or remain passive. Either way Sammy seemed to do about as he pleased.

The initial session closed after about one and one-half hours of meeting time. The teacher agreed to work with Sammy for up to two hours per day. It was six weeks before Sammy came to school long enough to stay for lunch. Several more weeks passed before Sammy put in a full day. Sammy was described as a "monster" of a social control problem in school. He was so excited about being with peers that his fatigue level would not permit a very long school day. His mother brought him to school and picked him up when school closed. It was nearly a year after the initial session before Sammy was permitted to ride the bus to and from school. He had several transfers to make because he lived out of the school neighborhood. Bus riding has been a success from the beginning. This contrast is one way to see the changes brought into Sammy's behavior. The initial session did give some clues to the possible future success of treatment.

Treatment Plan

Step One: Get the teacher to stay in the situation with Sammy in her classroom.

Step Two: Achieve the massive support of the mother over the three years forecast as essential to any degree of success with the case.*

Step Three: Mobilize the school counselor, principal, and district resources to provide the support for all of the special requests we might make. Provision for giving regular reports and the continuing involvement of the school counselor have made the whole activity a part of the school's responsibility.

Step Four: Mobilize professional counselors and teachers from among the graduate students in our department. The same key personnel should be involved all the way through the three years. The interpreter doubles as a reading tutor. Two men are counselors in charge of the special summer program.

Step Five: Complete the diagnosis to determine the possibility that interventions and treatment strategies available to us will make the differences necessary to assure reasonable chances for success.

Step Six: Train the counselors and specialists who come on the case to work directly with Sammy. The school counselor and classroom

---

*The mother reported after one year that she had wanted to quit many times but because she could see progress she stayed with it. In the Spring of 1970, Sammy began to phone Japan and visit with his father. He initiated the phone calls by himself.

teacher are important to the overall success. They are given continuing access to help when it is needed.

Step Seven: Evaluation at regular intervals by outside professional consultants is essential to reliable and valid measurement of progress. Evaluation prevents the forming of self-fulfilling hypotheses due to halo effect.

The treatment plan called for regular meetings with the family and all persons actively engaged with the case. The idea central to the treatment was the total overall effect on Sammy. We worked on socialization until Sammy was ready to be tested. Then we began to work on the academic gaps in achievement. Visual-motor development was a continuing area to treat. Once a phase began, the continuous effort to carry on the treatment was maintained. Intensity and frequency of treatment was varied to keep from overloading Sammy's ability to respond.

Several times a year Sammy would go home to Japan. The father comes to Honolulu on regular visits. The family finances the special tutoring and the special summer programs.

The treatment plan did not call on the mother for any major change in her life at home. She handled Sammy by providing everything he wanted, immediately. If she is able to change this pattern, school and peer group will be more effective. Neither school nor peer group is going to give Sammy what he wants. They will continue to expect Sammy to measure up to his age-mates.

Strategy for Coordination

The strategy we use is an open involvement policy. You can participate but we won't beg you. Once you are in the coordinated activities, the inputs from your agency, speciality, or professional service come to bear on the case. Whenever there is any money, the graduate students get first claim to it. If one of them cannot perform the service the money goes to purchase the service. My service and instructional role are paid by the university as part of my regular teaching, laboratory and practicum load. The family is able to underwrite the extra professional services we purchase from outside consultants.

The plan is to bring every resource to bear on the specific problem involved at a given time. This case may well be the only one of its kind, but I doubt it. Coordination, if adequately done, is a good opportunity to help students learn the management skills needed in counseling and consulting.

Maintaining Continuing Contact

The case of a family may come and go without much being accomplished. In the Suzuki case the need was great because they had been about everywhere. No one had helped. The public school in all of its most depressing ways shines as a jewel in the "one more chance" department. For us at the University the chance to learn and the chance to help usually come from terminal cases. If everyone else fails, we can't do any harm? Well, whatever the nostalgia of the martyr complex may be, the fact is that we came to this case mostly by chance factors.

Keeping any case in group counseling requires that we show progress. We did get results with Sammy that parents and others could see and comment about, both in Honolulu and in Japan. We continue to get results with our treatment plan for Sammy. This is what keeps the contact continuing.

Plateaus, Ridges, Valleys, and Peaks

The profile of Sammy's case is an expression of his personal-social-academic condition. The learning curves for Sammy run as uniquely as his case history. In the social-emotional and interpersonal areas, Sammy is able to learn many things with one trial. Whether one trial or many trials, the learning Sammy could do was directly dependent upon the counselors, teachers, tutors and others immediately involved. The next section will be devoted to this important topic of counselor development.

My task was twofold. Work on the diagnosis and analysis of Sammy's behavior, and train the counselors and significant others to work with Sammy. Managing the case was carried on a continuous basis. Management of the case was a small task compared to the training function. A peak (high point) in the profile of trainess appeared in May 1970. The mother took a stand and moved into physical encounter with Sammy. For a full thirty minutes the two of them carried on an intimate engagement, every bit as intimate as copulating. They were yelling, kicking, biting and restraining limbs and objects for throwing. Sammy was just past his eleventh birthday and his strength and stamina were enough to almost overwhelm the mother, but neither of them had to give up. We were in a regular family session the same as we hold every week. Sammy's half-sister (age 19) was present, the maid had previously returned to Japan. I was there along with all the regulars, the interpreter, school counselor, and the two male counselors.

This encounter was a new high point (peak) because we had not known the nature of the mother's involvement nor the strong emotional mother-son tie that had developed. Previously we had observed the mother as ineffective in an overt control of Sammy. The chief method employed was to give Sammy whatever it was he wanted. The incident that triggered the encounter was a quite simple thing. Sammy tossed the thermos bottle cap into the air and arched it back over his shoulder. A few drops of orange juice spilled on one of the male counselors. His response was an expression of mild annoyance—he had hesitated. The hesitation probably meant to Sammy that it was no big thing. But mother demanded Sammy apologize to "Mr. Counselor." The incident escalated to a direct physical encounter between Sammy and his mother. The daughter-sister became embarrassed and tried to intervene. We asked her to please not interfere, just let it run its course. She removed herself from the room. A week later, we confirmed her reasons and discussed the incident in full.

We do not stop intimate encounters unless there is danger of lethal injury. The verbal exchanges were in Japanese. The interpreter kept notes and shared with us observers. There is always a risk in intense emotional encounter but it is far less than the risk of intervention. Sammy was angry and the mother was determined. Together, they struggled to a point near enough to exhaustion to permit each to stop without losing face. A very few minutes after it was over, the two of them were examining each other's battle wounds consisting of bruises and bite marks. In group counseling, we work to build up relationships between persons. The relationship is only worth as much as it will withstand when demands are placed upon it. Suddenly, we saw for the first time how strongly the mother felt about Sammy. There was the reason she had stayed in family consultation at considerable cost to her usual way of life. The peak was for us as much as for anyone else. She was really a partner and not just another ineffective mother. All the hours we had spent discussing the strategy of setting limits for Sammy at home, at school, at the special treatment events, had paid off. Sammy had learned to handle anger, express it, and carry on—all in sequence. Socialization was progressing.

One year earlier, in May 1969, the record contains two reports of incidents that took place in the peer group. The plateau is a frequent condition in the profile. The one-year interval between the mother-son encounter and the peer group incidents detailed below, may be seen as a plateau.

> May 5, 1969, evening-family consultation session; I related our
> plan of changing the manner of handling Sammy's aggression. He sat

quietly and appeared to listen intently. His school teacher then told the following story: "This afternoon, Sammy hit a little girl on the head with a brush. She started to cry. Sammy was forced to say he was sorry." I asked the teacher if she thought Sammy was sorry or if he appeared guilty. She said, "No." While relating the story, Sammy sat in his chair and alternately raised and lowered his head with closed or squinting eyes—just enough to follow the action in the room. This was his usual position when we related something that in our interpretation deviated negatively from the cultural expectations.

When Sammy came to the play group the following Tuesday, I explained to the boys what we would do when Sammy acted out his aggression. I also explained why we had to change; that it would be important that the boys completely understood the concept of Sammy and his feelings of guilt and consciousness. They would probably be the most realistic and fair judges of its presence or absence. As an adult, my only guide was how I saw the other boys react in a situation to how Sammy related in a similar situation. The boys, on the other hand, would immediately be able to tell if Sammy's feelings fitted the context. This would also prepare the boys to think in terms of guilt and how to verbalize these feelings should the need for a more structured model arise.

The boys' reaction to the plan was rather negative at first: B. said, "Oh, we'll never be able to keep him from doing things now!" D.: "This is really junk—we have to pay him back if he does something! ... He'll get away with anything." We talked about the whole idea of guilt and being sorry some more and the boys finally agreed to go along with the plan. Sammy had listened very closely to the whole affair and appeared excited—at times not quite knowing what to do with himself. We then decided to go to D's park.

In the car, while driving up to the park, the boys interacted with each other as usual. Sammy interrupted them several times and successfully got their attention, explaining and restating what we had decided to do with his acts of violence. "You can't hit back" "Nobody can hit back" "You can't hit back either," said one boy. "You can't hit back if I do something—you just talk to me—yah!" When the boys had confirmed his questions and he seemed satisfied that they understood, he stopped asking and joined the usual interaction in the car.

The boys started to play when we arrived at the park. Later they instigated a new game by running down from the top of a slide, which faced the merry-go-round, some twenty yards away, and jumped on the merry-go-round while it was in motion. The merry-go-round was divided into eight pie-shaped slots separated by iron bars. This game required not only a sense of balance in order to run down without falling but also the ability to judge distance and speed. (I tried it once and had my pelvis nearly severed in half by the iron bar before being jarred onto the ground.) The boys quickly became good at this game but Sammy couldn't get up enough courage to try. They finally encouraged him to try in slow motion. He was successful—big cheer from the boys. Later he was eagerly awaiting his turn on top of the slide with the other boys. He did misjudge his jump on the merry-go-round several times, but that was the point of the game and it did not seem to bother him too much. When this game was exhausted they had their snack and played basketball with a coconut. Sammy stayed with the game for only a short while and went over to play with the water tap for the remainder of the period.

As I sat back and watched the boys interact, I wondered why all the verbal confirmation in the car was so important. How and when would Sammy test the reality of our new agreement on aggressive acting out? From past experience I knew he could set the situation up anytime he wanted to. I did not notice any acting out or testing today; on the contrary, he seemed to be more aware of his fair turn in line behind the slide. His withdrawal to play alone was not uncommon—the later game was much more complex socially than the first which was more motor oriented. Had he learned that our culture will accept a physical weakling if he is socially acceptable but not visa versa?

Two weeks later, May 19, we decided to explore a nearby creek. We found a storm-drain outlet, it was about four feet in diameter and several hundred yards inside a faint light from a drain was visible through the tunnel. The boys were afraid to enter the tunnel but wanted to explore it anyway, so we fumbled our way further in through the dark musty tunnel. There was tense excitement in the voices as we slowly moved on holding hands. Someone said, "What if we find a monster?" "There's a giant spider," said another. This was followed by screams and tense laughter. As we moved on, the boys and particularly Sammy, noticed the clear strong echo in the tunnel. It took several seconds for a sound to come back from the other end. This really amused Sammy, and he made the discovery that the echo came back in a deeper tone. He excitedly modulated his voice demonstrating to us how a high shrilly tone came back as normal and a deep sound came back as a monstrous groan.

When the boys later started to talk about imaginary dead men up ahead in the tunnel, they finally talked themselves out of going any further and started out. Once out they talked about how scary it had been and then started to play with the rocks and water. When it was time to go, Sammy threw his shoe into the water. The boys verbalized their disgust: "You stupid idiot. Go get it!" "Look what Sammy did." "You threw it in. Now get it." I told them we had to leave now or we'd be late and proceeded, with the other boys, to climb over the embankment. The boys kept looking back and hollering: "Hurry up Sammy or you'll be left behind." "Get your shoe." A short while later Sammy caught up with us, carrying his shoes.

In the evening at the family consultation session, we made Sammy retell the day's event. He emphasized the echo and being scared in the tunnel: "Boy, Mr. B., never take us there again—I was scared." It was obvious that he liked it, but he must have learned our cultural way of saying so. When I told him that I had been scared too, he said, "Yeah-that was scary, but the boys were scared too!" At the next play session, he brought the subject up again: "I was scared in the tunnel! You [the boys] were scared too?" It was too redundant for the boys to keep on that old subject and they soon dismissed the topic but for some reason it seemed important to Sammy—as if he were comparing or validating feelings. I wonder if he was unsure of the cues he had received in the tunnel. How could he be sure his feelings fitted the context?

Counselor Development

The case of Sammy Suzuki and his family is not typical. No intent is here to say to you that every counselor must work with family groups or one family like Sammy's. The case, in full, is illustrative of what counselors, teachers, and parents can do in cooperation because we are doing it. Learning how to cooperate and getting the school policies to encourage the strategy constitute another task the counselor must learn. Group counseling is a way of living and working to bring the right resources to bear on a given problem. No dependence on one model or method should be permitted to offset the treatment plan. Counselor development is necessary if the person called *counselor* will know how to coordinate the diverse resources resident in most of our communities. We shared this case of Sammy Suzuki because the psychotherapy-verbal model would not have achieved our goals. Frequently, we had to invent a way of working with Sammy. The qualifications of counselors were developed as the services were needed. Qualification implied the possibility of disqualification. The Suzuki family was especially effective at disqualification. It was not a conscious plot. It was a cultural difference in values. I found the task of preventing disqualification quite difficult. Suzuki's Japanese custom requires they give gifts to show appreciation for services given to them. We were working with Sammy, so gifts arrived for each of us. The violation of counseling ethics was a minor concern. We could rationalize that conflict by accepting their culture rule and respecting their wishes. However, it is not that benign. A gift obligates me in a very curious way which does interfere with my being free to express my professional opinion. Sammy's history was filled with examples of teachers giving reports to the mother affirming the satisfactory progress of Sammy in school because the teacher could not disappoint the mother after accepting the beautiful gifts. Being disqualified in such a pleasant way made gift giving and acceptance a tender trap.

Permission

We do not act without the permission of the person involved. We stay very close to the culture's rules about permission. Privacy is protected by the phenomenon of permission. It is probably true that anything can be abused, even permission. Counselors develop the intuitive quality (fourth-level abstraction) to know when permission is necessary and when it is being abused. In group counseling, permission at one level is not permission on all other levels. Once permission is given, it carries an obligation. The obligation is against violation of it.

Group Expectations

Group counseling depends upon the member's need to meet the group's expectation. Social control and social pressure stem from this force. The counselors become a group when they work in teams sharing a common task. Peer groups and family groups have a similar condition for social control. My expectation is that group counseling will become virtually identical with "natural" groups whenever expectations are important to behavior change.

Delivery System in Group Counseling

A delivery system is the key to success in a group counseling program. If I can deliver only when someone comes to me, I am severely limited by the delivery system. The counselor may find ways to bring people together and discover they are unable to deliver their service because the delivery system they depend upon is bankrupted by the new setting. For example, the counselor cannot bring the teacher out of the classroom. If the counselor's delivery system is bankrupt in the classroom, nothing more can happen. The counselor is faced with the fact that he cannot "get there from here."

We mobilize many resources and bring them to bear upon the problem Sammy has at a given moment. To do this we must be able to deliver whatever is necessary to accomplish the necessary conditions so the referral agent can deliver his service. In our referral system we keep primary responsibility for the case. The referral agent is in our employ and consults with us. However, we do not intervene in his performance of his specialty.

Our delivery system requires a follow-up procedure with each referral. Follow-up is closely tied in with evaluation and continuing treatment. Feedback is a continuous process at all levels in the delivery system. There is always the hazard of one service nullifying another if the coordination is off. The teacher is a key person. She may undo Sammy by the way she works with him or ignores him. Our goal is to have Sammy enrolled in his regular class. Classroom behavior is learned at school. We are depending on the teacher to deliver what we cannot possibly achieve in isolation.

Group work has a different problem with identity factors for the team members. I have the risk of failure. Others have the problem of being nameless in the group. This case abstract has left out everyone's name, except mine. But how do you know "I" refers to "me"? Perhaps the author has used the literary license to hide all the identities? When I do something by myself, I know it is mine. In a group I have no "mine," only "ours."

Mobilization and motivation are big and important concerns. I bring people together for my purposes. They come for their reasons. Whenever we can share the reasons and purposes in some complementary relationship, we then can enhance opportunities for each other. Graduate students want to learn about family group consultation. I want to continue to study group counseling method in a laboratory of human relations. These reasons can serve each other. Once we get underway, we become a group of our own, terminal by design. Like many contrived groups, for a time we share a piece of life.

Owari　　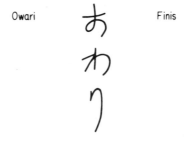　　Finis

Bibliography

ABERCROMBIE, M. L., 1960. *The Anatomy of Judgment.* New York: Basic Books.

ALEXANDER, F. M., 1963. *Fundamentals of Psychoanalysis.* New York: Norton.

ALLEN, R. D., 1931. "A Group Guidance Curriculum in the Senior High School," *Education* 52, 189–194.

ALLPORT, G. W., 1961. *Pattern and Growth in Personality.* New York: Holt.

ALPER, T. G. and G. D. KRONZLER, 1970. "A Comparison of the Effectiveness of Behavioral and Client-Centered Approaches for the Behavior Problems of Elementary School Children," *Elementary School Guidance and Counseling* 5(1), 35–43 (October).

APGA, 1970 (American Personnel and Guidance Association), Testimony before the U.S. Senate Subcommittee on Employment, Manpower and Poverty. March 18, 1970.

ARIETI, S., 1965. "Contributions to Cognition from Psychoanalytic Theory," in G. Massermon (ed.), *Science and Psychoanalysis,* Vol. 8. New York: Grune and Stratton.

AXLINE, V. M., 1964. *Dibs: In Search of Self.* Boston: Houghton Mifflin.

BACH, GEORGE R., 1966. "The Marathon Group: Intensive Practice of Intimate Interaction." *Psychological Reports* 18, 995–1002.

BACH, GEORGE R., 1968. "The Nature of Marathon Man," paper presented at the Western Psychological Association, San Diego, Calif.

BALES, R. F., 1950. *Interaction Process Analysis: A Method for the Study of Small Groups.* Reading, Mass.: Addison-Wesley.

BANDURA, A., 1964. "Social Learning through Imitation." in E. Page (ed.), *Readings for Educational Psychology.* New York: Harcourt.

BANDURA A., 1969. *Principles of Behavior Modification.* New York: Holt.

BANDURA, A., D. ROSS, and S. A. ROSS, 1961. "Transmission of Aggression through Imitation of Aggression Models," *Journal of Social Psychology* 63, 575–582.

BANDURA, A., D. ROSS, and S. A. ROSS, 1963. "A Comparative Test of Status

Envy, Social Power, and Secondary Reinforcement Theories of Identificatory Learning," *Journal of Abnormal and Social Psychology* 67, 527–534.

BATES, M., 1968. "The Fine Art of Groupsmanship or Surviving in Group Interaction," *Personnel and Guidance Journal* 47, 381–384.

BATESON, G., 1942. "Social Planning and the Concept of Deutera-Learning in Relation to the Democratic Way of Life," in *Science, Philosophy and Religion: Second Symposium.* New York: Harper, pp. 81–97.

BAYERL, J. A., 1970. Personal correspondence. Ann Arbor: University of Michigan graduate student.

BEAIRD, J. H., and J. T. STANDISH, 1964. "Audiosimulation in Counselor Training." Final Report, NDEA Title VII, No. 1245. Oregon System of Higher Education, Monmouth, Oreg.

BENEDICT, R., 1934. *Patterns of Culture.* New York: Mentor reprint (1946).

BENNE, K. D., 1964. "History of the T-Group in the Laboratory Setting." in L. P. Bradford, J. R. Gibb, and K. D. Benne (eds.), *T-Group Theory and Laboratory Method.* New York: Wiley.

BENNIS, W. G., E. H. SCHEIN, D. E. BERLEW, and F. I. STEELE (eds.), 1964. *Interpersonal Dynamics.* Homewood, Ill.: Dorsey.

BERNARD, H. W., 1970. *Human Development in Western Culture.* 3rd ed. Boston: Allyn and Bacon.

BERNARD, H. W., and D. W. FULLMER, 1969. *Principles of Guidance: A Basic Text.* Scranton, Pa.: International Textbook.

BERNARD, H. W., and W. C. HUCKINS, 1968. *I.D.E.A. Research Report.* Dayton, Ohio: Kettering Foundation.

BERNE, E., 1964. *Games People Play.* New York: Grove.

BERSTEIN, B., 1964. "Social Class, Speech Systems, and Psychotherapy," *British Journal of Sociology* 15, 54–64.

BERTALANFFY, L. VON, 1962. "General System Theory—a Critical Review," *General Systems Yearbook* 7, 1–20.

BERTALANFFY, L. VON, 1968. *General System Theory: Foundations, Development, Applications,* New York: Braziller.

BESTON, W. H., W. HERON, and T. H. SCOTT, 1954. "Effects of Decreased Variation in the Sensory Environment," *Canadian Journal of Psychology* 8, 70–76.

BETTLEHEIM, BRUNO, 1969. *Children of the Dream.* New York: Macmillan.

BEYMER, L., 1970. "Confrontation Groups: Hula-Hoops?" *Counselor Education and Supervision* 9, 75–86.

BIERER, J., 1962. "The Day Hospital: Therapy in a Guided Democracy," *Mental Hospital* 13, 246–252.

BILOVSKY, D., W. McMASTERS, J. E. SHORR, and S. L. SINGER, 1953. "Individual and Group Counseling," *Personnel and Guidance Journal* 31, 363–365.

BLACHLY, P. H., 1969. "Seduction as a Conceptual Model in the Drug Dependencies," Division of Psychiatry. University of Oregon Medical School, Portland, Oreg.

BLACHLY, P. H. (ed.), 1970. *Drug Abuse: Data and Debate.* Springfield, Ill.: Charles C Thomas.

BLAJAN-MARCUS, S., 1970. "Psychodrama in its Diverse Uses," *The Group Leader's Workshop,* Theory, V-16–20/34:1–5.

BRADFORD, L. P., J. R. GIBB, and K. D. BENNE, 1964. *T-Group Theory and Laboratory Method.* New York: Wiley.

BRADFORD, P., 1964. "Membership and the Learning Process," In L. P. Bradford, J. R. Gibb, and K. D. Benne (eds.), *T-Group Theory and Laboratory Method.* New York: Wiley, pp. 190–215.

BRONFENBRENNER, U., 1967. "Introduction," in A. S. Makarenko, *The Collective Family: A Handbook for Russian Parents.* Trans. by Robert Daglish. New York: Doubleday.

BRONFENBRENNER, U., 1969. "The Dream of the Kibbutz," *Saturday Review* 52, 72–73.

BRONFENBRENNER, U., 1970. *Two Worlds of Childhood: U.S. and U.S.S.R.* New York: Russell Sage Foundation.

BRUNVAND, J. H., 1968. *The Study of American Folklore.* Norton.

BURKS, H. M., JR. and R. H. PATE, JR., 1970. "Group Procedures Terminology: Babel Revisited." *The School Counselor.* 18(1), 53–60 (September).

BURTON, A., 1969a. "Encounter, Existence, and Psychotherapy," in Arthur Burton (ed.), *Encounter.* San Francisco: Jossey-Bass, pp. 7–26.

BURTON, A., 1969b. "Encounter: An Overview," in Arthur Burton (ed.), *Encounter.* San Francisco: Jossey-Bass, pp. 1–6.

CAMPBELL, P., and M. D. DUNNETTE, 1968. "Effectiveness of T-Group Experiences in Managerial Training and Development," *Psychological Bulletin* 70, 73–104.

CAPLAN, S. W., 1957. "Effect of Group Counseling on Junior High School Boys' Concepts of Themselves in School," *Journal of Counseling Psychology* 4, 124–128.

CARMICHAEL, L. (ed.), 1954. *Manual of Child Psychology.* 2nd ed. New York: Wiley.

COLEMAN, S. S., 1966. *Equality of Educational Opportunity.* Washington, D.C.: Government Printing Office, EO–38001.

CORSINI, R. J., 1952. "Immediate Therapy." *Group Psychotherapy* 4, 322–330.

CORSINI, R. J., 1957. *Methods of Group Psychotherapy.* Chicago: William James Press.

CORSINI, R. J., 1965. *Roleplaying in Psychotherapy.* Chicago: Aldine.

CRUTCHFIELD, R. S., 1955. "Conformity and Character." *American Psychologist* 10, 191–198.

CULBERT, S. A., 1968a. "Trainer Self-Disclosure and Member Growth in Two

T-Groups," *Journal of Applied Behavioral Science* 4, 47–72.

CULBERT, S. A., 1968b. "The Interpersonal Process of Self-Disclosure: It Takes Two to See One," in J. T. Hart and T. M. Tomlinson (eds.), *New Directions in Client-Centered Therapy*. Boston: Houghton Mifflin.

CULKIN, J. M., 1967. "A Schoolman's Guide to Marshall McLuhan." *Saturday Review* 11, 51ff. (March 18).

DABROWSKI, K., 1964. *Positive Disintegration*. Boston: Little, Brown.

DANSKIN, D. G., C. E. KENNEDY, JR., and FRIESEN, 1965. "Guidance: The Ecology of Students." *Personnel and Guidance Journal* 44, 130–135.

DELANEY, D. J., 1969. "Simulation Techniques in Counselor Education: Proposal of a Unique Approach," *Counselor Education and Supervision* 8, 183–188.

DICKSON, W. J., 1945. "The Hawthorne Plan of Personnel Counseling," *American Journal of Orthopsychiatry* 15, 344–347.

DICKSON, W. J., and F. J. ROETHLISHERGER, 1946. *Management and the Worker*. Cambridge: Harvard. U.P.

DICKSON, W. J., and F. J. ROETHLISBERGER, 1966. *Counseling in an Organization*. Cambridge: Harvard U.P.

DINKMEYER, W., and R. DREIKURS, 1963. *Encouraging Children to Learn*. Englewood Cliffs, N.J.: Prentice-Hall.

DOXIADIS, C. A., 1966. "Learning How to Learn," *Saturday Review*. 49, 16–17 (January 1).

DREIKURS, R., 1948. *The Challenge of Parenthood*. New York: Duell.

DREIKURS, R., R. CORSINI, and M. SONSTEGARD (eds.), 1959. *Adlerian Family Counseling—A Manual for Counseling Centers*. Eugene, Oreg.: University of Oregon (mimeo).

DREIKURS, R., and L. GREY, 1968. *Logical Consequences*. New York: Meredith.

DREIKURS, R., and V. SOLTZ, 1964. *Children: The Challenge*. New York: Duell.

DREIKURS, R., and M. SONSTEGARD, 1968. "The Adlerian or Teleoanalytic Group Counseling Approach," in G. M. Gazda (ed.), *Basic Approaches to Group Psychotherapy and Group Counseling*. Springfield, Ill.: Thomas.

DRUCKER, P. F., 1968. "A Warning to the Rich White World," *Harper's* 237, 67–75 (December).

DRUCKER, P. F., 1969. *The Age of Discontinuity: Guidelines to our Changing Society*. New York: Harper.

DUNDES, A. (ed.), 1965. *The Study of Folklore*. Englewood Cliffs, N.J.: Prentice-Hall.

DUNDES, A., 1969. "Folklore in the Modern World," address at the California Personnel and Guidance Convention, Anaheim, Calif. February 15. (CPGA, 654 E. Commonwealth Ave., Fullerton, Calif., 92631).

DUNLOP, R. S., 1968. "Pre-practicum Education: Use of Simulation Program," *Counselor Education and Supervision* 7, 145–146.

EITINGTON, J. E., 1969. "T-Group Learnings for Group Effectiveness." *Training and Development Journal* (May).

ELLIOTT, J., 1970. "Guided Imagery," *The Group Leader's Workshop,* V–21/34:1–7.

ELLIS, A., 1970. "Discussant: The Marathon: Efficacy of Intensive Physical and Emotional Contact," APGA Convention Program, New Orleans, March 23, 1970 (Program 171).

ENGEBRETSON, D. E., 1969. *Cross-cultural Variations in Territoriality.* Unpublished Doctoral Dissertation. University of Hawaii, Honolulu.

ENGEBRETSON, D. E., 1970. "Interactional Distance—A Definition of Relationship," research paper delivered at the Hawaii Psychological Association Convention, Honolulu, Hawaii, May 1, 1970.

ENGEBRETSON, D. E., and D. FULLMER, 1970. "Cross-cultural Differences in Territoriality: Interaction Distances of Native Japanese, Hawaii Japanese, and American Caucasians." *Journal of Cross-cultural Psychology* 1(3), 261–269 (September).

ENGEBRETSON, D. E., H. KOZUMA, E. FUJIOKA, and A. FARMER, 1970. "The Counselor's Week: What Is and What Could Be for Elementary and Secondary School Counselors in Hawaii," Department of Educational Psychology, University of Hawaii, Honolulu.

EYSENCK, H. J., 1965a. *A Fact and Fiction in Psychotherapy.* Middlesex: Penguin Books.

EYSENCK, H. J., 1965b. "The Effects of Psychotherapy," *International Journal of Psychiatry* 1, 97–143 (January).

FANTINI, M. D., 1970. "Institutional Reform: Schools for the Seventies," *Today's Education* 59, 43–44 (April).

FARSON, R. E., 1968. "The Education of Jeremy Farson," address, *IMPACT,* Phoenix, Ariz. John A. Gutherie, ed., University of Pittsburgh, April, pp. 22–51.

FIEDLER, F. E., 1950a. "A Comparison of Psychoanalytic, Non-Directive and Adlerian Therapeutic Relationships," *Journal of Consulting Psychology* 14, 436–445.

FIEDLER, F. E., 1950b. "The Concept of an Ideal Therapeutic Relationship," *Journal of Consulting Psychology* 14, 239–245.

FOA, U. G., 1967. "Differentiation in Cross-Cultural Communication," in L. Thayer (ed.) *Communication: Concepts and Perspectives.* Washington, D.C.: Spartan Books, pp. 135–152.

FORER, B. R., 1969a. "Therapeutic Relationships in Groups," in Arthur Burton (ed.), *Encounter.* San Francisco: Jossey-Bass, pp. 27–41.

FORER, B. R., 1969b. "Encounter Group Theory Symposium," *The Group Leader's Workshop.* Report from the 1969 APA Convention.

FRANKL, V. E., 1955. *The Doctor and the Soul.* New York: Knopf.

FRANKL, V. E., 1959. *From Death Camp to Existentialism.* Boston: Beacon Press.

FRANKL, V. E., 1962. *Man's Search for Meaning.* Boston: Beacon Press.

FRENCH, J. R. P., JR., 1956. "A Formal Theory of Social Power," *Psychological Review* 63, 181–194.

FREUD, S., 1929. *Introductory Lectures on Psychoanalysis.* London: Allen and Unwin.

FREUD, S., 1935. *A General Introduction to Psychoanalysis.* New York: Liveright.

FREUD, S., 1938. *The Basic Writings of Sigmund Freud.* Trans. and edited by A. A. Brill. New York: Modern Library.

FULLMER, D. W., 1964a. "Working with Parents," in D. Schreiter (ed.), *Guidance and the School Dropout.* Washington, D.C.: National Education Association and American Personnel and Guidance Association.

FULLMER, D. W., 1964b. Lecture, NDEA Institute. Portland, Oreg.: Oregon System of Higher Education.

FULLMER, D. W., 1968. "An Evolving Model for Group Work in the Elementary School: Counselor-Teacher-Parent Teams," *Elementary School Guidance and Counseling* 3, 58–64 (October).

FULLMER, D. W., 1969a. "Family Group Consultation," in G. M. Gazda (ed.), *Theories and Methods of Group Counseling in the Schools.* Springfield, Ill.: Thomas.

FULLMER, D. W., 1969b. "Group Therapy—Interaction Model," Report, Contract 82–13068022, Department of Labor, K. Seixas, Project Director. Manpower Training, Rehabilitation Center of Hawaii, 1969.

FULLMER, D. W., 1969c. Book review of G. Gazda (ed.) *Basic Approaches to Group Psychotherapy and Group Counseling, Personnel and Guidance Journal* 47, 921–924 (May).

FULLMER, D. W., 1969d. "Alienation in our Living Room," address, California Personnel and Guidance Association Convention, Anaheim, Calif., February 14. (CPGA, 654 E. Commonwealth Ave., Fullerton, Calif., 92631).

FULLMER, D. W., 1970a. "Future of Counseling and Personnel Services in the State of Hawaii," *Proceedings,* Second Annual Conference HPGA-HSCA. Honolulu: Hawaii Personnel and Guidance Association.

FULLMER, D. W., 1970b. "Selection and Retention of Students of Counseling," APGA Convention, New Orleans.

FULLMER, D. W., 1971. "Counseling with Parents of Students." in *The Encyclopedia of Education.* New York: Macmillan.

FULLMER, D. W., and H. W. BERNARD, 1964. *Counseling: Content and Process.* Chicago: Science Research Associates.

FULLMER, D. W., and H. W. BERNARD, 1968. *Family Consultation.* Boston: Houghton Mifflin.

FULLMER, D. W., and H. W. BERNARD, 1971 *The School Counselor-Consultant.* Boston: Houghton Mifflin.

GAZDA, G. M., and M. J. LARSEN, 1968. "A Comprehensive Appraisal of Group and Multiple Counseling Research," *Journal of Research and Development in Education* 1, 57–132.

GIBB, J. R., 1965. "Fear and Facade: Defensive Management." In R. E. Farson (ed.), *Science and Human Affairs.* Palo Alto, Calif.: Science and Behavior Books, pp. 197–214.

GIBB, J. R., 1968. "Using Groups in an Educational Setting." (April-May). *IMPACT,* National Seminar, Phoenix, Ariz. U.S.O.E. and University of Pittsburgh, sponsors. (John A. Guthrie, ed., University of Pittsburgh).

GIBB, J. R., and L. M. GIBB, 1967. "Humanistic Elements in Group Growth." In James F. T. Bugental (ed.), *Challenges of Humanistic Psychology.* New York: McGraw-Hill, pp. 160–170.

GIBB, J. R., and L. M. GIBB, 1969. "Role Freedom in a TORI Group." In Arthur Burton (ed.), *Encounter.* San Francisco: Jossey-Bass, pp. 42–57.

GINOTT, H. G., 1961. *Group Psychotherapy with Children.* New York: McGraw-Hill.

GINOTT, H. G., 1968. "Group Therapy with Children," in G. M. Gazda (ed.), *Basic Approaches to Group Psychotherapy and Group Counseling.* Springfield, Ill. Thomas.

GLASSER, W., 1965. *Reality Therapy: A New Approach to Psychiatry.* New York: Harper.

GLASSER, W., 1970. Address. ASCD Convention. Honolulu, Hawaii, July 20, 1970.

GLATTHORN, A. A., 1966. "Learning in the Small Group," *I.D.E.A.* (Institute for Development of Educational Activities). Dayton, Ohio.

GLUCKSON, L., 1968. "The Marathon as a Growth and Learning Experience for the Therapist," paper presented at the Western Psychological Association, San Diego, Calif. March 30, 1968.

GOFFMAN, E., 1967. *Interaction Ritual.* New York: Doubleday.

GORDON, E., 1970. " Introduction: Education for Socially Disadvantaged Children." *Review of Educational Research* 40, 1–12 (February).

GUNTHER, B., 1968. *Sense Relaxation: Below Your Mind.* New York: Macmillan.

GURMAN, E., 1967. "Research Evaluations of Marathons," paper presented at the Western Psychological Association, San Diego, Calif., March 30, 1968.

HAIGH, G. V., 1967. "Psychotherapy as Interpersonal Encounter," in James F. T. Bugental (ed.), *Challenges in Humanistic Psychology.* New York: McGraw-Hill, pp. 218–224.

HALL, E., 1970. "A Conversation with Jean Piaget and Barbell Inhelder," *Psychology Today* 3, 25–32, 54–56.

HALL, E. T., 1959. *The Silent Language.* New York: Doubleday.

HAMILTON, C., 1969. "Black Power and Its Alternative," California Personnel and Guidance Convention, Anaheim, Calif. (CPGA, 654 E. Commonwealth Ave., Fullerton, Calif., 92631).

HANDEL, G., 1965. "Psychological Study of Whole Families," *Psychological Bulletin* 63, 19–41.

HANSEN, J. C., T. M. NILAND, and L. P. ZANI, 1969. "Model Reinforcement in Group Counseling of Elementary School Children," *Personnel and Guidance Journal* 47, 741–744.

HARLOW, H. G., and M. K. HARLOW, 1962. "Social Deprivation in Monkeys," *Scientific American* 207, 136–146.

HARRISON, C. H., 1970. "South Brunswick, N.J.: Schools Put a Town on the Map," *Saturday Review* 53, 66–68 (February 21).

HAVIGHURST, R. J., and F. L. NEUGARTEN, 1962. *Society and Education.* 2nd ed. Boston: Allyn and Bacon.

HAVIGHURST, R. J., 1970. "Minority Subcultures and the Law of Effect," *American Psychologist* 25, 313–322.

HEBB, D. O., 1949. *The Organization of Behavior.* New York: Wiley.

HEBB, D. O., 1955. "Drives and the Conceptual Nervous System," *Psychological Review* 62, 243–254.

HELLER, W., 1970. "A Letter from the Publisher." *Time* 95:6 (March 9).

HENRY, J., 1963. *Culture Against Man.* New York: Random House.

HOBBS, N., 1956. "Curing Unreason by Reason," review of H. S. Sullivan, *The Psychiatric Interview, Contemporary Psychology* 1, 44–45.

HORA, T., 1968. "Existential Psychiatry and Group Psychotherapy," in G. M. Gazda (ed.), *Basic Approaches to Group Psychotherapy and Group Counseling.* Springfield, Ill. Thomas.

HOSFORD, R. E., 1969a. "Behavioral Counseling—A Contemporary View," *The Counseling Psychologist* 1, 1–33.

HOSFORD, R. E., 1969b. "Rejoinder: Some Reactions and Comments," *The Counseling Psychologist* 1, 89–95.

HUBBARD, L. R., 1951. *Dianetics: The Modern Science of Mental Health.* New York: Random House.

IRISH, G., 1966. "Behavioral Change of Participants in Family Group Consultation," unpublished doctoral dissertation, Oregon State University, Corvallis, Oreg.

IVEY, A. E., 1969. "The Intentional Individual: A Process-Outcome View of Behavioral Psychology," *Counseling Psychologist* 1, 56–60.

JACKSON, D. D., 1965. "The Study of the Family," *Family Process* 4, 1–20.

JENSEN, A. R., 1968. "Social Class, Race, and Genetics: Implications for Education," *American Educational Research Journal* 5, 1–42.

JOURARD, S. M., 1964. *The Transparent Self.* Princeton, N.J.: Van Nostrand.

KAGAN, N. (principal investigator), 1967. *Studies in Human Interaction: Interpersonal Process Recall Simulated by Videotape.* David R. Krathwohl, consultant. Michigan State University (a five-year study). Final Report. Project No. 5–0800/U.S. Department of Health, Education, and Welfare, Office of Education. Bureau of Research, Washington, D.C.

KAGAN, N., 1968. "Supervision as a Developmental Process." "Supervision: A Few Techniques and a Model." in *Impact, Invitational Meeting on the Preparation of Administrators, Counselors and Teachers.* pp. 82–98. University of Pittsburgh and U.S. Office of Education, John A. Guthrie, Director. Phoenix, Ariz., April 27–May 2, 1968.

KAGAN, N. 1970. Personal interview at New Orleans, March 23, 1970.

KAGAN, N., D. R. KRATHWOHL, and W. W. FARQUHAR, 1965. "I.P.R.—Interpersonal Process Recall: Stimulated Recall by Videotape," *Education Research Series,* Michigan State University, East Lansing, Mich.

KELLY, G. A., 1955. *The Psychology of Personal Constructs:* Vol. 1: *A Theory of Personality.* New York: Norton.

KEMP, C. G., 1967. *Intangibles in Counseling.* Boston: Houghton Mifflin.

KEMP, C. G., 1970a. "The T-Group," in C. Gratton Kemp (ed.), *Perspectives on the Group Process.* Boston: Houghton Mifflin, pp. 70–72.

KEMP, C. G., 1970b. "Foundations of the T-Group," in C. Gratton Kemp (ed.), *Perspectives on the Group Process.* Boston: Houghton Mifflin, pp. 183–184.

KEMP, C. G., 1970c. "T-Group Leadership," in C. Gratton Kemp (ed.), *Perspectives on the Group Process.* Boston: Houghton Mifflin, pp. 203–204.

KRUMBOLTZ, J. D., and C. E. THORESEN (eds), 1969. *Behavioral Counseling: Cases and Techniques.* New York: Holt.

LAKIN, M., 1969. "Some Ethical Issues in Sensitivity Training," *American Psychologist,* 923–928.

LAZARUS, A. A., 1968. "Behavioral Therapy in Groups," in G. M. Gazda (ed.), *Basic Approaches to Group Psychotherapy and Group Counseling.* Springfield, Il. Thomas.

LENNARD, H. L., and A. BERNSTEIN, 1969. *Patterns in Human Interaction.* San Francisco: Jossey-Bass.

Life Magazine, 1970. Anonymous, "What Heroin Did to a Family." 68, 50–56 (March 20).

LINTON, R., 1936. *The Study of Man.* New York: Appleton.

LONDON, P., 1969. *Behavior Control.* New York: Harper.

LOUGHARY, J. A. (ed.), 1966. *Man-Machine Systems in Education.* New York: Harper.

LOUKES, H., 1964. "Passport to Maturity," *Phi Delta Kappan* 46, 54–57 (October).

LOW, B. P., 1967. "A Preliminary Study of the Adjustment Problems of East-West Center Students," Department of Educational Psychology, University of Hawaii, Honolulu.

MAHL, G. F., B. DANET, and N. NORTON, 1959. "Reflections of Major Personality Characteristics in Gestures and Body Movements," Yale University ISPHS Grant M–1052. Also reported in American Psychological Association Annual Meeting, 1959.

MASTERS, W. H., and V. E. JOHNSON, 1970. *Human Sexual Inadequacy.* Boston: Little, Brown.

MATSON, F., 1964. *The Broken Image.* New York: Braziller.

MATSUMOTO, S., 1970. Public Address, Honolulu, University of Hawaii.

MCGREGOR, R., et al., 1964. *Multiple Impact Therapy with Families.* New York: McGraw-Hill.

McKnown, H. C., 1934. *Home Room Guidance.* New York: McGraw-Hill.

McLuhan, M., 1964. *Understanding Media: The Extensions of Man.* New York: McGraw-Hill.

McMahon, E. M., and P. Campbell, 1969. *Please Touch.* New York: Sheed and Ward.

Mead, M., and K. Heyman, 1965. *Family.* New York: Macmillan.

Menninger, K., H. Ellenberger, P. Pruyser, and M. Mayman, 1958. "The Unitary Concept of Mental Illness," *Bulletin of the Menninger Clinic* 22, 4–12.

Menninger, K., M. Mayman, and P. Pruyser, 1963. *The Vital Balance.* New York: Viking.

Miles, M. B., 1965. "Changes During and Following Laboratory Training: A Clinical-Experimental Study," *Journal of Applied Behavioral Science* 1, 215–242.

Montagu, A., 1970. "A Scientist Looks at Love," Phi Delta Kappan 51, 463–467 (May).

Moreno, J. L., 1923. *Das Stegreiftheater.* Potsdam: Keipenheur. (English trans.: *The Theater of Spontaneity.*) Boston: Beacon, 1946.

Moreno, J. L., 1946a. *Psychodrama.* Vol. I. Beacon, N.Y.: Beacon House.

Moreno, J. L., 1946b. *The Theatre of Spontaneity.* Beacon, N.Y.: Beacon House.

Moreno, J. L., 1953. *Who Shall Survive?* 2nd ed. Beacon, N.Y.: Beacon House.

Moreno, J. L., 1958. *Psychodrama: Volume II.* Beacon, N.Y.: Beacon House.

Moreno, J. L. (ed.), 1966. *The International Handbook of Group Psychotherapy.* New York: Philosophical Library.

Morris, D., 1967. *The Naked Ape.* New York: McGraw-Hill.

Mower, O. H. (ed.), 1953. *Psychotherapy: Theory and Research.* New York: Ronald.

Mowrer, O. H., 1964. *The New Group Therapy.* Princeton, N.J.: Van Nostrand.

Mowrer, O. H., 1966. "Integrity Therapy: A Self-Help Approach," *Psychotherapy, Theory, Research and Practice* 3, 114–119.

Mowrer, O. H., 1968. "Loss and Recovery of Community," in G. M. Gazda, (ed.), *Innovations to Group Psychotherapy.* Springfield, Ill.: Thomas, pp. 130–189.

Murray, H., 1962. "The Personality and Career of Satan," *Journal of Social Issues* 18, 36–54.

Nelson, B., 1968. "The Psychoanalyst as Mediator and Double Agent: An Overview," in M. C. Nelson et al., *Roles and Paradigms in Psychotherapy.* New York: Grune and Stratton.

Ohlsen, M. M., 1970. *Group Counseling.* New York: Holt.

Ohlsen, M. M., and H. Johnson, 1962a. "Group Counseling Evaluated by Blind Analysis and Projective Techniques," *Journal of Counseling Psychology* 9, 359.

Ohlsen, M. M., and M. C. Oelke, 1962b. "An Evaluation of Discussion Topics

OLCH, D., and D. L. SNOW, 1970. "Personality Characteristics of Sensitivity Group Volunteers," *Personnel and Guidance Journal* 48, 848–850.

PACKER, P., 1970. *Death of the Other Self.* New York: Cowles.

PARIS, N. M., 1968. "T-Grouping: A Helping Movement," *Phi Delta Kappan,* 460–463 (April).

PAVLOV, I. P., 1927. *Conditioned Reflexes.* Trans. by G. V. Anrep. London: Oxford U.P.

PIERSON, G. A., 1965. *An Evaluation: Counselor Education in Regular Session Institutes.* Washington, D.C.: U.S. Department of Health, Education, and Welfare (OE–25042).

POLING, E., 1968. "Video Tape Recordings in Counseling Practicum: II—Critique Considerations," *Counselor Education and Supervision* 8, 33–38.

PRATT, S., and J. TOOLEY, 1964. "Contract Psychology and the Actualizing Transactional Field," First International Congress of Social Psychiatry, London. (August).

PUFFER, J. A., 1913. *Vocational Guidance.* Chicago: Rand McNally, pp. 23–24.

RAKSTIS, T. J., 1970. "Sensitivity Training: Fad, Fraud or New Frontier?" *Today's Health,* 21–25, 86–88 (January).

ROGERS, C. R., 1951. *Client-Centered Therapy.* Boston: Houghton Mifflin.

ROGERS, C. R., 1959. "A Tentative Scale for the Measurement of Process in Psychotherapy," in E. Rubestein (ed.), *Research in Psychotherapy.* Washington, D.C.: American Psychological Association, pp. 96–107.

ROGERS, C. R., 1961. "The Place of the Person in the New World of Behavioral Sciences," *Personnel and Guidance Journal* 39, 442–451 (February).

ROGERS, Carl R., 1967. "The Process of the Basic Encounter Group," in James F. T. Bugental (ed.), *Challenges in Humanistic Psychology.* New York: McGraw-Hill, pp. 260–276.

ROGERS, C. R., 1968. "Interpersonal Relationships: U.S.A. 2000," *Journal of Applied Behavioral Science* 4, 265–280.

ROGERS, E. M., 1962. *Diffusion of Innovations.* New York: Free Press.

RYAN, C. W., 1969. "Video Aids in Practicum Supervision," *Counselor Education and Supervision* 8, 125–129.

SCHEFLEN, A. E., 1961. *A Psychotherapy of Schizophrenia: Direct Analysis.* Springfield, Ill.: Thomas.

SCHEIN, E., 1965. "Reaction Patterns to Severe Chronic Stress in American Army Prisoners of War of the Chinese," in O. Milton, (ed.), *Behavior Disorders: Perspectives and Trends.* Philadelphia: Lippincott.

SCHEIN, E. H. and W. G. BENNIS, 1965. *Personal and Organizational Changes Through Group Methods: The Laboratory Approach.* New York: Wiley.

SCHILLER, C. (ed. and trans.), 1957. *Instinctive Behavior.* London: Methuen.

SCHNEIDER, L., 1949. "Some Psychiatric Views on Freedom," and "The Theory of Social Systems," *Psychiatry* 12, 251–264.

SCHUTZ, C., 1967. *Joy: Expanding Human Awareness.* Grove P.

SHERIF M., and C. W. SHERIF, 1964. *Reference Groups: Explorations into Conformity and Deviations in Adolescents.* New York: Harper.

SHOCKLEY, W., 1967. "Articulated Science Teaching and Balanced Emphasis," in L. Thayer (ed.), *Communication: Concepts and Perspectives.* Washington, D.C.: Spartan Books, pp. 113–179.

SKINNER, B. F., 1938. *The Behavior of Organisms.* New York: Appleton.

SKINNER, B. F., 1948. *Walden Two.* New York: Macmillan.

SKINNER, B. F., 1951. "How to Teach Animals," *Scientific American* 186, 1–6.

SKINNER, B. F., 1953. *Science and Human Behavior.* New York: Macmillan.

SKINNER, B. F., 1965. "Why Teachers Fail," *Saturday Review.* 40, 80–81 (October 16).

SMITH, G. J. W., D. F. SPENCE, and G. S. KLEIN, 1959. "Subliminal Effects of Verbal Stimuli," *Journal of Abnormal and Social Psychology* 59, 167–176.

SONSTEGARD, M. A., 1970. "The Basic Principles and Rationale of Group Counseling," *Idaho Guidance News and Views* 11, 15–23 (April).

SORENSON, G., 1969. "A Reaction to Hosford's Version of Behavioral Counseling," *The Counseling Psychologist* 1, 33–37.

SPEILBERGER, C. D., H. WEITZ, and J. P. DENNY, 1962. "Group Counseling and the Academic Performances of Anxious College Freshmen," *Journal of Counseling Psychology* 9, 195–204.

SPRINGER, H., 1968. "Therapeutic Groups and Conformity." Seattle: University of Washington. Unpublished paper.

STOCK, D. A., 1964. "A Survey of Research on T-Groups," in L. P. Bradford, J. R. Gibb and K. D. Benne (eds.), *T-Group Theory and Laboratory Method.* New York: Wiley, pp. 395–441.

STOLLER, F. H., 1966. "Accelerated Interaction: A Time-Limited Approach Based on the Brief, Intensive Group." Department of Mental Hygiene, State of California, Bureau of Research, No. 352.

STOLLER, F. H., 1967. "The Long Weekend," *Psychology Today* 1, 29–33 (December).

STOLLER, F. H., 1968a. "Marathon Group Therapy," in G. M. Gazda (ed.), *Innovations to Group Psychotherapy.* Springfield, Ill.: Thomas.

STOLLER, F. H., 1968b. "Focused Feedback with Video Tape: Extending the Group's Functions," in G. M. Gazda (ed.), *Innovations to Group Psychotherapy.* Springfield, Ill.: Thomas, pp. 207–255.

STOLLER, F. H., 1968c. "Use of Video Tape (Focused Feedback) In Group Counseling and Group Therapy," *Journal of Research and Development in Education* 1, 30–44.

STOLLER, F. H., 1969. "A Stage for Trust," in Arthur Burton (ed.), *Encounter.* San Francisco: Jossey-Bass, pp. 81–96.

STOLLER, F. H., 1970. "The Marathon: Efficacy of Intensive Physical and Emotional Contact," presentation at APGA Convention Program 171, New Orleans, March 23.

SULLIVAN, H. S., 1947. *Conceptions of Modern Psychiatry.* 2nd ed. Washington D.C.: William Alanson White Psychiatric Foundation.

SULLIVAN, H. S., 1953. *The Interpersonal Theory of Psychiatry.* Edited by H. S. Perry, and M. L. Gawel. New York: Norton.

SULLIVAN, H. S., 1954. *The Psychiatric Interview.* Edited by H. S. Perry, and M. L. Gawel. New York: W. W. Norton.

SZASZ, T., 1965. "The Myth of Mental Illness," in O. Milton, and R. Wahler, *Behavior Disorders, Prescriptives and Trends.* Philadelphia: Lippincott.

THAYER, L. (ed.), 1967. *Communication: Concepts and Perspectives.* Washington, D.C.: Spartan Books.

THEOBALD, R., 1961. *The Challenge of Abundance.* New York: Mentor.

THEOBALD, R., 1970. "The Challenge for the Year 2000," address: Honolulu, Hawaii, February 28, 1970, Governor's Conference on the year 2000.

THOMAS, D., 1968. "T-Grouping: The White-Collar Hippie Movement," *Phi Delta Kappan,* 458–460.

TRUAX, C. B., 1966. "Reinforcement and Non-Reinforcement in Rogerian Psychotherapy," *Journal of Abnormal Psychology* 71, 1–9.

TYLER, L. E., 1969. *The Work of the Counselor.* 3rd ed. New York: Appleton.

TYLOR, E. B., 1924. *Primitive Culture.* 7th ed. New York: Brentano.

ULLMAN, L. P., and L. KRASNER, 1969. *A Psychological Approach to Abnormal Behavior.* Englewood Cliffs, N.Y.: Prentice-Hall.

UNGERSMAN, A. J., 1961. *The Search for Meaning.* Philadelphia: Westminster.

VARENHORST, B. B., 1969. "Behavioral Group Counseling," in G. M. Gazda (ed.), *Theories and Methods of Group Counseling in the Schools.* Springfield, Ill.: Thomas.

VOSEN, L. M., 1966. "The Relationship Between Self-Disclosure and Self-Esteem," unpublished doctoral dissertation, University of California (Los Angeles).

WALKER, E. L., 1967. *Conditioning and Instrumental Learning.* Belmont Calif.: Brooks/Cole.

WALSMITH, C. R., 1970. Professional-personal correspondence, May 5.

WATSON, G., 1960. "What Psychology Can We Feel Sure About?" *Teachers College Record* 60, 253–257.

WATZLAWICK, P., J. BEAVIN, and D. JACKSON, 1967. *Pragmatics of Human Communication.* New York: Norton.

WEIGEL, R. G., 1968. "Marathon Group Counseling and Marathon Group Discussion with University Client Population," APA Convention Report on Session 103, Detroit, Mich.

WHITAKER, C. A., 1970. "Recent Advances in Family Therapy." Address, *Interim Session,* University of Hawaii, Honolulu (January).

WHITMAN, R. M., 1964. "Psychodynamic Principles Underlying T-Group Processes," in L. P. Bradford, J. R. Gibb, and K. D. Benne (eds.), *T-Group Theory and Laboratory Method.* New York: Wiley, pp. 310–335.

WIKLER, A., 1961. "On the Nature of Addiction and Habituation," *British Journal of Addiction* 57, 73–79.

WOLF, A., and E. SCHWARTZ, 1962. *Psychoanalysis in Groups.* New York: Grune and Stratton.

WOLFF, W. (ed.), 1952. *Success in Psychotherapy.* New York: Grune and Stratton.

WOLPE, J., 1958. *Psychotherapy by Reciprocal Inhibition.* Stanford, Calif.: Stanford U.P.

WOODYARD, J.E., 1970. "Employee Counseling in Industry," master's paper, Department of Educational Psychology, University of Hawaii.

WRENN, C. G., 1969. Lecture, University of Hawaii, Honolulu.

YABLONSKY, L., 1965. *The Tunnel Back: Synanon.* New York: Macmillan.

ZIGLER, E., 1970. "Social Class and the Socialization Process," *Review of Educational Research* 40, 87–110.

ZIMPFER, D., 1967. "Expression of Feelings in Group Counseling," *Personnel and Guidance Journal* 45, 703–708.

ZWETSCHKE, E. T., and J. E. GRENFELL, 1965. "Family Group Consultation: A Description and a Rationale," *Personnel and Guidance Journal* 43, 974–980 (June).

Glossary

Accountability. The next level beyond responsibility involving the action or behavior essential to resolve the life event and bring closure. Accountability carries a continuing obligation. Responsibility can be dismissed by a feeling with no action e.g., feeling responsible to others. Accountability is the act of doing some specific behavior to account to others.

Acculturation. The process of acquiring a culture with all of its values, social-physical conditioning, and symbol systems.

Acting-out models. Systems of human organizations such as groups for specific tasks and are essentially different from passive and spectator models of human organization, e.g. audiences at baseball games, operas, or school classrooms.

Active psychology. The counter concept to reactive psychology. Instead of seeing the person as a reactor, active psychology sees the person also as a seeker of stimulation.

Alienation. The condition of separation from intimate involvement in significant relationships at the personal or social level.

Analysis of interaction. A way of assessing the nature of the relationship between two or more persons. (See Watzlawick, et al. (1967) for more complete analysis of communication.)

Base line. The beginning point in measuring increments of behavior, learning, or skill achievement.

Behaviorism. A term associated with a particular type of psychology particularly important in contemporary learning theory. Schedules of reinforcement are manipulated to effect behavior modifications.

Behavior modification. The particular application of schedules of reinforcement to modify the behavior of a target person or population.

Bio-social community. A group like a family or a group of families in which biological reproduction and social acculturation can happen.

"Black Box" designs. Characterized by inputs and outputs that are known but the processes intervening between input and output are unknown; thus, the "Black Box" designs concept. An example could be the human brain.

315

Catharsis. Reliving a situation and "letting go" of it by verbal and/or dramatic expression to significant others.

Comfort level. Level at which anxiety is felt with respect to a particular life situation well within tolerance limits for stress and anxiety in a given person.

Communities. Group or groups of persons gathered together with some common underlying bond.

Coached clients. Used in counselor training to simulate actual counseling life situations under controlled conditions.

Concept of group. A way of seeing man in his human organization model. The dynamic nature of man forms and operates within a system of interrelated persons who are gathered together on some basis common to the interests, needs, backgrounds and identifying characteristics of each person.

Context of behavior. Those events which precede and supersede a particular overt act. The environment in which the behavior occurs.

Contingency. A stimulus event which is made conditional upon a specific response.

Contrived group. A group which is not "natural" in its origin such as is a family or peer group. A contrived group is brought together for a specific purpose which engineers its activities. It is artificial in its origin and is terminal. If it does not terminate, it changes into a natural group.

Control group designs. In an experiment the group whose behavior is not manipulated. The "as is" group.

Counter-transference. Projection of thoughts, feelings, emotions, or characteristics from the client to the counselor is Transference. Counter-transference is the action by which the counselor projects the transference back to the client.

Credibility. The margin of trust the reality of experience supports in a relationship.

Criterion. The behavior or other factor used to measure the quality or quantity of a phenomenon.

Cultural bias. The ability to perceive only in relation to one's own culture. The bias is spelled out in the expression of one's belief that his culture is the center of all cultures. Therefore all other cultures are perceived as inferior.

Cultural parameters. The limits placed upon the range of behavior acceptable under the rules of a given ethnic group.

Culture. A system of rules, beliefs, values, behavior and symbols sufficient to effect complete human organization.

Desensitization. Increasing exposure under controlled conditions to an anxiety-producing life situation which results in a reduction of anxiety.

Deutero-learning. Learning how to learn. Learning how to learn is systematically organized in each culture.

Double-bind communication. A communication in which the injunction is given and then restricted in such a way that the injunction can be activated only if the qualification placed upon it is violated. (See Watzlawick, et al. (1967) for a more complete definition.)

Enthnocentrism. See cultural bias.

Etiology. The beginning or cause of the behavior observed in a given person.

External intervention. Intervention from outside the group as opposed to an internal intervention originating from within a group.

Folklore. As it is used in group consultation and individual counseling, describes the "story" anyone will tell about himself and others.

Formal culture. Defined by E. T. Hall in *The Silent Language,* 1959, as the set of rules for which no alternatives are permitted.

Frame of reference. The context within which a given individual perceives reality.

Halo effect. The tendency to project positive characteristics or negative characteristics beyond those possessed by the subject.

Heterostasis. A condition of imbalance in a system, social or biological.

Homeostasis. A condition of balance in a system, social or biological.

Human Fix. The condition created by the circumstances imposed by nonchoice in the social system of a human organization.

Human organization. The model for systematizing the roles and functions of individual human beings.

Immaculate scientism. The state of pedantically following the form of science without regard for the substance of scientific method.

Indeterminacy. The inability to determine the limits or characteristics of a given phenomenon.

Informal culture. Defined by E. T. Hall in *The Silent Language,* 1959, as the nonexplicit rules and regulations used to guide behavior for which there are infinite alternatives.

Interaction. The process of talking, acting, or communicating with others.

Intervention. The external direct act associated with changing an environment, a person's behavior, or other dynamic and on-going phenomenon.

Intravention. The internal direct act associated with changing an environment, a person's behavior or other dynamics and on-going phenomenon.

Introspection. A paradoxical process of the mind looking at itself.

Invariance. The opposite of variable. The stable function of a culture rule is an example.

Kibbutz. A group method of child rearing employed by Israel for more than fifty years.

Level of knowing. Associated with the concept of levels of abstraction beginning with direct experience to language through inference, etc.

Life style. The preferred model of behaving.

Metacommunication. Communication about communication.

Microcosm. A miniature world.

Milieu. Or environment. Consists of all external factors affecting or potentially affecting a person or a group of persons.

Modeling. The patterning of behavior after a model.

Natural groups. Those formed spontaneously within a given culture.

Nuclear family. An institutionalized bio-social group made up of parents and their children.

Objective reality. A subjective reality which can be replicated for repeated observation.

Parsimony. The most frugal expenditure of energy to produce optimum results.

Pathogenic. The condition likely to generate disease.

Peter principle. The concept that every competent person will be promoted to new responsibilities for which he is not competent.

Projective technique. Kind of test whereby the subject perceives or manipulates some relatively unstructured stimulus and the examiner makes an interpretation about the subject's personality by studying the structure that the subject constructed.

Pseudo-encounter. The nonauthentic self-disclosure on the part of one member or a dyad.

Radical honesty. Complete and uncensored self-disclosure.

Reality check. The act of sharing with one or more others the perceptions derived from a common experience.

Reality test. The evaluation of self by the direct exposure of one's perceptions to the perceptions of others.

Reinforcement. Any stimulus event that increases the probability that a particular response will repeat.

St. Vitus dance. Type of nerve disease characterized by irregular, involuntary muscle movements in the limbs and face.

Self-authentication. The simple act of acknowledging one's successes and failures.

Self-confrontation. The complex process of facing the reality of one's impact on others.

Self-defeating behavior. Any behavior that enhances the perpetuation of behavior one wishes to avoid.

Self-disclosure. The process of revealing oneself to oneself and others.

Self-fulfilling prophecy. The act of believing and behaving in such a way as to create the predicted results.

Self-help group. Any group operating without external leadership.

Self-perception. What one thinks and feels about oneself.

Self-presentation. Technique used in psychodrama to help a person see how he is presenting himself to others. Their response to him will tend to confirm or disconfirm him.

Self-respect. The vital act of retaining respect for what one is.

Seduction. The act of taking a short term reward for something that has a long term consequence, usually negative. Examples include smoking, drinking, and sexual intercourse.

Simulation. The act of replicating reality without risking the consequences of reality.

Social isolates. The persons kept alone by the psychological barriers in their personalities.

Sociometry. Measurement of preference in interpersonal relationships in group.

Sub-culture. A culture inclusive of a larger culture which distinguishes itself from other cultures within the larger culture because of specific characteristics.

Subjective reality. The only reality in human experience.

Synanon. Kind of group therapy involving a particular contract between the client and the group defined in advance and enforced by specific techniques.

Therapeutic community. A milieu in which everyone becomes a member of the treatment team.

Venture group. A specific type of self-help group interested in personal development.

Name Index

Subject Index

Abstraction, 211, 213
  fourth-level, 297
  levels of, 67, 153, 158
Accelerated interaction, 232
Acceptance, 233
  as reinforcer, 47
Accountability, 9, 189, 206, 209, 265
Acculturation, 151
Addicts, drug, 6
Adlerian counseling, 147, 191, 196, 208
  group counseling, 218
  method, 192-196
  technique, 28
Alcoholic, 258
Alienation, 2, 8, 13, 50, 63, 133, 169,
  186, 187, 197, 228, 230, 235,
  238, 258, 259
All-at-once learning, 245
Ambiguity, 228
Analytic psychology, 192
Anger, 274
  repressed, 233
Anthropology, 5
  cultural, 5
Anti-intellectualism, 238
Anxiety, 242
  in interaction, 236
  level of, 225
Arena
  behavior, 257
  encounter, 231
  intervention, 259
  one-to-one, 202
  teaching, 272
  teaching-learning, 196
  treatment, 251
Asian, grantee, 2
Assumptions, 210, 270
  behavior, 223, 228, 233, 239-240, 244
  existential approaches, 207-8
  learning, 223
Attention span, 286

Attitude, 99, 144, 153, 163, 173, 174,
  187, 194, 209, 210, 212, 244, 261
  change, 159
Attitudinal value, 210, 212
Attraction, forces of, 181
Authenticity, 189, 190
Authority, 93, 196, 202, 203, 204, 218,
  254
  figure, 225
Autism, 167, 279, 291
Autonomy, 233
Awareness, 202, 224
  conscious, 205
  group, 137, 150
  learning, 247
  level of, 246
  sensory, 238-43
  training, 95

Basic encounter group, 227-32
  tool of, 229
Behavior, 187
  abnormal, 158, 173
  adaptive, 204, 211, 215
  analysis of, 75-6, 293
  analysis, levels of, 43
  and context, 46
  and information, 110
  appropriate, 69, 253
  as communication system, 261
  as language, 43, 262
  assumptions of, 179-182, 223, 228,
    233, 239-40, 244, 257
  autonomous, 66
  cause of, 208
  change, 7, 95, 105, 116, 141, 143,
    146, 151, 152, 156, 157, 159,
    160, 162, 165, 173, 178, 179,
    182, 184, 190, 191, 196, 197,
    199, 200, 202, 204, 210, 215,
    216, 217, 219, 225, 227, 229,
    231, 236, 242, 246, 251, 252,
    273, 276, 278, 298
  conditions of, 213
  classroom, 244

DATE DUE

FEB 23 1987			
MAY 0 4 2004			